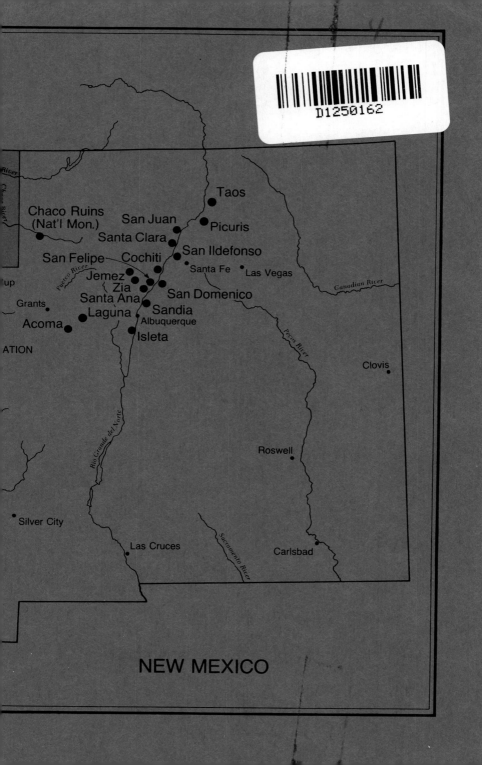

Taos

Chaco Ruins
(Nat'l Mon.)

San Juan

Picuris

Santa Clara

San Ildefonso

San Felipe

Cochiti

Santa Fe

Las Vegas

Jemez

Zia

San Domenico

Santa Ana

Grants

Sandia

Laguna

Albuquerque

Acoma

Isleta

ATION

Clovis

Roswell

Silver City

Las Cruces

Carlsbad

Chaco River

Puerco River

up

Canadian River

Pecos River

Rio Grande del Norte

Sacramento River

NEW MEXICO

D1250162

ZUÑI

Cushing in Zuñi Regalia. (Courtesy of the Smithsonian Institution National Anthropological Archives, Bureau of American Ethnology Collection)

ZUÑI

Selected Writings of
FRANK HAMILTON CUSHING

Edited, with an introduction, by
JESSE GREEN

Foreword by FRED EGGAN

UNIVERSITY OF NEBRASKA PRESS
Lincoln and London

Publishers on the Plains

UNP

Library of Congress Cataloging in Publication Data

Cushing, Frank Hamilton, 1857–1900.
  Zuñi : selected writings of Frank Hamilton Cushing.

  Bibliography: p. 431
  1. Zuñi Indians. I. Green, Jesse, 1928–
II. Title.
E99.Z9C93   1978   970'.004'97   78–14295
ISBN 0–8032–2100–2

Contents

Illustrations

FRED EGGAN

Foreword

I

WHEN Jesse Green published a sparkling review of Frank Hamilton Cushing's writings on Zuñi life and culture in the *New York Review of Books* (May 29, 1975) under the title "The Man Who Became an Indian," many of us hoped for a sequel and here it is. Cushing was a self-taught genius and the volume which follows represents the first comprehensive selection from his varied contributions to our understanding of the Middle Ant Hill, as the Zuñis characterize their central village in western New Mexico. Jesse Green's own Introduction provides a first-rate account of Cushing's scientific accomplishments at Zuñi and elsewhere in the context of nineteenth-century American anthropology. Here we might say something about the position of Zuñi in the Southwest and the historical factors which had affected its development.

It is almost a century since Cushing arrived at Zuñi as a fledgling member of the Smithsonian expedition sent out to collect specimens and inaugurate field research for the newly founded Bureau of Ethnology in the autumn of 1879. When he broke with precedent and moved into the Zuñi governor's household and proceeded to learn the language and participate in Pueblo activities, his companions left him without supplies and without even a farewell! In this crisis he became completely dependent on the Zuñis, who set out to make him into an Indian, patiently teaching him Zuñi customs and "hardening his meat." Cushing had been a frail child and the rigors of a Zuñi winter almost did him in, but he managed to survive by sheer will power.

Cushing had originally intended to stay only a few months, but in the end he remained for four and a half years, becoming a member of the tribe and obtaining a high position in the Priesthood of the Bow. During that period his main support was Spencer F. Baird, the secretary of the Smithsonian Institution, who had recognized the abilities of the young Cushing and sent him to Zuñi at the age of twenty-two. What Cushing did at Zuñi was nothing less than to develop a new method—"participant observation"—and a new view of what the ethnologist should do: "The day is fast approaching when it will be demonstrated that the personal equation is the supremely essential thing in such researches as this." By combining accurate observation with controlled imagination he was a century ahead of his time. Later students of Zuñi who couldn't see as far were critical of his results and only the French scholars of the *Année sociologique* took him seriously. Claude Lévi-Strauss has recently placed Cushing, along with Lewis Henry Morgan, "as one of the great forerunners of social structure studies," and has praised him as a pioneer in the construction of models illuminating Zuñi society.

II

By the time Cushing arrived at Zuñi, the Pueblo peoples of New Mexico had been under Spanish control for some three centuries. The six Zuñi villages had borne the brunt of Coronado's conquest in 1540 and had been forced to construct mission buildings and churches after 1629. Spanish excesses led to the Pueblo Rebellion in 1680, in which the Zuñis joined, and the Spaniards were driven out of New Mexico and were not able to return in force until 1692. The six Zuñi villages were abandoned during this period as the population took refuge on a nearby mesa top, Towayalane, where they made preparations to resist the Spanish forces. Here they centralized their war organization and began the process of integrating their social and ceremonial organization.

With the return of the Spaniards the Zuñis were forced to submit, but Spanish controls beyond the Rio Grande were less rigorous after 1692. The Zuñis coming down from Towayalane had decided to reside together in a single village, the better to deal with the Spanish authorities and to ward off the increasing incursions of the Apaches and Navajos. After Halona was built near its earlier site, a mission church was reconstructed, but during most of the eighteenth century the Zuñis were largely left alone.

The revolt of Mexico against Spain was successful in 1821 and Spanish soldiers and missions were withdrawn from New Mexico, cutting the Pueblos and Spanish settlements off from trade with the south and subjecting them to Indian raids. The inauguration of trade with the United States over the Sante Fe trail soon followed and led in 1846 to the bloodless conquest of New Mexico and its subsequent acquisition in the Treaty of Guadalupe Hidalgo two years later. The new owners set out to pacify the still wild tribes of the Plains and the Southwest and to explore their new possessions. Once this was accomplished, it was time to study them before their languages and customs were entirely gone.

When the Smithsonian expedition arrived in Zuñi in 1879, the population had been reduced from an estimated 2,500 in 1680 to about 1,700. They were still concentrated in a single village but had begun to expand into farming villages during the summer. A small Presbyterian mission had been established shortly before Cushing's arrival and the completion of the railroad through Gallup in the early 1880s led to an influx of traders and missionaries and the beginnings of a school system. The agency for Indian affairs was initially in Santa Fe, but the establishment of Fort Wingate, some forty miles to the northeast of Zuñi, soon led to military interference in the internal affairs of the pueblo.

III

In this situation the Zuñis needed mediators who could assist them in their dealings with the outside world, and hence their interest in Cushing. We see him aiding the Zuñis in retaining their land base and driving off intruders—whether Indians, Spanish-Mexicans, or Anglos. He had a hard time with the missionaries and some of the traders, but his loyalties to the Zuñis were always clear. In a critical incident in which he was accused of witchcraft, a serious offense, he dramatically took the offensive and shamed his accusers by a recital of what he had actually done for the Zuñis.

Almost a century later T. N. Pandey spent some three years

at Zuñi, where he studied modern political developments and changes in the Zuñi world view. He also inquired about their reactions to anthropologists, beginning with Cushing, and his account confirms many of Cushing's own statements as to his difficulties with Anglo missionaries and government agents, as well as illustrating the realistic views which the Zuñis held as to the value of his presence.[1] It is ironic that Cushing was ultimately forced to leave Zuñi for opposing attempts to take over Zuñi lands by U.S. army officers, including the son-in-law of Senator John A. Logan, who threatened to withhold funds for the Bureau of Ethnology.

Cushing was later able to return to the Southwest and Zuñi as the director of the Hemenway Expedition, the first organized archeological program in the region, but ill health and other difficulties led to his resignation and return to Washington. Between bouts of illness and some further archeological work in Florida at Key Marco he wrote the reports and unpublished papers that are presented in this volume. His work was cut short by his untimely death at the age of forty-three, when he choked on a fishbone.

In the pages which follow, Jesse Green has brought Cushing back as a living presence. As the first professional ethnologist his contributions to method and above all his contributions to our understanding of Zuñi and Pueblo behavior entitle him to a secure place in the history of anthropology. And if there is a certain flamboyance in signing official letters as "1st War Chief of Zuñi, U.S. Assistant Ethnologist," you will find that he had more than earned that dual title. And you might further note that the Zuñis apparently had a higher regard for his accomplishments than did the U.S. government. There is more in prospect with regard to Cushing and his contributions to scholarship, and we can thank Professor Green for providing the major directions and perspectives. To have this much of his work in one place is itself a major event.

Note

1. Triloki Nath Pandey, "Anthropologists at Zuñi."

ZUÑI

Introduction

Zuñi pueblo stands in the valley of a little tributary of the Colorado River high in the plateau country of western New Mexico, near the Arizona boundary. In the midst of a desert seemingly older than the continent itself, it too has a long past as perhaps the first still occupied settlement within the borders of the United States to have been discovered by Europeans. Known to its ancient inhabitants as *Hálona I'tiwana*, the Middle Ant Hill of the World, this little village, numbering then some two or three thousand persons, was one of the "Seven Cities of Cibola," stories of whose supposed wealth and splendor began to reach the Spanish rulers of Mexico in the early 1530s and led by 1540 to an expedition of conquest under the command of Francisco Vásquez de Coronado. While the spoils proved disappointing, the result, nevertheless, was that the Zuñi villages and the whole surrounding region, including over eighty pueblos altogether, came under Spanish—and Franciscan—rule.

In the course of time the eighty have dwindled to nineteen, and of those known to the Spanish as "Cibola" (an approximation of the Indians' own name of *"Shi-wona"*) only the single pueblo of Zuñi remains. Zuñi itself, which preserved into the present century its ancient character as an essentially autonomous and self-reliant farming village, has now, like virtually all such communities, come into its inheritance from the modern society of its

Substantial portions of this Introduction appeared earlier in the form of a review. Reprinted with permission from *The New York Review of Books.* Copyright © 1975, Nyrev, Inc.

conquerers—a rural version of urban blight. Instead of corn, its modern crops, someone has said, are welfare, various federal and tribal programs, and jewelry making. For all the cultural erosion, however, Zuñi communal life is still based in a ceremonial lore as ancient as it is extensive, detailed, and complex.

Because of this remarkable body of myth, ceremonial observance, and ritual drama—focal as it has been to the whole life and operation of the society—Zuñi has seen a great many anthropologists over the years. The author of this collection was the first—and not simply in the sense of being the first to arrive at Zuñi.

Frank Hamilton Cushing (1857–1900) was one of those pioneers who get buried by the rush of progress in the very territory they have opened up. Barely known today other than by specialists and a few buffs, Cushing is a figure of no little significance in the history of American anthropology. "Probably the first professional ethnologist" in the field,[1] he was without much doubt the most brilliant of the group associated with the Bureau of American Ethnology in its illustrious first years under the directorship of Major John Wesley Powell, and his work at Zuñi and later as director of the Hemenway Expedition in Arizona laid the foundations for scientific study of the ethnology and archeology of the American Southwest. Regarded as a man of genius (if somewhat erratic genius) by such contemporaries or near contemporaries as Powell, Adolph Bandelier, Franz Boas, and Alfred Kroeber, during his own lifetime he not only had a considerable and devoted following within the profession but enjoyed popular fame both as "the man who lived with the Indians" and as a kind of North American Schliemann, a discoverer of buried cities and ancient civilizations.

Through his writings, moreover, his influence extended beyond America to such seminal figures in European anthropology and sociology as Lucien Lévy-Bruhl, Emile Durkheim, and Marcel Mauss, and by way of their work ideas of his have filtered down to writers as current as Claude Lévi-Strauss and as far afield from anthropology as Owen Barfield. Naturally he was known to Edmund Wilson, who seems sooner or later to have discovered nearly everything. Cushing, Wilson informs us in his book *Red, Black, Blond, and Olive,*

> was an admirable writer—almost as much a literary man as he was a technical expert; and, if the historians of American literature had seriously done their work, he would be recognized not merely as a classic in the anthropological field but as an artist who had something in common with Doughty of Arabia. A good deal of Cushing's work has an autobiographical element, and his account of his queer dual life is a unique literary document on the struggle between white man and red man, not in the forest or on the plains, but in one dislocated human spirit.[2]

In 1879, the year of Cushing's arrival at Zuñi pueblo, the conquest of the Indians was nearly complete and the new Americans had begun to indulge an interest in the waning culture of the old. The Bureau of Ethnology had just been established as a branch of the Smithsonian Institution, and the "collecting party" to which Cushing was assigned as ethnologist, at the age of twenty-two, was its first expedition. The expectation was that he would spend about three months finding out all there was to know, camping the while with his colleagues in tents outside the pueblo. One of his first professional field experiences, however, was frustration at how little he could learn as an outsider, and he soon abandoned the tents of his colleagues and—to the consternation of everyone, including the Zuñis— moved in with the Indians, establishing himself, without invitation, in a room belonging to the governor, or secular chief, of the tribe. ("How long will it be before you go back to Washington?" asked the governor, upon discovering his guest.)

As it turned out, Cushing remained for four and a half years, became proficient in the language, and—partly winning his way through a combination of charm, luck, and stubbornness and partly being pulled along by the Indians' own determination to convert and absorb him—entered so far into the life of the pueblo that he not only was formally initiated into the tribe but became a member of the tribal council and of the Bow Priesthood. The original "participant observer," Cushing was the first anthropologist to have actually lived with his subjects over an extended period—and the only man in history entitled to sign himself, as he once did at the end of an official letter, "1st War Chief of Zuñi, U.S. Asst. Ethnologist."[3]

Such a figure, dashing and flamboyant as he was in his long hair and individual version of Zuñi dress, was clearly susceptible to mythologizing—even self-mythologizing.[4] In the contemporary accounts of Cushing's life and activities several romantic images converge with that of the scientific investigator: the frontier adventurer, the traveler among exotic peoples and convert to noble savagery, the individual moving to a different drummer. Sorting image from fact is not always easy, but even discounting the stories that appear too edifying to be true, it is remarkable how Cushing's career seems to have evolved from his earliest experiences.[5] Endowed both with frail health and an independent-minded physician father who hated conventionality, believed only in reason, and walked barefoot in the street when he pleased,[6] Cushing as a child seems to have eluded in large degree the convention of regular school attendance, spending much of his time instead alone in the woods and fields around the family farm in central New York learning, in the best Emersonian fashion, not from books but from nature. At about the age of ten, coming upon an arrowhead, he had become fascinated by the idea that Indians had once lived on that same ground, and from that time on, according to his own account, his life had become centered on the attempt to recreate for himself the life of those Indians.

Using as his headquarters the ruin of an ancient Indian fortification he had come upon in the woods, he communed with the spirits of the place for days, and nights, at a time. More than that, he not only gathered a large collection of artifacts (later deposited at the Smithsonian) but experimented tirelessly to reproduce those objects and thereby to recover knowledge of how they had been made and used originally. On one memorable occasion, carving with chips of flint on the bone handle of his toothbrush in the effort to reproduce a beautiful bone harpoon he had found, he accidentally reversed motions and discovered how to cut flint with bone. "I never finished that harpoon," he recalled later; turning it about and using it as an arrowflaker, he had made arrow after arrow in the excitement of his discovery, until his hands were blistered and lacerated.[7]

Developing thus on his own both a gift for handcrafts and the powers of close observation for which he was later famous, he became expert at making arrowheads and other implements, and he experimented as well with pottery, basket weaving, and the construction of birch-bark and log canoes. In doing so, according to Powell, he made a number of remarkable discoveries about Indian methods of workmanship, as well as recognizing for what they were a variety of relics that had never before been noticed. One admirer's story has it that Cushing introduced himself to Cornell University at age eighteen by bringing to a professor who had told him there were no Indian remains left in that neighborhood a whole bag full, collected in the course of an hour or so. When he started to empty the contents on the floor, the professor stared and then shouted, "Stop! What are you doing? Take care of those things! Bring them here to the table."[8] It was an auspicious beginning to a short academic career.

Even given capacities of this sort on Cushing's part, however, finding out all there was to know about the Zuñis involved a good deal more than anyone had bargained for. To begin with, as he tells the story in the most autobiographical of his writings, *My Adventures in Zuñi*, neither the Zuñi nor Cushing's white colleagues were prepared for the kind of enterprise he embarked on with his move into the pueblo; and if Cushing himself assumed that he could pursue it entirely on his own terms, he was to find otherwise. Far from according with any existing scientific—not to mention social—norm, his move in among the "savages" was apparently regarded by most of his associates as bizarre and absurd; and when he elected to remain in Zuñi rather than accompany the expedition on its further travels, he seems to have been left rather unceremoniously—and without provisions. More lonely and helpless than he had expected to be, Cushing thus found himself totally dependent on those upon whom he had been intruding. The Indians, in turn, out of pity and propriety, accepted him—but on *their* terms—vowing to make a Zuñi of him, taking away his eastern clothes and his comfortable hammock, dressing him in Zuñi garb, and undertaking to "harden his meat" by subjecting him to the rigors of their way of life.

Cushing complained of his miseries, but, accepting these

discomforts (as he did very much greater hardships later on in the course of various journeys of exploration in the area) despite his physical frailty and increasingly serious respiratory and digestive disorders, he made up his mind to let the Zuñis do with him what they wished.[9] He had already begun making friends, especially in the family of the governor, with whom he lived, and now the latter took him over as his particular charge, instructing Cushing to regard him as his elder brother. Still, serious strains could hardly be avoided—Cushing's central aim continuing to be to gather information and that of the Zuñis being to continue their way of life undisturbed by outsiders. As he relates in *My Adventures*, he was persistently finding his way past taboos into places where he did not belong, and his unyielding and sometimes fierce insistence on always taking notes and sketching everything came near to costing his life before the Indians satisfied themselves that he was basically harmless.

Also, adaptable as he was, taboos of his own conflicted sometimes with *their* demands—for example, their insistence, long resisted, that he allow them to pierce his ear lobes, an act whose importance he was slow to perceive but which turned out to be a prelude to the ceremony in which he was formally adopted and given his Indian name. To repeated attempts to get him married to a Zuñi girl he never did give in, managing to pass himself off (not quite convincingly but with acceptable courtesy) as being too young to think of it. And then there were the times when whatever resistance he felt to the other culture's tastes or values had simply to be swallowed unseen, as on the occasion he recalls in another book, *Zuñi Breadstuff*, when, still "fresh from the East, callow, and with as yet but limited notions as to what [his] experiments implied," he was invited to share his first Zuñi family meal—all hands in the stew pot. When he scalded his fingers trying to dip in with the rest, his alert and considerate hostess

> quietly rose and went hunting about for something. Presently she found that something on the floor where the baby had been playing with it. It was an old, broken-handled pewter spoon. She caught it up, and seeing that it was—not very clean—put it into her own mouth, good woman, licked it off thoroughly, then went to the waterjar and rinsed out that organ; but it never seemed to occur to

her to rinse off the spoon. At any rate, without doing so, she approached me and was about to hand it to me when the old man gave her dress-skirt a surreptitious jerk and whispered something. She gave me a quick, scared look, then reached for a brown, very old cotton mantle which was lying on the floor (the one she had on was too clean) and wiped the spoon off with it. Then with an air which seemed to say, "Could a *Melik* woman have done better than that?" she handed me the spoon.[10]

While appreciating her courtesy, the fastidious Cushing clearly took considerable satisfaction in his own courteous acceptance and use of that spoon (after stirring it about a good deal in the steaming pot) and in his subsequent enjoyment of the stew. So, of course, did the Zuñis. He was immediately inundated with dinner invitations and was known from then on as He-Who-Eats-From-One-Dish-With-One-Spoon.

From the beginning Cushing was impressed by the communal ceremonies he witnessed in Zuñi, and his interest was much aroused as he became aware before long of other activities going on—ceremonial meetings of various sacred societies or priesthoods—which he was not supposed to witness. The first glimpse he contrived to get into one of these meetings revealed, he wrote in *My Adventures*, "a mysterious life by which I had little dreamed I was surrounded." Gaining access to that "mysterious life," becoming himself a priest in one of the most prestigious of the sacred orders, the Priesthood of the Bow, was the work of years and involved, as well as arduous ordeals of motionlessness, silence, fasting, and dancing to exhaustion, a spiritual and psychological investment perhaps greater than Cushing himself cared to realize. Later on, when he had returned east and lapsed from the religious observances he had practiced as a Zuñi, he seems to have been visited by a troubling dream or vision about returning to the true way and his true self.

During this time Cushing became intimately involved in all aspects of Zuñi life. Dwelling in an apartment occupied by the governor and his wife, together with nine assorted relatives, he became like a member of the family, close to all the details of their domestic life and implicated in the intricacies of their personal relationships. In the village at large he took part in all the tasks, and through close observation and patient practice he became expert in the varous Zuñi handcrafts, to the point where, according to Major Powell, "there was nothing that a Zuñi could make he could not reproduce with greater skill." [11]

As he improved his knowledge of the language and assimilated the complexities of the Zuñi social order, he assumed an influential role in the government of the tribe. And, a gifted raconteur, he became not only a recognized authority in matters of Zuñi history, myth, and ceremony but a favorite among the tribal storytellers, making contributions of his own to the collective store. Translations into English utlimately followed, appearing both in his "Outlines of Zuñi Creation Myths" and in the posthumously published *Zuñi Folk Tales*. Not only are these the first translations to have been made of such a body of aboriginal American literature, but the latter, according to Edmund Wilson, is "one of the few first-rate things of the kind that have been produced in the United States." [12] In a contemporary review of the book, H. F. C. tenKate wrote that Cushing "indeed could think like the Indians who made those myths; he could speak like their priests and prophets as probably no white man before or after him ever could." [13]

So much, indeed, did Cushing come to think like a Zuñi that toward the end of his stay he got into trouble with a local Indian agent for shooting a trespassing Navajo horse. Certainly the role he played as resident anthropologist remains unique in the degree of his identification with the people he studied—and really of his responsibility to them and for them as not only a member of the tribe but a council leader and head war chief. It was as a Zuñi of responsible position, he argued, that he had fired his pistol at the Navajo ponies; their owners had been warned before to keep them off Zuñi lands, and action was required. [14] As head war chief, he was also obliged on one occasion to lead an attack against a gang of horse thieves—a success-crowned venture resulting, though the Zuñis were "mostly unarmed," in the death of two of the thieves, one an American, the other a Mexican. [15] Earlier, he had been involved in a skirmish with raiding Apaches, an adventure from which he had emerged with an enemy scalp. This was a prize long coveted as a prerequisite for his initiation into the Priesthood of the Bow, and while he left decorously vague the circumstances of his coming into possession of it, there was, according to his own account at any rate, no doubt about his ownership, and a special ceremony had to be performed to purge it of the taint of being taken with a steel rather than a flint knife.[16]

Among other things, such incidents may remind us of the larger historical scene in which Cushing's researches were being carried on. The battle of the Little Big Horn had occurred only three years before his arrival in Zuñi, and the Zuñi encounter with an Apache raiding party, while in keeping with ancient tribal enmities, was in the context of a general Apache uprising—the last major resistance to the white man's conquest of the continent—which was not finally suppressed until 1886, two years after Cushing's departure. Cushing's own attitude with respect to Apaches seems to have derived for the most part, in any case, from his Zuñi identity. In one of his letters of the period he reports defending in council "the rights of my adopted people against these wandering coyotes—driving them mercilessly from Zuñi territory and compelling them to return or pay for stolen property." Hence, as he goes on to say, "more than ordinary Americans, I am in danger when travelling solitarily about the country." He had been warned also of "some risk from the Mexicans," having testified to "the traitorous character of some of their relations with the Indians."[17]

Not surprisingly, however, the greatest trouble he encountered in defending his adopted Zuñis against encroachments on their hereditary lands came not from the Navajos, the Apaches, or the Mexicans, but from his fellow Americans. As a result of careless error when the reservation boundaries were established in 1877, an area containing essential springs, rich farming lands, and some sixty houses and fenced pastures had been omitted from the official description—though this area, whose Spanish name is Las Nutrias, or Nutria, had been occupied by Zuñis since long before the arrival of the conquistadores. Learning of this error in late 1882, two army officers stationed in the region entered claims for 800 acres each, declared their intention to establish cattle ranches, and requested the Indians to vacate the property. Through Cushing's covert intervention, and the help of his well-placed journalistic friends, the error was ultimately corrected and the attempted land grab exposed and forestalled;

but since one of the men was the son-in-law of a powerful and quarrelsome United States senator, General John A. Logan of Illinois, a lengthy struggle was required and there were consequences for Cushing. The level of the senator's argument is suggested by the rhetorical question he posed on one occasion: "If a civilized white man can now get only 160 acres of land as a homestead by paying for it, and an Indian can get over 1,000 acres without paying for it, had not the white man better adopt the Cushing plan and become one of the Zuñi Indians?" [18]

Warned by his superiors, who were of no mind to antagonize an important senator over a trivial issue of Indian land rights, Cushing remained strictly in the background, but he was nonetheless subjected to a personal vendetta by the angry senator, who apparently threatened finally to crush the Bureau of Ethnology itself unless Cushing was recalled from Zuñi. The recall notice came in January of 1884: "It is thought best that the valuable ethnological material collected by you at the Pueblo of Zuñi should be put in shape for publication at as early a day as practicable. . . . As soon, therefore, as you can settle your affairs at Zuñi, and make the necessary arrangements, you will proceed to Washington and report to the Director." [19]

All these episodes illustrate that Cushing's role at Zuñi went well beyond that of a collector of ethnological material. The first professional ethnologist in the field, he was also no doubt the last to collect his own scalps. It is all of a piece, however, and if the profession has had to place narrower limits on the observer's participation than Cushing submitted to, a price for these more scientific standards has been paid—even if the loss, as some would say, is only to "literature."

When Cushing left Zuñi in 1884, still under twenty-seven, he—and the bureau—expected that a compendious report would be the result of his stay there. Compendious reports were not, however, what he was fated to produce. While still at Zuñi he had published or completed several articles on special topics such as fetishism and pottery, as well as the *Century Magazine* series on his life in Zuñi and a two-part report in the *Atlantic* on a visit he had made to the Havasupais, whose village in a remote section of the Grand Canyon had never before been host to a white visitor,[20] and he had almost completed the series "Zuñi Breadstuff" appearing in an Indianapolis trade journal, the *Millstone*. Back in Washington, he set to work putting his notes in order for the larger task. But his health, increasingly fragile during the years in Zuñi, now gave way, and a long leave of absence from the bureau ensued, culminating in his being sponsored by a wealthy Boston patroness for a return to the Southwest, this time as director of the ambitious Hemenway Southwestern Archaeological Expedition.

The aim of this enterprise was to trace the ancient sources of the culture Cushing had studied at Zuñi; the means were to be the systematic excavation of ruins, both on the Cibola town sites near Zuñi and those which the Zuñi migration legends led him to expect to find in the valleys of the Gila and Salt rivers in Arizona. A staff was recruited, including Adolph Bandelier, to research the Spanish history of the area; H. F. C. tenKate, to be responsible for matters of physical anthropology; and Frederick W. Hodge (Cushing's future brother-in-law) to provide general assistance;[21] and after elaborate preparations and much arduous journeying, operations were commenced in February of 1887 at a mound near Tempe, Arizona. Excavations on this site, overgrown with mesquite and undisturbed by prior relic diggers, disclosed what was, according to Emil W. Haury, "probably the largest community in southern Arizona in pre-Spanish times."[22] Not only extensive architectural remains but an elaborate system of irrigation canals and some five thousand archeological specimens were uncovered during the fifteen months of activity in the area.

Again, however, the compendious report which would have brought to fulfillment this pioneer enterprise—the first of its kind in the Southwest—was not fated for completion. Recurrence of Cushing's illness seriously impaired his direction of necessary activities and ultimately, in the winter of 1888–89, forced his return to the East. Management passed briefly to other hands, and then, amid recriminations about Cushing's administration (or misadministration), the expedition was terminated. Cushing remained almost totally inactive for the next several years; and in the end, beyond a "Preliminary Report" he had written for the 1888 meeting in Berlin of the International Congress of Americanists, he published nothing on the Hemenway project, though in 1892 or 1893 he did write some two hundred pages of a work titled "Field Notes and Journal of Exploration and Discoveries in Arizona and New Mexico during the Years 1887–1888"—an introductory account which carries only through the second day of actual excavation (and depends extensively, even within that scope, on notes taken by Hodge).[23] It is generally assumed that Cushing simply failed to maintain the field notes necessary for completing this report, having trusted, in his quirky way, that memory would suffice. Among his papers, however, is an account of the dissolution of the Hemenway Expedition in which he refers to the seizure by his successor, J. Walter Fewkes, of "more than 1,000 pages of notes, . . . all of my most important papers, maps, sketches, etc." The loss of these, he adds, "deprived me of any opportunity there might have been for working up and publishing the results of that really magnificent and splendidly successful piece of work. I have never since been able to see any of my collections or any of the data we so carefully gathered and saved."[24] Eventually the collection of artifacts themselves was deposited in the Peabody Museum at Harvard, along with some sketches and miscellaneous notes. But to date no cache of one thousand pages of Cushing field notes has turned up. Whatever the truth may be, the result for Cushing was a lost opportunity for what might have been a monumental achievement. As for the excavated town itself, named Los Muertos by the diggers on account of the quantity of skeletons turned up, its discovery excited great public interest for a time; but not being Ninevah, it soon succumbed to the farmer's plow and not a trace of it remains.

When his health was sufficiently recovered, Cushing returned to the bureau and spent the next several years at various writing and research projects, museum work, and preparations for the bureau exhibit at the 1893 World Columbian Exposition in Chicago. The lengthy "Outlines of Zuñi Creation Myths" is a product of this period; others include the important "Manual Concepts: A Study of the Influence of Hand-Usage on Culture-Growth," "Primitive Copper Working: An Experimental Study," and a paper on the evolution and cultural role of the arrow.

Seriously ill again in the spring of 1895, Cushing was referred to Dr. William Pepper in Philadelphia, and the outcome of their meeting was not only an improvement in Cushing's condition but a new archeological expedition. Pepper, who was much interested in both Cushing and the study of ancient cultures, financed a trip by his patient to the Florida Keys—partly for the sake of his health—to investigate reports of Indian ruins in the area. What Cushing found on this first trip, in May of 1895, was so promising that a second, more ambitious venture was underwritten by Pepper, this time with support from Mrs. Phoebe Hearst and joint official sponsorship by the bureau and the University of Pennsylvania.

What Cushing had discovered, and proceeded to excavate in the winter and spring of 1896, were the remains of an Indian civilization, then entirely unknown, whose settlements had been constructed over the water on mounds artificially built up out of seashells. Preserved in the underwater muck amid the ruins of what had been elaborate garden terraces, canoe channels, and water courts were thousands of artifacts, many of great beauty. The finds were spectacular, suggesting links hitherto unestablished between the cultures of Central America and those of the Mississippi Valley.

Retrieving and drying articles so long immersed that they had been reduced to little more than spongy mush presented considerable difficulties, and despite painstaking care and ingenuity, the technology Cushing could draw on or improvise was not sufficient to prevent the loss of a large number of items in the process. Nevertheless, in the course of several months he and his crew amassed enough relics to fill some eleven barrels and fifty-nine boxes—a rich collection and a unique one, since none of the efforts over the years to duplicate Cushing's finds has succeeded.

With this collection he returned north in the summer of 1896, and he continued to work with it through most of the next four years, making further efforts at preservation and restoration, studying and cataloging the specimens, and preparing for publication. A "Preliminary Report," based on a talk before the American Philosophical Society, was published in the *Proceedings* of that society for 1896. He was still working on a larger report when he died in April of 1900, at the age of forty-three.[25]

Cushing's peculiar genius and his unique place in the annals of anthropology are really epitomized by his odd double title as both war chief and ethnologist. No "participant" before him had been an observer disciplined with anything like his scientific aims and methods; nor has participation in tribal life by any scientific observer after him extended so far or been so central to the very modes of observation, let alone—barring a few recent exceptions—so admissible to the record. For a proper eastern gentleman of the Victorian age, and for an undoubting believer in science and progress dedicated first and last to the gathering of data, he was a remarkable man. What he brought to his science at this juncture in its history were the imagination and talents, and some of the quirks, of an artist. "Intensive, intuitional, mystic, neurotic and in chronic ill health, with a streak of exhibitionism"—thus Kroeber describes him in his brief article on Cushing in the 1930 edition of the *Encyclopaedia of the Social Sciences*. Cushing, Kroeber goes on to say, with some exasperation, was capable of "vivid insight amounting at times to genius, . . . [and] he had an extraordinary knowledge of Zuñi. . . . His observations were of the keenest, but almost impossible to disentangle from his imaginings." It was of course this overlapping of observation and imagination, of U.S. Ethnologist and adoptive Zuñi, in Cushing's work that made him an anachronistic figure as twentieth-century anthropology came to identify more and more with the "exact" sciences and the ideal of a nonsubjective methodology. Not surprisingly, on the other hand, it was precisely upon this same highly individual combination of characteristics, extending into his theoretical concepts, that Cushing's reputation and influence among his own contemporaries both in the United States and abroad were based.

Cushing himself, moreover, was quite aware of the questions raised by his radically participatory methods. Indeed, he was far ahead of his time in recognizing as inherent in the nature of anthropology itself as a discipline the problem of the observers' "tendency . . . to read into their renderings of things their [own] personalities." Nevertheless, he wrote, "the day is fast approaching when it will be demonstrated that the personal equation is the supremely essential thing in such researches as this, provided it has been abundantly [saturated] with the primitive elements it is dealing with—has absorbed at all points practical, sensational or emotional."[26]

In the matter of handcrafts Cushing's method as a mature archeologist was the direct outgrowth of his boyhood experiments at arrowhead making. It was also sufficiently unorthodox from the standpoint of science even in his own time to warrant the following explanation in a talk he gave in 1895 before the American Association for the Advancement of Science:

> If I am at times seemingly too personal in style of statement, let it be rememberd that well-nigh all anthropology is personal history; that even the *things* of past man were personal, like as never they are to ourselves now. They must, therefore, be both treated and worked at, not solely according to ordinary methods of procedure or rules of logic, or to any given canons of learning, but in a profoundly personal mood and way. If I would study any old, lost art, let us say, I must make myself the artisan of it—must, by examining its products, learn both to see and to feel as much as may be the conditions under which they were produced and the needs they supplied or satisfied; then, rigidly adhering to those conditions and constrained by their resources alone, as ignorantly and anxiously strive with my own hands to reproduce, not to imitate, these things as ever strove primitive man to produce them. I have virtually the same hands he had, the same physique, [and] generally or fundamentally the same activial and mental functions, that men had in ages gone by, no matter how remote. If, then, I dominate myself with their needs, surround myself with their material conditions, aim to do as they did, the chances are that I shall restore their acts and their arts, however lost or hidden, rediscovering what they discovered precisely as they discovered it. Thus may I reproduce an art in all its stages; see how it began, grew, developed into, and affected other arts and things.[27]

In "this new method of research by experimental reproduction," Major Powell wrote in 1900, "Cushing laid the foundation of a system of investigation which has since proved of marvelous efficiency and which has been successfully developed by other laborers"[28] —a foundation, it should be added, which has stood the test of time, for the experimental method is perhaps the basis for more serious work in archeology today, both in Europe and in America, than it has been at any time in the past.

What primitive conditions and resources implied to Cush-

ing was not confined, of course, simply to material considerations. Among his more influential contributions, in fact,
were his observations concerning the significance carried in the
forms of things, because of the Zuñi way of perceiving all things
as living, including "the things made or born in their special
forms by the hands of men." Cushing gives every evidence of
having wholeheartedly shared with his Indians this sense of
what is alive—and has a meaning that needs only to be divined—in all things born, made, or performed. And the work of
reproduction to which he patiently disciplined himself
amounted to seeking, so to speak, the divinations which might be
performed by his own hands. Reviving the primitive function of
the hands, he could, as Lévy-Bruhl paraphrases him, "live over
again with them their experience of prehistoric days . . . *when
the hands were so at one with the mind that they really formed a
part of it*" (Lévy-Bruhl's italics).[29] The thesis that various basic
linguistic, numerical, and distributional concepts originate in
the form and functioning of the hands is one that Cushing de-
velops in his "Manual Concepts."

What Lévy-Bruhl found in Cushing was a rich source both of
insight and of documentation basic to the development of his
own concept of the "law of participation," i.e., his theory of
primitive cognition as based on "collective representations" or
projections of communally shared psychic values onto the external world (a concept taken up by such writers as Ernst Cassirer
and Owen Barfield). Not only recognizing the collectively invested potency in individual forms, moreover, Cushing perceived a coherent order in this Zuñi world of circumambient
powers. Based on a conception of the cosmos as divided sevenfold into "spirit quarters," each related to the center or "Middle
of the World," it was an order which he saw as underlying and
defining every aspect of pueblo life. The elemental forces of
nature, plants, and animals, seasonal changes, birth, growth, and
death all are identified according to this fundamental division
which Cushing found to be evident likewise in the design of the
buildings, the agricultural practices, the symbols and ritual observances, the totemic associations and clan and priesthood organizations, the housing arrangements, in short, in all aspects of
the culture.

It was his exposition of this intricate and detailed correspondence between the Zuñi world picture and the "mytho-
sociologic organization" of their culture, and his view of this
correspondence as typifying the way cultures generally may be
shaped by "an *Idea* conceived during the incipient stages" of
their development,[30] that Cushing passed on to Durkheim and
Mauss—a contribution observed by Claude Lévi-Strauss in a
discussion of their pioneer work *Primitive Classifications*. Noting that Durkheim and Mauss "received their inspiration from
the work of Cushing, which it has become fashionable in recent
years to belittle," Lévi-Strauss goes on to remark that

> Cushing's insight and sociological imagination make him deserv-
> ing of a seat on [Lewis Henry] Morgan's right, as one of the great
> forerunners of social structure studies. The gaps and inaccuracies
> in his descriptions, less serious than the indictment of having
> "over-interpreted" some of his materials, will be viewed in their
> true proportions when it is realized that, albeit in an unconscious
> fashion, Cushing was aiming less at giving an actual description of
> Zuñi society than at elaborating a model (his famous sevenfold
> division) which could explain most of its processes and structure.[31]

It is questionable whether Cushing would have been altogether pleased with this compliment (however well deserved),
since whatever he may have been up to unconsciously, his conscious aim in general really was to give actual description.
Indeed, to view him against the background of the computer-
oriented analyses of structures and functions now dominating
the field of anthropology is to see that his greatest distinction is to
have conveyed always a sense of the presence of living people
and real things. But that, perhaps, is a literary distinction more
than a scientific one; and in truth, when all is said about Cushing's significance in the history of anthropology, it may be that
one should admit, if pressed, that it is primarily as literature that
his writings continue to merit attention—though they have received even less of it in the literary world than in the anthropological.

Interestingly enough, however, even from the literary
standpoint, Cushing turns out to have been a prophetic figure in
the history of anthropology, for a number of contemporary anthropologists like Laura Bohannan and Hortense Powdermaker

have reintroduced "the personal equation" by writing literature off-duty, so to speak, in the form of anthropological novels and memoirs. "Field work," Powdermaker writes in her *Stranger and Friend: The Way of an Anthropologist,*

> is a deeply human as well as a scientific experience and a detailed knowledge of both aspects is an important source of data in itself, and necessary for any comparative study of methodology. Yet we know less about participant observation than about almost any other method in the social sciences. . . . To openly recognize and use as part of the research the humanness of the investigator, as well as of the people he studies, is sometimes considered old-fashioned by those who would depersonalize both. But the constants underlying effective field work know no fashion.[32]

Of course, as everyone now knows, what is really old-fashioned is the notion, carried over from the natural into the behavioral sciences but outgrown sooner in the former than in the latter, that *any* science can be so "exact" as to preclude the element of subjectivity in the human investigator. A sort of circle is completed by the work of George Devereaux and other psychoanalytically or philosophically oriented anthropologists whose theoretical explorations are predicated on the central role of that subjectivity.[33] These more recent writers, to be sure, are sophisticated in ways that Cushing was not. He does not seem to have been particularly introspective. Nor was he really very concerned with the epistemological ramifications of "the personal equation." He simply recognized his own person as the medium in which the "saturation" of "primitive elements" essential to his research must take place—recognized, that is, the essentiality of his participation as adoptive Zuñi to any observation he might make as ethnologist.

"The keynote of Mr. Cushing's personality," his friend Alice Fletcher observed, "seems to have been an unconscious sympathy." What she had in mind included the kind of intuitive capacity for getting inside primitive craftways and ways of seeing and thinking that almost all of Cushing's associates found so remarkable in him—the ability to draw forth from "the crude ceremony, the archaic thought, the mnemonic symbol . . . the secret meaning which through them was struggling for expression." But she seems also to have been referring to something at once simpler and more inclusive, a quality of vitality and responsiveness conveyed in everything about him—his facial expressions, the deftness of his hands, the "peculiar wealth of his mental imagery." To him, as to the Indians who adopted him, "everything was alive." [34]

For the reader of Cushing, all this may be taken as a comment upon his writing. It is possible too, however, that it may express something of the feeling of the Indians themselves who gave him the name *Tenatsali*, or Medicine Flower, after a plant whose vital healing qualities made it for them the most sacred of all plants. They loved him; and when the archaeologist and writer Bertha Dutton visited Zuñi in 1938, fifty years after his last departure, she "found that the older people were still mourning because Cushing was not able to return from Washington." And on various occasions in the course of her work there, her informant, an old man named Zna'ote, told her: "What Cushy says, that is right." [35] Coming from a people grown weary and suspicious of anthropologists, that is a remarkable tribute.

It is often regretted that Cushing wrote no more than he did. Frequent illness, premature death, and undeniably mercurial ways with respect to the management of time and energy resulted in his leaving a written record that, by subsequent anthropological standards, did not do justice to his actual experience. His career, according to one recent estimation,

> was in fact a series of brilliant failures, a string of exciting promises followed by inability to execute systematically. Illness was usually the excuse, but the fact is that Cushing could never get beyond the brilliant flash of insight and the far-reaching hypothesis to the methodical treatments that were increasingly in demand in American anthropology at the end of the [nineteenth] century.[36]

If such is the case, it is also true that what Cushing could and did accomplish is increasingly of interest at this point in our own century. The record is by no means paltry: on Zuñi alone his published work includes a host of important and substantial studies of a range of subjects such as creation myths, the lore of fetishism, the social, mythic, and religious systems, copper working, and the development of pottery and pottery design, not to mention the three still classic books, *Zuñi Breadstuff*, *Zuñi Folk Tales*, and *My Adventures in Zuñi*. And the sum of his work is hardly exhausted by Zuñi, as the bibliography shows.

A more serious problem with respect to Cushing's work has been that of accessibility or exposure. While a number of his writings—*My Adventures in Zuñi*, *Zuñi Breadstuff*, *Zuñi Folk Tales*, *Zuñi Fetiches*, *The Nation of the Willows*, *Outlines of Zuñi Creation Myths*, and *Explorations of Key Dwellers' Remains on the Gulf Coast of Florida*—have in recent years become available in facsimile reprint (all but *My Adventures*, *Zuñi Breadstuff*, and *Zuñi Folk Tales* for the first time since their original publication in the 1880s and 1890s and the latter two of these for the first time, respectively, since 1920 and 1931), these reprints are all the product of small specialty presses with limited circulation. The rest of Cushing's writings, apart from these seven titles, either are available only in the government reports, professional journals, or other periodicals in which they originally appeared—which means in the large research libraries which house such publications—or have never been published at all. (To the latter category belongs a huge store of manuscripts, some quite lengthy, in various stages of completion, and on a variety of subjects from Zuñi to Florida and from oral history to primitive music, craftsmanship, and symbolism, which he left behind at his death.)[37]

Unlike the reprints brought out to date, which serve a small but growing body of readers for the most part already acquainted with Cushing, the present volume aims at introducing his work to new readers, by way of a compact yet representative selection. Zuñi presented itself as a natural focus for such a selection. While by no means Cushing's only important subject, it was doubtless his central one and engaged his sensibilities and interests on so many fronts as to make possible an exclusively Zuñi book that would also be amply representative of the range of his contributions.

One last note: Cushing's orthographic practices, particularly in the use of italics and intersyllable or intermorpheme hyphenation or spacing in the reproduction of Zuñi words, were somewhat various. In some pieces, all Zuñi words, including proper names, are italicized; in others, proper names and sometimes other words are not italicized. In marking divisions within words he is more, but not altogether, consistent: except in *Zuñi Folk Tales* and the "Notes Made . . . 1886," where no internal divisions are shown, his practice was normally to space, if not hyphenate, between syllables or morphemes in all Zuñi words. Confronted with a seeming need for principles, I have chosen to regularize the use of italics throughout the selections by employing them for all Zuñi words except the proper names for individual persons and places—a practice Cushing himself seems to have followed most of the time. In the case of hyphens, I have regularized among the selections to the extent of inserting them wherever internal divisions appeared in the form of spacing (since Cushing himself more often hyphenated than not). In practice, this means that Zuñi words are generally hyphenated throughout the text, with the exceptions indicated above in *Zuñi Folk Tales* and "Notes Made . . . 1886." In the interest of consistency, I have also made slight changes, as needed, in diacritical marking or spelling of one or two particular Zuñi terms which appear variously in different Cushing texts (e.g., *Kâ'-kâ*, *Kâ-Kâ* *Kā* *Kā*, etc.). Except for these changes in the Zuñi words, plus some minor regularizations or corrections of spelling or punctuation and another few clearly marked insertions or adjustments of Cushing's English syntax in the interest of clarity, the selections here included are printed in the form in which Cushing left them or in which they were originally published. I have, however, provided titles for a number of the selections which are excerpted from larger works.[38] Brackets in the text are Cushing's when they appear in material being quoted by him, mine when they appear among Cushing's own words. The reader may likewise differentiate easily between Cushing's footnotes and notes I have appended to the selections; while both appear at the end of the selections to which they pertain, his are marked "F.H.C." As for the illustrations, those not otherwise credited are from the original editions of the selections in which they appear.[39] Finally, in deference to Cushing's usage and for the sake of consistency, the name *Zuñi* itself is printed throughout with the tilde—the form generally followed also in modern dictionaries, though currently less in favor than the plain *Zuni* among both scholars and Zuñis.[40]

Notes

1. Fred Eggan, "One Hundred Years of Ethnology and Social Anthropology," in *One Hundred Years of Anthropology*, ed. J. O. Brew, p. 125. One should also mention Alice Fletcher, whose almost equally early work with the Omaha Indians began in 1881.

2. Edmund Wilson, *Red, Black, Blond, and Olive*, pp. 15–19. A number of substantial academic studies of Cushing should also be mentioned: Raymond Stewart Brandes, "Frank Hamilton Cushing: Pioneer Americanist"; Bernard L. Fontana, "Pioneers in Ideas: Three Early Southwestern Ethnologists"; Clarissa P. Fuller, "Frank Hamilton Cushing's Relations to Zuñi and the Hemenway Southwestern Expedition"; Marion Spjut Gilliland, *The Material Culture of Key Marco, Florida*; Emil W. Haury, *The Excavations at Los Muertos and Neighboring Ruins in the Salt River Valley, Southern Arizona*; and Triloki Nath Pandey, "Anthropologists at Zuni;" and, most recent, Joan Mark, "Frank Hamilton Cushing and an American Science of Anthropology" (an essay presenting an impressive case for Cushing's importance in the history of anthropology, most notably as the originator of the modern concept of cultural pluralism and as the practitioner of what he called the "reciprocal method" of relating to the subjects of ethnological study). Finally, I should mention the section on Cushing—quite critical but full of fresh and challenging perceptions—in Curtis M. Hinsley, Jr., "The Development of a Profession: Anthropology in Washington, D.C., 1846–1903."

3. The letter is one of several quoted in Arthur Woodward, "Frank Cushing—'First War-Chief of Zuñi,'" *Masterkey* (Southwest Museum) 13 (1939): 172–79.

4. A note by another member of the original BAE expedition to Zuñi, Mrs. Matilda Coxe Stevenson, written on the back of a photograph of Cushing in his Zuñi clothing, should enter the record here as an example of *counter*-mythologizing: "Frank Hamilton Cushing in his fantastic dress worn while among the Zuñi Indians. This man was the biggest fool and charlatan I ever knew. He even put his hair up in curl papers every night. How could a man walk weighted down with so much toggery?" (Box no. 1, Hodge-Cushing Collection, Southwest Museum, Los Angeles). Between Cushing and Mrs. Stevenson, who outlasted him in the Southwest and whose later work on Zuñi and Sia was far more compendious, and more strictly descriptive, than his own,

competition seems to have been sharp and ill-natured from the beginning. More than one of his early letters from Zuñi refer to her efforts to belittle, malign, and interfere with his work. See, for example, the oblique but clear reference in his letter of December 14, 1879 (below). An aggressive and domineering person, Mrs. Stevenson pretty clearly had no sympathy for Cushing's participant approach; her own way of gathering ethnological information was more direct. In addition to buying it (at least on occasion), she seems also (at least occasionally) to have bullied it, marching in on kiva ceremonies without invitation and threatening the Indians with the militia if they interfered with her. As well as her own account in "The Zuñi Indians," see Nancy O. Lurie, "Women in Early American Anthropology," in *Pioneers of American Anthropology*, ed. June Helm, pp. 29–81, and Pandey, "Anthropologists at Zuñi." So far as I know, she is Cushing's only accuser with respect to the curl papers.

5. For a set of particularly vivid stories of this sort, see the "Remarks" William H. Holmes read at the Cushing memorial meeting of the American Anthropological Association—a source for various other authoritative accounts. We read here, for example, that Cushing "at birth was a mere mite of humanity, weighing only a pound and a half. For a year or two he grew but little, and was kept always on a pillow; but it is said that his mind developed more rapidly than his body—that in after years he could remember faces seen and aches felt before he was able to form words or to move from his place on the pillow. When he finally got a start he was so tiny and weak that he found no place among the hardy and boisterous brothers and sister, and sought to avoid them and be alone. Even thus early the characteristics of his unusual personality began to take form" (Frederick Webb Hodge, ed., "In Memoriam: Frank Hamilton Cushing," p. 356). One may make an educated guess that it was from Cushing himself that Holmes learned this remarkable "history."

6. George Kennan, "Frank Cushing," *Medina Tribune*, December 6, 1923, p. 1.

7. "The Arrow," pp. 312–13.

8. Holmes, "Remarks," p. 360.

9. Neil M. Judd in his book *The Bureau of American Ethnology: A Partial History* (p. 59) rightly points out that Cushing had a reputation in the BAE as a chronic complainer; his letters to Baird, Powell, and others abound with stories of hardships and privations. Examples will be found in the letters selected for inclusion in the present volume. That Cushing wrote of such matters should not, however, obscure the fact that hardships and privations were a regular feature of his life in the field and that he suffered them willingly if not silently.

10. *Zuñi Breadstuff*, pp. 553–54.

11. "Remarks by J. W. Powell," in Hodge, "In Memoriam," p. 366. This is a claim which latter-day cynics assume Powell took over, on face value, from Cushing himself. Evidence here and there of such vanities on Cushing's part should not, however, detract from the impressiveness of his achievements as a craftsman, recognized by all of his contemporary associates. Indeed, his skill—or its reputation—involved him in serious embarrassment in the notorious incidents of the painted shell and the mosaic frog—items he was accused of fabricating himself and then fraudulently passing off as genuine relics. In the case of the frog— included among the Hemenway finds and still displayed in the Peabody collection—Cushing's chief accuser was his brother-in-law, Frederick W. Hodge, who in a letter written years later described how Cushing had secreted himself in his tent at Los Muertos to do the deed and had tried to fool Hodge himself with the product before succeeding with a more gullible visitor, who then took the object back east to present to Mrs. Hemenway (Hodge to Haury, October 5, 1931, Envelope 138, Hodge-Cushing Collection, Southwest Museum). Cushing himself insisted that he had merely done a bit of restoration on an authentically Indian article (Cushing to Powell, March 29, 1897, Envelope 249, Hodge-Cushing Collection). Hodge's account is very circumstantial, but it is curious that he made no mention of the incident in a copious diary he kept throughout the period in question (Envelope 169, Hodge-Cushing Collection). In any case, his initial "disclosure," sometime before March of 1897, was particularly awkward for Cushing, since it was made in support of another accusation of the same order: that Cushing had fabricated a painted shell in the Key Marco collection. A major scandal threatened, and a group within the bureau, including Hodge, Mrs. Stevenson, and J. Walter Fewkes (see note 24 below) were evidently prepared to testify against Cushing—with what purity or mixture of motives it is not possible to be certain from the documents so far available (letters by Cushing, Fewkes, Hodge, Powell, Boas, and others, both in the Smithsonian Anthropological Archives and in the Hodge-Cushing Collection). Cushing's explanations were plausible, as were the specimens themselves, and he was officially exonerated. But a residue of misgivings seems to have remained—perhaps not so much about any actual fraudulence suspected as about the way in which, with Cushing, "personality" seemed to intrude upon sober science. It is interesting to speculate how much this episode may have contributed to the virtual collapse of Cushing's professional reputation following his death. It seems to have been in reference to this affair that Boas remarked that Cushing's "greatest enemy is his genius" (letter from Boas to W. J. McGee, January 1, 1897, Unclassified BAE History file, National

Anthropological Archives). For a full review of the painted shell case and texts of the major correspondence involved, see Gilliland, *The Material Culture of Key Marco, Florida*, pp. 179–84.

12. Wilson, *Red, Black, Blond, and Olive*, p. 17.

13. H.F.C. tenKate, "The Indian in Literature," p. 518.

14. As a student—and partisan—of Zuñi traditionalism, Cushing found himself at odds not only with some government functionaries but with the local missionaries, who strongly resented his presence and influence. Accounts of some of his difficulties with these people, including the horse episode, may be found in both Brandes, "Frank Hamilton Cushing" (pp. 90–92) and Pandy, "Anthropologists at Zuñi," (pp. 324–25). However Cushing's own personality may have complicated matters, life could not have been simple for a resident anthropologist in the Southwest in the early 1880s.

15. Draft of Cushing's annual report for the year ending June 30, 1884, p. 2 (2427-b, Cushing file, National Anthropological Archives).

16. As to what actually happened in this matter of the Apache scalp, no authoritative source of information other than Cushing himself has appeared. It is known that he had already obtained two scalps from the East in an effort to promote his initiation (see Brandes, "Frank Hamilton Cushing," p. 68). There is no particular reason to doubt his account of the encounter with the Apache raiders, including the acquisition of this third scalp (see "A Scalp and Initiation," below); he simply doesn't tell us, and we don't know, how it came into his hands.

17. See Cushing's letter of June 20, 1880, below.

18. William E. Curtis, *Children of the Sun*, p. 52. Also see discussion in Brandes, "Frank Hamilton Cushing," pp. 99–107, and Pandey, "Anthropologists at Zuñi," pp. 325–26.

19. James C. Pilling, BAE Chief Clerk, to Cushing, January 19, 1884 (BAE microfilm reel no. 27). No absolute proof as to the motives for this order, other than those stated in it, has as yet turned up; but it is hard to resist the inference that trepidation about Logan was a prime one. In earlier correspondence Baird had requested Cushing to write an "authoritative denial" that he had done anything to offend Senator Logan, and the letter leaves no doubt about the degree of the secretary's nervous concern (December 23, 1882, BAE History 4677). Years later, in a letter to E. DeGolyer, Fredrick W. Hodge, who was probably in a position to know, wrote that Cushing "returned to Washington not by reason of his health but because Senator John A. Logan demanded his return under threat of 'killing' the Bureau of Ethnology's appropriation" (April 3, 1946, Box no. 1, Hodge-Cushing Collection, Southwest Museum).

20. In his introduction to a reprint of this report, Robert C. Euler

comments that Cushing should never have made the journey to Havasupai, given his delicate health and the nature of the terrain. Yet he "rode that trail, endured hardships which today border on the incredible, and thus became the first anthropologist to record and publish an account of 'the Nation of the Willows.'" "Most of Cushing's records," he adds, "have been substantiated, and his text needs little correction or elaboration" (Frank Hamilton Cushing, *The Nation of the Willows*, p. 7).

21. Hodge, who went on to a distinguished career including leadership positions in the BAE and the Heye Museum of the American Indian in New York, as well as the directorship of the Southwest Museum, was then a junior employee at the BAE. He was recommended to Cushing by Powell, and it would seem he almost immediately became a Cushing family intimate, taking on a sort of filial role in relating to Cushing himself and that of a young gallant in relating to Mrs. Cushing and her younger sister, Margaret Magill, who accompanied the expedition. A diary he kept of the expedition from the time of his appointment, in December of 1886, until mid-May of 1888 includes a charming—and almost daily—account of the progress of his courtship with Miss Magill (Envelope 169, Hodge-Cushing Collection, Southwest Museum). When it became known that she and Hodge had become engaged, they were subjected to a "confidential lecture" by Cushing, the purport of which seems to have been that the ardors must be banked for the duration of the expedition and until Hodge had established a position in his field. Despite whatever irritation this paternal check may have occasioned, however, the tone of references to Cushing throughout the diary is one of respect and affection—rather markedly in contrast to that of his later comments on Cushing, even in reference to the period covered by the diary. However much he may have built on the experience gained in service with Cushing on the Hemenway Expedition, as Hodge came into his own professionally, he formed allegiances independently of Cushing with colleagues he apparently considered more rigorous than Cushing in their science. Notably, as between Cushing and his successor as director of the Hemenway Expedition, J. Walter Fewkes, Hodge seems to have become more comfortable with Fewkes, with whom he continued a friendly correspondence and whom he joined or at least visited on various other digs. Indeed, he sided with Fewkes against Cushing both in criticism of the latter's management of the Hemenway Expedition generally and in a particular case in which Cushing's professional integrity was at stake (see note 11 above). For a retrospective view, expressing respect on the one hand for Cushing's "visionary" capacities and for his development of "a new method of Southwestern archaeological research" but on the other hand blaming

the "woefully small body of descriptive data" resulting from the Hemenway Expedition on his egotistic reliance on his own memory and imagination instead of scientific record keeping, see Hodge's foreword to Emil Haury's monograph on the expedition, *The Excavations at Los Muertos*. Since Hodge was certainly in a position to know whether and in what quantity Cushing kept field notes, he must be regarded as a direct witness with respect to Cushing's own claims in this matter (see note 24 below)—which means his own veracity is as much on the line as Cushing's or Fewkes's. Whatever differences there may have been between them, however, it should be added that Hodge seems to have been the person chiefly responsible for arranging the publication, after Cushing's death, of *Zuñi Folk Tales* and the reissue of *Zuñi Breadstuff* as a book in 1920 during his tenure at the Heye Museum. It was of course Hodge's collection of Cushing's papers, inherited from Mrs. Cushing, that was acquired by the Southwest Museum, along with his own papers, after his death.

22. Emil Haury, *The Excavations at Los Muertos* (1945), p. 3. This study of Haury's, pursued under all the difficulties presented by the absence of field notes and records, represents the first published report of Cushing's Hemenway excavations—of the actual fruits, that is to say, of the expedition to which, as Haury says, "we largely owe the awakening of interest in the archaeology of southern Arizona" (p. 3).

23. This manuscript is in the Hemenway collection of the Peabody Museum. Another manuscript, titled "Itinerary of the Initial Work at the Ruin Cluster of Los Muertos," is among Cushing's papers at the Southwest Museum (Envelope 156, Hodge-Cushing Collection). The latter, typed double-spaced and running to 121 pages, seems to be a draft of the same work as that deposited at the Peabody. This version, however sketchily, does extend to April 14, 1887—covering something over two months of excavation.

24. Hodge-Cushing Collection, Envelope 393, Southwest Museum. See also letter of August 27, 1891, to an unnamed "dear friend," Envelope 333, Hodge-Cushing Collection. For studies of the Hemenway Expedition, see Brandes, "Frank Hamilton Cushing"; Fuller, "Cushing's Relations with Zuñi and the Hemenway Southwestern Expedition"; and Haury, *The Excavations at Los Muertos*; and for a particularly sharp commentary on the nature of Cushing's feud with Fewkes, see Hinsley, "The Development of a Profession," pp. 250–51. Given the recurrent pattern of Cushing's performance when faced with the challenge of producing full reports of his field activities, one may doubt that the loss of the materials referred to, whatever they may have been, was all that prevented him from "working up and publishing" his

results. One may also be skeptical about Cushing's claim as to the quantity and substance of the loss. On the other hand, it is probably also wise to suspend total disbelief so far as Cushing's accusation of Fewkes is concerned. Competition among early field workers could be fierce and sometimes unscrupulous, and judging by surviving letters from John G. Bourke, Washington Matthews, and Adolph Bandelier to Cushing and others and from Fewkes himself to Mrs. Hemenway's son, Fewkes was sufficiently devious and self-serving to have been capable of purloining the papers Cushing said he left behind in New Mexico—and worse. In a letter to Cushing of April 5, 1892 (Envelope 286, Hodge-Cushing Collection, Southwest Museum), Matthews accused Fewkes of having grossly plagiarized in his article "A Few Tusayan Pictographs," which had just appeared in *American Anthropologist* 5 (1892): 9–26. Bourke made a similar accusation writing to the journalist Sylvester Baxter, October 20, 1895, in reference to an article in the *Boston Herald* about "Dr. J. Walter Fewkes's great discovery of 'Hwahibi'"—which ruin, according to Bourke, had been known to others for years and been identified and named by Bourke himself long since in his *Snake Dance of the Navajoes*. Fewkes, by Bourke's account, had "gone out at the 11th hour, with a superb equipment in men and money and material, and tooted his brass band, ignoring every other work in the same field. If he has advanced a single new idea about the Tusayan country, I'd like to know about it" (Envelope 264, Hodge-Cushing Collection). In other letters, both Matthews (January 21, 1897, Envelope 286, Hodge-Cushing Collection) and Bandelier (*Unpublished Letters of Adolph Bandelier*, p. 30) refer to Fewkes as a "snake in the grass," and Bandelier writes of his "villainous intrigues" and "peculiar underhanded ways," mentioning also that Major Powell had told him "that Fewkes was understood, and everybody on his guard against him." Such remarks perhaps add some plausibility to Cushing's own bitter complaint to Bandelier that Fewkes's article "A Reconnoissance of Ruins in or Near the Zuñi Reservation" (*Journal of American Ethnology and Archaeology* 1 (1891): 95–132) had been "taken bodily or in brief" from the very papers in question, "without official or personal credit, without even quotation marks—to say nothing of the use, however ill applied, that has been made all the way through of this material of mine" (Cushing to Bandelier, June 17, 1891, Envelope 91, Hodge-Cushing Collection). Interestingly enough in this connection, I am informed in a letter from Richard B. Woodbury that Fewkes himself, "when he took over the Hemenway Expedition and dug at Zuñi [as reported in 'A Reconnoissance'], left virtually no significant field notes or records, so far as the files and archives of the Peabody Museum and the Smithsonian reveal." Were there notes, not his, that Fewkes took advantage of and then destroyed? Or was he, on the other hand (or as well), no better a note taker than Cushing—a possibility that would leave the whole issue of Cushing's Hemenway records shrouded in irony? According to Woodbury, Fewkes "also left few records or notes for his other archaeological work in the Southwest. He wasn't a very good archaeologist, in fact, being not even up to the standards of his day." Whatever the truth may be in the matter of the Hemenway notes, it is but one of the issues dividing Cushing and his friends from Fewkes, Mrs. Stevenson, and other rivals, and it is perhaps worth adding that from the historical perspective the acrimony generated may have been reflective not only of these particular persons but of the times in general. According to James K. Flack, "unrelenting antipathies were almost the rule rather than the exception in the pursuit of natural science in late nineteenth century America" ("The Formation of the Washington Intellectual Community, 1870–1898," p. 141).

25. Cushing's final enterprise thus represents again a case of unfinished business, and his work in Florida has been subjected to the same kind of criticism that has been aimed at his work in the Southwest: unsystematic field methods and note keeping and no redeeming final report with the necessary details. He did not, for example, describe items which he was unable to remove or preserve; nor did he systematically keep track of where he had located the items he did preserve, let alone maintain a stratigraphic register of his finds. To some extent such shortcomings simply reflect the state of the science in Cushing's lifetime; to some extent they are accountable to his personality. How much detailed observation of the sort in question might have found its way into his final report on Key Marco, Florida, had he lived to complete it, is impossible to say. In his final years, at any rate, Cushing seems to have suffered a losing battle between declining health and demands for finished work. According to a letter to Pepper dated September 20, 1896, he had already by that time "dictated considerably more than a thousand closely typewritten pages—more than half of what will become a large book" (Envelope 245, Hodge-Cushing Collection Southwest Museum). This was prior, however, to the long delayed and crisis-fraught publication of the *preliminary* report; the struggle continued for another three and a half years; and as in the case of the Hemenway report, no such large-scale manuscript has as yet turned up. Of the materials he did leave, however, a report by Wells M. Sawyer to Major Powell, dated January 1901, comments that with editing, and printed together with the "Preliminary Report," they would "make a most creditable and valuable volume" ("List of manuscript material left by Frank Hamilton Cushing,"

32   INTRODUCTION

p. 4, 1844-b, Cushing files, National Anthropological Archives). This volume, of course, never saw publication. For a full study of Cushing's work in Florida and its significance, see Gilliland, *The Material Culture of Key Marco, Florida.*

26. Untitled handwritten notes filed under "Notes on Myth and Folklore," pp. 3a–5a, Box no. 1, Hodge-Cushing Collection, Southwest Museum.

27. "The Arrow," pp. 309–10. Cushing's "Primitive Copper Working" is a particularly pure example of the approach described here.

28. "Remarks by J. W. Powell," in Hodge, "In Memoriam," p. 361.

29. Lucien Lévy-Bruhl, *How Natives Think,* p. 161.

30. See "Preliminary Notes on the Origin, Working Hypothesis and Primary Researches of the Hemenway Southwestern Archaeological Expedition," p. 151.

31. Claude Lévi-Strauss, "Social Structure," p. 532.

32. Hortense Powdermaker, *Stranger and Friend: The Way of an Anthropologist,* pp. 9, 306.

33. For an extreme statement of this position, see George Devereaux's *From Anxiety to Method in the Behavioral Sciences* (New York: Humanities Press, 1967). For other meditations more specifically on the inner dynamics of the anthropologist's involvement with the subjects of his observation, see Claude Lévi-Strauss, *Tristes Tropiques,* trans. John Russell (New York: Criterion Books, 1961); Gregory Bateson, *Naven* (Cambridge, England: Cambridge University Press, 1936); and Kurt H. Wolff, "Surrender and Community Study: The Study of Loma," in *Reflections on Community Studies,* ed. Arthur J. Vidich, Joseph Bensman, Maurice R. Stein, (New York: John Wiley and Sons, 1964), pp. 233–63.

34. "Remarks by Alice C. Fletcher," in Hodge, "In Memoriam," pp. 367, 369. Various examples of what Fletcher calls Cushing's "divining power" have been recorded. Hers concerns a characteristic she had noticed in the way the woodpecker is represented on the sacred peace calumet. "I *know* why they turned the mandral back," Cushing had said, after pondering the question; "it was to prevent the crest from rising, to show that the bird could not be angry; he must serve the cause of peace"—an explanation confirmed for her later by an old priest (ibid., pp. 369–70). Hodge reports another example of what he calls Cushing's "almost uncanny insight into that which to others would be the unseen": Cushing had asserted "that were it possible to remove the elaborate wrappings from a ceremonial atlatl in the University Museum in Philadelphia, a turquoise bead, the 'heart' of the implement, would be found within. Some time later the atlatl was exposed to X-rays, when,

behold, the outline of a bead was clearly visible" (foreword to Haury, *The Excavations at Los Muertos*, p. viii).

35. Bertha Pauline Dutton, *Sun Father's Way: The Kiva Murals of Kuaua*, p. 42n.

36. Hinsley, "The Development of a Profession," p. 243.

37. The bulk of Cushing's papers (manuscripts, correspondence, notes, drawings, and other miscellaneous matter) is divided between the National Anthropological Archives of the Smithsonian Institution and the Hodge-Cushing Collection of the Southwest Museum in Los Angeles. The Peabody Museum at Harvard also has a collection of Cushing materials, relating chiefly to the Hemenway Expedition, as do the University of Pennsylvania Library and the American Philosophical Society Library, the latter both relating to the Florida expeditions. For a partial listing of these and other holdings of Cushing's papers, as well as an extensive listing of published works by and about Cushing, see the bibliography in Brandes's "Frank Hamilton Cushing."

38. I have supplied the following titles, for selections either not separately titled in their original appearance or titled somewhat differently because of the broader scope of the works from which they were excerpted: "Zuñi and the Missionaries: Keeping the Old Ways," "Remarks on Shamanism" (short title), "Form," "Form and the Dance-Drama," "Origins of Pueblo Pottery," "Pottery in the Making," "Zuñi Farming: Starting a New Field," "Corn and the Early Kitchen," "And Some Recipes," "Wafer Bread and the Baking Stone," "Wheat Farming," "Zuñi Etiquette," "On the Trail," and "Clowns, Priests, and Festivals of the *Kâ'-kâ*."

39. Many (or most) of the engravings, incidentally, are based on actual photographs—technology for reproducing the latter themselves in printed matter having not yet been developed in Cushing's day. The curious reader may find various of these photographs, particularly those used for the illustrations in "My Adventures in Zuñi," in the collection of the Anthropological Archives at the Smithsonian. Those I have so far identified with these illustrations are, with one exception, the work of John K. Hillers, official photographer for the 1879 BAE expedition which brought Cushing to the Southwest, and were taken in that year (though not all in Zuñi). The frontispiece photograph of Cushing, taken later, was also Hillers's work. In his own field, Hillers was as much of a pioneer as Cushing. Having got his start with the camera on the 1871–75 Colorado River expeditions with Major Powell, he produced both some of the first and some of the best photographs of the area and its native inhabitants. For his own account of the earlier ventures and a collection of his photographs of the Southwest, see *"Photographed all the Best*

Scenery": Jack Hillers's Diary of the Powell Expeditions, 1871–1875, ed. Don D. Fowler (Salt Lake City: University of Utah Press, 1972).

40. The case for plain *Zuni* is put most succinctly by Dennis Tedlock—in a piece in which he himself felt obliged to use the ñ: "The English-speaking residents of the Zuñi area, including bilingual Zuñis, use 'Zuni' in both spelling and pronunciation. Academics frequently render 'Zuñi' as 'zoonyee' (rather than the Spanish 'soonyee'), so that the final result after retaining the ñ is still an English corruption of what is already a Spanish corruption of the Keresan corruption of the Zuñis' word for themselves, which is Shiwi" ("On the Translation of Style in Oral Literature," p. 115, n. 5).

I. BECOMING AN INDIAN

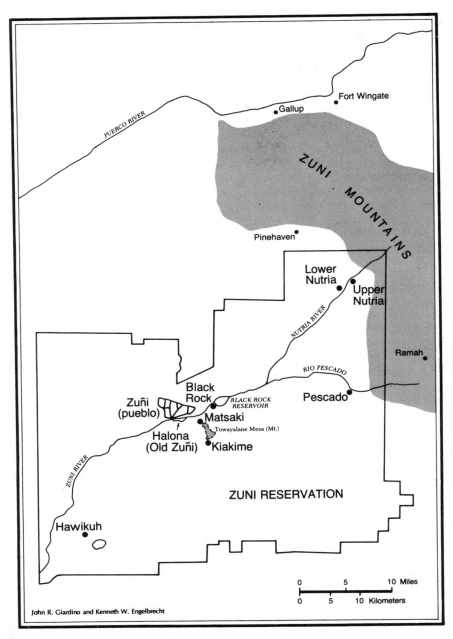

Zuñi Country. (Based on map in *Second Annual Report of the Bureau of American Ethnology, 1880–1881*)

Becoming an Indian

INCLUDED in this section are a number of accounts of life in Zuñi in which the autobiographical element predominates. Very little introduction is needed, since it is provided by Cushing himself both in the excerpt from his 1890 lecture and in the opening pages of "My Adventures in Zuñi," and that latter work, in turn, introduces the letters and other selections.

"My Adventures in Zuñi" was published originally as a three-part series in the *Century Magazine* in 1882–83—one of them appearing, as if to represent the *other* pole of exotica, next to a piece by Henry James on "Du Maurier and London Society." Of the same generation as Gaugin and Robert Louis Stevenson, writing less than forty years after Melville reported his experiences among the South Sea Island cannibals in his "nonfiction" novel *Typee* and less than thirty years after Thoreau's quite different but related account of his journey back to nature in *Walden*, Cushing must have appealed to his *Century Magazine* readers not only as a representative of science but as a recognizable type of romantic author- or artist-adventurer, evoking in his case the special mystique of the great American Southwest with its associations not only of the frontier land wrested from the Mexicans but of the old Spanish past and in the farther distance the strange ancient splendors of the Aztecs and the Incas.

Nor does Cushing's work suffer by its near adjacence in the *Century* to that of the literary master, James. Simply as a writer, Cushing is first-rate, combining a sure instinct for the dramatic with a gift for vivid description and for conveying an immediate sense of the individual personalities of those who figure in his story. After reading "My Adventures," one is not likely to forget the old governor, Palowahtiwa, or the members of his family. As the account of Cushing's own experience of crossing cultural boundaries, moreover, "My Adventures," as Edmund Wilson saw, is a unique record—not of struggle alone but of dual initiation, both as Zuñi and as professional field worker. Like *Walden*, I might add, it is not without an overall design: it too condenses the events of several years into the span of one cycle of the seasons and follows a progress not only outward but inward and of a kind, albeit remotely, with that spiritual development which the sequence of the seasons in *Walden* serves to symbolize. What is represented here is the rhythm of the Zuñi year, and, as a recent essay on Cushing perceptively points out, "a careful description of the cycles of Zuñi life [is] interwoven with the story of his own slow penetration into it, . . . the cycle of human life, from his own 'birth' into Zuñi society to, at the end, the death and burial of an aged Zuñi who had been his friend."[1]

Since its first appearance, "My Adventures in Zuñi" has been brought out in book form by three different presses (by two of them in limited editions for collectors). A bound facsimile reprint of the original articles, with an introduction by Okah L. Jones, Jr., is currently available from Filter Press. What is included here is likewise the text of the original *Century* articles.

Cushing's letters, on the other hand, have hitherto been entirely unpublished, though many of those written from Zuñi and elsewhere provide a view of the experiences of a pioneer field worker, close up, that is unavailable elsewhere. The selections included here, perforce a pitifully small sample, are drawn from his extensive correspondence with the Smithsonian during his stay in Zuñi. More particularly, they belong also to the series, initiated in 1874, when Cushing was not yet seventeen, addressed to Professor Spencer F. Baird, secretary of the Smithsonian from 1878 to 1888. Baird, who had taken an early interest in the young Cushing, supplying him with books, soliciting and publishing his first professional article (in 1875),[2] and then appointing him at age nineteen to the Smithsonian, remained for Cushing a sort of parental eminence (one of a series of such figures) to whom he looked for approval and to whom he held himself accountable. The letters printed here are in the National

Anthropological Archives, with the exception of one draft, which belongs to the Hodge-Cushing Collection at the Southwest Museum, Los Angeles. The passage at the opening of this section, which I have titled "Going to Zuñi," and the two at the end, for which I have provided other titles, are taken from a sheaf of drafts, partly handwritten, partly typed, labeled "Buffalo Lecture: Life in Zuñi." This, too, belongs to the Hodge-Cushing Collection and has never before been published.

Notes

1. Mark, "Frank Hamilton Cushing and an American Science of Anthropology," pp. 455–56.

2. "Antiquities of Orleans County, N.Y." This little article, a report on the earthwork ruin near Medina (the Indian fortification mentioned in the general Introduction, where Cushing had set up a hut and workshop), is a solidly professional piece of work in its precise description and analysis of the remains and their physical setting and what these reveal about the lives of the ancient occupants. It also reveals some acquaintance with the literature of archeology and geology then extant. The young Cushing had been making good use both of the books provided by Baird and of those he was borrowing from another older friend, George Kennan. See Kennan's four-part reminiscence in the *Medina* (New York) *Tribune* (December 6, 1923–January 3, 1924, Cushing file, National Anthropological Archives).

FIG. 1. Cushing in Washington, July 28, 1879. (Courtesy of Emilyn Magill Hodge)

Going to Zuñi

FIFTEEN years ago, one winter night, I fell asleep before my desk in the old tower of the Smithsonian Institution. I dreamed that I was far away in a country I had never seen or heard of. There the sun was brighter, the air clearer; the valleys, vast and twilit, were like cracks down to the foundation rocks of the world. The mountains rising from these ruptured plains were as flat as the plains they rose from, and rising from the level tops of these were others whence towered here and there, smaller mountains hundreds of feet high, rock-bound yet at first sight as round and pointed as the tent of a titan. But when one climbed to their tops, the points were broken off, revealing great craters yawning wider and wider downward into darkness, whence the voice of man or the cry of beast rolled back like the sonorous tones of far-off Buddhist bells.

On the edge of the smallest of these hollow mountains I was contending with two strangers, a rope around my body; they were holding me back and I straining forward. All at once I was spinning and dangling at the end of the rope, my hands burning, my heart beating, my eyes staring down into the twilight. Then I stood on a solid rock-strewn bottom, at my feet a strange, time-eaten idol, while, my vision slowly clearing, farther down in a smoky nook I saw a pagan altar surrounded by hundreds of painted wands, some with half-decayed plumes fastened to them, still faintly fluttering in the chill, chill eddies of the subterranean air which seemed the echo wind of another age. All was so wonderful, so strange and silent and ancient down there, the whole land was so solemn and weird and desolate and still that I was awed beyond measure, yet happy to the verge of ecstasy, as I stooped to pick up the great-headed, greenish, flat-faced, square-eyed, crooked little idol at my feet—so happy that I awoke, dazed to find myself empty-handed, my head pillowed among the papers on my writing table in the tower of the old Smithsonian! Again and again thereafter I dreamed this dream, and others like it, until weary of its weird fascination.

One day, six months later, as I was passing a great screen of photographs displayed in the government exhibit of the geological surveys at the Centennial Exhibition [Philadelphia, 1876] next to the one that I had charge of, my eye chanced to fall on a little water color sketch of a dancing Indian. As I looked, I became fascinated, for in the mask this figure wore—flat-faced, green paint, and all—I descried a face like that of the idol I had dreamed of. Beneath the figure was written "Katchina Dancer of Zuñi, New Mexico."

It may be that the chill of a windy winter night caused me to dream of wild and desolate lands, the height of my tower home, of mountains, the clang of an iron door left unlatched six flights below, of hollow, reverberating mountains, and my studies among the relics and idols of primitive man gathered the world over, of an idol stranger than any I have studied—while my joy was only that of every born collector and student of olden things. Again it may be that these things only aided me to see the things that resembled them far away in time and station; who knows? Be all this as it may, my eyes were first turned towards Zuñi by a vision of the night, else it is more than likely the exploration which I was bent year in and year out on accomplishing would have led me almost anywhere else than Zuñi; for at that time I longed to study the old dead cultures and monuments of Mexico, Central America, and Peru, told of by Stephen Prescott and others. I had conceived the idea of seeking among still existing tribes of those southern lands the descendants of the ancient builders and of living their lives, if need be, to overcome their secrecy in regard to the lore of their land. Now my fancy took another turn. I began to hear of the cliff and mesa ruins of our great southwest. I heard also that the race who reared them were supposed to be related to the peoples I had wished so much to study. When I learned the little then known of the Zuñi and other pueblo Indians of New Mexico and Arizona, I believed some of them would turn out to be themselves the children of the cliff dwellers. Never after that did I abandon the idea of someday visiting them to acquire knowledge which would guide me farther on in my quest of the golden sun worship.

Three years later I was off with the Powell Smithsonian party under Col. James Stevenson, for the wilds and canyons of the southwestern Sierra Madres. I suppose I reached the western plains in time to see the very last of two much described things, tent-topped emigrant wagons snailing along the great Santa Fe trail and a disappearing land of buffalo—the bones of whose ancestry strewed the plains throughout which their wallows still held reign. But these, the wolves, and the ever curious prairie dog villages have been better described a dozen times than I could describe them, and I shall follow the railroad silently to the plain, just this side of Las Vegas, in New Mexico, where was laid two days before our arrival the last tie southwestward on the Atchison, Topeka and Santa Fe Railroad.

Already a small town of unplaned pine timber and unbleached factory cotton had sprung up, boasting seventeen saloons, several gambling establishments, two or three stores, and as many hotels, arranged like the actors quarters in a Chinese theater, with rooms six feet by eight. In each of these rooms one could hear the lightest sounds of the whole town, while diaphanous and semi-transparent as the cloth partitions were, they sheltered quite a colony of unwelcome bed-fellows—the season being summer.

And now begins my story of experiences in the southwest! On the night of our arrival, I innocently set forth to see—not knowing how soon we might leave, one of those strange old Spanish churches, the sun-dried mud or adobe of which I saw peering up above the flat roofs of Mexican houses across the plain in the middle of old Las Vegas. The sun was just setting. The plain, dry and covered with sagebrush, looked all but level between where I emerged from the unbleached village of the railroad end. The olden town seemingly so near seemingly grew no nearer as I plowed along a beaten mule road toward it, until dusk began to deepen. Presently I paused. Directly in front of me was a black arroyo, one of those earth canyons which seam the southwestern valley plains, as many feet deep as wide, straight sides save where crossed by the deep pitching roads or trails. This one was so crooked that one could not see straight in it anywhere, or more than two rods around its corners even. I descended into it. Just as I was about to set foot in the sandy bottom, a dark figure stood up and stepped around one of those mud-cliff corners. A fist with something gleaming in it was thrust toward me, and a voice peremptorily said, "Hold up your hands, sonny."

I don't think any insult ever made me so indignant as that demand. I was so mad that I did not have time to get afraid. Pretending to raise my hands, I made a grab for the pistol I had luckily thrust into my hip pocket. Alas, it came out butt foremost. I was too unskillful to reverse it. I made a lunge with it as one would with a club and came down with the weight of my body and such suddenness that it hit the man somewhere so hard that he staggered still for a second, too amazed to utter even a curse, then scooted up the arroyo like a dog trying to dodge a brickbat, while I too stood perfectly still for a moment, then laughed aloud, like a madman, till my voice, sounding down in that straight-walled gulch like the bark of a woodchuck at bay in a stone pile, called me to my senses. For I was as much surprised as the man I had hit. I insanely began to marvel that I, so fresh from Washington, should get the better of a practiced foot thief before I had time to fairly know how I did it, and musing on how surprised too the man must have been, I assure you I quite forgot to turn back as I had momentarily thought of doing, and plodded on toward the old town, alternately keeping an eye out, then lapsing into merriment and absent-mindedness. Before the evening was over, I fell in with our renowned photographer, Jack Hillers [a member of the expedition], and he led me off to a Spanish dancing place, none too good of its kind, where behold! I met my man, with a ragged bandana over his right eye and cheek and a very sharp, very red nose—but whether red as the result of my work or of dissipation, which was rife there, I couldn't tell.

Oh the glory of those days on the trail over the plains and mountains from Las Vegas to Santa Fe. The misery of my first mule back did nought, no, nor our hard earthen beds under cedar trees by the wayside, to curtail it.

From a lecture, "Life in Zuñi," delivered in Buffalo, New York, December 10, 1890. Envelope 214, Hodge-Cushing Collection, Southwest Museum, Los Angeles. Printed with the permission of the Southwest Museum.

My Adventures in Zuñi

O<small>NE</small> hot summer day in 1879, as I was sitting in my office in the ivy-mantled old South Tower of the Smithsonian Institution, a messenger boy tapped at my door, and said:

"Professor Baird wishes to see you, sir."

The professor, picking up his umbrella and papers, came toward the door as I entered.

"Haven't I heard you say you would like to go to New Mexico to study the cliff-houses and Pueblo Indians?"

"Yes, sir."

"Would you still like to go?"

"Yes, sir."

"Very well then, be ready to accompany Colonel Stevenson's collecting party, as ethnologist, within four days. I want you to find out all you can about some typical tribe of Pueblo Indians. Make your own choice of field, and use your own methods; only, get the information. You will probably be gone three months. Write me frequently. I'm in a hurry this evening. Look to Major Powell, of the Bureau of Ethnology, if you want further directions. Good-day."

Thus it happened that, on a sultry afternoon in late September, by no means firmly seated in the first saddle I had ever bestridden, I was belaboring a lazy Government mule just at the entrance of a pass between two great banded red-and-gray sandstone mesas, in the midst of a waterless wilderness. I had ridden from Las Vegas, then the southern terminus of the railway across New Mexico, to Fort Wingate, and over a spur of the Sierra Madres, until here I was far in advance of our little caravan, and nearer the close of my long journey than I had dreamed. Beyond the pass I followed the winding road up a series of cedar-clad sand-hills to where they abruptly terminated in a black lava descent of nearly two hundred feet.

Below and beyond me was suddenly revealed a great red and yellow sand-plain. It merged into long stretches of gray, indistinct hill-lands in the western distance, distorted by mirages and sand-clouds, and overshadowed toward the north by two grand, solitary buttes of rock. From the bases of the latter to a spire-encircled, bare-faced promontory to the right, stretched a succession of cañon-seamed, brown, sandstone mesas, which, with their mantle of piñon and cedar, formed a high, dark boundary for the entire northern side of the basin.

To the left, a mile or two away, crowning numberless red foot-hills, rose a huge rock-mountain, a thousand feet high and at least two miles in length along its flat top, which showed, even in the distance, fanciful chiselings by wind, sand, and weather. Beyond its column-sentineled western end the low sand-basin spread far away to the foot-hills of the gray-and-white southern mesas, which, broken by deep cañons, stretched, cliff after cliff, westward to the hills of the horizon.

Out from the middle of the rock-wall and line of sand-hills on which I stood, through a gate of its own opening, flowed a little rivulet. Emerging from a succession of low mounds beneath me, it wound, like a long whip-lash or the track of an earth-worm, westward through the middle of the sandy plain and out almost to the horizon, where, just midway between the northern buttes and the opposite gray mesas, it was lost in the southern shadows of a terraced hill.

Down behind this hill the sun was sinking, transforming it into a jagged pyramid of silhouette, crowned with a brilliant halo, whence a seeming midnight aurora burst forth through broken clouds, bordering each misty blue island with crimson and gold, then blazing upward in widening lines of light, as if to repeat in the high heavens its earthly splendor.

A banner of smoke, as though fed from a thousand crater-fires, balanced over this seeming volcano, floating off, in many a circle and surge, on the evening breeze. But I did not realize that this hill, so strange and picturesque, was a city of the habitations of men, until I saw, on the topmost terrace, little specks of black and red moving about against the sky. It seemed still a little island of mesas, one upon the other, smaller and smaller, reared from a sea of sand, in mock rivalry of the surrounding grander mesas of Nature's rearing.

Descending, I chanced to meet, over toward the river, an Indian. He was bare-headed, his hair banged even with his eyebrows in front, and done up in a neat knot behind, with long locks hanging down either side. He wore a red shirt and white cotton pantalets, slitted at the sides from the knees down so as to expose his bare legs, and raw-hide soled moccasins. Strings of shell-beads around his neck, and a leather belt around his waist, into which were stuck a boomerang or two, completed his costume. Knitting-work in hand, he left his band of dirty white and black sheep and snuffling goats in charge of a wise-looking, grizzled-faced, bob-tailed mongrel cur, and came, with a sort of shuffling dog-trot, toward the road, calling out, "Hai! hai!" and extending his hand with a most good-natured smile.

I shook the proffered hand warmly, and said, "Zuñi?"

"E!" exlaimed the Indian, as he reverentially breathed on my hand and from his own, and then, with a nod of his head and a fling of his chin toward the still distant smoky terraces, made his exclamation more intelligible.

I hastened on with all the speed I could scourge out of my obstinate, kicking mule, down the road to where the rivulet crossed it, and up again, nearer and nearer to the strange structures.

Imagine numberless long, box-shaped, adobe ranches, connected with one another in extended rows and squares, with others, less and less numerous, piled up on them lengthwise and crosswise, in two, three, even six stories, each receding from the one below it like the steps of a broken stairflight—as it were, a gigantic pyramidal mud honey-comb with far outstretching base,—and you can gain a fair conception of the architecture of Zuñi.

Everywhere this structure bristled with ladder-poles, chimneys, and rafters. The ladders were heavy and long, with carved slab cross-pieces at the tops, and leaned at all angles against the roofs. The chimneys looked more like huge bamboo-joints than

FIG. 2. General View of Zuñi. (From the *Twenty-Third Annual Report of the Bureau of American Ethnology, 1901–1902*)

anything else I can compare them with, for they were made of bottomless earthen pots, set one upon the other and cemented together with mud, so that they stood up, like many-lobed, oriental spires, from every roof-top. Wonderfully like the holes in an ant-hill seemed the little windows and door-ways which everywhere pierced the walls of this gigantic habitation; and like ant-hills themselves seemed the curious little round-topped ovens which stood here and there along these walls or on the terrace edges.

All round the town could be seen irregular, large and small adobe or dried-mud fences, inclosing gardens in which melon, pumpkin and squash vines, pepper plants and onions were most conspicuous. Forming an almost impregnable belt nearer the village were numerous stock corrals of bare cedar posts and sticks. In some of these, burros, or little gray, white-nosed, black-shouldered donkeys, were kept; while many others, with front legs tied closely together, were nosing about over the refuse heaps. Bob-tailed curs of all sizes, a few swift-footed, worried-looking black hogs, some scrawny chickens, and many eagles—the latter confined in wattled stick cages, diminutive corrals, in the corners and on the house-tops—made up the visible life about the place.

Not an Indian was anywhere to be seen, save on the topmost terraces of this strange city. There hundreds of them were congregated, gazing so intently down into one of the plazas beyond that none of them observed my approach, until I had hastily dismounted, tied my mule to a corral post, climbed the refuse-strewn hill and two or three ladders leading up to the house-tops. The regular *thud, thud* of rattles and drum, the cadence of rude music which sounded more like the soughing of a storm wind amid the forests of a mountain than the accompaniment of a dance, urged me forward, until I was suddenly confronted by forty or fifty of the men, who came rushing toward me with excited discussion and gesticulation. One of them approached and spoke something in Spanish, motioning me away; but I did not understand him, so I grasped his hand and breathed on it as I had seen the herder do. Lucky thought! The old man was pleased; smiled, breathed in turn on my hand, and then hastily addressed the others, who, after watching me with approving curiosity, gathered around to shake hands and exchange breaths, until I might have regarded myself as the President, had not an uproar in the court attracted them all away,—all, save one, a young, cadaverous-looking fellow with strange, monkey-like little eyes, who lingered behind and ventured:

"How-li-loo?"

"Pretty well," I replied. "How are you?"

"'At's good," said he, and this useful phrase he employed in every answer to my crowded queries, until I reluctantly concluded that it was the extent of his English. It was amusing to see his efforts, by constantly repeating this phrase, ducking his head and grinning, to convince the other Indians that he was carrying on a lively conversation with me.

At last, gaining my wished-for position on the edge of the terrace, I came face to face with nearly the whole population of Zuñi. The music had ceased, and the dancers had temporarily retired, but all over the upper terraces were young men in groups and pairs, jauntily mantled in red, green, blue, black, and figured blankets, only the upper portions of their painted faces and occasional patches of their silver-bedecked persons being exposed. Here and there an elaborately plumed straw hat surmounted one of these enveloped statues, aside from which not an article of civilized apparel appeared. Opposite, women and girls, attired in clean, blue-black, embroidered blanket dresses, neat, softly draped head-shawls, and huge-legged, white buckskin moccasins, were standing and sitting on the lower terraces, or in one side of the court below. The older ones were holding their children and talking to them; the younger, intently watching for the dance, or slyly glancing from under their banged hair, which, black as jet and glossy with oil, was combed down over the eyes and parted a little to one side. Old, gray-headed men, muffled in heavy, striped serapes, sat or squatted around, or leaned on their crooked stocks. Innumerable children, some naked, others half clad in tattered cotton shirts and short trousers, were chasing one another about the terraces, wrestling, screeching, or pelting any stray dog that came around, while a few imitated the older people by sitting in silent expectation.

After a brief interval, a priest, with plumed head and trailing white buckskin mantle, gravely stepped in through a tunnel under the houses, scattering on the ground, as he came, sacred meal from a vessel which he held in one hand, while with the other he waved a beautiful wand of macaw plumes. He was followed by some twenty dancers elaborately costumed from head to foot. Close-fitting plumed wigs covered their heads, and black, long-bearded, yellow-eyed masks, with huge rows of teeth from ear to ear, red tongues lolling out between them, gave frightful grinning expressions to their faces. Their half-nude bodies were painted black and yellow, while badges of buckskin were crossed over their shoulders, and skirts of the same material, secured at the waists with elaborately embroidered and fringed sashes, depended to the ankles. Their feet were incased in green and red buskins, and to the legs were bound clanging rattles of tortoise-shell and deer-hoofs. Their necks were decorated with heavy necklaces of shell beads and coral, shining disks of *haliotis* hanging from them in front and behind; while the arms were bedecked with green bands, fluttering turkey plumes, silver bangles and wrist-guards of the same material.

Each carried in his right hand a painted gourd rattle, in his left, bow, arrows and long wands of yucca.

As the leader sounded his rattle they all fell into a semicircular line across the plaza, and began stepping rapidly up and down, swaying from side to side, facing first one way, then the other, in perfect unison, and in exact time to their rattles and strange measures of wild music.

Sprawling about the ground in front of and behind the row of dancers, in attitudes grotesque yet graceful, I observed for the first time ten most ludicrous characters, nude save for their skirts and neck-cloths of black tattered blanketing, their heads entirely covered with flexible, round, warty masks. Both masks and persons were smeared over with pink mud, giving them the appearance of reptiles in human form that had ascended from the bottom of some muddy pool and dried so nearly the color of the ground and the surrounding houses that at first it had been difficult to distinguish them.

One of them seated himself a little way off and began pounding with a short, knotty war-club a buffalo-skin bale, which he held between his knees, while the others, motionless save for their heads, which they were continually twisting and screwing about, or nodding in time to the drummer's strokes, kept up a series of comments and banterings which sometimes convulsed the whole throng of spectators with laughter.

In a few moments the leader shook his rattle again, and the dancers ceased as promptly as they had begun, breaking up irregularly and bellowing out long war-cries, brandishing their weapons, and retiring, as they had entered, one by one in the wake of the priest, through the tunnel. Suddenly the motionless, warty-headed figures sprang up, running against one another, crying out in loud tones, and motioning wildly with their long, naked arms. One moment they would all gather around one of their number, as if intensely interested in something he was saying; then as suddenly they would run confusedly about. They would catch up balls and pelt one another most vehemently, such as were struck making great ado about it. One of them discovered me. Immediately he stretched his fingers out and called excitedly to his companions, who pretended to hide behind him and the ladders, peering at me with one or the other of their black, wen-shaped eyes with the most frightened, and, at the same time, ridiculous looks and expression. Their antics were cut short by a renewal of the dance. While one commenced the drumming, another whirled a whizzing stick, and as soon as the others had arranged the costumes of some of the dancers, and had seen them fairly in line, they resumed their sprawling attitudes on the ground.[1]

Meanwhile, our party had arrived, and the escort had pitched camp in the corral of the mission and school down on the plain about a quarter of a mile north from the pueblo. In one corner, Mr. Hillers, our photographer, and I found a cozy little tent. I spread blankets over the ground, hung pictures and toilet-case on the wind-swayed walls, and thus, with a trunk in either corner, a cot along either side, we made a snug little home for ourselves.

We had not been there long when, to Hillers' disgust and my delight, two or three Indians approached, peered through the fly, and then came in, and squatted on their haunches near the entrance. They took the cigarettes I offered them, and made the interior blue with smoke within a few minutes. They were jolly, talkative fellows, and taught me all sorts of words in their strange, clicky language. Whenever they talked for any length of time, it seemed as if each sentence, long or short, was said in a single breath. At the end of each the speaker would pause, draw a long whiff of smoke from the cigarette, gulp it all into his lungs and begin again, the smoke and words issuing simultaneously from his throat.

Toward sunset, the Gobernador, or head chief, Pa-lo-wah-ti-wa, with some of his *tinieutes*, or sub-chiefs, and the herald of the town, came down to our camp. He was about forty-five years of age, of medium stature, and stooped slightly when walking. He was a grave man of but few words, yet with a kindly expression in his face, which was so finely molded, that in profile it appeared like an Egyptian cameo, the resemblance being heightened by the deep lines of character about his eyes, hollow cheeks, and large, fine mouth, as well as by his rather broad ears shaded with locks of soft jet-black hair. After partaking sparingly of the food we offered him, he thanked us simply and inquired if we wished anything. Learning our desiderata, he gave a few

FIG. 3. Palowahtiwa, Governor of Zuñi

quiet directions to the herald and *tinieutes*, and then departed, not, however, before inviting us to come up on the morrow, to eat peaches and melons with him. Soon after a long musical call proclaimed the governor's orders. From my tent door I could see, on the topmost house of the pueblo, the distant, erect figure of the herald against the twilight sky, a serape thrown gracefully over his shoulders like a Roman toga,—an example of Indian obedience.

Some of us, a young officer and several ladies who had joined our party, strolled up to the pueblo, through a sandy lane and along the winding pathway that led down the hill to a well. As I sat watching the women coming and going to and from the well, "How strangely parallel," I thought, "have been the lines of development in this curious civilization of an American desert, with those of Eastern nations and deserts." Clad in blanket dresses, mantles thrown gracefully over their heads, each with a curiously decorated jar in her hand, they came one after another down the crooked path. A little passage-way through the gardens, between two adobe walls to our right, led down rude steps into the well, which, dug deeply in the sands, had been walled up with rocks, like the Pools of Palestine, and roofed over with

FIG. 4. A Midsummer Terrace

reeds and dirt. Into this passage-way and down to the dark, covered spring they turned, or lingered outside to gossip with new comers while awaiting their chances, meanwhile slyly watching, from under their black hair, the strange visitors from "Wa-sin-to-na." These water-carriers were a picturesque sight, as, with stately step and fine carriage they followed one another up into the evening light, balancing their great shining water-jars on their heads.

We attempted to penetrate a narrow street or two, to enter one of the strange, terrace-bounded courts, but the myriad dogs, with barks and howls in concert, created such a yelping pandemonium that the ladies were frightened, and we returned to camp.

The next morning I climbed to the top of the pueblo. As I passed terrace after terrace the little children scampered for sundry sky-holes, through which long ladder-arms protruded, and disappeared down the black apertures like frightened prairie dogs; while the women, unaccustomed to the sound of shoes on their roofs, as suddenly appeared head and shoulders through the openings, gazed a moment, and then dropped out of sight. Five long flights passed, I stood on the topmost roof.

Spread out below us were the blocks of smoothly plastered, flat-roofed, adobe cells, red and yellow as the miles of plain from which they rose, pierced by many a black sky-hole, and ladder-

FIG. 5. Returning from the Field

poles and smoke-bannered chimneys were everywhere to be seen. In abrupt steps they descended toward the west, north, and central plaza, while eastward they were spread out in broad flats, broken here and there by deep courts. The whole mass was threaded through and through by narrow, often crooked, passage-ways or streets, more of them lengthwise than crosswise, and some, like tunnels leading under the houses from court to court or street to street.

The view extended grandly from the outlying, flat lower terraces, miles away to the encircling mesa boundaries north, east, and south, while westward a long, slanting notch in the low hills was invaded to the horizon by the sand-plain through which, like molten silver, the little river ran.

Every school-boy sketches a map of the Zuñi basin when he attempts with uncertain stroke to draw on his slate a cart-wheel. The city itself represents the jagged hub, whence the radiating, wavering trails form the spokes, and the surrounding mesas and hills, the rim. Let some crack across the slate and through the middle of the picture indicate the river, and your map is complete.

In and out, on the diverging trails, the Indians were passing to and from their distant fields, some on foot, some on burro-back, with others of the little beasts loaded from tail to ears with wood,

FIG. 6. Decorating Pottery

blankets full of melons, pumpkins and corn, or great panniers of peaches. A series of them away out on the bare plain, mere moving specks in the distance, appeared like a caravan crossing a desert waste. Occasionally a half-nude rider, mounted on a swift-footed pony would come dashing in from the hills. Far away he seemed a black object with a long trail of golden dust behind, but his nearer approach revealed remarkable grace of motion and confusion of streaming hair and mane. There was an occasional heavily laden ox-cart, with urchins sprawling over the top, a driver on either side, and leading up the rear a mounted donkey or two; while away to one side, more picturesque than all this, a band of dust-shrouded sheep straggled over the slopes toward their mesa pastures, followed by their solitary herder and his dog.

Strangely out of keeping with the known characteristics of the Indian race were the busy scenes about the smoky pueblo. All over the terraces were women, some busy in the alleys or at the corners below, husking great heaps of many-colored corn, buried to their bushy, black bare heads in the golden husks, while children romped in, out, over and under the flaky piles; others, bringing the grain up the ladders in blankets strapped over their foreheads, spread it out on the terraced roofs to dry. Many, in little groups, were cutting up peaches and placing them on squares of white cloth, or slicing pumpkins into long spiral ropes to be suspended to dry from the protruding rafters.

One of these busy workers stopped, deposited her burden, and hailed a neighboring house-top. Almost immediately an answering echo issued from the red stony walls, and forthwith a pair of bare shoulders seem to shove a tangled head and expectant countenance up through an unsuspected sky-hole into the sunshine. In one place, with feet over-hanging the roof, a woman was gracefully decorating some newly made jars, and heaps of the rude, but exquisite bric-à-brac scattered around her,—while, over in a convenient shadow, sat an old blind man, busy spinning on his knee with a quaint bobbin-shaped spindle-whorl.

Out near the corrals old women were building round-topped heaps of dried sheep dung, and depositing therein with nice care their freshly painted pots and bowls for burning. Others, blankets in hand, were screening their already blazing kilns from the wind, or poking the fires until eddying columns of black pungent smoke half hid them from my view, and made them seem like the "witches and cauldrons" of child-lore.

Children were everywhere, chasing one another over the terraces, up and down ladders, through alleys, and out again into the sunlight. Some, with bows and arrows, sticks and stones, were persecuting in mock chase dogs and hogs alike, as attested by their wild shrieks of delight, or the respondent ceaseless yelps arising seemingly from all quarters of the town at once.

Along the muddy river below the long southern side of the pueblo, more of these youngsters were ducking one another, or playing at various games on the smooth, sandy banks. Women, too, were there engaged in washing wool or blankets on flat stones, or in cleansing great baskets of corn. I was attracted thither and observed that these primitive laundresses had to raise the water with little dams of sand. I smiled as the thought occurred that the first expedition of Americans to Zuñi had been sent here by Government to explore this self-same river, "relative to its navigability."

At the south-western corner of the town, on the river bank, stood the house of the governor. The herald had called a council, and beckoned me to enter. In one of the large rooms the tribal dignitaries were assembling. Some came wrapped closely in their blankets, bearing old canes in their arms,—relics of a forgotten Spanish rule. In a stately, grave manner they approached each of us, shook hands, and took their seats along the northern side of the room. Others, evidently unofficial persons, sauntered inside the door and dropped on their haunches as near to it as possible. Immediately on sitting down, each took out a small piece of plug tobacco, picked it to powder, then, cutting a suitable length of corn-husk with his thumb-nail, rolled a cigarette, and began a protracted smoke. The older ones usually blew the smoke in different directions, closing their eyes, dropping their heads, and muttering a few words which I regarded as invocations.

We told them, as well as we could through our Mexican interpreter, that we were from Washington, whereupon several arose, advanced, and taking our hands breathed from them as though desirous of drinking in the influence of the reverenced name;[2] that their father was anxious to see how they lived, and to get some of their beautiful articles to show his white children; therefore he had sent us there with many fine things to trade. To everything they replied, *"We-no" (Bueno)*. So, securing the large room of the governor's house for Hillers' use, Colonel Stevenson closed the council by giving the multitude a liberal feast of coffee and sugar.

Not many days after, the Indians began to bring all sorts of their odd belongings down to the mission. Through the courtesy of Dr. Ealy, the missionary, Colonel Stevenson occupied two of the rear rooms as a trading establishment, and day after day, assisted by his enthusiastic wife, gathered in treasures, ancient and modern, of Indian art and industry. Meanwhile, Hillers and I were busy about the pueblo, the former with photographing, myself with measuring, sketching, and note-taking.

Within a week the Indians could be heard every night singing, and pounding a great drum, in preparation for a dance. It was of a semi-social character, and when, on the morning of the great day, before the assembled multitude, I began sketching in colors

FIG. 7. Zuñi Spinning

the gayly costumed figures below, only lively curiosity was excited and young people gathered so closely around me that it was almost impossible to work. For a long time afterward, as I climbed to the house-tops or sat down in shady old nooks to take notes, the women would gather near, and ask me, with incessant jabber and significant looks, to show them the colored drawings. They were wonder-struck, and would pass their fingers over the figures as though they expected to feel them. Failing in this, they would look at the backs of the leaves, as children look behind mirrors to see what had become of the images.

    With a dance that occurred soon after, I was not so successful. It was the sacred water-dance. The long, embroidered cotton garments and strange masks of this wonderful ceremonial would have claimed space in my sketch-books, even had I not been intent on representing everything I saw. When I took my station on a house-top, sketch-books and colors in hand, I was surprised to see frowns and hear explosive, angry expostulations in every direction. As the day wore on this indignation increased, until at last an old, bush-headed hag approached me, and scowling into my face made a grab at my book and pantomimically tore it to pieces. I was chagrined, but paid no attention to her, forced a good-natured smile, and continued my sketching. Discouraged, yet far from satisfied, the natives made no further demonstrations.

Among my drawings was the portrait of a pretty little girl. An old white-headed grandmother, looking the sketches over one day, recognized this. She shook her head, frowned, and, covering her face with her withered hands, began to cry and howl most dolefully, leaving me abruptly and disappearing into a room adjoining the governor's. At intervals during the remainder of the day, I could hear her talking, scolding, and sobbing over what she regarded as a great misfortune to her family.

I was exercised by this state of feeling, which became, as time went on—especially with those conservators of the ancient régime the world over, old women—more and more virulent. The sketching and note-taking were essential to my work. I was determined not to give them up, but was desirous, so far as possible, of conciliating the Indians. I therefore began with the children. They would scamper up ladders and stand on the roof-tops as I passed, but for all that had a lively curiosity concerning me, and would shout to one another, "*Is-ta-shí, Me-lik-i-a!*"—which I rightly divined was, "Just look, the little American is coming!" I began carrying sugar and pretty trinkets in my pockets, and whenever I could tempt some of them near with a lump of the rare delicacy, would pat them on the head and give them the pretty trinkets, or even take the less shy and dirty of them in my arms. I grew in their favor, and within a few days had a crowd of them always at my heels. The parents were delighted, and began to share the affection of their children. Nevertheless, the next time I sketched a dance, all this went for nothing.

Much discouraged, at last I determined to try living with the Indians. Accordingly I moved books, papers, and blankets to the governor's house. On the dirt floor in one corner I spread the blankets, and to the rafters slung a hammock. When the old chief came in that evening and saw that I had made myself at home, he shrugged his shoulders.

"How long will it be before you go back to Washington?" he attempted to ask.

"Two months," I signified.

"*Tuh!*" (damn) was his only exclamation as he climbed to the roof and disappeared through the sky-hole.

The room was forty feet in length by twelve in width. The white-washed walls and smooth, well swept floor of plastered mud, paved near the center and at the entrance with slabs of sandstone, gave it a neat appearance. Huge round rafters supported the high, pine-stave ceiling, pierced near one end with a square hole for entrance and exit, and along the center with lesser apertures for the admission of light. Two or three silenite glazed port-holes in the walls served as additional windows, and as many square openings led into other rooms. A carved pine slab, hung on heavy wooden hinges and secured by a knotted string, served as the door of one, while a suspended blanket closed another. A low adobe bench around the room appeared to be the family sitting-place. It was interrupted near one end by the mealing trough and fire-place. The latter consisted of a thin adobe wall, about five feet high by as many wide, which stood at right angles with the main wall of the house, and was capped by a structure overhead of thin sandstone slabs, not unlike the cover of a box, from the corner of which next to the wall rose a flue of long flag-stones to the ceiling. On one side, at its base, a commodious square space was inclosed by narrow stones set edgewise in the ground.

Between the fire-place and the end of the room, eight or ten *metlatls* were slantingly set side by side in a trough of stone,—the mills, coarse and fine, of the household. Along the opposite side of the room was suspended from the rafters a smooth pole, upon which hung blankets, articles of clothing, and various other family belongings. More of the like, including quivers and bows, war-clubs, and boomerangs or "rabbit-sticks," disks of haliotis shell, and other ornaments, depended from pegs, and deer or antelope-horns on the walls. Some large, finely decorated water-jars, and a black earthen cooking-pot by the fire-place, two or three four-pronged stools of wood, sundry blanket rugs and robes, made up the furniture of the apartment. Furnishings and all, it differed not from hundreds of its kind throughout the pueblo, save that conspicuous in one corner was the governor's staff of office,—a silver-knobbed ebony cane, suspended by a faded red ribbon, a present to the tribe, as I afterward learned, from President Lincoln. I did not observe, until I had thrown myself into the hammock, that between the rafters and staves over the center of the room were some beautifully painted and plumed sticks, the guardian gods and goddesses of the household.

As night approached I tried to build a fire and cook supper, but I made but sorry work of it. Unsavory fumes rose from my badly burned bacon, and presently the governor's face appeared at one of the openings in the roof. He regarded operations silently a minute, and then vanished. Soon he followed his feet down the ladder, approached the fire-place, and without a word shoved me aside. Taking my skillet he marched down to the river. When he returned, every trace of the odious bacon had been removed, and replaced by a liberal quantity of mutton and abundant suet. Poking up the fire, the old fellow dexterously cooked the contents brown. Then, placing skillet and all in the center of the floor, he hastened away, soon to return with a tray of curious paper bread in one hand, while in the other, to my surprise, he held a steaming pot of thoroughly boiled coffee.

"*Hamon no bueno*," he remarked. "*Este k' ók-shi, í-tâ,*" he added; from which amalgamation of Spanish and Zuñi, augmented by suggestive gesticulation, I inferred that he regarded bacon as vile, but Zuñi food prepared in Zuñi fashion as worthy of emphatic recommendation. He did all this after the manner of a man who was performing an unpleasant duty, and when by gesture and incoherent Spanish phrases I expressed my gratitude most extravagantly he merely nodded his head, climbed the ladder, and remarked in Spanish, "Poor fellow," as he disappeared through the sky-hole as before. He probably commiserated me, for I was awakened next morning at the peep of day by the sound of breaking sticks, and turning over in my hammock saw the old fellow busily engaged in preparing a breakfast for me. Nor did he, throughout my long stay among the Zuñis, ever willingly permit me to prepare another meal.

I soon became better acquainted with the domestic life of the Zuñis, and learned where the governor went when he vanished through the sky-hole. His wife's family lived in the second story. There a room much wider than the one below, though not quite so long, accommodated all of them. A large beam through

FIG. 8. Cooking Breakfast

the center gave additional support to the rafters. Against it I struck my head the first time I entered, and, for that matter, nearly every time. I verily believe the Indians, though amused by this, sympathized with me so much that they were kinder than they otherwise would have been. Especially was this the case with the old chief's younger brother, a constant visitor, himself taller than most of them, who frequently experienced my difficulty, swearing the explosive oaths of his mother tongue with rare and increasing vehemence with every added experience. Indeed, a bond of sympathy thus arose between us. He soon realized that "Oh!" in American meant "Ai-ii," in Zuñi, and that "Damn" represented "Tuh!" He became morally—or immorally—even more certain, for he occasionally alternated the two expressions, or combined them with more presence of mind than I could have commanded under like circumstances.

The family consisted of the governor's ugly wife, a short-statured, large-mouthed, slant-eyed, bush-haired hypochondriac, yet the soul of obedience to her husband, and ultimately of kindness to me, for she conceived a violent fancy for me, because I petted her noisy, dirty, and adored little niece. Not so was her old aunt, a fine-looking, straight little old woman of sixty winters, which had bleached her abundant hair as white as snow. She would stand half an hour at a time before me in the middle of the floor, holding the little girl in a blanket on her back, and varying her snatches of lullaby with sighs, meanwhile regarding me with large eyes and half-moon shaped mouth, as though I were a wizard, or a persistent nightmare. The governor did not love her. He called her "Old Ten," which, as he explained after I began to pick up Zuñi and his regards, referred to the number of men she had jilted, and which appellation, when judiciously employed, usually brought hot tears from the old lady's eyes, or unloosed a tongue that the governor avowed "knew how to talk smarting words."

Then there was the governor's brother-in-law, a short, rather thick and greasy man, excessively conceited, ignorant, narrow, and moreover, so ceaselessly talkative, that he merited the name the inventive and sarcastic chief had given him, "Who-talks-himself-dry." I have known him, while dressing in the morning (usually a short process with the Zuñi), to forget, in the ardor of some new scandal, the most important articles of apparel, and issue forth from his couch of skins and robes, very like a half-picked chicken, still talking, and blissfully unaware of his dutifully uncriticised condition.

If the governor loved not "Old Ten," he despised her favorite nephew. This fellow's wife, however, was good-looking, dignified, quiet, modest, and altogether one of the most even-tempered women, red or white, it has been my lot to know. She was always busy with her children, or with the meal-grinding and cookery, occasionally varying these duties with belt-making or weaving. The little niece and her older brother were the only children. The former was a little child, rather too small for her age, bright-eyed, slant-headed like her father, and at once pursy and dirty with abundant food. Though she could not speak plainly, she even thus early gave promise of her father's character, in her ability to make much noise. She was the small "head of the household." All matters, however important, had to be calculated with reference to her. If she slept, the household duties had to be performed on tiptoe, or suspended. If she woke and howled, the mother or aunt would have to hold her, while "Old Ten" procured something bright-colored and waved it frantically before her. If she spoke, the whole family must be silent as the tomb, or else bear the indignation of three women and one man. The governor despised the father too much to join in this family worship. Indeed, while the rest delighted in speaking of this short specimen of humanity by the womanly name of "*Iu-í-si-a-wih-si-wih-ti-tsa*," the governor called her a "bag of hard howls," and said that she had the habit of storing up breath like a horned toad, which accounted for her extraordinary circumference, and her ability to make a noise in the world.

Little Iú-ní, her brother, was as handsome and as nearly like his mother as boy could be, save that he was rather inconsiderate to dumb things, and to his little sister's hideous dolls.

The aged grandfather of this group was usually absent after wood, or else puttering near the fire-place, or on the sunny terrace, with bits of raw hide, strands of buckskin, or head-scratching. He was lean as Disease, and black as his daughter—which expressed a good deal to her husband, the governor,—with toothless under-jaw and weeping eyes. The Navajos had treated him roughly in his youth, which he showed by the odd mixture of limp, shuffle, and jump in his gait. The asthma had tried for years to kill him; but he only coughed and wheezed harder and harder, as winter succeeded winter. So explained his son-in-law, the governor, who, if he ever mentioned him at all, called him "the Ancient Hummer" (*U-mumu-thlä-shi-kia*)—or, to translate into news-boy slang, "Old Buster."

There were two unmarried members of the house; a nephew and an adopted girl. The nephew was an over-grown, heavy-faced, thick-lipped, yellow-haired, blue-eyed blonde,—a specimen of the tribal albinism, a dandy, and the darling of the white-haired "Old Ten." One day, after I had presented the latter with a pane of ruined negative glass, she ventured to compare her favorite with me. My flattering acknowledgments of this compliment made decided winnings of the old woman's hitherto restrained affections. The governor spared this youth no more than the others. With characteristic irony, he called him "The Family Milkman," or "The Night Bird," the latter term referring to his eyes, "which," the governor usually added, "wiggled like those of an owl in strong sunlight." The maiden was jolly, pretty, and coquettish—the belle of "Riverside street." Her lovers were many, but soon, of the long row who waited under the moonlit eaves, only one was admitted—the governor's younger brother, my sympathetic friend. There was but one room in the house in which the two could hope to be left to themselves—mine. Here they came night after night. They paid no attention to the lonely *Mé-lik* in his hammock, but sat opposite in the darkness on the low adobe bench, hour after hour, stroking each other's hands, giggling and cooing in low tones just like so many of my own people of the same age, only in a different language. An occasional smack, followed by feminine indignation, taught me the meaning of "Stop that!" in Zuñi, and the peculiarities of the Pueblo kiss. If the blissful pair remained too late, the slab door would rumble on its wooden hinges, and the governor, preceded by a lighted torch of cedar splints, would stalk in, and, as near as I could make out, rate the young man soundly for his want of respect to the *Wa-sin-to-na Me-li-kana*, whereupon the pair would vanish, the maiden giggling and the young man cursing.

I made fair progress in the good graces of this odd group, but still by them, as by the rest of the tribe, I was regarded as a sort of black sheep on account of my sketching and note-taking, and suspicions seemed to increase in proportion to the evident liking they began to have for me. Day after day, night after night, they followed me about the pueblo, or gathered in my room. I soon realized that they were systematically watching me. They were, however, pleasant about it, and constantly taught me Mexican and Indian words, so that I soon became able to carry on a conversation with them. My apparent estrangement from the other members of our party aroused in some of them sympathy, in others only additional suspicions. It thus happened that the Indians began to watch me still more strictly, not only by day, but throughout whole nights. No matter how late I lay in the corner of my room, writing, the governor always sat beside me. Not until the last word had been written and I was stretched out in my hammock would he leave. Nor was I even then by myself, for either the governor, or, when he was absent, some one of his relatives or sub-chiefs, slept across the doorway of the room.

Realizing that until I could overcome the suspicion and secure the full confidence of the Indians, it would be impossible to gain any knowledge of importance regarding their inner life, I determined to remain among them until the return of our party from Moqui, whither it was soon to go. It was, therefore with feelings akin to those of a doomed exile that I watched the busy preparations one evening for the departure. This feeling was heightened by the fact that I was by no means intimate with the missionary, and Mr. Graham, the trader, was then temporarily absent from the pueblo. Moreover, I received from most of my party little sympathy in my self-imposed undertaking.

Next morning, when at sunrise I started toward the mission to bid them good-bye, a glance at the distant corral showed that they had all gone; and as I strained my eyes to catch a glimpse of them, the last white-topped wagon of the train disappeared over the far-off lava hills whence I had first caught sight of the Valley of Zuñi.

It had been arranged that my provisions should be left with the missionary. When I applied to him that dreary morning for my coffee, sugar, flour, and other necessaries, he simply replied that he had nothing for me; that the things the Colonel had left were designed for himself. It was with the most gloomy forebodings that I turned toward the pueblo. As I passed along the western end of the town the Indians watched me and commented on my sadness, but several of them assured me that "Zuñi was a good place to live in. So long as one had plenty to eat, why should he feel sad?" I entered my lonely room, and sat down in the hammock, burying my face in my hands. I heard no moccasin footstep, but when I roused up again the old governor was standing before me.

"Why is our little brother sad?" he asked.

"Alas!" I replied, "my friends are all gone, and they have left me nothing."

He looked at me a moment and said,

"Little brother, you may be a Washington man, but it seems you are very poor. Now, if you do as we tell you, and will only make up your mind to be a Zuñi, you shall be rich, for you shall have fathers and mothers, brothers and sisters, and the best food in the world. But if you do not do as we tell you, you will be very, very, very poor, indeed."

"Why should I not be a Zuñi?" I replied in despair; and the old man quickly answered,

"Why not?"

Leaving me for a few minutes, he soon returned with a steaming bowl of boiled mutton, followed by his kindly old wife, bearing a tray of corn-cakes mixed with *chili* and sliced beef, which, wrapped in husks, had been boiled like meat dumplings.

"There, try that," said the old man, as he placed the bowl in the center of the floor. "Fill your stomach, and your face will brighten."

And the old woman stood admiringly by as I heartily ate my first genuine Zuñi meal.

Although kinder than ever, the governor continued just as faithfully his nightly vigils. One night, after sitting close beside me examining every word I wrote, he threw away his cigarette, and informed me that "it was not well for me to make any more marks on the paper—it was of no use." As I calmly persisted, the next night a grave council was held. It was in the same room, and as I lay in my hammock listening to the proceedings, the discussion grew louder and more and more excited, the subjects evidently being my papers and myself.

When at a late hour the council broke up, the governor approached me, candle in hand, and intently regarded my face for several minutes. He then said:

"The *Keá-k'ok-shi* (Sacred Dance) is coming to-morrow. What think you?"

"I think it will rain."

"And *I* think," said he, as he set his mouth and glared at me with his black eyes, "that you will not see the *Keá-k'ok-shi* when it comes to-morrow."

"*I* think I *shall*," was my reply.

Next morning before I was awake, the herald and two or three *tinieutes* had come in, and, as I arose, were sitting along the side of the house. The old head chief had just prepared my morning meal, and gone out after something. I greeted all pleasantly and sat down to eat. Before I had half finished I heard the rattle and drum of the coming dance. I hastily jumped up, took my leather book-pouch from the antlers, and strapping it across my shoulder, started for the door. Two of the chiefs rushed ahead of me, caught me by the arms, and quietly remarked that it would be well for me to finish my breakfast. I asked them if the dance was coming. They said they didn't know. I replied that I did, and that I was going out to see it.

"Leave your books and pencils behind, then," said they.

"No, I must carry them wherever I go."

"If you put the shadows of the great dance down on the leaves of your books to-day, we shall cut them to pieces," they threatened.

Suddenly wrenching away from them, I pulled a knife out from the bottom of my pouch, and, bracing up against the wall, brandished it, and said that whatever hand grabbed my arm again would be cut off, that whoever cut my books to pieces would only cut himself to pieces with my knife. It was a doubtful game of bluff, but the chiefs fell back a little, and I darted through the door. Although they followed me throughout the whole day, they did not again offer to molest me, but the people gathered so closely around me that I could scarcely find opportunity for sketching.

As the month of November approached, the cold rains began to fall. Frost destroyed the corn-plants and vines. Ice formed over the river by night to linger a little while in the morning, then be chased away by the midday sun. Not in the least did these forerunners of a severe winter cause the dance ceremonials to abate. The Indians were, to some extent reassured when on the occasion of the next dance, which happened to be a repetition of the first, I did little or no sketching. At another dance, however, I resumed the hated practice, which made matters worse than before. A second council was called. Of this, however, I knew nothing, until afterward told by the old chief. It seems that it was a secret. It discussed various plans for either disposing of me, or compelling me to desist. Among others was the proposal that I be thrown off the great mesa, as were the two "children of the angry waters,"[3] but it was urged that should this be done, "*Wa-sin-to-na*" might visit my death on the whole nation. In order to avoid this difficulty, others suggested that I be *há-thli-kwïsh-k'ia* (condemned of sorcery) and executed. They claimed that sorcery was such a heinous crime that my execution would be pardoned, if represented to the Americans as the consequence of it. But some of the councilors reminded the others that the Americans had no sorcerers among them, and were ignorant of witchcraft.

FIG. 9. The Dance of the Great Knife

At last a plan was hit upon which the simple natives thought would free them from all their perplexities. Surely, no objection would be offered to the "death of a Navajo." [4] Forthwith the Knife Dance was ordered, as it was thought possible that the appearance of this dance would be sufficient to intimidate me, without recourse to additional violence.

One morning thereafter, the old chief appeared graver and more affectionate toward me than usual. He told me the "*Ho-mah-tchi* was coming,—a very *sa-mu* (ill-natured) dance," and suggested that "it would be well for me not to sketch it." Unaware either of the council or of the functions of the angry dance, I persisted. The old man, a little vexed, exclaimed, "Oh, well, of course, a fool always makes a fool of himself." But he said no more, and I assigned, as the cause of his remarks, superstitious reasons, rather than any solicitude for my safety.

When the great dance appeared, the governor seemed desirous of keeping me at home. During most of the morning I humored him in this. At last, however, fearing I would miss some important ceremonial, I stole out across the house-tops and took a position on one of the terraces of the dance court.

The dancers filed in through the covered way, preceded by a priest, and arranged themselves in a line across the court. Their costumes were not unlike those of the first dance I had witnessed, save that the masks were flatter and smeared with blood, and the beards and hair were long and streaming. In their right hands the performers carried huge, leaf-shaped, blood-stained knives of stone, which, during the movements of the dance, they brandished wildly in the air, in time and accompaniment to their wild song and regular steps, often pointing them toward me.

As the day advanced, spectators began to throng the terraces and court, few, however, approaching to where I was sitting; and the masked clowns made their appearance.

I had been busy with memoranda and had succeeded in sketching three or four of the costumes, when there dashed into the court two remarkable characters. Their bodies, nude save for short breech-clouts, were painted with ashes. Skull-caps, tufted with split corn-husks, and heavy streaks of black under their eyes and over their mouths, gave them a most ghastly and ferocious appearance. Each wore around his neck a short, twisted rope of black fiber, and each was armed with a war-club or ladder-round.

A brief intermission in the dance was the signal for a loud and excited harangue on the part of the two, which, at first greeted with laughter, was soon received with absolute silence, even by the children. Soon they began to point wildly at me with their clubs. Unable as I was to understand all they had been saying, I at first regarded it all as a joke, like those of the *Keó-yi-mo-shi*, until one shouted out to the other, "Kill him! kill him!" and the women and children excitedly rising rushed for the doorways or gathered closer to one another. Instantly, the larger one approached the ladder near the top of which I sat, brandishing his war-club at me. Savagely striking the rounds and poles, he began to ascend. A few Indians had collected behind me, and a host of them stood all around in front. Therefore, I realized that in case of violence, escape would be impossible.

I forced a laugh, quickly drew my hunting-knife from the bottom of the pouch, waved it two or three times in the air so that it flashed in the sunlight, and laid it conspicuously in front of me. Still smiling, I carefully placed my book—open—by the side of the pouch and laid a stone on it to show that I intended to resume the sketching. Then I half rose, clinging to the ladder-pole with one hand, and holding the other in readiness to clutch the knife. The one below suddenly grabbed the skirt of the other and shouted, "Hold on, he is a *kí-he!* a *kí-he!*⁵ We have been mistaken. This is no Navajo." Jumping down to the ground, the one thus addressed glanced up at me for an instant, waved his war-club in the air, breathed from it, and echoed the words of his companion, while the spectators wildly shouted applause. The two held a hurried conference. They swore they must "kill a Navajo," and dashed through the crowd and passage-way out of the court.

The *Keó-yi-mo-shi* freed from their restraint, rushed about with incessant jabber, and turned their warty eyes constantly in my direction. As I replaced my knife and resumed the sketching, the eyes of nearly the whole assemblage were turned toward me, and the applause, mingled with loud remarks, was redoubled. Some of the old men even came up and patted me on the head, or breathed on my hands and from their own.

Presently a prolonged howl outside the court attracted the attention of all, and the frantic pair rushed in through the covered way, dragging by the tail and hind legs a big, yelping, snapping, shaggy yellow dog. "We have found a Navajo," exclaimed one, as they threw the dog violently against the ground. While he was cringing before them, they began an erratic dance, wildly gesticulating and brandishing their clubs, and interjecting their snatches of song with short speeches. Suddenly, one of them struck the brute across the muzzle with his war-club, and a well-directed blow from the other broke its back. While it was yet gasping and struggling, the smaller one of the two rushed about frantically, yelling, "A knife, a knife." One was thrown down to him. Snatching it up, he grabbed the animal and made a gash in its viscera. The scene which followed was too disgusting

FIG. 10. Dance Paraphernalia

for description. It finds parallel only in some of the war ceremonials of the Aztecs, or in the animal sacrifices of the savages of the
far North-west. Let it suffice that what remained of the dog at
sunset, when the dance ended, was reluctantly given over to its
former owner by the hideous pair.[6]

Whether the Indians had really designed to murder me, or
merely to intimidate me, my coolness, as well as my waving of
the knife toward the sun, both largely accidental, had made a
great impression on them. For never afterward was I molested to
any serious extent in attempting to make notes and sketches.

That night, the old chief was profuse in his congratulations
and words of praise. I had completed in him, that day, the
winning of the truest of friends; and by so doing had decided the
fate of my mission among the Zuñi Indians.

II

When the frost first crackles the corn-leaves in the valley of
Zuñi, it is, to the dweller in that desert land, what the first April
shower is to husbandmen of New England. For in Zuñi autumn
is spring-time. It is the time of soft breezes and hazy beauty of
sky, not the days of blazing sun, driving sand-blasts and dust-
hidden clouds and distances. You may stand on the topmost
terraces of the old pueblo and see the busy harvesters bringing in

FIG. 11. Kolowissi, God of the Plumed Serpent

their last crops, and the old women who have been off among the mountains gathering peaches all day, staggering home at sunset, under huge baskets, strapped across their foreheads, full of the most delicious fruit. As you stroll through the narrow terrace-bounded streets your foot slips on pulpy melon-rinds, and from every dark window-hole dusky faces grin at your mishap. From as many door-ways welcomes greet you in unpronounceable clicks and guttural aspirations, which you are not long in comprehending, for basket after basket of the fruit brought in last evening is set before you. Day after day you may hear from the open plazas the sound of the drum and rattle, telling in strange cadences of the general joy of the time when "the corn grows aged, and the summer birds chase the butterfly to the land of everlasting summer."

It was toward the close of these merry days, one bleak evening in November, just as the red sun had set behind heavy black-bordered clouds at the western end of the plain of Zuñi, and the wind was wildly rushing to the opposite end, with its heavy freightage of sand, dead corn-leaves, and dried grasses, that the herald of Zuñi and I were walking down past the scalp-house toward the buildings of the mission. My companion turned to me with a pleasant smile on his face, and, tucking the corner of his *serape* more closely under one arm, raised his fingers as if to count them.

"Little brother, make your heart glad," said he, "a great festival is now every one's thought. Eighteen days more, and from the west will come the *Shá-la-k'o*; it welcomes the return of

FIG. 12. The Return of the Flocks

the *Kâ⸗kâ* and speeds the departure of the Sun. Make your heart glad, for you shall see it too."

Elated with the change of spirit toward men which this indicated on the part of the Indians, who had previously constantly opposed my presence at their ceremonies, I turned to reply, but he was shading his eyes and gazing intently off toward the road over the eastern mesas.

"Look! I wonder who are coming," said he.

A train of wagons was appearing at the crest of the black, distant head-lands. It came but slowly in the dusk, and against the wind-storm, so we returned to the pueblo.

My room was no longer lonely as at first. Huge blocks of piñon blazed on the hearth, and the Governor, now my inseparable friend, with his watchful, industrious wife, were there to welcome me. Night grew black outside. The wind howled in the chimneys. Rain and hail pelted fiercely down on the roof and against the plates of selenite in the windows. But the fire burned

FIG. 13. Zuñi Weaving

only the more brightly, shooting red tongues of flame up into the black, box-shaped flue, and casting dancing shadows against the white walls and over the stone-paved floor.

Next morning I crossed the pueblo, and looked down over the plain. The storm had ceased. Tents were pitched in the corral of the mission; white-topped wagons stood around, and smoke rose from a little fire in the corner. By these signs I knew that the caravan we had seen was my party returning from Moqui.

Hastening back to tell the good news to my "old brother," as the Governor insisted I should call him now, I met at the entrance Colonel Stevenson. Inquiries exchanged, he drew forth and handed me a letter from the Smithsonian Institution, informing me that a continuation of leave had been granted as I requested.

That night, doubtful of the results, I told the Governor that Washington wished me to remain there some months longer, to write all about his children, the Zuñis, and to sketch their dances and dresses.

"Hai!" said the old man. "Why does Washington want to know about our *Kâ'-kâ*? The Zuñis have their religion and the Americans have theirs."

"Do you want Washington to be a friend to the Zuñis? How can you expect a people to like others without knowing something about them? Some fools and bad men have said 'the Zuñis have no religion.' It is because they are always saying such things of some Indians, that we do not understand them. Hence, instead of all being brothers, we fight."

"My little brother speaks wisely, but many of my people are fools, too. He may get in touble if he pictures the *Kâ'-kâ* too much."

"Suppose I do."

"Well, then, what makes you puff up your face with sad thoughts?" asked the old man impatiently. "Don't you have plenty to eat? When you came here you lived on pig's grease and baked dough, but I threw the light of my favor on you and cooked some mutton. Have you ever had to ask for more? Sister would make all the paper-bread, corn-cakes, and dumplings you could eat, but you will not eat them, and she has grown ashamed. What's the matter anyway?" he persisted. "Do you want to see your mother? Pah? Well, you can't, for if Washington says 'You stay here,' what have *you* to say? Now go to bed. You had better cut down that hanging bed of strings, though, and sleep on a couple of sheepskins, like a man. Some night you will dream of 'Short Nose' [my mule], and tumble out of that 'rabbit net,' and then Washington will say I killed you. You just wait till 'Teem-sy' [Colonel Stevenson] and his beasts [the Mexican cook and drivers] go away, I'll make a man of you then;" and with this he leaned back against the adobe bench, with all the complacency of a tolerant, dutiful, and very responsible guardian.

A day or two afterward he approached me with a designing look in his eyes, and snatched off my helmet hat and threw it among some rubbish in the corner, producing from behind his back a red silk handkerchief. Folding this carefully, he tied it around his knee, and then placed it on my head. With a remark denoting disgust, he hastily removed it, and disappeared

FIG. 14. Chief Priest of the Bow

through a blanket-closed door into a quaint mud-plastered little room. After rummaging about for a time, he came out with a long black silken scarf, fringed at either end, which must have belonged once to some Mexican officer. He wound this round and round my head, and tied the ends in a bow-knot at my temple, meanwhile turning his head from side to side critically. "Good! good!" said the old man. "There, now, go out and show the Zuñis, then travel down to the camp and show the 'Teem-sy-kwe' [Stevenson people] what a sensible man you are, and how much better an *othl-pan* is than a mouse-head-shaped hat." He also insisted on replacing my "squeaking foot-packs," as he

FIG. 15. Women Grinding Corn

called a pair of English walking shoes, with neat red buckskin moccasins.

Thus, in a blue flannel shirt, corduroy breeches, long canvas leggings, Zuñi moccasins and head-band, heartily ashamed of my mongrel costume, I had to walk across the whole pueblo and down to camp, the old man peering proudly around the corner of an eagle-cage at me as I started. The Zuñis greeted me enthusiastically, but when I reached camp great game was made of me. I returned thoroughly disgusted, determined never to wear the head-band again; but, when I looked for the hat and shoes, they were nowhere to be found. When I asked for them, the Governor said, "No-o-o-o! The Americans are asses. Don't you suppose I know what becomes a man? Here, what have you got that on sidewise for? You Americans *will* stick things on your heads as though your skulls were flat on one side; are they? Well, then! wear your head-band straight and don't make a hat of it. There!" said he, straightening the band. And every morning, just as I was about to go out, he would carefully equip me in the black silk head-band. He took so much satisfaction in this, and it pleased the other Indians so much, that I decided to permit them thenceforth to do with me as they pleased.

One night, toward the close of the month, there appeared in the pueblo the ten *Keó-yi-mo-shis*. It was for the last time, the Indians told me, for during the old Sun ceremonials others would be elected for the ensuing year. Followed by a great crowd, they went from court to court, repeating in a sing-song, measured tone prayers to the gods and instructions to the people, whom they directed to prepare within four days for the coming festivities. Each of these clowns, save one, their reputed father, would start out soberly and properly enough in his recitation, but would soon, as if confused, wander off to some ridiculous, childish nonsense, which would bring down the rebuke of the older one. Forthwith the culprit was hunted forth from the line and replaced by one of his companions. This one, in turn, repeated the failure of the first. Each sally of rude wit was greeted with loud laughter and shouts of applause from the by-standers, who crowded around the little circle and lined the house-tops in the dark. Those near the *Keó-yi-mo-shis* held torches in order that the grotesque faces might be seen. As soon as the prayer of the oldest one began, however, the torches were lowered, and the whole court hushed until it was finished. Then the ceremony, varied only in the jokes, was repeated in some other plaza or court.

After all the plazas had been visited, I stealthily followed the retiring *Keó-yi-mo-shis* to a large room on the south side of the pueblo. A sentinel stood at the door, and no one but these clowns was permitted to enter. Nor could I catch more than a glimpse of the fire-lit interior, as the windows were heavily curtained with blankets. I learned that the group had been confined in this room four days and nights, engaged in fasting, prayer, and sacred incantations; so I determined to visit them.

Two days later I collected some tobacco and candles. The evening meal over, I asked where the *Keó-yi-mo-shis* were.

"They are tabooed," was the reply.

"I know," said I, "but where are they?"

"How do you know? What do you want with them?" the Indians glumly asked.

"They are good men," said I, "and I wish to give them some candles and tobacco."

It happened that an old man whom I knew, was one of the ten. He had temporarily come home after some plumes, and was standing aloof from the rest. A little while after his departure, a messenger came from the high-priest, with the request that I visit them, as "no harm would come from the presence of a *kí-he*." Forthwith, I was instructed how to behave.

"When you go in, little brother, you must breathe on your hand and, as you step into the fire-light, you must say, 'My fathers, how are you these many days?' They will reply, 'Happy, happy'! You must not touch one of them, nor utter a single word in Spanish or American, nor whistle. But you must behave very gravely, for it is *ák-ta-ni* [fearful] in the presence of the gods. If you should happen to forget and say a Spanish word, hold out your left hand and then your right, one foot and then the other, and they will strike them very hard with a wand of yucca."

The messenger guided me to the low door, which I entered, breathing audibly on my hand. Stepping into the brightly lighted center of the room, I started off very well with, "My fathers" (*Hóm a tá-tchu*), but here broke down, and placing the candles and tobacco on the floor, with a muttered apology, I unfortunately finished, partly in Spanish. Instantly two or three of the sprawling priests started up exclaiming, "*Shu! shu!*" and stretched their hands excitedly toward me. One of them took a wand from the front of the altar, and gravely advanced toward me. Without a word I stretched out my hand, and he hit me a terrific blow directly across the wrist. Never wincing, however, although the pain was excruciating, I stretched out the other hand and my two feet in succession, receiving the hard blows on each. I breathed on my hand and said, *É-lah-kwa* (thanks!). The priest spat on the wand, smiled, and waved it four or five times around my head. The white-haired father of the ten then approached me, placing his finger on his lips as a warning, thanked me for the presents, and asked that the "light of the gods might shine on my path of life." But he directed that I be hustled away, for fear I might commit some other indiscretion.

I had gained my object, however, in merely entering the room. It was large. At the western end stood an altar, composed of tablets of various heights and widths, strangely carved and painted in representation of gods, and set up in the form of a square. At the back were larger tablets, on and through which figures of the sun, moon, and stars were painted and cut. Within the square stood a number of sacred wands of long macaw feathers inserted into beautiful wicker-work handles. Overhead hung the figure of a winged god, a little in front of and below which was suspended horizontally an elaborate cross. It was composed of two tablets, carved to zigzag points at the ends, and joined at the center, so as to resemble a wind-mill with four arms. Numerous eagle-plumes depended from the lower edges of the four arms, on each of which was perched the effigy of a swallow.[7] Underneath this stood a large medicine-bowl with terraced edges. It was covered with figures of frogs, tadpoles, and dragon-flies, and contained a clear, yellowish fluid. Over this two of the priests were crouching and muttering incantations. Behind the altar, partly covered with little, embroidered cotton kilts, were the warty masks and the neck-cloths of these priestly clowns. Almost immediately on entering, my guide had uttered prayers and scattered medicine flour over them. All along the walls of the great room, now vivid in the fire-light, now indistinct in the flickering shadows, were painted in red, green, blue and yellow, the figures of animals, birds, human monsters, demons and significant pictographs.

This little glimpse revealed to me a mysterious life by which I had little dreamed I was surrounded, and I looked forward with curious anxiety to the coming ceremonials.

That night, on my way home, I saw great fires blazing on the south-western hills. I could hear the sound of rattles, and the long, weird cries of the dancers, whose forms were too distant to be seen even against the snow-sprinkled slopes. "The Long-horn and the Hooter, the wand-bearers and the sacred guardians, whom you shall see four days hence," said my brother, as he opened the door to let me in, and motioned with his head in the direction of the sounds.

During the next day, hundreds of Navajos, Moquis, and Indians from the Rio Grande pueblos, gathered in from the surrounding country. Everybody was busy. Oxen were slaughtered by the dozen, sheep by the hundred. In every

FIG. 16. The Tower of the Shadows and the Road of the Red Door

household some of the men could be seen sewing garments both for themselves and the women. The latter were busily engaged in grinding corn, cooking paper-bread over great polished, black stones, cutting up meat, bringing water, and weaving new blankets and belts. Outside, continual streams of burros, heavily laden with wood, came pouring in from the surrounding mesas.

My old brother, however, was none too busy to insist constantly that I should not sketch the "fearful *Shá-la-k'o*," when they came in from the west. If I would promise this, the party and I should be permitted to see the great ceremonial, which never before had the white man been allowed to look upon.

Toward evening, on the second day following, people began to gather all over the southern terraces, and away out over the plain there appeared seven gigantic, black-headed, white forms, towering high above their crowd of attendants. Gradually they came toward the pueblo, stopping, however, midway in the plain across the river, to perform some curious ceremonials. Meanwhile, eight remarkably costumed figures preceded them, crossed the river, and passed along the western end of the pueblo. These were the same the Governor had told me of. The "Long-horn" and the "Hooter" were clothed in embroidered white garments, and their faces were covered by horrible,

FIG. 17. Arrival of the *Sha-la-k'o*

ghastly, white masks, with square, black eye and mouth-holes. Their head-dresses were distinguished from each other only by the large white appendages, like bat-ears, attached to one of them, while the other was furnished with a long, green horn, from which depended a fringe of wavy black hair, tufts of which covered the heads of both. They bore in their right hands clattering rattles made from the shoulder-blades of deer, and in their left, painted plumed sticks. Following came two red-bodied, elaborately costumed and ornamented characters wearing round, green helmets, across the tops of which were attached painted round sticks with shell-rattles at either end. They bore in their hands white deer-horns and plumed sticks, and were, with the others, guarded by two nearly nude figures with round-topped, long-snouted, red masks, surrounded at the neck by collars of crow-feathers. They carried rattles like those of the chief figures, and long yucca wands with which to chastise spectators who might approach too near.

All of these were preceded by a gorgeously costumed, bare-headed priest, with streaks of black, shining paint across his eyes and chin, and profusely decorated with turquoise ear-rings and shell necklaces. A snow white deerskin mantle was thrown gracefully over his shoulders and trailed in the dust behind. He carried a tray of sacred plumes in his hand, and was closely followed by a representation of the fire-god. This was an entirely nude boy, the body painted black and covered all over with many-colored round spots. His face and head were entirely concealed by a round-topped, equally black and speckled mask or helmet. Slung across his shoulder was a pouch made from the skin of a fawn, and in his hand a long, large, smoking torch of cedar bark, which he kept gracefully waving from side to side.

The whole party passed rapidly toward one of the plazas, where a square hole had been dug by the Priest of the Sun. After dancing back and forth four times to the clang of their rattles, uttering at intervals cries of hoo too! hoo too! the four principal characters, with long prayers and ceremonials,[8] deposited sacrifices of some of the plumed sticks. This ceremonial was repeated in the chief plazas of the pueblo, and outside of it north, south and east, after which the whole party, just at sunset, retired into one of the immense sacred rooms at the southern side of the town.

After dusk, the giant figures which had been left on the plain across the river came in one by one. They were, by all odds, the most monstrous conceptions I had seen among the Zuñi dances. They were at least twelve feet high. Their giantic heads were shocks of long black hair with great horns at the sides, green masks with huge, protruding eye-balls, and long, pointed, square-ended, wooden beaks; and their bodies were draped with embroidered and tasseled cotton blankets, underneath which only the tiny, bare, painted feet of the actor could be seen. The spasmodic rolling of the great eyeballs and the sharp snapping of the beak as it rapidly opened and closed, together with a fan-shaped arrangement of eagle-feathers at the back of the head, gave these figures the appearance of angry monster-birds.

To each new house of the pueblo one of these monsters was

FIG. 18. A Night with the *Sha'-la-k'o*

guided by two priests. The latter were clad in closely fitting buckskin armor and round, helmet-like skull-caps of the same material. Several elaborately costumed flute-players together with a *Keó-yi-mo-shi* or two, attended. After prayers and ceremonials before the ladders of the houses to be entered, each, with his two attendant priests, mounted with great difficulty, descended through the sky-hole, and was stationed at one end of the room, near the side of an altar, differing only in details from the one already described as belonging to the *Keó-yi-mo-shis*. Immense fires of sputtering piñon-wood, and rude, bowl-shaped lamps of grease, brilliantly lighted up each one of these closely curtained rooms.

Toward midnight, my brother explained to me that, in each new room and sacred house of Zuñi, the twelve "medicine" orders of the tribe were to meet, and that, as he was a priest of one of them, I could go with him, if I would sit very quiet in one corner, and not move, sleep, or speak during the entire night.

As we entered the closely crowded, spacious room into which the first party of dancers had retired, a space was being cleared lengthwise through the center, from the altar down toward the opposite end. With many a hasty admonition, the Governor placed me in a corner so near the hearth that, for a long time, controlled by his directions, I was nearly suffocated by the heat. Along the northern side of the room were the dancers, their masks now laid aside. Conspicuous among them were the two priests, who were engaged in a long, rhythmical prayer, chant, or ritual, over eight or ten nearly prostrate Indians who squatted on the floor at their feet. As soon as this prayer was ended, great steaming bowls of meat, trays of paper-bread, and baskets of melons were placed in rows along the cleared space. A loud prayer was uttered over them by an old priest, who held in his hands a bow, some arrows, and a war-club, and who wore over one shoulder a strange badge of buckskin ornamented with sea-shells and flint arrow-heads.[9] He was followed by the Priest of the Sun, from the other end of the room. The little fire-god then passed along the array of victuals, waving his torch over them, with which the feast was pronounced ready.

Many of the dishes were placed before the dancers and priests and a group of singers whose nearly nude bodies were grotesquely painted with streaks and daubs of white. They were gathered, rattles in hand, around an immense earthen kettle-drum at the left side of the altar, opposite the now crouching monster. As soon as the feast was concluded, many of the women bore away on their heads, in huge bowls, such of the food as remained.

The singers then drawing closely around the drum, facing one another, struck up a loud chant, which, accompanied by the drumming and the rattles, filled the whole apartment with a reverberating din, to me almost unendurable. Two by two the dancers would rise, step rapidly and high from one foot to the other, until, covered with perspiration and almost exhausted, they were relieved by others. At the close of each verse in the endless chant, the great figure by the altar would start up from its half-sitting posture, until its head nearly touched the ceiling, and, with a startling series of reports, would clap its long beak and roll its protruding eyes in time to the music.

When the little fire-god took his place in the center of the room, no one relieved him for more than an hour and a half, and I feared momentarily that he would drop from sheer exhaustion. But I learned later that this was a trial ceremonial, and that it was one of the series of preparations which he had to pass through before becoming a priest, to which rank his birth rendered him eligible.

Just as the morning star was rising, the music ceased, the congregation became silent, and the chief dancer was led to the center of the room, where he was elaborately costumed. Then the Priest of the Sun took him up the ladder to the roof, where, facing the east, he pronounced in measured, solemn tones a long prayer to the waning Sun of the Old Year. Descending, he pronounced before the multitude (signalizing the end of each sentence with a clang of his rattles) a metrical ritual of even greater length. Then the spectators gathered around the altar, and hastily said their prayers, the sound of which reminded me of a recitation in concert in a large school-room. The sun rose, and they dispersed to their various homes.

Some time after, the dancers, one by one, still in costume, passed over the river toward the southward; and the monsters, to the sounds of chants, acompanied by rude music on the flutes, were guided across to a flat, snow-covered plain, where, in the presence of the assembled priests of Zuñi,—but no others,— they ran back and forth, one after another, over a great square, planted plumed sticks at either end of it, and, forming a procession, slowly marched away and vanished among the southern hills. Toward evening no fewer than seven curious dance-lines of the *Kâ⁺kâ* at one time occupied the principal court. Most of that, as well as of the three succeeding nights, were passed in ceremonials at the sacred houses and estufas. With this the great festival was over. The assembled Indian visitors, laden with food and the products of Zuñi looms, departed for their various tribal homes.

During the evening of the last day, just as I was sitting down with the rest around the family supper-bowl, Colonel and Mrs. Stevenson came in to bid me good-bye. And on the following morning, long before daylight, their train passed over the lava-hills, and I was once more alone in Zuñi.

During the day I told the Governor that I would follow my friends before two months were over. With great emphasis and a smile of triumph, he replied, "I *guess not.*"

On the evening of the second day he beckoned me to follow, as he led the way into the mud-plastered little room, whither he had unearthed my head-band. In one corner stood a forge, over which a blanket had been spread. All trappings had been removed, and the floor had been freshly plastered. A little arched fire-place in the corner opposite the forge was aglow with piñon, which lighted even the smoky old rafters and the wattled willow ceiling. Two sheepskins and my few belongings, a jar of water and a wooden poker, were all the furnishings. "There," said he, "now you have a little house, what more do you want? Here, take these two blankets,—they are all you can have. If you get cold, take off all your clothes and sleep next to the sheepskins and *think* you are warm, as the Zuñi does. You must sleep in the cold and on a hard bed; that will harden your meat. And you must never go to Dust-eye's house [the Mission], or to Black-beard's [the trader's] to eat; for I want to make a Zuñi of you. How can I do that if you eat American food?" With this he left me for the night.

I suffered immeasurably that night. The cold was intense, and the pain from my hard bed excruciating. Although next morning, with a mental reservation, I told the Governor I had passed a good night, yet I insisted on slinging my hammock lengthwise of the little room. To this the Governor's reply was: "It would not be good for it to hang in a smoky room, so I have packed it away." I resigned myself to my hard fate and harder bed, and suffered throughout long nights of many weeks rather than complain or show any unwillingness to have my "meat hardened."

An old priest, whom I had seen at the head of one of the dances, and whose fine bearing and classic, genial face had impressed me, used to come and chat occasionally of an evening with the Governor, in the other room. Often, as he sat in the fire-light, his profile against the blazing background made me wonder if the ghost of Dante had not displaced the old Indian for a moment, so like the profile of the great poet was the one I looked upon. He had conceived a great affection for me, and his visits became more and more frequent, until at last one day he told me his name was Laí-iu-ah-tsai-lun-kia, but that I must forget his name whenever I spoke to him, and call him "father." Now that I wore the head-band and moccasins of his people, his attentions were redoubled, and he insisted constantly that I should dress entirely in the native costume, and have my ears pierced. That would make a complete Zuñi of me, for had I not eaten Zuñi food long enough to have starved four times, and was not my flesh, therefore, of the soil of Zuñi?'

I strongly opposed his often repeated suggestions, and at last he so rarely made them that I thought he had altogether given up the idea.

One day, however, the Governor's wife came through the door-way with a dark blue bundle of cloth, and a long, embroidered red belt. She threw the latter on the floor, and unrolled the former, which proved to be a strip of diagonal stuff about five feet long by a yard in width. Through the middle a hole was cut, and to the edges, either side of this hole, were stitched, with brightly colored strips of fabric, a pair of sleeves. With a patronizing smile, the old woman said,—

"Put this on. Your brother will make you a pair of breeches, and then you will be a handsome young man."

Under her instructions I stuck my head through the central hole, pushed my arms down into the little blanket sleeves, and gathered the ends around my waist, closely securing them with the embroidered belt. The sudden appearance of the Governor was the signal for the hasty removal of the garment. He folded it up and put it away under the blanket on the forge. Long before night he had completed a pair of short, thin, black cotton trowsers, and secured a pair of long, knitted blue woolen leggins.

"Take off that blue coat and rag necklace," said he, referring to my blue flannel shirt and a tie of gray silk. "What! *another* coat under that. Take it off."

I removed it.

"There, now! Go over into that corner and put these breeches on. Don't wear anything under them."

Then the coarse woolen blanket shirt was again put on as

FIG. 19. Ancient Mines in the Valley of the Pines

before, only next to my skin. There were no seams in this remarkable garment, save where the sleeves were attached to the
shoulders and from the elbows down to the wrists. The sides, a
little below the armpits, and the arms inside down to the elbow,
were left entirely exposed. I asked the Governor if I could not
wear the under-coat.

"No," said he. "Didn't I say you must have your meat hardened?"

Fortunately, however, a heavy gray serape, striped with
blue and black, and fringed with red and blue, was added to this
costume. One of the young men gave me a crude copper bracelet,
and the old priest presented me with one or two strings of black
stone beads for a necklace.

The first time I appeared in the streets in full costume the
Zuñis were delighted. Little children gathered around me; old
women patronizingly bestowed compliments on me as their
"new son, the child of Wa-sin-to-na." I found the impression was
good, and permitted the old Governor to have his way. In fact, it
would have been rather difficult to have done otherwise, for, on
returning to my room, I found that every article of civilized
clothing had disappeared from it.

During my absence for several days on an expedition to the Valley of the Pines in search of mines which had formerly been worked by the Zuñis, the old Governor and his wife industriously plastered my room, whitewashed the walls and even the rafters, spread blankets over the floor, and furnished it in Indian style more luxuriously than any other room in Zuñi. On the wall at one end, the Governor, in recollection of the pictures in officers' quarters which he had seen, had pasted bright gilt and red prints, which no one knows how many years past had been torn from bales of Mexican *bayeta*. Above, carefully secured by little pegs, was a photograph of Colonel Stevenson, which the latter had given the Governor before leaving, and which the Indians had designed as my companion. On my return I was so cordially greeted that I could no longer doubt the good intentions of the Zuñis toward me.

My foster father and many other of the principal men of the tribe, now insisted that my ears be pierced. I steadily refused; but they persisted, until at last it occurred to me that there must be some meaning in their urgency, and I determined to yield to their request. They procured some raw Moqui cotton, which they twisted into rolls about as large as an ordinary lead-pencil. Then they brought a large bowl of clear cold water and placed it before a rug in the eastern part of the room. K'iawu presently came through the door-way, arrayed in her best dress, with a sacred cotton mantle thrown over her shoulders and abundant white shell beads on her neck. I was placed kneeling on the rug, my face toward the east. My old father, then solemnly removing his moccasins, approached me, needle and cotton in hand. He began a little shuffling dance around me, in time to a prayer chant to the sun. At the pauses in the chant he would reach out and grasp gently the lobe of my left ear. Each time he grasped, I braced up to endure the prick, until finally, when I least expected it, he ran the needle through. The chant was repeated, and the other ear grasped and pierced in the same way. As soon as the rolls of cotton had been drawn through, both the old man and K'iawu dipped their hands in the water, prayed over them, and, at the close of the prayer, sprinkled my head, and scattered the water about like rain-drops on the floor, after which they washed my hands and face, and dried them with the cotton mantle.

FIG. 20. The God of War

I could not understand the whole prayer; but it contained beautiful passages, recommending me to the gods as a "Child of the Sun," and a "Son of the Corn people of earth" (the sacred name for the priests of Zuñi). At the close, the old man said— "And thus become thou my son, Té-na-tsa-li," and the old woman followed him with, "This day thou art made my younger brother, Té-na-tsa-li." Various other members of the little group then came forward, repeating the ceremonial and prayer, and closing with one or the other of the above sentences, and the distinct pronunciation of my new name.

When all was over, my father took me to the window, and, looking down with a smile on his face, explained that I was "named after a magical plant which grew on a single mountain in the west, the flowers of which were the most beautiful in the world, and of many colors, and the roots and juices of which were a panacea for all injuries to the flesh of man. That by this name,—which only one man in a generation could bear,—would I be known, as long as the sun rose and set and smiled on the Corn people of earth, as a *Shi wi* (Zuñi)."

III

"The rattled-tailed serpents
Have gone into council;
For the god of the Ice-caves,
From his home where the white down
Of wind in the north-land
Lies spread out forever,
Breathes over our country
And breaks down the pine-boughs."[10]

Thus say the grandfathers of Zuñi children when the snow-storms whiten the distant mountains and mesas. Next to autumn, winter is the merriest season of the year; merry to the lazy Indians, because a time of rest, festivity, and ceremonial. There is not much to be done; only the wood to be gathered from the mesas and cañons and brought in on "burro-back," the herds to be looked after, and the snow, when it happens to get piled up on the terraces, to be shoveled with wooden spades into blankets, and carried on the head down ladders to the outer edge of the pueblo, and there banked against the corrals. The days, save when some national observance claims the time, or betting over elaborate games in the plazas runs high, are dreary and monotonous enough; but the firelit evenings lengthen into hours of merry conversation. Old gray-heads sit around the hearths, telling their children of the adventures of men and the gods "when the world was young in the days of the new."

When the new-year of 1880 brought such times as these, I had been four months in Zuñi, and was counted one of the Children of the Sun. As I strolled through the streets or over the house-tops, children stopped pelting dogs with snow-balls, or playing checkers with bits of pottery on flat stones, and shouted my new name, "Te-na-tsa-li! Te-na-tsa-li!" at the tops of their shrill little voices. I was able, too, to share somewhat in the conversations and councils of the older ones; no longer did the cigarette of my "brother," the old governor of the tribe, gleam alone when the blazes on the hearth shrank back into the red embers, leaving only the shadows of the night in my little room. No; a dozen red stars glowed and perished with every whiff of as many eager visitors, or burned in concert at the end of each joke or story, revealing strange features which started forth from the darkness, like the ruddy ghosts of some pre-Columbian decade. "Shake the blazes out of the brands," one of these ghosts would say; and another, with a long cedar stick, would poke the brands, till the flames would dart up the black chimney anew, the cigarette stars would fade into ashes in the sunlight of the piñon, when lo! the ancient ghosts became sprawling, half-nude Indians again.

No sooner had I begun to enjoy these evening diversions of the pueblo home than they were interrupted for several days. I then first learned of the existence of thirteen orders or societies, some of which were actually esoteric, others of a less strict nature, but all most elaborately organized and of definitely graded rank, relative to one another. For the introduction here of a few words relative to these organizations, I beg the pardon of the reader; since their existence is a fact of ethnologic importance, and moreover my statements relative to them have been most acrimoniously criticised and persistently disputed.

Functionally they are divisible into four classes: Those of War, of the Priesthood, of Medicine, and of the Chase; yet the elements of every one of these classes may be traced in each of all the others.

Of the first class (Martial) there is but one society—the "*A-pi-thlan-shi-wa-ni,*" or the "Priests of the Bow," at once the most powerful and the most perfectly organized of all native associations, in some respects resembling the Masonic order, being strictly secret or esoteric; it is possessed of twelve degrees, distinguished by distinctive badges.

Of the second class (Ecclesiastical) there is also but one order—the "*Shi-wa-ni-kwe,* or society of priests, of the utmost sacred importance, yet less strictly secret than the first.

Of the third class (Medical) are the "*Ka-shi-kwe*" and "*A-tchi-a-kwe,*" or cactus and knife orders—the martial and civil surgeons of the nation; the "*Ne-we-kwe*" and "*Thle-we-kwe,*" or the gourmands and stick-swallowers; "Bearers of the Wand," who treat diseases of the digestive system; the "*Ka-ka-thla-na-kwe*" and "*Ma-ke-thla-na-kwe,*" or grand *ka-ka* (dance) and grand fire orders, who treat inflammatory diseases; the "*Ma-ke-tsa-na-kwe*" and "*Pe-sho-tsi-lo-kwe,*" or the lesser fire and insect orders, who treat burns, ulcers, cancers, and parasitic complaints; the "*U-hu-hu-kwe,*" or "Ahem" (cough) order, who treat colds, etc.; and lastly, the "*Tchi-to-la-kwe,*" or rattlesnake order, who treat the results of poisoning, actual or supposed, resulting from sorcery or venomous wounds.

Of the fourth class (Hunters) there is again but one order—the "*San-ia-k'ia-kwe,*" or "*Tus-ki-kwe,*" blood or coyote order—the hunters of the nation.

To all these a fourteenth organization might be added, were

it not too general to be regarded as esoteric, notwithstanding its operations are strictly secret and sacred. I refer to the much quoted, misspelled, and otherwise abused *"Kâ⸍-kâ,"* "the Dance," which is wonderfully perfect in structure, and may be regarded as the national church, and, like the church with ourselves, is rather a sect than a society.

Perhaps the Priesthood of the Bow is the only truly esoteric of all these bodies, since members of it may be admitted to meetings of all the others, while members of the other societies are strictly excluded from the meetings of this.

Early learning this, I strove for nearly two years to gain membership in it, which would secure at once standing with the tribe and entrance to all sacred meetings, as well as eligibility to the Head Chieftaincies. I succeeded, and the memory of my experiences in this connection are to me the most interesting chapter of my Zuñi life.

These orders were engaged in their annual ceremonials, of which little was told or shown me; but, at the end of four days, I heard one morning a deep whirring noise. Running out, I saw a procession of three priests of the bow, in plumed helmets and closely-fitting cuirasses, both of thick buckskin,—gorgeous and solemn with sacred embroideries and war-paint, begirt with bows, arrows, and war-clubs, and each distinguished by his badge of degree,—coming down one of the narrow streets. The principal priest carried in his arms a wooden idol, ferocious in aspect, yet beautiful with its decorations of shell, turquoise, and brilliant paint. It was nearly hidden by symbolic slats and prayer-sticks most elaborately plumed. He was preceded by a guardian with drawn bow and arrows, while another followed, twirling the sounding slat which had attracted alike my attention and that of hundreds of the Indians, who hurriedly flocked to the roofs of the adjacent houses or lined the street, bowing their heads in adoration, and scattering sacred prayer-meal on the god and his attendant priests. Slowly they wound their way down the hill, across the river, and off toward the mountain of Thunder. Soon an identical procession followed and took its way toward the western hills. I watched them long until they disappeared, and a few hours afterward there arose from the top of "Thunder

Mountain" a dense column of smoke, simultaneously with another from the more distant western mesa of "U-ha-na-mi," or "Mount of the Beloved."

Then they told me that for four days I must neither touch nor eat flesh or oil of any kind, and for ten days neither throw any refuse from my doors, nor permit a spark to leave my house, for "This was the season of the year when the 'grandmother of men' (fire) was precious."

Since my admission to the Priesthood of the Bow, I have been elected to the office of guardian to these gods; have twice accompanied them to their distant lofty shrines, where, with many prayers, chants, and invocations, they are placed in front of their predecessors of centuries' accumulation. Poetic in name and ascribed nature are these cherished and adored gods of war: one is called "Á-hai-iú-ta," and the other "Má-tsai-lé-ma," and they are believed to be single in spirit, yet dual in form, the child or children of the God of the Sun, and to guard from year to year, from sunrise to sunset, the vale and children of those they were first sent to redeem and guide. These children receive without question the messages interpreted by their priests from year to year, which unfailingly shape the destinies of their nation toward the "encircling cities of mankind."

When the fast was over and the nation had gladly thrown aside its yoke of restriction with the plumed sacrifices, which were cast into the river or planted on the sandy plain, the nightly sittings were again resumed in my little home. One night, at the pause of a long story, I heard a priest counting his fingers to fix the date of the ceremonials of initiation to be performed, he said, "by the rattlesnakes and fire-eaters." He lamented greatly the loss of some sacred black paint, with which he wished to decorate afresh the tablets of his altar, and was wondering what he would do about it. Conversation recurred to the stories, and I fell to thinking how I could turn the priest's difficulties to account. At last a plan struck me: I took from my trunk a book illustrated with colored prints and pretended to read it before the dim fire-light. As I had designed, the curiosity of my companions was excited. Then I told them how the pictures had first been painted, and getting my water-color box, which contained some India ink, proceeded to illustrate what I had said. In describing how the

FIG. 21. Zuñi Ceremony (left); Thunder Mountain (right)

colors were made, I dwelt particularly on the ink, saying that it was "made only by the *Chi-ni-kwe*, who were a Celestial people and lived on the back side of the world." I then painted with it a tablet of wood, and the deep black gloss excited their admiration. When I saw this, I hastened to add that "the *black* pigment was most precious; that they might use the other tints, but I could not part with that for an instant." At their usual late hour the company broke up. The priest, on leaving, looked longingly toward the corner wherein I had placed the box of paints, but said nothing. I awaited further developments most anxiously.

Four or five days later he came to me in company with one or two others. It was quite early in the day. As I had hoped, he asked for a "small piece of the Chi-ni-kwe ink." I refused it, repeating what I had already said. For a time he looked blank, but finally asked if I would not *lend* him some of it. Again I refused, saying "I could not trust it out of my sight." Finally, after much consultation with the others, he asked me if I "liked the Mexicans and other fools." I said "No"; then he begged that I should come to the "Chamber of the Rattlesnakes," and bring with me some of the "Chi-ni-kwe black." I purposely hesitated a long time, but finally said that "may-be" I would.

As soon as the embassy had departed, I made up a package of tobacco, candles, etc., with the black paint and an elaborate Chinese ink-stone. Near noon I took my way to the Chamber. I stepped down the ladder with perfect assurance, and observing that all the members were barefooted, drew my own moccasins off and went up to the front of the altar; at the same time speaking the greeting which had been taught me when I visited the "Keó-yi-mo-shi," I deposited the articles one by one, last of all the paint.

Had a ghost appeared in their midst he would not have caused more surprise than my assurance and seeming familiarity with the forms excited in the members of the order. They occupied one of the largest rooms in the town, along the walls of which were painted figures of the gods, among them a winged human monster with masked face, and a giant corn-plant which reached from floor to ceiling and was grasped on either side by a mythologic being. Toward the western end of the room stood the altar, with attendant priests before, behind, and on either side of it. Above all was suspended a winged figure, like the painting on the wall. Between the altar and the blazing hearth were gathered the members, all of whom save the women, were nearly nude; but elaborate devices in red, white, and yellow paint, representing serpents, suns, and stars, made them appear dressed in skin-fitting costumes. They were at work grinding and mixing paint, adorning costumes, and cleaving blocks of straight-grained cedar into splints about a yard in length, and nearly as thin as grass straws. Others, again, were tying, with strips of "yucca" leaf, the splints thus prepared into bundles about as large as one's arm.

As soon as I had deposited the presents, I approached and saluted the chief-priest, grasped his hands with both my own, and telling him I would "return at evening for the paint," breathed on them and hastily withdrew. On my way home an Indian who had seen me enter cursed me heartily, and said I would suffer for my imprudence, but I paid no attention to him. He told my old brother, however, and when long after dark I threw my serape over my shoulders, the latter asked where I was going. I said "To see the rattlesnakes." "No!" said the old man.

"Yes," said I; "if the priest be willing, why should *you* object?" and amid family imprecations I darted out of the door and hurried along the dark streets to the place of meeting. I climbed the ladder and entered, blinking at the flood of light with which the place was aglow. Several of the members started up and motioned me out with their flat hands; but I only breathed deeply from my own, until I reached the place of the old priest. Knowing that Mexican was forbidden, I pretended not to understand what was said, when the latter advised me, in his own language, to go home: on the contrary, I wrung his hand, and, as I pulled off my moccasins, incoherently expressed my thanks for the privilege of remaining, and immediately seated myself as if for the night. It was a heavy "game of bluff"; but utterly bewildered by it, the old priest said nothing for some moments, until, evidently in despair, he lighted a cigarette, blew smoke into the air, uttered a prayer, and then handed the cigarette to me. I smoked a whiff or two, said a prayer in English, and handed the cigarette to the nearest member. I had the satisfaction of hearing them say, "Let him stay; he is no fool, and what if he be—he is our Ki-he, and the 'Beings' will throw the light of their favor upon him, because he cannot understand and knows no better." So they rolled another cigarette and told me I "must smoke all night, and help to make clouds for their little world"; that I "must occasionally give to the fathers (priests and song-masters) my cigarettes, roll more, and never be idle, nor cease smoking." I had never smoked before. The first cigarette made me desperately sick; the second, sicker; so that, when I rose to present it, I reeled and had to sit down again; with the third, the sickness disappeared, and with the fourth I first came to feel the dreamy pleasures of the smoker.

At midnight, a long succession of cries like the voices of strange night-birds penetrated our smoky den. The musicians began to beat their great drum and sing a weird, noisy song, celebrating the origin of their order. Soon a grand company of dancers filed in, costumed like the members of the Rattlesnake order, save that black streaks of paint encircled their mouths, bordered and heightened by lines and daubs of yellow pigment. After passing through a rapid dance, which was attended by the round-headed "*Sa-la-mo-pi-a,*" they settled down along the op-

FIG. 22. A Zuñi War-Party

posite side of the room. Only the "Sa-la-mo-pi-a" now remained, dancing wildly up and down before the altar, waving his wand of yucca and willow, with which, on occasion, he soundly thrashed the unfortunate sleepers whom his keen little round eyes failed not to discover.

There was now a sudden pause in the music. The Sa-la-mo-pi-a retired, and only members of the two orders remained. Two lads who were undergoing their novitiate, were brought into the middle of the room. The fires and huge grease lamps were freshly kindled and lighted, until the smoke near the ceiling looked almost like the clouds of sunset. A nude functionary brought great armfuls of the splint bundles, and deposited them in front of the hearth. The music struck up—wilder, more mysterious and deafening than ever. The two boys looked wistfully about; one trembled visibly, while the other, more imbued with the spirit of his race, seemed possessed, after the first movements, with a dogged apathy. Two members of the order approached them from behind, pinioned their arms, and stood holding them. All the other members rose, each procured a bundle of the splints, breathed on it, prayed over it, and all, save the leading priests, sat down again; these set up long, terrific cries, rushed toward the fire, howled at it as if in defiance, and stuffed the ends of the splints into the flames and embers. Soon their torches set the place more aglow than ever. They approached the terrified boys, danced, and joined in the wild song, brandishing their flambeaux, and yelling more and more vociferously. Suddenly, two by two, they stepped into the light, thrust the blazing splints into their mouths and throats, drew them forth still aglow with coals, and put the latter out in the mouths of the boys. The stoic stood unmoved, but the other writhed and turned his head piteously; to no purpose, however, for the stalwart priests held him firmly to the fiery ordeal. Two by two, all the members in order of their rank, even the songmasters, went through this process, until just before day-break there remained only the prayers to be said over the wretched pair to complete their initiation. This completed, they were conducted to seats, and all present said their prayers before the altar; meal was thrust into my hand and I was dragged up with the rest. A long silence ensued. Sleepy participants nodded, grimaced, fell against one another, re-straightened up, only to repeat again and again the same experience, before daylight sifted in and sunbeams followed through the holes in the blanket curtains. Finally, a woman's voice called down from the roof. One by one she passed down huge bowls of meat broth, red with chili, guava and Indian delicacies, until four rows extended from the end of the room to the altar. She then came in accompanied by a plumed priest of another order; together they said a prayer of presentation, which the priests present replied to with one of thanksgiving. The "bad influence" of the feast was skimmed off with eagle plumes and "thrown up" the altar by a medicine priest. Then the leader called out, "Eat all!" The weary crowd woke up of one accord, and with boisterous jokes, loud smacking, and gurgling exclamations of satisfaction, soon cleared away a good portion of the liberal feast. A bowl of hot broth and meat was set before the novices. It was red with pepper, powder, or chili. They took a mouthful each, and with tears in their eyes desisted, for their lips were as black with cinders as their tongues were white with blisters, but they were bidden to eat. The more timid one refusing was grasped by the nape of the neck by one priest, while another stuffed the hot smoking food down his throat.

Horrible as are these ordeals, they are less so than those of the Cactus order, where the young candidate is scourged with willow wands and cactus thorns, until his naked body is covered with a net-work of ridges and punctures. Far from blaming my foster-people for these things, I look rather to the spirit of their at first imposed, but afterward voluntary sufferings, that they may place themselves beyond the evil they strive to overcome in others; may strengthen the faith of their patients to the sublime power of their medicines, given, they aver, by the gods themselves for the relief of suffering humanity. So, annually, they and their brother orders give public exhibitions of their various powers—sometimes, as is the case with the slat swallowers (or "Bearers of the Wand"), producing injuries for life, or even suffering death; but, nevertheless unflinchingly, year after year, performing their excruciating rites.

When all was over I followed the little ray of golden sunshine, which shot down through the neat covering of the sky-hole, up the slanting ladder and out into the cold winter morning air. A chill seized me before I had reached my little room. Several Indians who noticed my pallor attributed it to my transgressions. They were not long in communicating their thoughts to my old brother, who lamented having allowed me to go. As days passed I grew little better, and a few colds—the result of my scant costume and almost constantly damp, cold feet—at last prostrated me with pneumonia. When I began to recover, I was for weeks almost confined to my room. A walk across the pueblo would exhaust me. During this long illness and convalescence, I was constantly attended by my old brother and K'ia-wu ("sister"). My hammock was once more brought out and strung, and I was allowed more blankets. An almost constant crowd of visitors assembled during the day in my little room, leaving only with the late hours of night. They kept up a steady conversation, and I determined to improve the time by studies of the language. My old brother was delighted. Hour after hour he would sit by my bedside, drilling me in pronunciation and compelling me to say, over and over, the hard new words which he continually produced and explained for my benefit.

I now began to learn that the language spoken by my foster-people is by no means either meager or crude. It has most of the cases, moods, and tenses of the Greek, and like it possessed the singular, dual-plural, plural, and collective-plural numbers. It abounds in synonyms. For instance, the word *much* or *many* is expressed by no fewer than three words: *Em-ma, te-u-tcha, ko-ho-ma-sho-ko*. For our verb *to know*, five expressions occur, strikingly delicate in their distinctive shades of meaning. *To know*—intentively or abstractly, self-evident knowledge, *ai-yu-ya-na; to know* through the understanding, acquired knowledge, *iu-he-ta; to know*—how to act, speak, think, do or make anything,—methodic knowledge, *an-i-kwa; to know*—a country, road, river, mountain or place—geographic knowledge, *te-na-di; to know*—a place, person, animal, or personified object—knowledge of acquaintance, *a-na-pi*. Each of these expressions is again capable of modification by grammatic prefixes, suffixes, or interjections; so that more than fifteen almost distinct terms for the one English verb, *to know*, can be produced. Nor are these refinements of meaning limited to this one example; they extend through the whole range of verbs, adverbs, and adjectives of the language. I was at first overwhelmed; but my old brother so invariably pounced upon a wrong use of any apparent synonym, that I soon overcame the difficulty.

To get used to the proper number, however, was not so easy. A friend's face would smile in at my open door. I would say *Kwa-ta* (Come in). He would thank me and obey instantly. Three or four, old and young, would appear; I would address them in the same way. They would look at one another and then at me, and finally begin a discussion as to which of their number I had meant. My old brother would look up and remark *U-kwa-ta*. They would troop in, and he would rate me soundly before them all for such a blunder. But if it happened that two appeared at the door, and I repeated the plural expression, they would unfailingly look over their shoulders as though they expected some one else to follow. Then the old man would laugh at me, swear a little, and call out *"Atch-kwa-ta."* Imagine my surprise when I thought I had mastered these distinctions to find myself yet again sharply rebuked by my old teacher. Several dancers came to my door-way. I said *U-kwa-ta*; they looked offended. *"An-samu-kwa-ta,"* said my old brother; the looks vanished before smiles at my ignorance, and my brother explained that they all belonged to "one class" (*ta-nan-ne*).

He trained me diligently in another peculiarity of his speech. A man may say for "I want" *ha-anti-shi-ma*, but he must not say *ha-kwa-anti-shi-ma* for "I do not want." He must say *kwa* (not) *ha* (I) *anti-shi-ma* (want) *nam-me*, negative ending. "Good" was *k'ok-shi*; "not good," *kwa-k'ok-sham-me*; and this double negative was a sore perplexity, especially when *Kwa* initiated a long sentence and the negative ending was added to each subject verb or adverb as well as to the close of the whole sentence. After I had gained an insight into case, mood, and tense, endings, prefixes, and interjections, my progress was more rapid. The tenses presented the greatest obstacle. One night I went to bed rather discouraged. I dreamed of having gained a clear conception of the tenses (which probably resulted from my long thinking on the subject), and of speaking at great length many of the roots I already knew, with their *proper* prefixes and endings. Next morning I spoke according to my dream, and found to my surprise that the fogs about the whole subject had cleared; for it proved that nearly all Zuñi verbs are regular, my subsequent studies having revealed only four or five exceptions to this rule. Wonder of wonders—a language of regular verbs!

And now began my most interesting studies—in which, alas, my teacher could not help me—of the etymology of the language.

Advocates of the "Bow-wow" theory of the origin of language may find convincing facts among the Zuñis. Take, for instance, the root *a-ti*. It is primarily an exclamation of mortal fear. As *a'-ti*, it means blood. It is a termination expressing violence, as in *la-pa-a-ti*—to shake violently—from *la-pa*, the sound of a shaken blanket, and *ati*. *Ta-pa-at-i*—to rap or pound, as at a door, from *ta-pa*—to tap—and *a-ti*. *Tsi-a-a-ti*—to cut or tear flesh or soft substance—from *tsi-a*, in imitation of the sound of cutting flesh, and *a-ti*. *Teshl-a-ti*—to fear; from *teshl*—to breathe hard, and *a-ti*. *A ͗-tu*—dark blood—from *a-ti*, the exclamation, and *u-e*—painful, —since black blood is supposed to cause inflammation. *A ͗-tu*, again, is a violent expression for "get out"; and *tuh* becomes an exclamation of anger, equivalent to our word damn. In fact, the number of words in which elements and roots occur derived from this one exclamation, *a-ti*, are so numerous as to become tedious to others than specialists. I venture, however, on one or two additional examples of derivation through imitation. *Pi-wi-wi-k'e-a* is the sound of a string or thread drawn over a resisting body or through the damp fingers. From this the word *pi-le*—a string—is derived. *Tsu-nu-nu-k'e-a* is the sound of air escaping from the punctured paunch of a slain animal. From it the word *tsu-le* (paunch) is derived. These two words shortened and combined, *pi-tsu-li-a*, signify a round line, a circle—from string and the shape of a paunch, which is round. Thus almost throughout is this remarkable archaic language of the Zuñis built up, bearing in itself no small portion of the primitive history, especially of the intellectual development of the people by whom it is spoken.

During my illness, I was brought into very close contact with the people. I began to think, from the domestic harmony by which I was surrounded, that I had found the long-sought-for social Utopia. One day, however, the governor had a quarrel with his brother-in-law, and with a few sarcastic and telling epithets gathered up his sheep-skins and blankets, came into my room, slammed the door after him, and did not cross the threshold again for months. The weeping but faithful K'ia-wu followed, and thenceforth they took up quarters with me. More than a year elapsed before I had any more privacy while in Zuñi.

The governor was a rare and singular character. I never tire of speaking or writing of him. He was long-suffering to a degree incredible, but silent, emotionless, and unswerving when he had determined. One of his traits was cleanliness. One sunny afternoon he was pottering about the eagle-cage, picking up some hard-wood sticks, and carrying them to the oven, behind which he was carefully piling them. K'ia-wu was on the roof sifting corn, and chatting with some neighboring women. Presently I heard a whine; looking round I saw a large, fine dog limping along, his knee, left eye, lips, mouth, and whole face covered with the yellow spines of a porcupine.

"Ha! a yellow beard comes, and is unhappy," I cried.

"A yellow mustache?" echoed and queried the governor.

"Why did you tell him?" called K'ia-wu from the roof, for she had just espied the miserable creature.

But the emotionless governor paid attention to neither dog nor remarks. He had just loaded his arms full of the sticks. K'ia-wu, encouraged, warned him that it was his "own uncle's dog." The governor approached the oven with his load; suddenly choosing from it a suitable club, he edged toward the dog, dropped the others, and with two blows across the muzzle dispatched it. Then catching the still struggling brute by the hind-legs, he dragged it toward the river, remarking: "Yellow beards sometimes make little children crazy, and cause thoughts," with which he threw him over the bank, and bade him "go west to the spirit-land of dogs," where he assured him "it would be well to hunt other game than porcupines." Then, under the full shower of K'ia-wu's reproaches, he anxiously asked, "Is supper ready?"

If any of the numerous aggrieved complained to him, he listened gravely with an expression of sympathetic interest, until the plaint was spent, then replied: "I have heard; indeed!" And if this somewhat unsatisfactory reply provoked further remarks, he usually went about what he had to do, or with his characteristic summary manner sent the malcontent home, or left him to plead to an empty room.

K'ia-wu troubled herself much with her husband's actions. They usually slept along the opposite side of my little room. Night after night, hour after hour, I have heard her, in the peculiar sing-song tone of her race and sex, lecture the silent governor. The darkness would grow deeper, the embers on the hearth fade to ashes, but the theme lost neither interest nor voice. It used sorely to provoke me; and in my own language, hopelessly striving to sleep, I would sometimes curse both the persistency of the Zuñi Caudle and the silence of the matrimonial stoic. The voice would change, but not cease. "Ho! the younger brother is thoughtful; to-morrow I will fix his bed better," it would say; and the governor, filling the exclamation with the most perfect understanding of the situation, would ejaculate, "Humph!" but no more. Undisturbed, the current would then flow on until later, by considerable distance of the stars, the tone would die away. A moment of dead silence, then a cough from the governor, followed by the bland inquiry:

"Is that all?"

"What more should I say, talkless?"the old woman would reply, in a most injured and ill-controlled tone.

"Well, then" (with a yawn), "let's go to sleep, old girl (*o'ka-si-ki*), for it is time, and the younger brother is restless." With which he would turn over, cough again, and lapse into silence, hopeless to the tongue-weary woman, as evinced by her long-continued, half-smothered sobs.

I had nearly given up seeing a pair of garters which had been promised me, when one day, all bustle and smiles, the "Little mother" came in bearing them.

They were beautiful and well made,—they endure even yet,—and with matronly pride she laid them before me. I paid her liberally, that the subject of Lai-iu-lut-sa should not be resumed. But it was broached to the governor. That night when we were alone, he came and lay down by my side where I was writing.

"Get a big piece of paper," said he, and knowing him, I obeyed.

"Now write." I seized a pencil.

"'Thou comest?'" said he, in his own language.

I wrote it and pronounced it.

"Good," said he; then added:

"'Yes; how are you these many days?'"

"'Happy!' 'Sit down,' 'Eat.' (Then a tray of bread will be placed before you, but you must be polite, and eat but little, and soon say:) 'Thanks.'"

"'Eat enough. You must have come thinking of something. What have you to say?'"

"'I don't know.'"

"'Oh! yes, you do; tell me.'"

"'I'm thinking of you' (in a whisper)."

"'Indeed! You must be mistaken.'"

" 'No!'

" 'Aha! do you love me?'

" 'Ay, I love you.'

" 'Truly?'

" 'Yes!'

" 'Possibly; we will see. What think you, father?'

" 'As you think, my child' (the father will say)."

"What in the name of the moon does all this mean, brother?" I asked him when he had made me read the questions and answers over two or three times, and said I had pronounced them all right.

"It means what you will say to Lai-iu-lut-sa tomorrow night when you go to see her."

I was perplexed. I knew not what to say, as I feared offending the good old man.

"Look here, brother, I can't go to see her; she would laugh at me because I can't speak good Zuñi yet."

"Now that's all I have to say to you," he replied, angrily. "I've done my best for you; if fools will be fools, not even their brothers can help it. I see you propose to live single and have everybody say: 'There goes a man that no woman will have; not even when his brother helps him. No! Do you suppose I am blind? You are no Zuñi; you want to go back to Washington; but you can't, I tell you. You might as well get married; you *are* a Zuñi; do you hear me? You are a fool, too!'"

With this, he left me; nor would he speak to me again for many days, save on the most commonplace affairs of life, and then but briefly.

My old father here came to my relief. He persuaded the vexed governor that perhaps Lai-iu-lut-sa did not suit me, and that my refusal of her was no argument against my love for her people. With a sublime sense of his power of diplomacy, he also sat down to have a talk with me the same evening. "You see, my son, I had nothing to say about Lai-iu-lut-sa; don't like her myself," said he, with a smile. "Now had it been Iu-i-tsaih-ti-e-tsa, I should have said, 'Be it well!'" and he waited for me to ask who she was. I kept a wise silence; my old brother kept a sulky one. "She is the finest being in our nation; and *my own niece*," he added, with emphasis.

"I never saw her," said I.

"Is that all?" he exclaimed, eagerly. "Well! she shall bring you a bundle of candle-wood to-morrow evening," he remarked.

"What shall I pay her for it?" I asked.

"Pay her! Nothing, my son; do you wish her to think you a fool, and cover me with shame?"

Next evening, I went to see Mr. Graham, the trader, and staid late. When I returned, a little bundle of pitch-pine was lying by the door-way, and the old governor, getting up with an oath, left the house. Again the girl brought wood, at a time unexpected to me, yet I happened to be absent; and the matter, with many vexatious remarks on my strange behavior, was for a time given up.

The Zuñi customs connected with courtship are curious. Regularly, a girl expresses a fancy for a young man. Her parents or her relatives inform those of the youth, and the latter is encouraged. If suited, he casually drops into the house of the girl, when much the same conversation as the governor tried to teach me ensues; and "if it be well," the girl becomes his affianced, or *Yi-lu-k'ia-ni-ha* (His to be). Thereafter the young couple may be seen frequently together, the girl combing his hair on the sunny terraces, or, in winter, near the hearth, while he sits and sews on articles of apparel for her. When he has "made his bundle," or gathered a sufficient number of presents together, invariably including a pair of moccasins made from a whole deer-skin, he takes it to her, and if they are accepted he is adopted as a son by her father, or, in Zuñi language, "as a ward," *Ta-la-h'i*; and with the beginning of his residence with her commences his married life. With the woman rests the security of the marriage ties; and it must be said, in her high honor, that she rarely abuses the privilege; that is, never sends her husband "to the home of his fathers," unless he richly deserves it. Much is said of the inferior position of women among Indians. With all advanced tribes, as with the Zuñis, the woman not only controls the situation, but her serfdom is customary, self-imposed, and willing absolutely. To her belong, also, all the children; and descent, including inheritance, is on her side.

I did not learn, until late in the season, that the midnight *Kâ⁻kâ* were held thrice monthly during two of the winter

FIG. 23. Zuñi Courtship

months, in all the estufas, or *ki-wi-tsi-we*, of the pueblo, of which
there were six, corresponding in Zuñi mythology to the six regions of the universe, North, West, South, East, Upper, and
Lower. One day, however, there came past my house two costumed and masked "Runners of the *Kâ⸲-kâ*." I followed them into
a *ki-wi-tsin*. A group of priests near the smoky, rude, stone altar,
were gathered, bare-footed and praying. I drew my moccasins
off, and joined them. A friend among them told me, as we left,
that I had "behaved so wisely I could come with him that night
and see the *Kâ⸲-kâs*."

What a wonderful night it was! The blazes of the splinter-lit
fire on the stone altar, sometimes licking the very ladder-poles in
their flight upward toward the sky-hole, which served at once as
door-way, chimney, and window; the painted tablets in one end,
with priests and musicians grouped around; the spectators opposite and along the sides; the thin, upward streams of blue smoke
from hundreds of cigarettes; the shrill calls of the rapidly coming
and departing dancers, their wild songs, and the din of the great
drum, which fairly jarred the ancient, smoke-blackened rafters;
the less distinguishable but terribly thrilling "swirr-r" of the
yucca-whips, when brought down on some luckless sleeper's

head and shoulders; the odors of the burning sacrifices, the tobacco, and of evergreen. All this was impressed indelibly on my memory,—the more impressive, that I was the first of my race to witness it. Wonderful, too, were the costumes and masks. Scaly monsters, bristling with weapons and terrible of voice and manner, with reptile heads; warrior demons, with grinning teeth, glaring eyes, long horns, mats of grizzly hair and beard; grotesque *Ne-wes*; ludicrous *Keó-yi-mo-shis*; ridiculous caricatures of all things in earth, and of men's strange conceptions. Such made up the sights of the *ki-wi-tsin* of the midnight *Kâ⸍-kâs*. Prayers near morning, distribution of the medicine-water to each of us, and, in Zuñi language, "like leaves in a sand-storm the people severed."

With February came the season of general abandonment to games, when old men and young children were busy with the chances of the thrown stick, the hidden ball, or the contest of matched strength. Even the non-participants, the women, were intensely excited with these peaceful contests; betting, in common with their at all other times less temperate husbands, the choicest articles of apparel, or the most valued items of possession.

One remarkable feature of the Zuñi had impressed me—the well-regulated life they lead. At one season they are absorbed in harvesting, at another in the sacred obligations; now games lead the day, while previously they have been of such rare occurrence—even among little children—that I had written in my November notes, "The Zuñis have few if any games of chance"; while, had my observations been confined to February, I would have written "A nation of gamesters."

Like most things else in Zuñi, their games were of a sacred nature. Now that the nation "had straightened the thoughts of the impossibly terrible 'A-hai-iu-ta' and Ma-tsai-le-ma, the 'beloved two' smiled and willed that, with the plays wherewith they themselves had whiled away the eons of times ancient, should their children be made happy with one another."

So one morning the two chief priests of the bow (Pi-thlan-shi-wan-mo-so-na-tchi) climbed to the top of the houses, and just at sunrise called out a "prayer-message" from the mount-enshrined gods. Eight players went into a *ki-wi-tsin* to fast, and

FIG. 24. A Zuñi Farmhouse

four days later issued forth, bearing four large wooden tubes, a
ball of stone, and a bundle of thirty-six counting straws. With
great ceremony, many prayers and incantations, the tubes were
deposited on two mock mountains of sand, either side of the
"grand plaza." A crowd began to gather. Larger and noisier it
grew, until it became a surging clamorous black mass. Gradually
two piles of fabrics,—vessels, silver ornaments, necklaces, embroideries, and symbols representing horses, cattle, and
sheep,—grew to large proportions. Women gathered on the roofs
around, wildly stretching forth articles for the betting; until one
of the presiding priests called out a brief message. The crowd
became silent. A booth was raised, under which two of the
players retired; and when it was removed, the four tubes were
standing on the mound of sand. A song and dance began. One by
one, three of the four opposing players were summoned to guess
under which tube the ball was hidden. At each guess the cries of
the opposing parties became deafening, and their mock
struggles approached the violence of mortal combat. The last
guesser found the ball; and as he victoriously carried the latter
and the tubes across to his own mound, his side scored ten. The
process was repeated. The second guesser found the ball; his
side scored fifteen, setting the others back five. The counts
numbered one hundred; but so complicated were the winnings

and losings on both sides, with each guess of either, that hour after hour the game went on and night closed in. Fires were built in the plaza, cigarettes lighted, but still the game continued. Noisier and noisier grew the dancers, more and more insulting and defiant their songs and epithets to the opposing crowd, until they fairly gnashed their teeth at one another, but no blows! Day dawned on the still uncertain contest; nor was it until the sun again touched the western horizon, that the hoarse, still defiant voices died away, and the victorious party bore off their "mountains of gifts from the gods."

Another game of the gods was ordered later, in the same way—*Ti-kwa-we,* or the race of the "kicked stick."

Twelve runners were chosen and for four days duly "trained" in the estufas. On the fourth morning, the same noisy, surging crowd was gathered in the principal plaza, the same opposing mountains of goods were piled up. At noon, the crowd surged over to the level, sandy plain beyond the river. They were soon followed by the nude contestants, in two single-file processions, led and closed in by the training-masters. Each had his hair done up in a knot over his forehead, and a strong belt girded tightly about his waist. Either leader carried a small round stick, one painted at the center, the other at either end, with red. When all was ready, each leader placed his stick across his right foot, and, when word was given, kicked it, amid the deafening shouts of the spectators, a prodigious distance into the air and along the trail. Off dashed the runners vying with each other for possession of the stick, and followed by dozens of the wild crowd on foot and on horseback. The course of their race was shaped not unlike a bangle, with either end bent into the center. That is, starting from the river-bank, it went to the southern foot-hills, followed the edge of the valley entirely around, and back whence it had started, in all a distance of nearly twenty-five miles. During the progress of the distant circling race, spectators, including hundreds of the women, lined the house-tops. In much less than two hours and a half the victorious party returned, kicked their stick triumphantly across the river, ran into the plaza, circled around the goods, breathed on their hands, exclaimed, "Thanks! this day we win," and hurried to their estufa, where with great ceremony they were vomited, rubbed, rolled in blankets, and prayed over.

Notwithstanding these precautions, they were so stiff within half an hour they could hardly move; yet no one can witness these tremendous races without admiration for the physical endurance of the Indian.

These two games, varied with others which, equally interesting, would require even more space for description, filled the days and nights thenceforward for many weeks. Although I faithfully studied and practiced many of the more complicated of them that I might the better understand them, I remain, notwithstanding many losings and few winnings, yet unable to perfectly master their intricacies. The game of cane-cards, or the "Sacred Arrows," would grace the most civilized society with a refined source of amusement; yet though I have played it repeatedly, I cannot half record its mythic passes, facetious and archaic proverbs, and almost numberless counts. The successful *shos-li*, or cane-player, is as much respected for his knowledge as he is despised for his abandoned, gambling propensities. Great though their passion for game be, the Zuñis condemn, as unsparingly as do we, great excesses in it.

With the waning of winter the snows had disappeared, and now terrific winds swept daily down from the western "Sierra Blanco," until the plain was parched, and the stinging blasts of sand flew fairly over the top of Ta-ai-yal-lon-ne. Still the races and games went on, until one morning the Priest of the Sun declared aloud that the sun was returning. "Our father has called and his father answers," said the people to one another. The games ceased as if by magic; and the late profligate might now have been seen, early each morning, with hoe and spade in hand, wending his way out to the fields to prepare them for the planting time.

Each morning, too, just at dawn, the Sun Priest, followed by the Master Priest of the Bow, went along the eastern trail to the ruined city of Ma-tsa-ki, by the river-side, where, awaited at a distance by his companion, he slowly approached a square open tower and seated himself just inside upon a rude, ancient stone chair, and before a pillar sculptured with the face of the sun, the sacred hand, the morning star, and the new moon. There he awaited with prayer and sacred song the rising of the sun. Not many such pilgrimages are made ere the "Suns look at each

FIG. 25. Zuñi Planting

other," and the shadows of the solar monolith, the monument of Thunder Mountain, and the pillar of the gardens of Zuñi, "lie along the same trail." Then the priest blesses, thanks, and exhorts his father, while the warrior guardian responds as he cuts the last notch in his pine-wood calendar, and both hasten back to call from the house-tops the glad tidings of the return of spring. Nor may the Sun Priest err in his watch of Time's flight; for many are the houses in Zuñi with scores on their walls or ancient plates imbedded therein, while opposite, a convenient window or small port-hole lets in the light of the rising sun, which shines but two mornings in the three hundred and sixty-five on the same place. Wonderfully reliable and ingenious are these rude systems of orientation, by which the religion, the labors, and even the pastimes of the Zuñis are regulated.

Each day whole families hastened away to their planting pueblos, or distant farm-houses, but the sand-storms abated not. At night there was not a zephyr, but soon after sunrise, away off over the western rim of the plain, a golden, writhing wave of dust could be seen, followed by another and another, and rising higher and higher, until as it swirled over the pueblo it fairly darkened the sky, increasing in column and height until the sun went down; then retreating after him and covering the plain, not with golden, but with blood-red waves, matching in brilliancy and shifting beauty the blazing clouds of the evening skies.

I well remember the morning my old brother and I parted for the first time. He lingered by me long after the others had gone and his burros had strayed far up the valley trail. Finally, he took me gently by the hand, saying

"Ah! little brother, my heart is like the clods I go to break— heavy! For I have grown to you as one stalk grows to another when they are planted together. Poor little brother, may the light of their favors fall upon you, for you will live long alone with the white-headed 'old Ten.' Come with me a little."

Then he dropped my hand, and folded his own behind his bent back, and I followed him slowly along the dusty street. As we were crossing the principal plaza, we met Iu-i-tsaih-ti-e-tsa. She drew her head-mantle over her eyes, and was about to pass us when the governor straightened up, smiled, and greeted her.

"Ha?" inquired the bashful maiden, when he told her something was on his mind.

"Only this," he added: "my little brother will be lonely while I am gone; perhaps he would be less so if you took him a tray of *he-we* once in a while, you know it is 'home-sick' to eat alone."

"Ya," assented the girl, as she tripped past us, and we plodded along.

"Now, little brother, stay at home like a man of dignity, while I am gone. Don't you know it is shameless to run all round the streets and over the house-tops as you do? Better your thoughts, and make your heart good, and remember that your brother speaks for you *once more*."

Poor old brother! Good old brother! He never had occasion to mention Iu-i-tsaih-ti-e-tsa to me again, and for many months a shade passed over his face whenever he saw her or heard her name.

We went on past the gardens, and far out into the plain. Then he stopped me.

"Little brother," said he, and he laid one hand on my shoulder, while with the other he removed his head-band, and pressed both of mine,"*This day we have a father who, from his ancient place, rises hard holding his course; grasping us that we may stumble not in the trails of our lives. If it be well, may his grasp be firm until, happily, our paths join together again, and we look one upon the other.* Thus much I make prayer,—I go."

With this he turned suddenly, a tear in his eye, and walked hastily along the river-side. And I stood there watching him, until his bent form disappeared, and trying hard to bear the loneliest moment of all my exile in Zuñi. God bless my Indian brother!

I expected to have a hard time with my "white-headed mother," as I called her; but she was the soul of tenderness and attention. Only one circumstance occurred to jar our peace; that, happily, the second day. I was not in the house when the crash came; but entering soon after, I saw the cause of it, and heard from the mother. Something stood in the middle of my room, with a white mantle of cotton spread over it. I lifted the mantle, and discovered a handsome tray of flaky *he-we*. The mother was awaiting me—much as a spider waits for a fly—just inside the next room.

"Who brought it, mother?" said I, in mock surprise.

"*You* ask who brought it? Well! Who should it be but that shameless wench who lives over the covered way, whose mother has clog feet, and whose father is so poor that no one knows how they live? No matter if young fools do grow crazy over her; she's nothing, nothing at all, Medicine Flower, nothing but a common creature that is not human enough to know what shame is."

"Indeed, was it Iu-i-tsaih-ti-e-tsa?"

"Then I knew it!" she rejoined. "You knew all about it. You are not going to let her make a fool of *you*, are you, Medicine Flower? (I was usually her *child*, but on this occasion I was *Medicine Flower*, emphatically pronounced.) She doesn't *near* to you at all; she only thinks of what you have and of your fine buttons."

"Where does she live, mother?"

"Why do you ask?"

"I wish to go and see her."

"I'll have nothing to do with it. Shame myself? Not I!"

"But I wish to *pay* her."

"Ha! my child? Right over the covered way, up two ladders, and down the first sky-hole," replied the old lady, suddenly as bland as though spite had never caused her heart to beat the faster during her long life.

"I'm going to have her come here."

"*No!* She shall not come into—"

"Wait, mother, wait. Have her come here to eat, and then refuse to eat with her, and pay her sugar; but mind, don't you tell my good old brother."

"Your brother! Aha! Then *he* was mixed up in it, was he? Poor child! I thought it was you. So it was Pa-lo-wah-ti-wa. Ah, well! he's a *Pino*, you know—the family is all alike; he belongs to a good clan, but his father's blood is *his* blood."

Peace was made with the mother, and I went to the house of Iu-i-tsaih-ti-e-tsa. She was not at home. I left word for her to come and eat with me at sunset. When she came, I was writing. She was accompanied by her aunt. I bade them enter, set coffee, bread, *he-we*, sugar, and other delicacies before them. Then I merely broke a crust, sacrificed some of it to the fire, ate a mouthful, and left them, resuming my writing. The girl dropped her half-eaten bread, threw her head-mantle over her face, and started for the door. I called to her and offered her a bag of sugar in payment, I said, for the *he-we*. At first she angrily refused; then bethinking herself that I was an American and possibly knew no better, she took the sugar and hastened away, mortified and almost ready to cry with vexation. Poor girl! I knew I was offering her a great dishonor,—as runs the custom of her people,—but it was my only way out of a difficulty far more serious than it could have possibly appeared to her people. The aunt was an old friend of mine. She had frequently come to our house to help grind corn, or make *he-we*, and thought much of me,—calling me, always, *ha-ni* (a sister's younger brother). She remained a few moments; then rising, thanked me, and was about to go when I said to her: "Sister, Iu-i-tsaih-ti-e-tsa is a good and pretty girl. I like her; but it will be many days before I think of women save as sisters and mothers." The woman hesitated a moment, then said:

"Ha-ni, you are a good being, but an unknowable sort of a man. You have caused me to think much this night and made me

FIG. 26. A Zuñi Silversmith

ashamed, but then! may you sit happily, even alone," she added, as she passed out of the door.

(However out of place these statements may seem, I deem them not only essential to the narrative, but characteristic of the Zuñis, and of their early attitude toward me. Possibly, too, they may disarm charges and criticisms which are as narrow, unrefined, and malicious, as they are false.)

The old mother entered immediately, and without further remark than a sigh of relief, cleared the things away.

During our lonely life together, I often helped her to split wood, or lift heavy burdens, wind yarn, or bring water. She never failed to thank me for the least of these services. Once she came in, looking tired; I arose and offered her my seat by the hearth. She hesitated a moment, laughed hysterically, then sat down; but in trying to thank me, burst into tears. "Ah!" said she, "*tsa-wai-k'i* (son), don't be so kind to me; I am old." But she never ceased to mention the little circumstance; and I know that of all services I ever did her, such as that ranked in her estimation foremost. It taught me that even "squaws" could sometimes appreciate such attentions.

During my lonely life that spring, a few young men fell into the habit of visiting me occasionally, to "hear about the world." They would light their cigarettes, square themselves along the opposite wall, their faces beaming with expectation and satisfaction. An amusing chapter could be written on their questions and comments. I give here but one instance.

One of them asked me, "How the sun could travel so constantly over the world by day and back under it at night, without getting tired and giving it up?"

I explained that the earth revolved and the sun stood still, which caused day and night and made the sun appear to move, illustrating the statement as well as I could; also telling them, that "twice a year the earth wagged back and forth, which made winter come and go and the sun move from one side of Thunder Mountain to the other."

For a few moments they sat still and puffed vigorously at their cigarettes, as thoughtful men are apt to do. Of a sudden, one of them cried out:

"Listen! the Medicine Flower is right. If you gallop past Thunder Mountain, Thunder Mountain moves, and you stand still; and besides, I have noticed that in summer the great hanging snow-bank (Milky Way) drifts from the left of the Land of Daylight (N.E.) to the right of the World of Waters (S.W.), and in winter, from the left of the World of Waters (N.W.) to the right of the Land of Daylight (S.E.). Now! how could they move the great hanging snow-drift without moving the sky too? It would be easier to wag the world than to turn the sky around."

"Ah! but our ancients taught us . . . "

"No matter what our ancients taught us," said the young philosopher; "why do you speak the words of dead men? They lied, and Medicine Flower speaks straight, for why should the sun go so far and let the earth stand still, when, by merely rolling her over, he could save himself all that trouble?"

Meanwhile, three times word came from my old brother that he was "homesick for me." Finally he sent a horse, with the message that "if I did not ride it back the next day he should cease to speak to me, believing, that in forgetting him I had found another brother." But when I rode down the neatly tilled and irrigated fields, the old man, who was breaking clods, dropped his hoe, ran up to my side, pulled me from the saddle, embraced me, and that night sat up until nearly daylight, close by my side, in the low room of his quaint farm-house, talking. When time came for me to return, he gave up his work, and with K'ia-wu accompanied me, leaving the fields to the brother-in-law, with whom K'ia-wu told me delightedly, "peace had been made."

It was well that we returned! The wind-storms were growing worse: day after day they had drifted the scorching sand over the valley, until the springs were choked up and the river was so dry that a stranger could not have distinguished it from a streamless arroyo. The nation was threatened with famine. Many were the grave speculations and councils relative to the "meaning of the gods in thus punishing their children."

Strange to say, I was given a prominent place in these, and was often appealed to, on account of my reputed "knowledge of the world." More and more frequent and desperate grew these gatherings, until at last a poor fellow named "Big Belly" was seized and brought up before them, accused of "heresy!" The trial—in which I had taken no part—lasted a whole day and part of night, when to my surprise a body of elders summoned me, and placed me at the head of their council. They addressed and treated me as chief counselor of their nation, which office I held thenceforward for nearly two years. Among other things, they asked what should be done. I inquired minutely into the case, and learned that the culprit had opened one of the sand-choked springs, which proved to be sacred. The gods were supposed to be angry with the nation on account of his transgression,—demanding the sacrifice of his life. As impassionately as possible, I pleaded that the wind-storms had set in long before he opened the spring, and suggested that he be made to fill it up again and to sacrifice bits of shells and turquoise to it. The suggestion was adopted! The additional penalty of ostracism, however, was laid upon him; and to this day he lives in the farming pueblo of K'iap-kwai-na-kwin, or Ojo Caliente.

One evil followed another. Many deaths occurred, among them, that of a beautiful girl, who had been universally liked. Nor did the wind-storms abate. As a consequence, I heard one night a peculiar, long war-cry. It was joined by another and another, until the sound grew strangely weird and ominous.

Then three or four men rushed past my door yelling: "A wizard! a wizard!" The tribe was soon in an uproar. The priests of the Bow had seized an old man named the "Bat," and in one of their secret chambers were trying him for sorcery. I was not present, of course, at the trial; but at three o'clock in the morning they dragged him forth to the hill on the north side of the pueblo. There they tied his hands behind him with a rawhide rope; and passing the end of the latter over a pole, supported by high crotched posts, they drew him up until his toes barely touched the ground and he was bent almost double.

Then the four chief-priests of the Bow approached and harangued him one by one, but provoked no reply save the most piteous moans. Day dawned; yet still he hung there. The speeches grew louder and more furious, until, fearing violence, I ran home, buckled on my pistol, and returned. I went straight to the old man's side.

"Go back," said the accusers.

"I will not go back; for I come with words."

"Speak them," said they.

"These," said I. "You may try the old man, but you must not kill him. The Americans will see you, or find it out, and tell their people, who will say: 'The Zuñis murdered one of their own grandfathers.' That will bring trouble on you all."

"What! murder a wizard?" they exclaimed. "Ho!" and for a few moments I grew hopeless; for the chief-priest turned to the old man, and asked, with mock tenderness.

"Father, does it hurt?"

"Ai-o," moaned the old man, in a weak voice. "I die, I am dying."

"That's right," retorted the priest. "Pull him up a little higher, my son," said he, addressing an assistant. "He says it hurts, and I have hopes he will speak." Then he turned to me again.

"This is our way, my son, of bringing bad men to wisdom; I have worn my throat out urging him to speak; now I am trying another way. If he but speak, he shall be let to go."

"What shall I say?" piteously moaned the suffering man.

"Say *yes* or NO! dotard," howled the priest.

"Speak, grandfather, speak!" said I, as re-assuringly as I

could, at the same time laying my hand on his withered arm.

"Tell them to let me down, then," he pleaded, "for I can speak not long as I am; I shall die. Oh! I shall die."

"Thanks! father, thanks!" said the priest, briskly. "Let him down; he is coming to his senses, I see."

They let the sufferer down for a moment; and gazing on the ground, he began: "True! I have been bad. My father taught me fifty years ago, in the mountains of the summer snows. It was medicine that I used. You will find a bundle of it over the rafters, in my highest room."

One of the attendants was immediately dispatched, and soon returned with a little bunch of twigs.

"Ay! that it is, I used that. It has covered me with shame; but I will be better. I will rejoin my *ti-k'ia* (sacred order). It will surely rain within four days; for if you but let me go, I shall join my *ti-k'ia* again."

"Will you be wise?"

"Yes! believe me."

"Will you stay in Zuñi?"

"Yes! believe me."

"Will you never more cause tears?"

"No! It were a shame."

"Will you never teach to others your magic?"

"No! believe me—"

"Thanks! You have spoken. Let him go!" said the priest, as he walked hastily through the crowd toward his home.

Four days passed, and no rain came; nor did the "Bat" do as he had promised, for he returned home only to threaten revenge on the priesthood, and since the fifth day no one outside of that priesthood has ever seen a trace of the "Bat."

In Zuñi law-custom there are but two crimes punishable by death—sorcery and cowardice in battle. If, however, a man attempt the life of another, or even threaten it, he is regarded as a wizard; but no immediate measures are taken for his correction. Should crops fail, wind-storms prevail, or should the threatened man die, even from natural causes, the reputed wizard is, when he least expects it, dragged from his bed at night by the secret council of the *A-pi-thlan-shi-wa-ni*, taken to their chamber and tried long and fairly. Should the culprit persist in silence, he is

FIG. 27. Torturing a Sorcerer

taken forth and tortured by the simple yet excruciatingly painful method I have described, throughout a "single course of the sun"; and if still silent, again taken to the chamber of the priesthood, whence he never comes forth alive; nor do others than members of the dread organization ever know what becomes of him. Rare indeed is the execution for which no other than superstitious reasons may be adduced. Even in case of the "Bat," I learned that he had attempted to poison his own niece, the girl heretofore mentioned, the death of whom, a few weeks afterward, rendered him a criminal and liable to condemnation, not only as such, but as a sorcerer. Thus, like a vigilance committee, the priesthood of the Bow secretly tries all cases of capital crime under the name of sorcery or witchcraft,—the war-chief of the nation, himself necessarily a prominent priest of the Bow, acting as executioner, and, with the aid of his sub-chiefs, as secretly disposing of the body. On account of this mysterious method of justice crime is rare in Zuñi.

At last, in late June, rains came. As if by magic, the dust-storms ceased, and the plains were overspread with bright green. The Zuñis became uproariously happy. The members of the little "bees," that were formed for mutual assistance in the field labors, laughed and joked at their work from sunrise till supper-time. The river flowed broad and clear again. Thither again flocked the urchin population as I had seen them the autumn before.

One day I saw some of the children playing at "breaking horses." One juvenile demon was leading a band of four or five others, in the pursuit of a big bristling boar. Lasso in hand, the little fellow watched his chance, and, twirling the flexible cord once or twice rapidly in the air, sent it like lightning toward the head of the boar. The latter made a desperate dash only to run his snout and forefoot into the coil, which, held by the combined efforts of all, quickly precipitated him, in a succession of entangling somersaults, into the shallow river. In an instant another lasso was dexterously thrown over his hind feet, and his captors, heedless of mud and water, wild with vociferous glee, bestraddled him, and held him down. The leader tore off one of the legs of his cotton trowsers, and with this he bandaged the eyes of the squealing animal, wrapping another piece tightly around his snout so as to smother his cries. Thus equipped, the hog was set at liberty. Two of the little wretches jumped astride him, while the others prodded him behind and at the sides. Thus goaded, the poor beast ran uncertainly in all directions, into corrals, over logs, headlong into deep holes, precipitating his adventuresome riders; not, however, to their discomfiture, for they would immediately scamper up, drive, push, lead, or haul him out, and mount him again. The last I saw of them was toward evening; they were ruefully regarding the dead carcass of their novel horse.

With midsummer the heat became intense. My brother and

FIG. 28. The Demon of Childhood

I sat, day after day, in the cool under-rooms of our house,—the latter busy with his quaint forge and crude appliances, working Mexican coins over into bangles, girdles, ear-rings, buttons, and what not, for savage adornment. Though his tools were wonderfully rude, the work he turned out by dint of combined patience and ingenuity was remarkably beautiful. One day as I sat watching him, a procession of fifty men went hastily down the hill, and off westward over the plain. They were solemnly led by a painted and shell-bedecked priest, and followed by the torch-bearing *Shu-lu-wit-si*, or God of Fire. After they had vanished, I asked old brother what it all meant.

"They are going," said he, "to the city of the *Kâ'-kâ* and the home of our others."

Four days after, toward sunset, costumed and masked in the beautiful paraphernalia of the *Ka-k'ok-shi*, or "Good Dance," they returned in file up the same pathway, each bearing in his arms a basket filled with living, squirming turtles, which he regarded and carried as tenderly as a mother would her infant. Some of the wretched reptiles were carefully wrapped in soft blankets, their heads and forefeet protruding—and, mounted on the backs of the plume-bedecked pilgrims, made ludicrous but solemn caricatures of little children in the same position.

While I was at supper upstairs, that evening, the governor's brother-in-law came in. He was welcomed by the family as if a messenger from heaven. He bore in his tremulous fingers one of the much-abused and rebellious turtles. Paint still adhered to his hands and bare feet, which led me to infer that he had formed one of the sacred embassy.

"So you went to Ka-thlu-el-lon, did you?" I asked.

"E'e," replied the weary man, in a voice husky with long chanting, as he sank almost exhausted, on a roll of skins which had been placed for him, and tenderly laid the turtle on the floor. No sooner did the creature find itself at liberty than it made off as fast as its lame legs would take it. Of one accord, the family forsook dish, spoon, and drinking-cup, and grabbing from a sacred meal bowl whole handfuls of the contents, hurriedly followed the turtle about the room, into dark corners, around water-jars, behind the grinding-troughs, and out into the middle of the floor again, praying and scattering meal on its back as they went. At last, strange to say, it approached the foot-sore man who had brought it.

"Ha!" he exclaimed, with emotion; "see, it comes to me again; ah, what great favors the fathers of all grant me this day," and passing his hand gently over the sprawling animal, he inhaled from his palm deeply and long, at the same time invoking the favor of the gods. Then he leaned his chin upon his hand, and with large, wistful eyes regarded his ugly captive as it sprawled about blinking its meal-bedimmed eyes, and clawing the smooth floor in memory of its native element. At this juncture, I ventured a question:

"Why do you not let him go, or give him some water?"

Slowly the man turned his eyes toward me, an odd mixture of pain, indignation, and pity on his face, while the worshipful family stared at me with holy horror.

"Poor younger brother!" he said, at last; "know you not how precious it is? It die? It will *not* die; I tell you, it *cannot* die."

"But it will die if you don't feed it and give it water."

"I tell you it *cannot* die; it will only change houses tomorrow, and go back to the home of its brothers. Ah, well! How should *you* know?" he mused. Turning to the blinded turtle again: "Ah! my poor dear lost child or parent, my sister or brother to have been! Who knows which? May be my own great-grand-father or mother!" And with this he fell to weeping most patheti-cally, and, tremulous with sobs, which were echoed by the women and children, he buried his face in his hands. Filled with sympathy for his grief, however mistaken, I raised the turtle to my lips and kissed its cold shell; then depositing it on the floor, hastily left the grief-stricken family to their sorrows.

Next day, with prayers and tender beseechings, plumes and offerings, the poor turtle was killed, and its flesh and bones were removed and deposited in the little river, that it might "return once more to eternal life among its comrades in the dark waters of the lake of the dead." The shell, carefully scraped and dried, was made into a dance-rattle, and, covered by a piece of buckskin, it still hangs from the smoke-stained rafters of my brother's house.

Once a Navajo tried to buy it for a ladle; loaded with indig-nant reproaches, he was turned out of the house. Were any one to venture the suggestion that the turtle no longer lived, his remark would cause a flood of tears, and he would be reminded that it had only "changed houses and had gone to live forever in the home of 'our lost others.'"

This persistent adherence to the phrase, "our lost others," struck me as significant. Had they believed in the transmigration of the soul, they would have said "our brothers, our fathers, our children," I reasoned; and yet it was long before I learned the true meaning of it. At last, a wonderful epic, including the genesis and sacred history of the Zuñi ancestry, was repeated in my hearing by an old blind priest, through which I came to understand the regard my adopted people had for the turtle. I give a portion of the tradition as afterward explained to me:

> In the days of the new, after the times when all mankind had come forth from one to the other of the "four great cavern wombs of earth" (*a-wi-ten-te-huthl-na-kwin*), and had come out into the light of our father, the sun, they journeyed, under the guidance of A-hai-iu-ta and Ma-tsai-le-ma, twin children of the sun, immortal youths, toward the father of all men and things, eastward.
>
> In those times, a day meant four years and a night the same; so

FIG. 29. A Zuñi Burial

that, in the speech of the ancients, "Between one sunrise and another" means eight years.

After many days and nights, the people settled near the mountain of the Medicine Flower, and a great cazique sent forward his two children, a young man and a young girl—the passing beautiful of all children—to explore for a better country. When they had journeyed as far as the region where now flow the red waters [Colorado Chiquito], they paused to rest from their journey. Ah! they sinned and were changed to a demon god and goddess.

The world was damp. Plant corn on the mountain-tops, and it grew. Dig a hole into the sands at will, and water filled it.

The woman in her anger drew her foot through the sands, that she might—from shame—separate herself from her people; and the waters, collecting, flowed off until they were a deep channel; yet they settled most about the place where she stood, and it became a lake which is there to this day. And the mark in the sands is the valley where now flow the red waters.

No tidings came from the young messengers; and after many days the nation again journeyed eastward, carrying upon their backs not only their things precious, but also their little children.

When they reached the waters they were dismayed; but some ventured in to cross over. Fear filled the hearts of many mothers, for their children grew cold and strange, like others than human creatures, and they dropped them into the waters, changed indeed; they floated away, crying and moaning, as even now they cry and moan when the night comes on and the hunter camps near their shores. But those who loved their children and were strong of heart passed safely over the flood and found them the same as before.

Thus it came to be that only part of our nation ever arrived at the "middle of the world." But it is well, as all things are; for others were left to remember us and to make a home, not of strangers, but of "our others," for those who should die, and to intercede with the "Holders of the Waters of the World" that all mankind and unfinished creatures, even flying and creeping beings, might have food to eat and water to drink when the world should harden and the land should dry up. And in that lake is a descending ladder, down which even the smallest may enter fearlessly, who has passed its borders in death; where it is delightful, and filled with songs and dances; where all men are brothers, and whence they wander whither they will, to minister to and guide those whom they have left behind them—that is the lake where live "our others" and whither go our dead. At night, he who wanders on the hills of the *Ka-ko'k-shi* may sometimes see the light shining forth and hear strange voices of music coming up from the depths of those waters.

For the Zuñi, therefore, there is a city of the living and another of the dead. As the living may wander through far countries, so may the dead return to their birthland, or pass over from one ocean to another.

Possibly, at some remote period, the ancestors of the Zuñis have believed in the transmigration of the soul, of which belief these particular superstitions relative to the turtle remain as survivals. Their belief to-day, however, relative to the future life is spiritualistic. As illustrative of this and of their funeral customs, I conclude with an account of the death and burial, toward the close of my first year among them, of my adopted uncle.

For more than a year he had been wasting with consumption, when, on account of a medical reputation which had greatly aided me and had, indeed, given rise to my name, I was called to see him. I gave him such simple remedies as I had at hand, and he became very fond of me, at last adopting me as his nephew, and naming me Hai-iu-tsaih-ti-wa.

Toward the last, the old man talked often of his approaching death, speaking of the future life with an amount of conviction which surprised me.

"To dwell with my relatives, even those whose names were wasted before my birth, is that painful to the thought?" said the old man. "Often, when we dream not, yet we see and hear them as in dreams." "A man is like a grain of corn—bury him, and he molds; yet his heart lives, and springs out on the breath of life [the soul] to make him as he was, so again."

He grew rapidly feebler. For two or three days I did not see him. Hearing that he was worse, I hastened to his side. He was unconscious, and a crowd of relatives were thickly gathered around him, wringing their hands and wailing. Presently he opened his eyes.

"Hush," said he, and he raised his hand weakly with a smile of recognition, not of me, but of something he seemed to see. Then he turned to me. "My boy, I *thought* you would come," he murmured. "Now I can bid you, 'I go'; for they are—all around me—and I know—they have come for me—*this* time. My heart makes happy. *No,*" said he, as a medicine-man tried to force breath into his mouth. "No, I go not alone! Let me go! *E-lu-ia* (Delightful!)"

Then he closed his eyes and became unconscious again, smiling even in his dying sleep.

Two hours after, the women of the same clan which had sprinkled water and meal on him when a baby, adopting him as "their child of the sun," bathed his body and broke a vessel of water by its side, thus renouncing all claim to him forever and returning his being to the sun. Then four men took the blanket-roll by the corners and carried it, amid the mourning wails of the women, to the ancient burial-place. They hastily lowered it into a shallow grave, while one standing to the east said a prayer, scattered meal, food, and other offerings upon it; then they as hastily covered it over, clearing away all traces of the new-made grave. *Now* I know not the bone-strewn grave of "my uncle" from those of a thousand others, for the "silent majority" of the Zuñi nation lie in the same small square. Four days later, down by the river, a little group of mourners sacrificed, with beseeching in the name of the dead, the only flowers their poor land affords— the beautiful prayer-plumes of the "birds of summerland."

"My Adventures in Zuñi," *Century Illustrated Monthly Magazine* 25 (1882): 191–207, 500–511, and 26 (1883): 28–47.

Notes

1. These were the *Keó-yi-mo-shi*, or "Guardians of the 'Sacred Dance,'" whose business is to entertain the spectators during the intervals of the dance, by rude buffoonery and jokes, in which comic speeches and puns play an important part. The office is sacred, and elective annually from among the priesthood of the nation. [F.H.C.]

2. "Washington" is a term used by nearly all the south-western Indians, not as the name of a place or person, but as that of a government. [F.H.C.]

3. A beautiful bit of folk-lore concerning *Tá-ai-yál-lon-ne*, or Thunder Mountain, and the deluge of the land of Zuñi. [F.H.C.]

4. Figurative expression for any sacrifice of life, either animal or human, at the *Ho-mah-tchi*, or Great Knife Dance and ceremonial—the ancient war *Kâ'-kâ* of the Zuñis. [F.H.C.]

5. *Kí-he* is an archaic term for "friend." It is now used to signify a spiritual friend, or one who is endowed with sacred powers for the good of mankind—a spiritual friend to the *Kâ'-kâ*. [F.H.C.]

6. I have since learned that the two, whom I now know very well, belonged to a secret order, members of which are obliged on such occasions to go through this horrible ceremonial. [F.H.C.]

7. I have since learned that this represented the great morning star, and that the swallows were emblematic of the summer rains. [F.H.C.]

8. The purification of the pueblos. [F.H.C.]

9. This, as I afterward learned, was *Nai-iu-tchi*, the Chief Priest of the Bow, a powerful sacred order of war. [F.H.C.]

10. An almost literal translation from a Zuñi folk-lore tale of winter. [F.H.C.]

Letters from Zuñi

Zuñi, New Mexico
October 29, 1879

My dear Professor Baird—

As a wagon leaves for Wingate in the morning, I take the occasion afforded by the evening of a busy day to write you a few words.

As the winter approaches and the corn is gathered in, the dances become more frequent, and unlike those of other Indians, they are all *observances* which, without variation, year after year, have been repeated by this people for centuries. In these strange festivities the Zuñian throws off everything foreign. His dress, where not fantastic, is primitive, his axe and knife are of stone; his gorgeous scarfs and feather ornaments are much as Cabeza de Vaca saw when first he climbed the mesa and saw the city which afterward was Niça's Cibola.[1] No less are the names designating the characters and forms in these ceremonies primitive; hence I find them teeming with suggestions of the Pre-Columbian Pueblo.

In view of these things, on all days and nights when these dances take place, I note the important details, and sketch at least faithfully and in color, all personages or characters figuring in them and all minutiae of costume. And it is in view of these facts that I am using every argument in my power to induce Col. Stevenson to make arrangements for my sojourn here until mid-winter—if such prove not an unfavorable plan to you and to Maj. Powell. My anxiety would not be so great were there not a possibility that I am among the last who will ever witness all this in its purity, as the proposed advent of the Rail Road next fall will, with its foreign influence, introduce all sorts of innovations. Even when, with our party a company of officers and ladies from Wingate came here for a day or two, the Indians varied the *Tchā'-kwī-nā* or blanket dance which we found them dancing and which I have since witnessed in full, not only cutting it short but also casting out of it all obscenities—or rather indecent observances—on account of their presence.

As gradually their language dawns upon my intellect, not the significance of things alone but many other dark things are lighted up by its morning. They are the people who built the ruins of Cañon Bonita in De Chelly. In their language is told the strange history of these heretofore mysterious cities, each one of which has its definite name and story in their lore. The hand marks on the rock faces, and the "Pictographs of a 'Primitive Civilization'" in the light of this language and tradition thus reveal their mysteries at once with their *proof*. Each mark of conventional ornament on their earthen vases, I recently learned, has its name, and this name its significance. Perhaps not a more conventional people can be found than are in many respects these Pueblos. I lately discover that their apparently endless variety (in ornamentation) of *Tinajas* or ollas may be reduced to from seven to ten types, each bearing its definite name, and the ornaments of which you never find occurring in foreign forms.

Before these investigations too, if long enough continued, much of error must be swept away. Already the eagle which "is to bear Montezuma back" becomes a bird kept in common with the wild turkey—for its feathers—the latter sacred, but the bird no more so than is the soil on which is grown the sacred corn.

The literature on these people, with the exception of one or two recent brief articles, is utterly worthless and if again I turn my face to the field, I shall hardly be faint hearted because an authority tells me he can do more with books than I can with ears and eyes; and a filibuster says that the tribe scientifically is "bed-ridden." I do not count myself a man of as much ability as those possessed who have preceded me; but my *method* must succeed. I live among the Indians, I eat their food, and sleep in their houses. Because I will unhesitatingly plunge my hand in common with their dusty ones and dirtier children's into a great kind of hot, miscellaneous food; will sit close to them having neither vermin nor disease, will fondle and talk sweet Indian to their bright eyed little babies; will wear the blanket and tie the Pania around my long hair; will look with unfeigned reverence on their beautiful and ancient ceremonies, never laughing at any absurd observance, they love me, and I learn. On account of this, the women name me *Cushie K'ok-shī Kū-shi Tīhi Nīma* (the good Cushing, the sweet Cushing) and the speakers of the dance call me (in Zuñi of course) the little Capitan Cuzique. On account of this, thank God, my notes will contain much which those of all other explorers have failed to communicate. But do not fancy that all this is lightly purchased. Were I to paint you the picture of my daily life here—of my *meals*—you would, I fear, for some days, enjoy yours as little as on all days, does your poor servant his. I am the "good Kushie" for I take a child, dark with inherited disease, and cleanse and annoint its great sores that they heal. As such, therefore, I am entitled to distinguished courtesy. Hence a woman at a meal picks up from the floor (which is our table) a wooden spoon. It is *not* clean. She therefore wipes it across her moccasin (I do not tell you what that moccasin has repeatedly stepped on today), she draws it along her mantle (which was once white), and bethinking that it is the Good Cushing who is to eat with it, she quickly raises it to her mouth (I will not tell you what that mouth has been used for today—wait till my Report comes out) and in a manner most natural and expeditious, cleans (?) and immediately with the most irresistible smile hands it to me. Do you suppose that I refuse it? No! I plunge it into the huge bowl of steaming food, for I only know that her hands squeezed up the *Hé-we* [wafer bread] not how dirty they were, and trusting to its abundance and heat to cleanse the utensil sufficiently for my blunted perceptions—and, thinking that on this very day while I was doctoring her baby, I was indebted to her for show-ing me how she loosed it from the cradle board and—etc. I utter between my gulps of hot soup *E'lū'kwa'h, E'lū'kwa'h*, with a smile quite out-rivaling her own in breadth, if not in genuine-ness. Is this all of my price? Ah! no. I told you that my capital in the bank of health was large (would to God the other kind were equal). *More* than that, I have drawn on it, like the worst of spendthrifts since I began to eat Indian food. Never a Prize fighter through weeks of training who was more "Devilishly physicked" than I have been, never! and if Providence spare me to ever reach Washington again, it must be with but half a stomach.

Well it is very late. Two Cuziques who have been discussing "affairs of state" with the Governor and a Medicine Man who has been kneading the Governor's sick wife are about to depart and I must close. . . .

Zuñi Mts., N. M.
December 3rd, 1879

My dear Professor Baird—

Three days since, in the company of a Prospector named Jonathan Williams of Albuquerque, and a wanderer named Buck (Miller) I started for these Mountains to explore the supposed jade and turquoise mines of which I had received information. These I have found, together with interesting ruins in connection with them, and the sketches, notes and specimens which I have made and secured, form important additions to our collections and facts concerning the aborigines.

While I was searching for ancient remains yesterday morning, my two companions changed a knotted old rope for the magnificent lariat which I procured from Mr. Graham of Zuñi just before leaving. With this rope I was compelled to picket my mule last night, although before doing so Mr. Tyzeck, the young man in charge of the mining cabin here, and I carefully examined and strengthened every knot. After I had finished my notes last evening, I went out to once more look after the mule, and he had broken the rope and stampeded. This morning I shall track him if possible; if not, I shall strike off over the mountains for Zuñi, where he has probably gone.

In this altitude among strange mountains, and with scant provisions the chances are about equal that I get caught by a snow storm and freeze, get lost and starve, or reach my destination in safety. I therefore leave with Mr. Tyzeck this letter with the request that he, if I do not return after two weeks for my saddle, bridle, specimens, etc., may conclude I am lost and forward this letter to you by the first opportunity.

Therefore should this reach you, you may conclude that I have perished, and I would suggest, as the easiest way of informing all my friends and relations, that a paragraph be put in the press to that effect. In case this happen, I regret that the material I have collected this summer, much of which is new, may never be worked up, as my notes in the hands of another would be unintelligible. I am not much troubled about my difficulty. My philosophy is that every thing happens for the best, if not for the individual, yet for others and that's all I have to say save to thank you for all kindnesses. . . .

Fort Wingate, N. M.
December 14, 1879

My dear Professor Baird:

The prompt receipt of your kind letter of the 6th inst. is very gratifying, as it assures me at once that my lonely work receives your much needed approval, and that you are willing to allow me time for satisfactorily completing this work, and that the money which I asked for will reach me, at a time when I was arranging to sell my clothes for the purposes of raising means.

I have recently passed through a series of most trying and unlucky events and adventures. In my last (of the 27th inst.) I believe I mentioned my desire to visit an ancient mining region in the heart of the Zuñi Mountain. On the first of the month, accompanied by my informant, a prospector of Albuquerque named Williams and a stranger named Buck (alias Miller), who were to pass within a few miles of the region, I set out. . . . [See previous letter for account of the stolen lariat and the runaway mule.]

The mule had broken loose and gone, leaving me, my specimens, and equipage seventy five miles from Zuñi, in the highest, snow covered, most untraveled portion of the Zuñi Mountains, and thirty five miles from the last inhabited place.[2] I searched in vain, by the moonlight, the cañons and valleys of the neighborhood, then hastened back to our camping place of the previous night, and finding no trace, returned to get all the rest I could, determining to start on the morrow for Zuñi. In the morning I searched again until nearly eleven o'clock, but all tracks being obscured by snow etc., I could not determine definitely the direction which the mule had taken. Knowing that to be at all safe I must make at least thirty miles before the following midday, I made up my pack and wrote you the enclosed hasty note. This note, from my haste and condition of mind, was neither well considered nor detailed; yet, as it was sealed I send it you, not caring to re-read it from fear that I should condemn its sending, and thus fail to present the facts it bears witness to.

I need detail neither my adventures nor sufferings in that walk to Zuñi. Overtaken at night by snow storms, by day following deep covered trails, I reached, after two days' wanderings, the first ranch—weak with hands and arms rendered useless by cold and the tension of my pack but with spirits cheerful. Two days more brought me to Zuñi, where I was received with kindness and every demonstration of joy by my Indian hosts— a fact which I mention as in contrast with what I shall be compelled to record presently. I told them of my intention to again start within three days. After no little trouble, they procured me horses, and, never heeding my wishes to the contrary, detailed a man to go with me. The trader, Mr. Graham, also started, but, unable to endure the severe cold, left us on the second day. . . . On the third day we reached the cabin in which my things and letter were deposited. Most unfortunately, during the night and on the following morning, snow fell to such an extent that it was impractical to re-cross the divide. I was thus forced to come down the eastern slope and return toward Zuñi via Fort Wingate—a distance of more than a hundred miles. On my arrival here (a few hours since) I was met by indifference and insult such as I can never cease either to remember or to resent. Nor would I have had extended to me even the constrained courtesy which I am now compelled to suffer, had not my conversation convinced the commanding officer that I am still a civilized being and not the beast and savage—nor the "merely tolerated boy" that idle gossip and intentional malice have represented me as, to the conservative society of Fort Wingate. This experience is one more of the many which I owe to a presence in our party of which I have before made mention—a presence which, from the beginning, has been incapable of recognizing in my self-inflicted degradation to the daily life of savages any motives other than such as, from their rather low character, I trust I shall in future be, as I have in past been, quite incapable of. Could I have fore-known the experiences of today, I would have turned back over the threatening divide; for I had rather have faced the storms of the highest peaks in the Sierras of Zuñi than the contempt that I have this day faced. The one chills only the body and freezes the skin, but the other chills all faith in humanity and freezes the heart. Yet this is but one more of the little things which the course I have adopted calls upon me to endure. Need I feel surprised if, on the strength of the same gossip and conjectural representa-tions, which I naturally expect must precede me in Washington as they have in Wingate, my friends there come to class me—in desires and motives—with drunken sailors or enlisted soldiers. I should think one thing might appear quite plain—that desires of the nature above hinted at could lend but little enthusiasm to a solitary mountain trip of two hundred miles through the hostile Apache country or to the exploration in mid-winter of mountain mines and uninhabited caves, or at least that the man who bent his whole heart toward doing those things was sometimes ca-pable of a purer enthusiasm. Pardon me, I know that much which I have said is out of place in a letter to you; but I feel stung through and through with mortification and must say something to one who I believe *knows* why I have adopted the means I have. . . .

Draft of letter dated
June 20, 1880

Dear Professor Baird—

. . . I doubt not you have been perfectly informed by the press, of the condition of the Apaches. Gradually, during the past nine months, they have extended their raids in all directions from their Sierra strongholds until, only a short time past they spread terror and devastation throughout the region sixty miles southwest from here. News which I get of them later is that fleeting across the Sierras they have come down on the valleys of Mesilla and Eastern Rio Grande, all about Silver City, and left the country, with the exception of the latter and two or three other of the larger towns, an uninhabited waste. Taking their cue from these Apaches, the Navajos have become bold and arro-gant, some of them threatening to take the war path. Only two weeks since, they killed one and severely wounded another American (the latter an acquaintance of mine), and more recently two or three men were killed within ten miles of Fort Wingate. I do not, however, share in the general fear that they will break out—a fear which has driven dozens of families to the Post, and others to desert their homes; and which has caused the almost entire temporary suspension of trade, travel and freighting on the road through this valley. Nor have I ever ceased to vindicate in council the rights of my adopted people against these wandering coyotes—driving them mercilessly from Zuñi territory and compelling them to return or repay stolen property. Thus more than ordinary Americans, I am in danger when traveling solitarily about the country. No less am I, in the opinion of men of these parts, in at least some risk from the Mexicans who, on account of the restraint which my presence imposes upon them, and on account of my revealing . . . the traitorous character of some of their relations with the Indians, would on first occasion of finding me alone either cause me to be killed by Navajos or do it themselves.

While I fear neither of these cases, I value just now the fruits of the opportunities I have enjoyed, too much to run any unnecessary risks, and I am informed by gentlemen in both official and civil life that I must arm myself securely—for effect if nothing more. . . .

Zuñi
July 2nd, 1880

Dear Professor Baird—

. . . Two dances have recently taken place, together with important ceremonies relative to the Sun, thus introducing once more my old, ever interesting but very wearing task of watching, recording, and sketching.

It is my good fortune to have here one of the R. R. Route Exploration volumes containing occasional extracts in quotation from the journals of early Spanish Adventurers.[3] Also I have recently, through the courtesy of Padre Brun, enjoyed the privilege of searching over some of the Mss. records of the now

deserted Zuñi church—which was one of the earliest established by the Franciscans in New Spain.

Through studies of these ancient records I have been drawn
into a department of research in reference to the Zuñis—interesting from its connections with History, and important from the
light its results throw on early conditions and still existing traditions.

This line of investigation is founded mostly on the comparison of old Spanish names of People, Kingdoms, and Towns, with
corresponding terms in the Zuñi language of today—a task
which, heretofore impossible, is now comparatively easy to me.
By this means I have already *definitely* located the celebrated
City or Kingdom of "Civola," discovered three hundred and forty
years ago by Padre Marcos Niça, the ruins of which stand within
rifle range of the present pueblo of Zuñi. This ancient town,
having been first of the pueblos subdued by the efforts of
Coronado, and the centre of all subsequent early operations, it
occurred to me that many of the native names to be found
throughout the first Spanish accounts must have been derived
from the language of the Civolatese—or Zuñis—and this I find to
have been the case, more than two thirds that I know of or have in
hand being directly traceable to this source.

For example, the principle "Citie of Cibola—according to
Casteñeda—Muzaque (pronounced *Mū-tsa-kī*) finds a correspondence in the Zuñi name of a ruined pueblo [nearby] called
Mā'-tsā-kī. Also the largest city of the "Kingdome of Civola"
according to Niça and Coronado, Ahacus (Spanish pron. aspi-
rated *Hā-hā-kūs*) cannot but be represented by the splendid
ruins ten miles west from here—called by the Indians *Hā'-wī-
kuh.* . . .

I am now in the heart of the country treated of in all those
works; I speak the language which the writers of them listened
to, and took the names of Kingdoms and Cities from. In my rides
throughout these deserts, I constantly stumble upon the half
buried ruins of the identical towns to which these names related—and daily, I pass under the shadows of the first church
which the zealous hands of those old authors fashioned and
established in the outlying realms of their Nuevo España. If I

may have access to [a number of old Spanish texts] . . . I will pass whole nights with the old men of the tribe, translating passages to them, eliciting tradition from them, comparing Spanish names with theirs, or listening to their suggestions. . . .

Zuñi
July 18, 1880

My dear Professor Baird—
 . . . The matter of superstition which I above alluded to is, while very interesting and all that, not very pleasant. The Zuñis have, within the past ten days, killed one of their own men from its dictates. His trial on the absurd ground of sorcery, I attended personally and as in every other public debate of the tribe, had more or less to say—of course, so far as possible, for the defense. His death was horribly violent—although partaking more of the character of a sacrifice than of an execution. *I* have been more than once—on the ground that I had become a Zuñi—Americans being considered free from sorcery—subject to the same accusation. But I hold my friends from doing me violence by a bond of brotherhood which, you have but to be conversant with the Indian character to appreciate the strength of; and my enemies I have equal power over from their absolute dread of me.

 I have never flinched from their worst demonstrations— have hence established a reputation—very valuable among Indians, of absolute fearlessness. . . .

 I never espouse any cause in which there is not justice— never have any trouble which is not connected with my work—which with the other I always carry through, no matter what the risk. . . . I don't mind the risk of this thing; however, I cannot help recognizing the fact that there is some in it. I have no fear. Only the superstitions of these fellows and the things they ask me to do in conformity to them are at times exasperating in the extreme.

 My living is simply horrible, unmentionable. I thought I couldn't bear too lightly on that subject last Autumn; but the Spring living of the Zuñi I'd better not mention at all. Until now (July 18th) no green has appeared in all this valley.

 The rains have at last come, and, with the dying away of the sand storms, my health has been on the gain constantly, although

I continue to lose flesh rapidly. I hope, nevertheless, that Major Powell will not pass lightly over the consideration of my ration assignment.

Although on my arrival here I understood neither Spanish nor Zuñi, could converse with nobody save my books and by signs for many days and weeks, I do not remember during all my Zuñi experience having had a single attack of genuine nostalgia. And, however full my life be of hardships (from the civilized standpoint of view) and my work of discouragements (from the scientific), yet both have their bright sides, and the only actual depression I ever suffer from is when I see my health failing, and I sometimes recognize my inability to fill the time properly with work. For instance—when I make a long sought discovery, the pleasure is fairly so intense that I forget how I live and all. Besides, the Indians, though exteriorly so reticent and apparently gloomy a people, are when known and when viewed from the standpoint of one of themselves, about the merriest race I have ever known.

When the evening comes and we all sit round the meal of the day, no Christmas dinners I have known have been filled or seasoned with so much badinage, repartée, and hearty laughter as these. In stoic wit excellent; in repartée scarcely surpassed; in punning unconquerable, the Zuñi are not such bad companions after all. Yet if they hate one, all these points or traits only go to make them the more unendurable.

I can sum up in one sentence what my life here has been— Physically, so far as the appetites are concerned, paralysis; Socially, exile; Ethically, theoretically, a feast, a peace of mind unapproached in all my previous experience.

And as to results—probable impaired health during life; a strengthening and development of moral character in *every respect*, and aside from a more practical and cosmopolitan view of humanity and its institutions, I hope and pray (though sometimes dubiously) that it will make *a worker* of me.

On the whole, then, while it is a pretty hard thing, I am *far* from sorry you have decided to keep me down here till I've done something. I have made this long digression from proper official correspondence with you, neither complainingly nor, I trust, from egotistic motives, but that you may the more freely grant me

pardon if I seem sometimes disposed to ask too much consideration, which, *realizing* my situation you would not find it hard to
do. . . .

Zuñi
March 12, 1881

My dear Professor Baird:
The receipt of your letter dated February 24th must have
been delayed by the late snow storms and irregularity of the
buckboard, as it has only recently come to hand.

I am surprised and disheartened at the fate which all of my
more important communications to yourself and Major Powell
are attended by. The one which you refer to as missing consisted
of about sixty-eight closely written pages, accompanied by plans
and sections, giving an account of my recent operations in four
rich ancient caves, and of my discovery of seven others equally
deserving of exhaustive overhauling. Two sheets of it were devoted to the description of a *new* Pueblo tribe, of which I had at
first learned among my Zuñis, and afterward from travellers and
prospectors through these territories. In only one instance has
this tribe ever been visited by white men—two years since—by
a couple of gold hunters—one of whom lost his life in consequence. It referred to an invitation which I had received only a
short time before through the Moquis, directly from this people
(the *Kuh-ni-kwe*) [Havasupais] to visit them with an embassy of
my tribe, of the partial arrangement of the latter, and urged the
desirable nature of such a visit for the purpose of investigating
linguistic affinities said to exist between the Kuh-ni and the
Zuñi, by the latter, as well as other ethnographic features, and
finally asked your advice on the subject together with the transportation facilities to be used not only for this purpose but also
for exploring some twenty-nine ruined pueblos and the caves.

I cannot enter into such a thorough account either of this
matter or of the caves in the present letter, as I have not slept for
thirty-six hours, and the mail carrier is at this moment awaiting
my motions. I will, however, during the present week, try to
re-write as well as possible the letter, which to no purpose I
finished at the expense of considerable time and labor.

The money referred to came to hand a month since, and I

hope the receipts I signed therefor have long ere this been received. I shall, however, require more money very soon.

With regard to collections, I have on hand, not only that which I consider a very valuable although incomplete series of modern Zuñi specimens but the five or six hundred ancient articles which I brought home, at the expense of walking, on our burros. While I am aware of the War Department transportation facilities to which you call my attention, it is impossible for me to send in any of my collections for the simple reason that I can get them neither to [Fort] Wingate nor to any other military post. I am supplied with no transportation, nor with authority for commanding it such as Mr. Stevenson had at his disposal, while the means with which I am supplied are far from sufficient to secure the freighters of this country. True, I might secure the boxes and lumber (entirely lacking here of course) for packing such collections, from the Post, had I the proper papers, but it still would be necessary to have transportation from the latter place to this, as well as from here to there.

Moreover, as my letter informed you, I have cached at one of the caves more than a thousand specimens, at another, five hundred, and at a third a trifle more than at the latter. It is not only expensive but very dangerous to transport such things on horseback, and it would be quite impossible thus to carry the collecting and investigations at these places much further.

The Indians have only within the past ten days consented to my collecting any of the paraphernalia of their sacred dances, or of the ancient trophies of their tribe. They now promise to *help* me get such things together, and I expect as the result, one of the finest of ethnographic collections, although time will be required for its completion, and additional stratagems and watchfulness.

Of the collections "made by Col. Stevenson" few specimens were such as possessed great intrinsic value among the Indians.[4] Such alone were left for me to collect, with but a fraction of the means and facilities. Of the money which I have received during the past eighteen months all or nearly all has been expended incidentally—my whole strictly private account probably covered by *less* than twenty five dollars. The fine lot of imitation turquoises and corals sent me by Mr. Stevenson consisted simply of *three* of the former, of the size here given ●[and]●, and of a quantity of wax beads, which though of interest at first, very nearly ruined my reputation when they came to melt upon their wearer's necks—not withstanding the fact that I warned the Indians of their character.

Of the really magnificent series of shells which you sent me, I find I can make disposition to a very much greater advantage in the worked condition, and hence sent East at the expense (private) of nearly a hundred dollars for a lathe, turner, knives, etc. of my designing, with which to work up this rich material—which will show at once whether I am in earnest, and that I want, laboring under the disadvantages I do, to come out as honorably as possible.

This machine, I am informed by letter, was shipped from the railroad several days since, and I am expecting it with every sunset. . . .

I am terribly weary, terribly cast down. It does not seem at times as though I could endure longer this terrible work, or wait longer for the call which shall summon me to Washington. Yet with the acquisition of the Zuñi language, I have laid open a field which without presumption I can say is the richest ever within the reach or sight of an American investigator, but it widens with each step and to leave it *now*, after my struggle to acquire it, would seem not short of sacrilege to me.

I fear that by all and after all, I have not won the commendation of those for whose opinion I care most. . . .

P.S. I am at work by day constantly on the Herculean census designed by Major Powell, and put into my hands by Agent Thomas.[5] By night I am as busy with my more proper pursuits. I am making more rapid progress in the study of the *inner life* of these wonderful savages during the past few days than ever before. Familiar as I am with their language, and one of them by adoption, I have not until within a week secured anything like a complete vocabulary of their consanguinity terms, or any conception of their *true* belief in immortality and its conditions. Notwithstanding the fact that this has been one of the facts I have constantly searched for during a year and half.

Why is it that Major Powell designs every thing on such a

grand scale that the very object he aims so well to cover is defeated at the outset. An example is his census. In this he leaves for most enumerators—except they have limitless time and thorough familiarity with the native language—only two alternatives: either to turn in incorrect results—worse than none—or deceitful ones—worse than either.

Were it not that my honor was involved, I should have given it up long ago, for this extra work has been the source of many personal as well as official sacrifices. . . .

Zuñi
October 12, 1881

My dear Professor Baird:

I am glad to write you of great successes recently in the line of our researches. As hinted in my last letter, I have just been passed through the ceremonials of initiation into the secret order of the *A-Pi-Thlan Shi-Wa-Ni* or Priests of the Bow. In order that I might be made eligible to this position, I had first to be made "son of the Parrots," . . . [by adoption into gentile clan of the Macaw]. I have now the position of "Junior Priest of the Bow," with the privilege of taking the twelve other degrees of the society, or entering any of the ten medicine orders of the tribe. This order is the Masonry of the North American Indians, if for the sake of happy, yet not misleading comparison, it may be referred to as such. It exists among many, if not all, of the advanced Indian tribes, as with all Pueblos, the Navajos, the Mandans, Arickarees, and Hidatsas of the north, the remnants of the civilized Indians of Mexico in the south. There are prayers and songs in this order, embodied in ancient and obsolete language, which would require many pages of foolscap for their transmission, and which I was compelled to vow sacredly I would never weary of until I had acquired or written them. The priests above me have required me already to write carefully ten of them, and these alone are worth all sacrifices I have been compelled to go through in entering the order: the four days—first the day of motionless attitude and silence, the three nights of dancing in the estufa, the last of which was continued until physical exhaustion compelled some of the members to retire, giving me the same privilege. The feast I had to give in common with my four brothers, was expensive, but not so much as I had anticipated and has been a hundred-fold repaid. As a consequence of my initiation I have had a world of facts opened up to me, which I had despaired of ever reaching. I had from my former standpoint exhausted the subject with the exception of a few details, and was preparing to come home permanently during early January of 1882, in case your decision would prove favorable; but from the present I see nothing but the most constant work, with the best of facilities for at least four years to make my work *exhaustive*. I can never give this amount of time to the work, even with your heartiest concurrence, however important it may seem, as I have interests in life apart from Zuñi. But I would be willing to devote, say, a year or two more to it, or at least parts of such a period. Indeed, my disappointment would be almost irreparable, were I unable to study for a period almost as great, from the *inside*, the life of the Zuñis, as I have from the outside. After having secured the two necessities, the absolute confidence and the language of the Indian, I feel it my duty to use these necessities or advantages to the fullest extent of their value, toward the end which I acquired them for.

I have decided to ask your permission to my return in January with four or five Indians to Washington, and with this view, I have begun negotiations for securing free passage for myself and party via Omaha and Chicago. Some excellent connections which I have made during the past two years, will, I think, render this easy. Some of my enthusiastic friends in the two cities mentioned will aid me strongly; and the ladies of Boston have extended cordial invitations to me, to bring my party on if not to Boston, as far east as New York and Washington, promising their aid, etc.; also I wish to make this move principally to advance my future work in Zuñi, as the Indians have for each day, more than a year, spoken of this, begging that I should bring it to pass. They wish to see my great cacique's house, see what we will do with their things, and if in the end they prove satisfied, they promise to furnish me a series of their sacred costumes for the dances, etc., than which nothing can be more interesting, beautiful, or valuable for an ethnographic museum. Inasmuch as after the new sun festivities and ceremonials, nothing save the night *Kâ'-kâs*,—which I have faithfully seen for two seasons—occurs during the months of January, February, March, and April, I could remain in Washington during those months, retaining my brother, the head chief, working with him on the dictionary and grammar and a part of the ethnography and getting together material for the final work in Zuñi.

Through the promised aid of Col. Stevenson and my friends, the completion of this scheme would not involve great expense, would be the last remaining policy-stroke with the Indians, and, according to the colonel, would aid immensely in popularizing—not more mine than his own part of the ethnographic work. . . .

All letters save that of June 20, 1880, are from microfilm reel no. 27, National Anthropological Archives, Smithsonian Institution, Washington, D.C. Printed with the permission of the Smithsonian Institution. The letter of June 20, 1880, from Envelope 44, Hodge-Cushing Collection, Southwest Museum, Los Angeles, is printed with the permission of the Southwest Museum.

Notes

1. See "A Lesson in History" and notes for the introduction to the section "Observations and Participations." Alvar Nuñez Cabeza de Vaca was a member of the first Spanish party to discover the Zuñi towns, and his account of this and other famous adventures was one of Cushing's sources. Fray Marcos de Niça, sent by the Spanish viceroy of Mexico to investigate the reported "cities," is another early Spanish source. [Ed. note]

2. Cushing's figure seems a bit exaggerated, since the distance from the center of the Zuñi Mountains to Zuñi pueblo cannot be more than forty miles. [Ed. note]

3. Cushing doubtless refers here to the *Report of the Secretary of War Communicating the Several Pacific Railroad Explorations*, 3 vols. (Washington, D.C., 1855). [Ed. note]

4. "Illustrated Catalogues" of Stevenson's huge collections from Zuñi and other pueblos, prepared with Cushing's help, appeared in the BAE *Annual Reports* for 1880–81, (pp. 307–465) and 1881–82 (pp. 511–94). [Ed. note]

5. Among the papers in the Southwest Museum is a cover sheet labeled "Tenth Census of the United States: Indian Division . . . People of Zuñi," dated March 28, 1881, and signed by Frank Hamilton Cushing. A note on the envelope states, "Ms. of Zuñi census of 1880 is in the BAE" (Box no. 1, Hodge-Cushing Collection). Among Cushing's papers at the

BAE is a "Schedule of Zuñi Material Collected by Frank Hamilton Cushing and Turned In to BAE," dated January 27, 1885. This schedule includes a section "On the Sociology of the Zuñis" with a list of headings as follows. I will quote in full, both to indicate the nature of the data, which, in spite of his grousing, Cushing recognized as "indispensible to the results" of his research (letter to Baird of November 28, 1880, BAE microfilm reel no. 27) and to illustrate the capacity which he does seem to have had for the systematic collection and recording of such data.

1st. Census of the tribe as made for the Dept. of the Interior, with notes (pp. 210);

2nd. Name and Number census of the Gentes giving also distribution of lands and habitations to individuals as members of the gentes (on 1619 cards);

3rd. Name Census of the Esoteric Societies, giving also ranks and titles of Priests appertaining to them;

4th. D[itt]o of the Estufa memberships (on cards accompanying census of the gentes);

5th. Names of all individuals of the tribe, arranged in the order of gentile rank, and for linguistic comparison with the name-entries of baptisms and marriages in the Records of the Franciscan Mission of "Our Lady of Guadalupé" of the last century;

6th. Notes relative to:

a) The Gentile organizations

b) Dance organizations (Cachina of Kâ'-kâ)

c) Esoteric organizations

d) Priesthoods or ecclesiastical chieftains

e) Officers or secular chieftains

f) Sacred ceremonials

g) Secular and judicial councils

h) The regulation of relationship (marital and consanguinial) and conduct. (Contained in Diurnal & Miscellaneous Memoranda, Census schedules, Relationship charts, and Marginal Notes on *Ancient Society* and Bandelier's three works on Ancient Mexico [BAE microfilm reel no. 27]. [Ed. note]

A Scalp and Initiation

AFTER I had been, next to my elder brother, chief councillor of the tribe for almost a year, I undertook with two or three of my adopted kinsmen a journey over the great San Francisco plateau and desert in Arizona to the deep cañon home of the *Hava-supai*, or Nation of the Willows, a people then even less known than were the Zuñis. In that fearful journey of over 1100 miles in the saddle, we almost perished for the want of water and food, traveling day and night at one time during more than 50 hours without either, through forests grander than any I had ever seen, and great glades beautiful with waving desert grass and flowers (for dews fall there, but no rains). We emerged from that journey mere skeletons, our animals unable for days to bear us farther. I wish that I might tell of the strange people we encountered down in one of the side cañons of the Colorado. It was so abrupt and narrow that we knew not of its existence until we had ridden almost to its vertical brink. Over that we looked down upon rock below rock at the scattered huts of a little village, dots on the twilit plain, scarce half a mile wide, more than half a mile straight below us. In going down to that village we passed through a turn of the cañon where the rocks above us, six thousand feet high, seemed to be falling together to swallow us forever. It was dim twilight down there, and though but little after mid-day, we saw in the little strip of sky overhead, pale, yet distinctly visible, stars of the constellations of winter time.

When, after weeks, we were returning, we passed through the region of the Apache depredations of 1881 in eastern Arizona. Well did I learn of Zuñi modes of camping, trailing, warfare and concealment on that long trip; for one day we came into a broad valley, one of the arms of the Colorado Chiquito, in which we saw trails of a suspicious kind. A band of shepherdless sheep had been encountered by us early in the morning. We stopped therefore to examine the trail. We saw the tracks of fifteen or sixteen horses and mules, Indian animals, for only two, led evidently, had shoes. The ridden horse makes a trail of one kind to Indian eyes, the pack horse of another, and the led horse of yet another. The trails of mules also are perfectly distinguishable from those of horses, whether shod or unshod. We could not determine quite whether there were 11 or 13 of the animals ridden, but two things we determined that were very important to us: first that the trails were those of raiding Apaches and, second, they were so fresh that we must have been seen farther up before the Apaches had reached the cover of the opposite foothills. Hence we knew that when we camped that night we would certainly be followed and set upon. Our plans were laid accordingly. We traveled on until sunset, and selected a spot near the brink of an arroyo, under a clump of cedar trees; but with our eyes we selected another spot across that arroyo, which was steep and difficult to pass. Then we picketed our horses out beyond where we made camp, gathered together fire-wood, built a bright fire, and unconcernedly cooked our supper. When darkness had settled down we spread our blankets around the fire under the trees, ostentatiously, but not too much so, and laid ourselves down as though to rest. When the fire had burned low, however, one by one, almost imperceptibly, we crawled off backward, on our bellies, towards the arroyo, crossed it noiselessly and secreted ourselves under the bushes we had selected on the opposite bank. Hours passed. Our camp fire was but a glowing speck when the moon rose. I was new to it and more wakeful than my companions. Presently I heard a splash in the river. No other noise, except a little later a tinkling which immediately ceased. I knew that the Apaches were coming, for the tinkling sound was made by the ornaments of a bit. I pulled the blankets of my nearest companion, and he pulled those of the one next to him. Then we leveled our fire-arms and waited. Presently through a little moonlit opening in the trees came, almost silently, an Apache, bending low, on horseback; then exactly in his trail, another, and another, and another, until we counted thirteen. They never paused at our decoy camp, not they; nor did they utter a sound, but turned with the quickness of frightened game and scattered away among the bushes almost before we could fire a shot.

But I returned from that expedition, at the end of a hot day, with a scalp, sole remaining requisite for my initiation into the Priesthood of the Bow, or the order of war magicians; for I had been working with a few of the priests for more than nine months to gain even temporary admission.

Upon our arrival in Zuñi I was bidden to leave my scalp outside of the pueblo, however, for, said my brethren, it had not yet been taken. Then I learned that, as in surgical operations, so in the taking of a scalp, it was forbidden to make the first incision with a knife of metal. When it was decided after long and stormy debate that I should be admitted into the secret fraternity of the Bow, I was guarded all the rest of the night by four members of that priesthood. Just as the morning star appeared, dressed and painted as warriors, with skull caps of thick hide and cuirasses of doubled elk skins, bows, arrows, and shields, we silently stole out to the plain where lay my scalp. We went through all the manoeuvres of surprising the enemy, of offering hasty prayers, then shooting one of their number, finishing him with war clubs, and finally with elaborate rituals and ceremony taking his scalp, this time with flint knives, with which we were provided.

"O great White Beard of the Over World, who with Thy war magic and sharp nail, which is flint, taketh that which is vile and violent and maketh of it the cap of friendship and peace, this day through Thy favor, as Thou through the favor of the Sun Father, I take token from the enemy of his friendship. The light of Thy favor rest upon it."

After that I was brought in in triumph, bearing at the end of a long wand my scalp. Still fasting, bareheaded, and stripped nearly to the skin, I was set at sunrise on a large ant-hill of the red fire ants of the Southwest, so named because of their bites, and there all day long I had to sit, motionless, speechless, save to priests in reply to instructions. Toward evening my initiation began. A great triumphal procession was formed, of men, women, and children, headed in the regular order of their degrees and rank by the Priesthood of the Bow in battle array. More dogs were killed in our four-fold progress around the town that evening, toward the chambers of our priesthood than would serve to feed the eagles of Zuñi for two months. More fasting, more sleeplessness, purifications, vomitings each day, sacrificial pilgrimages, then silent motionless meditation again, filled up, with nightly instructions in the rituals and incantations, the time between this and the great day when the people assembled in the plaza to dance and feast, thus making complete in public my initiation, which in reality and in secret had been performed overnight by the Society. Every detail of this process is symbolic, poetic, intensely interesting, and its results on the mind of the man who passes through it more amazing than anything I could relate. No step that I ever achieved in Zuñi was so great a one as this, moreover, for it rendered me eligible to even higher priestly office, gained me entrance into every other esoteric society—this being the central organization of its kind—and raised me to the rank of head war chief.

From a lecture, "Life in Zuñi," delivered in Buffalo, New York, December 10, 1890. Envelope 214, Hodge-Cushing Collection, Southwest Museum, Los Angeles. Printed with the permission of the Southwest Museum.

Tried for Sorcery

THE day of my greatest ordeal came after more than two years of life among the Zuñis. Unknown to myself and because of enmity here and there, and whispered slanders from the outside world, from amongst Mormons, Mexicans, and even Americans who never liked my Indian experiment, I had been accused of sorcery, the most heinous crime this people knew of.

I was peacefully sleeping in my little room one night; late it was, the fire on the hearth had burned low. I had not noticed that those who gathered around as usual to talk, and listen, as they were always ready to do, to my stories of old world history, were somewhat more solemn than usual. Finally I felt a tapping at my feet and awoke. The room was nearly dark. Some one was bending over the fire and stirring up the embers to make light. As the glow became brighter I saw standing beside the doorway two men, ceremonial war clubs in their hands, badges of the war priesthood over their breasts. The one who was tapping me on the feet (their way of waking a sleeper, in order that his soul, if absent in dreams, will not be rudely shocked), as well as the one who was stirring the fire, was thus attired also.

One who lives the daily life of Indians becomes marvellously trained to take in details in an instant. Before I was fairly awake, I knew that I was suspected of sorcery. I thought I was doomed when the one at my foot said, "Come, Little Brother." Very gravely, but kindly, he said it. "Come, take your smoke." For it is customary when the priesthood is about to try a man for crime to bid him smoke, meaning his last smoke.

To gain time, I pretended ignorance. "You are pretty fellows," I said, "to be joking in this way, and pulling a fellow out of dreams from as far away as Washington." But I reached for my tobacco, and at the same time slipped an extra bag and some corn shucks and my pistol under my blanket, which I drew up around me, arose, and said suddenly, "So it is serious, is it? Then let us go, since go we must. Whither?"

One before me, one behind me, one on either side, they proceeded through the dark narrow ways of the pueblo to the other end, and led me deep down through a turning, tunnel-like entrance into a great low chamber, where a bright fire was burning, and where nearly a hundred members of the esoteric societies were gathered, row behind row. Down in the middle of the floor was a stool-block, a blanket already spread over it. My adopted father, my poor brother (Pa-lo-wah-ti-wa) and his father were sitting near it on the right hand side, the only defenders of the accused, who was quickly singled out, as they motioned me to sit down on the empty stool-block.

"Smoke," said I, joking again, as I threw the tobacco on the floor. "You must be sleepy, for you are not owls."

"You ought to know," said a voice gravely from their midst. He was alluding to the practice of sorcerers, who deal with owls' feathers and charms of the night.

But I kept on joking, talking out whatever came into my head, for I was endeavoring to gain time, when my old adopted father extended his hand, and said, "Son, pray do not joke; this is a grave matter."

"Grave," said I, changing again in a minute. "Come then," I said, sitting down, "let us hear what it is."

A man arose from the ranks on the other side, came forward and sat down. He accused me of practicing sorcery. Alas! that I had entered the meeting of the Fire Order when newly come to Zuñi, for the man before me was one of its chief priests. He alluded to that. He told the others how I had transgressed; how also I had stolen with brilliant colors the shadows of the sacred dance, and thereby disturbed the souls of the gods; how I had, not long before, put up a magic string, with tin cans at the ends of it, which extended farther than the steps of three arrows, yet which spoke at one end whatever had gone into the other; how I had brought strange medicines into the tribe, and predicted the deaths of children whom I would not cure, which predictions had invariably come true; had refused to treat their children when they were dying of the "red rash," as they called the measles; how the children had not died until those strange medicines were brought with which I had pretended to paint my doorway (they were merely boiled oil and turpentine, such as these people had never seen before, much less smelled). Then he said,

"We have referred the matter to the Mexicans, and they say he is an *ichesero*, or witch."

They had also referred to the Mormons, who shook their heads and did not dare to deny it; and they had referred even to other Americans, who had proven no less non-committal.

I listened to the long harangue, gathering my forces together. I had then been for more than a year a leading chief in the tribe, and had learned much of their ways. When he had finished speaking,

"Speak, my son," said my father.

"Yes, speak," echoed my brother.

"It seems, then," said I suddenly, "that you have all, men, as well as women and children, been such fools as not to see this long ago. Everything you have said is true. Why did I come here? Did you not notice that I left my weapons at your doorways when I entered your houses? You ought to have seen that was not for politeness but because I was a magician and fearless. Suppose that I did wear your dress and consent to call you brothers and fathers? Suppose that I did eat from one bowl with each one of you, as though born of the same mother?" My father and brother looked aghast. "No man who loved you," I continued, "would do such things as these."

Here, suddenly, my old father lifted his head and shouted: "Listen, fools, listen."

"Why did I counsel that the Mormons should not share your lands? Why did I lead your parties of young men to drive away the Mexicans from your pastures? No man who loved you would do such things as these. For the Mormons, who wear stems of red canvas for breeches (the Zuñi description for the poorest and most worthless of Americans), are, as you all know, the wisest and greatest of the Americans. They never lie. They love you so much that they long to live with you, and even to build their homes on your land."

"Listen, fools, listen," said my old father and my brother together now. Several of the men opposite raised their hands and cried,

"Enough! Shame is soiling the blankets that cover us."

"Go on," said my brother, with a flaming eye, and I continued:

"As for the Mexicans, you ought to have known that I was a sorcerer when I tried to drive them away; for they loved you so much that they came here to your pasture-grounds and brought thousands of their sheep, not to feed them on your grass but in order that they need not have to leave you. You have a proverb that the Mexican lies even when he prays,—But not to you, oh no!"

"Enough! Enough!" said one and all. "We are even as women in cold weather, and as weeping children."

"Yes, rise, Little Brother," said the old priest who had spoken against me, stepping over to where I was sitting and lifting me by the hand. He was trembling violently, but he solemnly embraced me and pronounced a prayer over me, as did every other one, except my brother and the two fathers, who accompanied me home and sat explaining and joking until the coming of dawn; and that was the last of my difficulties and dangers from superstitious causes among the Zuñis.

From a lecture, "Life in Zuñi," delivered in Buffalo, New York, December 10, 1890. Envelope 214, Hodge-Cushing Collection, Southwest Museum, Los Angeles. Printed with the permission of the Southwest Museum.

II. OBSERVATIONS AND PARTICIPATIONS

FIG. 30. Cushing in Washington. (Courtesy of the Smithsonian Institution National Anthropological Archives)

Observations and Participations

THE selections gathered under the heading of "observations and participations" are intended to represent both some of Cushing's distinct contributions and some of the variety of his approach as a reporter of Zuñi culture. The range extends in time from prehistory to current events, in focus from close factual description to broad generalization, in subject from mythology and social organization to surgery and agriculture, and in style from third person formality to first person familiarity.

The first two items concern Zuñi history, or the Zuñi way of keeping in touch with the past. With respect to the first of these, the reader of Cushing's letter of July 2, 1880, will already possess the background essential for comprehension. Only two things need to be added. One is that it is now regarded as established fact that the ruins Cushing refers to in the neighborhood of Zuñi *are* those of the "Cities of Cibola" which figure in the sixteenth-century Spanish accounts (though there is question whether these "cities" were really seven in number or six).[1] The other is that while Cushing is rarely included among the authorities referred to in this connection, it was he who discovered the fact, through the similarity he noticed between the names used for the towns in the early Spanish texts and the names used by the Zuñis themselves in reference to the ruins nearby.[2] A dual kind of excitement registers in this first abbreviated selection, responsive to the demonstration of Zuñi memory *and* to the age of their ancient dwelling place.

The second piece, on Zuñi resistance to imported Catholicism, comes to a more controversial conclusion. Later studies

FIG. 31. Cushing Demonstrating Coiled Pottery-Making Technique. (Courtesy of the Smithsonian Institution National Anthropological Archives, Bureau of American Ethnology Collection)

have tended to give greater emphasis to evidence of Spanish and more recent North American influences on Zuñi culture.[3] However that may be, Cushing's account, excerpted from "Outlines of Zuñi Creation Myths," continues to hold interest as contemporary witness, as of the 1880s.

The "Outline of Zuñi Mytho-Sociologic Organization," also excerpted from "Outlines of Zuñi Creation Myths," formulates succinctly the famous "sevenfold division" or principle of classification which Cushing saw as fundamental to the Zuñi conception of the world and to all phases of Zuñi cultural and social life. Reference has already been made to the well-recognized influence this notion, much elaborated by Cushing himself, has had in European, if not American, sociology and anthropology. As a perception simply of social organization in Zuñi itself, it now seems to have acquired respectability as well among American students of the southwest, having been either ignored or contested by Cushing's more immediate successors. Kroeber, in *Zuñi Kin and Clan* (1917), while acknowledging the consonance of Cushing's theory with Zuñi tradition and the way the old Zuñi priests themselves viewed their tribal organization, found nothing in the contemporary Zuñi social groupings to verify their derivation from an all-embracing directional system and generally discounted the notion as an esoteric fabrication too perfect to be true.[4] More recently, Fred Eggan has credited Cushing with having produced "the pioneer studies of social organization in the western Pueblos" and has made extensive use of the directional theory in his own book on Pueblo social organization, at the same time criticizing Kroeber for having underestimated its importance for understanding the complex structure of Zuñi society.[5] As for the slighting remarks several times reiterated by Kroeber about writers so enamored of their neat formulas that they mistake them for facts, the careful reader will note several warnings by Cushing that the system he is outlining is but approximated in the complicated overlapping network ("systems within systems") of actual clan, priesthood, sacred society, and kiva organizations known to him.[6] Here, indeed, and in a more conscious fashion than Lévi-Strauss recognized, Cushing's aim does seem to be not so much to give an actual description of Zuñi society as to elaborate "a model which could explain most of its processes and structure."

The essay on Zuñi animal fetishes, presented here in abridged form, may likewise be seen as an adumbration of the structural approach. As Dennis Tedlock has observed in a recent article on Pueblo literature, one of Cushing's main purposes in this work was "to convey, through an examination of the origin stories attached to the fetishes, what might be called the 'logic' of Zuñi fetishism."[7] Cushing, of course, was not the first to see a "logic" in primitive beliefs and practices. Edward B. Tylor's explanations of fetishism (and animism in general) as "savage philosophy" founded "on the very evidence of the senses" resonate behind Cushing's description of the Zuñis as "the closest of observers" and his statement that "theirs is a science of appearances and a philosophy of analogies."[8] Doubtless there is also an echo of Tylor in Cushing's reference to a "confusion of the subjective with the objective" as the reason for the Zuñi belief in the appearances and their faith in the living potency of images.[9] (That he could appreciate, too, as Tylor had, the difficulty—even for civilized folk like anthropologists—of avoiding this "confusion" has already been pointed out and may help to account for his respectful approach to the Zuñi beliefs.)

What Cushing added to the literature of fetishes, through prolonged intimate contact with a particular people, was a perception of a whole *system* of "savage philosophy" within its particular cultural context. He was able not merely to posit a general kind of "logicality" but to examine its structure as reflected in the body of lore associated with the fetishes. Moreover, while the directional division alluded to above figures here too as a controlling organizational principle, informing both the origin stories and the ritual practices for which they provide explanation and model, we are introduced as well to another structural conception which presages even more closely the approach of Lévi-Strauss. This conception emerges in Cushing's exposition of the "one great system of all-conscious and interrelated life, in which the degrees of relationship seem to be determined largely, if not wholly, by the degrees of resemblance." While there seem to be several aspects according to which any member or element of the Zuñi world may be placed relative to the others, the relationships indicated in the opening passage of the essay on fetishes all seem to register in linear form—as in a great chain of being. The structural principle or "chart" illustrated by the position of the animals *vis à vis* men and the gods is that in sets of three along this line the middle term mediates between the other two—a model both complementary to the directional division and expressive of the "notion of the 'middle' and its relation to the rest" which according to Cushing is "the central fact indeed of Zuñi organization." Cushing draws no diagrams in his essay, but we may see here in nascent form the method followed in Lévi-Strauss's own brief analysis of the Zuñi origin myths in terms of this mediation between gods and men, life and death, and other related oppositions and more recently in studies such as Alfonso Ortiz's "Ritual Drama and the Pueblo World View" and Louis A. Hieb's "Meaning and Mis-Meaning," particularly the section "The Zuñi: People of the Middle Place." [10]

The "Remarks on Shamanism" were made at a meeting of the American Philosophical Society in 1897 in response to a talk identifying a geometrically shaped stone found in Ohio as an artifact of Indian shamanism. Here again, as in the selections on "mytho-sociologic organization" and on fetishism, the general subject is the Zuñi world view; in this case, however, the focus is more particularly on the individual and his conception of himself and his world in relation to one another. The key terms in these remarks are force and form—apprehended everywhere by the Zuñis, according to Cushing, as manifestations of the "one great system of all-conscious and interrelated life" already spoken of. The individual himself is perceived as hardening or ripening into form by virtue of a series of connections which must be established, with the earth mother, the sun father, the clan, the totem animals, the spirit winds, in short with all the forces and forms on which his own life and breath depend. Because of their pertinence here, two short passages from "Outlines of Zuñi Creation Myths"—one on the life and force of forms as perceived by the Zuñis and another on the preservation of force through the reenactment of form in Zuñi dance-drama—are appended at the end of the selection.

The first of these latter passages, incidentally, is one of those quoted by Lèvy-Bruhl as illustrative of his thesis that people in so-called primitive cultures differ from those of "civilized" cultures not only in what they believe and how they think but in their very way of perceiving things. To the primitive, by virtue of Lévy-Bruhl's "law of participation" (his term for the "confusion of the subjective with the objective"),

> there is no phenomenon which is, strictly speaking, a physical one, in the sense in which we use the term. . . . His perceptive organs have indeed grasped the displacement of a mass of material as ours do; familiar objects are readily recognized according to previous experience; in short, all the physiological and psychological processes of perception have actually taken place in him as in ourselves. Its result, however, is immediately enveloped in a state of complex consciousness dominated by collective representations. . . . Primitive perception is fundamentally mystic. . . . Ours has ceased to be so, at any rate with regard to most of the objects which surround us. Nothing appears alike to them and to us.[11]

"No man," according to Powell, "has contributed more to our understanding of the doctrine [of mystical or magical powers] as believed and practiced by the Amerindian tribes than Cushing himself." [12] Everything he wrote concerning Zuñi culture is expressive of his interest in this "different" way of seeing things and of his own effort to participate in it, to experience it from within. In the piece on shamanism we find more particularly some sample observations of the kind of cultural conditioning which lies behind such differences in perception, producing the "collective representations" of which Durkheim and Lévy-Bruhl wrote.

The episode reported in "A Case of Primitive Surgery" is a remarkable instance of this cultural difference. Here, procedures which were not only successful but perfectly appropriate from the "rational" standpoint are examined in terms of the quite "irrational" ("from our point of view") perceptions and theories on which they were in fact based.

"A Study of Pueblo Pottery as Illustrative of Zuñi Cultural Growth" introduces again an element of controversy. Cushing's theory that the art of pottery making among the Pueblo people of the Southwest had evolved locally and independently, out of the use of clay-coated baskets, has never been a standard one. As Clark Wissler wrote in 1926, "Needless to say, this proposal on the part of Cushing, though eminently plausible, and upheld by a number of circumstantial facts, has from that day to this been the target of criticism and held up before the student as the horrible example of too much imagination and ingenuity in scientific writing. It was said that Cushing was a poet, or at least an essayist, this story of pottery evolution being one of his artistic creations." [13] That view seems still to obtain, for according to Paul S. Martin, in a pamphlet published in 1959, "no one at present credits the Mogollon Indians with the invention of pottery. We all agree that was a trait introduced from the south, as was agriculture." [14] Wissler, in his 1965 revision of *Indians of the United States*, is more skeptical, declaring that neither explanation can be proven from available evidence. Nevertheless, as he points out, the discoveries of later archeologists (Richard Wetherill in Utah and Earl H. Morris in Arizona) have established that hardened clay basket linings were used in the locality before the use of fired pottery, and "in some such way pottery must have been invented." [15] Whatever may be the current views on this subject, the paper—in condensed form—is presented here for its plausibility and charm, and as a sample of Cushing's work in the area of the crafts. While not primarily based here on his "experimental method" of actual reproduction under primitive conditions, the approach clearly illustrates his sympathetic and technical awareness of those conditions as an experienced craftsman used to working under them. Also illustrated, incidentally, in addition to his characteristically close observation of the artifacts themselves, is Cushing's use of etymology—his study of archaic Zuñi terms—as a resource for gaining insight into their history and meaning. His explanation of the origins of pueblo pottery owes not a little of its plausibility to this method; and whether or not the reliability of his information is beyond question in every instance, he is to be credited for applying to archeology the method itself, a kind of linguistic approximation to the stratigraphic core.

As for the selections from *Zuñi Breadstuff*, only hard necessity could force the editor to be selective at all with respect to this book. Published originally in 1884–85 as a series of articles in an Indianapolis trade journal (now long defunct) called the *Millstone*, rescued from oblivion by republication in 1920 as a volume in the Heye Foundation series of Indian Notes and Monographs, and now after half a century, available again in a Heye Foundation reprint, *Zuñi Breadstuff* is anything but the ordinary corn report its title suggests. A classic of very special order in the field of American Indian studies, it has for subject not merely the corn itself but the part it plays throughout Zuñi life and lore. The contents are various indeed, ranging from sacred creation myths and folk yarns to descriptions of contemporary planting techniques, festivals, and ceremonies, from discussions of ancient architectural, pottery, and basket-weaving designs to anecdotes of dinners, hunting trips, and other adventures—a teeming presence of persons, places, things, and events, held together throughout by their relation to the all-essential corn food. Reviewing the book in 1921, Kroeber wrote, "There seems to be no other piece of writing that renders so complete and true and powerful an impression of Zuñi as

Breadstuff."[16] The judgment is as true now as it was then, and the hope for the samples presented here is not that they will provide an adequate substitute for the book as a whole but that they will stimulate the reader to go in search for the rest.

Notes

1. The sixteenth-century Spanish accounts on which Cushing drew—those of Alvar Nuñez Cabeza de Vaca, Pedro Casteñeda, Fray Marcos de Niça, and Coronado himself—use the figure seven, as does Melchior Diaz, one of the leaders with Coronado of the conquering expedition. However, another of these early accounts, that of Juan Jaramillo, lists only six, and J. Walter Fewkes, in his "Reconnoissance of Ruins in or near the Zuñi Reservations," pp. 98–99, reports some uncertainties among the accounts of his contemporaries as to precisely which and how many of the Zuñi villages were known to the early Spaniards. Reviewing the question in 1937 in his *History of Hawiku,* Frederick W. Hodge makes a cogent case for six as the likely number—the figure seven in the Spanish accounts probably owing, as he points out, more to association of the pueblos with the "Seven Lost Cities" of earlier legend than to an actual count of the villages found in New Mexico in 1540 (see especially p. 57).

2. Cushing was, in fact, given credit at the time for his discovery by his friend Adolph Bandelier, who, doubtless on Cushing's prompting, seems to have been the first to advance in print a case for identifying the Zuñi villages with the "Seven Cities of Cibola." His accounts in *Contributions to the History of the Southwestern Portion of the United States* and *The Gilded Man* draw on the same Spanish sources as Cushing and cite Cushing both on the similarities of the Indian and Spanish place names and on the Zuñi story of the killing of the "Black Mexican" (see *Contributions,* p. 131, and *The Gilded Man,* pp. 141–49 and passim).

3. See, for example, the work of Edward P. Dozier—most recently, *The Pueblo Indians of North America.* Spanish influences were of course noted earlier by such students of the area as Elsie CleweParsons, A. L. Kroeber, and Leslie Spier.

4. Alfred L. Kroeber, *Zuñi Kin and Clan,* pp. 120, 147, and passim.

5. Fred Eggan, *Social Organization of the Western Pueblos,* p. 12. See also his chapter on Zuñi, pp. 176–222.

6. Cushing was also quite aware of the fact later pointed out by Kroeber as if in correction of Cushing: namely, that "the phratral combinations of clans [were] now modified or outgrown among the Zuñis" (*Zuñi Breadstuff,* p. 128), though, he adds, they "were well-nigh universal to aboriginal America."

Observations and Participations 171

7. Dennis Tedlock, "Pueblo Literature: Style and Verisimilitude," p. 220.

8. Edward B. Tylor, *Primitive Culture: Researches into the Development of Mythology, Philosophy, Religion, Language, Art, and Custom*, 2:478.

9. See Tylor, *Researches into the Early History of Mankind and the Development of Civilization*, pp. 100–4.

10. Claude Lévi-Strauss, *Structural Anthropology*, pp. 218–27. The Ortiz and Hieb pieces both appear in the volume edited by Ortiz in 1972, *New Perspectives on the Pueblos*.

11. Lévy-Bruhl, *How Natives Think*, pp. 43–44.

12. John Wesley Powell, introduction to *Zuñi Folk Tales*, pp. x–xi.

13. Clark Wissler, *The Relation of Nature to Man in Aboriginal America*, p. 113.

14. Paul S. Martin, *Digging into History: A Brief Account of Fifteen Years of Archaeological Work in New Mexico*, p. 81.

15. Clark Wissler, *Indians of the United States*, pp. 32–33

16. Alfred L. Kroeber, review of *Zuñi Breadstuff*, p. 479.

A Lesson in History

L IKE the teller of Indian tales, I bid you back more than three
hundred and fifty years, to the time "when the seven ruins of
Kiä-ki-me, Ma'-tsa-ki, Ha'-lo-na, A'-pina-wa, Háni-pas-sa, Ha'-
wi-k-kuh, and Kia'-na-we were peopled by the ancestors of the
Zuñis and towns stood where now are but old heaps of walls in
every direction about the old houses of our ancients."

[There follows a lengthy review of early Spanish accounts
bearing on the discovery and conquest of the "seven cities of
Cibola." The first contact had been made by the four survivors of
the ill-fated Narvaez expedition which had sailed from Spain in
1527 with the aim of conquering the Floridas but which, beset by
shipwreck and other disasters, had been reduced to a handful of
men who washed ashore on the coast of what is now Louisiana
and were captured by Indians. Four escaped, including an
officer (and ultimately author), Alvar Nuñez Cabeza de Vaca, and
a Barbary Black named Estavanico, and in the course of their
famous nine-year-long wanderings westward to the Gulf of
California they came upon the Pueblo towns. Their reports led to
further expeditions, culminating in that led by Coronado, who
conquered the territory and opened it, as well, for the Franciscan
missionaries. On one of these expeditions, meanwhile, Estevanico, who, according to the old Spanish account, had set off
carrying a mace decorated with red feathers, was killed by the
pueblo Indians. At the time of the episode recounted below,
however, Cushing (by his own report, at any rate, though see
letters of October 29, 1879, and July 2, 1880) had not yet come

across any of this earlier history, either from the Spanish or from the Pueblo point of view.]

One night as I sat reading an old work of travel by the firelight in the little room they had assigned me, one by one four old men came in, rolled their corn husk cigarettes, and fell to watching me. For a long time they smoked and nodded at one another. Finally one of them, acting as spokesman for the rest, punched my foot with his out-stretched fingers and exclaimed,

"Little Brother!"

"What?" I asked.

"Look here. What do the marks in that paper-fold say to you?"

"Old things," said I.

"How old?"

"Maybe three hundred years; maybe three hundred and fifty," I chanced to reply.

"Three hundred and fifty years," he repeated. "Three hundred and *fifty*! How long is that?"

"Why three hundred and fifty years."

"I know," said he. "I *know*! But three hundred and fifty sheep, that's easy! Three hundred and fifty *years—that* takes too *long*. Hold, little brother, lay out three hundred and fifty corn-grains on the floor in a straight line, then we can tell how long three hundred and fifty years is."

The corn was brought in a twinkling and curious to see the result, I began placing it, kernel by kernel, in a straight line across the floor. Meanwhile, the old men bent eagerly over my back, wrinkling their foreheads, counting up their long-nailed fingers, conferring together, and sliding the corn grains here and there with little slivers. When I had nearly completed the number, they began, wholly after their own fashion, to reckon.

"Now that's one father," said they, "and his son growing up; *one*! *two*!"

So they went on until they reached nearly the end of the row, when suddenly the eldest jumped up, his face beaming with inner light, and exclaimed,

"Why *here*, brothers, ten men's ages, *eleven*! That must have been when our ancients killed the Black Mexican at Kiä-ki-me.

Hold, little brother, does your old book tell anything about that?"

"No," said I to him most eagerly, "but you must."

"Why yes, of course," he replied, while the others settled back to their cigarettes. And he began:

"It is to be believed," said he, "that a long time ago, when roofs lay over the walls of Kiä-ki-me, when smoke hung over the house-tops, and the ladder-rounds were still unbroken—It was then that the Black Mexicans came from their abodes in Everlasting Summerland. One day, unexpected, out of 'Hemlock Cañon,' they came, and descended to Kiä-ki-me. But when they said they would enter the covered way, it seems that our ancients looked not gently on them, but with these Black Mexicans came many Indians of Sónō-li, as they call it now, who carried war feathers and long bows and cane arrows like the Apaches, who were enemies of our ancients; therefore these our ancients, being always bad tempered and quick to anger, made fools of themselves after their fashion, rushed into their town and out of their town, shouting, skipping and shooting with sling-stones and arrows and war clubs. Then the Indians of Sónō-li set up a great howl, and then they and our ancients did much ill to one another. Then and thus, was killed by our ancients, right where the stone stands down by the arroyo of Kiä-ki-me, one of the Black Mexicans. . . . Then the rest ran away, chased by our grandfathers, and went back toward their country in the Land of Everlasting Summer. But after they had steadied themselves and stopped talking, our ancients felt sorry; for they thought, 'Now we have made bad business, for after a while, these people, being angered, will come again.' So they felt always in danger and went about watching the bushes. By and by they did come back, those black Mexicans, and with them many men of Sónō-li. They wore coats of iron and even bonnets of metal and carried for weapons short canes that spit fire and made thunder. Thus it was in the days of Kiä-ki-me."

. . . .

If we but call to mind the red feathers on Estevanico's mace, which to the Zuñi is a symbol of violence, and if we further reflect that Indians seeing the Negro for the first time must have thought there were others like him, and been filled with the idea, the parallels in the two relations evidence how far we may, within certain limitations, trust to the accuracy of at least *Zuñi* Indian tradition. . . .

And I am guilty of no vain sentiment when I say that in this, the year of our Lord 1885, we have but to travel by rail six days, by diligence one day more, and in a flood of red sunset light, the glory of which the like is never known to these eastern slopes, we approach the site of Ha'-lo-na, the last of the Seven Lost Cities. As the shadows of night descend, and the stars like a thousand young moons come out, we turn into the northern court of that city. Save for dogs and the muffled tread of moccasins, it is as silent as are its sisters in ruin; save for the ruddy fire light at a few windows, the spark spangled banners of smoke from its house tops, as dreary and dusky. Yet by climbing two sky holes, behold there is life that we could not have dreamed of. Outside stands a wall that was old at the Conquest, that was seen by Coronado, near which rested Espejo. Inside are the rafters, stone-hewn and smoke-blackened, that stretched over the helmets of the first Spanish soldiers. The same mill is grating and scraping, the same song is crooned to its motion, in the same language questions and answers that were heard by those first Spanish soldiers, after Cibola bowed to their power.

Still, I hear someone ask, "*Is* the language the same, *are* the songs the same? And if so, are the religion, dances, customs, and character of those who now sit around that ancient hearthstone the same as they were in the days of those soldiers?"

Two hundred and fifty years of Franciscan teaching and Spanish rule; thirty years of American fraud and aggression; none of these things are as aught against the enduring genius of that ancient tongue and *tone*, and the philosophies and creeds framed in them a thousand years ago *must* endure and live, so long as, unwritten, that language endures and lives.

From "The Discovery of Zuñi, or the Ancient Provinces of Cibola and the Seven Lost Cities," a lecture given before the Geographic Society of Boston in 1885. Box No. 1, Hodge-Cushing Collection, Southwest Museum, Los Angeles. Printed with the permission of the Southwest Museum.

Zuñi and the Missionaries: Keeping the Old Ways

TOWARD the end of the century, between 1775 and 1780, the old Church of Our Lady of Guadalupe, which now harbors only burros and shivering dogs of cold winter nights and is toppling to ruin in the middle of the grand plaza of Zuñi, was built and beautifully decorated with carved altar pieces and paintings, gifts from the King of Spain to the Indies and work of resident monks as well. Its walls were painted—as the more recent plasterings scaling off here and there reveal—by Zuñi artists, who scrupled not to mingle many a pagan symbol of the gods of wind, rain, and lightning, sunlight, storm-dark and tempest, war and magic, and, more than all, emblems of their beloved goddess-virgins of corn-growing, with the bright-colored Christian decorations. And doubtless their sedulous teachers or masters, as the case may have been, understanding little, if aught, of the meanings of these things, were well pleased that these reluctant proselytes should manifest so much of zeal and bestow such loving care on this temple of the holy and only true faith.

In a measure, the padres were right. The Indians thenceforward did manifest not only more care for the mission, but more readiness to attend mass and observe the various holy days of the church. To be baptized and receive baptismal names they had ever been willing, nay, eager, for they were permitted, if only as a means of identification, to retain their own *tik'ya shiiwe* ("names totemic of the sacred assemblies"), which names the priests of the mission innocently adopted for them as surnames and scrupulously recorded in the quaint old leather-covered folios of their mission and church. Thus it chances that in these faded but beautifully and piously indicted pages of a century ago I find names so familiar, so like those I heard given only a few years since to aged Zuñi friends now passed away, that, standing out clearly from the midst of the formal Spanish phrases of these old-time books, they seem like the voices of the dead of other generations, and they tell even more clearly than such voices could tell of the causes which worked to render the Zuñis of those times apparently so reconciled to Spanish teaching and domination.

For it is manifest that when, as the meaning of his name informs us, the chief priest of the *Kâ'-kâ-kwe*, or mythic drama-dancers of a hundred years ago, entered the Church of Our Lady of Guadalupe and was registered as "Feliciano Pautiatzanilunquia" (Pautia-tsani-lun-k'ya), or "Felix Of-the-sacred-dancers-glorious-sun-god-youth," neither he nor any of his attendant clan relatives, whose names are also recorded, thought of renouncing their allegiance to the gods of Zuñi or the ever sacred *Kâ'-kâ*; but that they thought only of gaining the magic of purification and the name-potency of the gods of another people, as well as of securing the sanctification if not recognition of their own gods and priests by these other gods and priests.

That this was so is shown also by the sacred character almost invariably of even the less exalted tribal names they gave. Thus, those belonging not to the priesthood, yet to the "mid-most" or septuarchial clans, as "Francisco Kautzitihua" (Káutsi-tiwa), or "Francis Giver-of-the-midmost-dance," and "Angela Kahuitietza" (Káwiti Etsa), or "Angelina Of-the-midmost-dance Little maiden;" and those belonging to yet other clan divisions and the *Kâ'-kâ*, like "Manuel Layatzilunquia" (Laíyatsi Lúnk'ya), or "Emanuel Of-the-flowing plume Glorious-tall-bearer," and "María Laytzitilutza" (Laítsitilutsa), or "Mary Of-the-soft-flowing-plume Little-bearer;" and, finally, even the least sacred but mythical clan names, such as "Manuel Layujtigua" (Lá-yúhtiwa) or "Emanuel Plume-of-lightness," a name of the Eagle clan and upper division of the tribe; and "Lucia Jayatzemietza," (Haíya Tsemi Étsa) or "Lucy Of-green-growing-things-ever-thinking Little-maiden," which, alluding to the leaves of growing corn and vines when watched by the young unmarried girls, is one of the Corn or Seed clan names belonging to the southern division. Only very rarely were the colloquial names one hears most often in Zuñi (the sacred and totemic names are considered too precious for common use) given for baptismal registration. I have found but two or three. One of these is written "Estévan Nato Jasti" (Náto Hastin) or "Stephen Oldtobacco," a Navajo sobriquet which, in common with the few others like it, was undoubtedly offered reluctantly in place of the "true and sacred name," because some relative who had recently borne it was dead and therefore his name could not be pronounced aloud lest his spirit and the hearts of those who mourned him be disturbed.

But the presence of these ordinary names evidences no less than that of the more "idolatrous" ones, the uncompromisingly paganistic spirit of these supposedly converted Indians, and the unmodified fashion of their thoughts at the period of their truest apparent allegiance, or at least submission, to the church. . . . They evidence not merely the exceeding vitality of the native Zuñi cult, but at the same time present an explanation of the strange spectacle of earnest propagandists everywhere vigilantly seeking out and ruthlessly repressing the native priesthood and their dances and other ceremonials, yet, unconsciously to themselves, solemnizing these very things by their rites of baptism, officially recognizing, in the eyes of the Indians, the very names and titles of the officiators and offices they otherwise persecuted and denounced. It was quite of a piece with all this that during the acts of worship performed in the old church at that time by the Zuñis, whilst they knelt at mass or responded as taught to the mysterious and to them magic, but otherwise meaningless, credo, they scattered in secret their sacred white prayer-meal, and invoked not only the souls of their dead priests—who as caciques or rulers of the pueblo were accorded the distinction of burial in the church, under their very feet—but also, the tribal medicine-plumes and fetiches hidden away under the very altar where stood the archenemy of their religion!

So, in following further the Spanish history of Zuñi, we need not be surprised that all went well for a while after the completion of the church, and that more than twenty priests were at one time and another resident missionaries of Zuñi. Nor, on the other hand, need we be surprised that when in the early part of the present century these missionaries began to leave the pagan surnames out of their registers giving Spanish names instead—began to suspect, perhaps, the nature of the wall paintings, or for some other reason had them whitewashed away—and sought more assiduously than ever, in the deepest hiding places of the many-storied pueblo, to surprise the native priests at their unholy pagan practices, that the records of baptisms in the old books grew fewer and fewer, and that as the secular power withdrew more and more its support of the clergy, the latter could no longer control their disaffected flock, and that finally the old mission had to be abandoned, never again to be reoccupied save on occasions of the parochial visits of priests resident in far-away Mexican towns or in other Indian pueblos.

Nevertheless, although the old church was thus abandoned and is now utterly neglected, there lingers still with the Indians a singular sentiment for it, and this has been supposed to indicate that they retain some conscious remnant of the faith and teachings for which it once stood. . . . A few years since, a party of Americans who accompanied me to Zuñi desecrated the beautiful antique shrine of the church, carrying away "Our Lady of Guadalupe of the Sacred Heart," the guardian angels, and some of the painted bas-reliefs attached to the frame of the altar. When this was discovered by the Indians, consternation seized the whole tribe; council after council was held, at which I was alternately berated (because people who had come there with me had thus "plundered their fathers' house"), and entreated to plead with "Wasintona" to have these "precious saints and sacred masks of their fathers" returned to them.

Believing at the time that the Indians really reverenced these things as Christian emblems, and myself reverencing sincerely the memory of the noble missionaries who had braved death and labored so many years in the cause of their faith and for the good of these Indians, I promised either to have the original relics returned or to bring them new saints; and I also urged them to join me in cleaning out the old church, repairing the rents in its walls and roof, and plastering once more its rain-streaked interior. But at this point their mood seemed to change. The chiefs and old men puffed their cigarettes, unmoved by the most eloquent appeals I could make, save to say, quite irrelevantly, that I "talked well," and that all my thoughts were good, very good, but they could not heed them.

I asked them if they did not care for their *míssa k'yakwi* or mission-house. "Yea, verily," they replied, with fervor. "It was the sacred place of our fathers, even more sacred than were the things taken away therefrom."

I asked if they would not, then, in memory of those fathers, restore its beauty.

"Nay, " they replied, "we could not, alas! for it was the míssa-house of our fathers who are dead, and dead is the míssa-house! May the fathers be made to live again by the adding of meat to their bones? How, then, may the míssa-house be made alive again by the adding of mud to its walls?"

Not long afterward there was a furious night storm of wind and rain. On the following morning, great seams appeared in the northern walls of the old building. I called a council of the Indians and urged that since they would not repair the míssa-house, it be torn down; for it might fall over some day and kill the women and children as they passed through the narrow alley it overshadowed, on their way to and from the spring. Again I was told that my words were good, but alas! they could not heed them; that it was the míssa-house of their fathers! How, if they took it away, would the fathers know their own? It was well that the wind and rain wore it away, as time wasted away their fathers' bones. That mattered not, for it was the work of the beloved, whereof they, the fathers, were aware, but for themselves to move it suddenly away, that were worse than the despoiling of the shrine; for it was the house of the fathers, the shrine only a thing thereof, not a thing of the fathers as verily as was the house itself.

From their point of view this reasoning of the Indians was perfectly consistent, based as it was on their belief that the souls of their ancestors were mediators and that their mortal remains and the places and things thereof were means of invoking them, quite as sacrifices are supposed to be, for the time being, the mortal and mediate parts of the gods and spirits to which they have been offered, hence a potent means of invoking them. . . .

I need not add that this fully accounts for the contradictory behavior of the Indians in reference to the old church, the burial ground, and other things pertaining to it. The church could not be rebuilt. It had been dead so long that, rehabilitated, it would be no longer familiar to the "fathers" who in spirit had witnessed its decay. Nor could it be taken suddenly away. It had stood so long that, missing it, they would be sad, or might perhaps even abandon it.[1]

The Zuñi faith, as revealed in this sketch of more than three hundred and fifty years of Spanish intercourse, is as a drop of oil in water, surrounded and touched at every point, yet in no place penetrated or changed inwardly by the flood of alien belief that descended upon it. Herein is exemplified anew the tendency of primitive-minded man to interpret unfamiliar things more directly than simply, according to their appearances merely, not by analysis in our sense of the term; and to make his interpretations, no less than as we ourselves do, always in the light of what he already familiarly believes or habitually thinks he knows. Hence, of necessity he adjusts other beliefs and opinions to his own, but never his own beliefs and opinions to others; and even his usages are almost never changed in spirit, however much so in externals, until all else in his life is changed. Thus, he is slow to adopt from alien peoples any but material suggestions, these even, strictly according as they suit his ways of life; and whatever he does adopt, or rather absorb and assimilate, from the culture and lore of another people, neither distorts nor obscures his native culture, neither discolors nor displaces his original lore.

All of the foregoing suggests what might be more fully shown by further examples, the aboriginal and uncontaminated character—so far as a modern like myself can represent it—of the myths delineated in ["Outlines of Zuñi Creation Myths"]. Yet a casual visitor to Zuñi, seeing but unable to analyze the signs above noted, would be led to infer quite the contrary by other and more patent signs. He would see horses, cattle and donkeys, sheep and goats, to say nothing of swine and a few scrawny chickens. He would see peach orchards and wheat fields, carts (and wagons now), and tools of metal; would find, too, in queer out-of-the-way little rooms native silversmiths plying their primitive bellows and deftly using a few crude tools of iron and stone to turn their scant silver coins into bright buttons, bosses, beads, and bracelets, which every well-conditioned Zuñi wears; and he would see worn also, especially by the men, clothing of gaudy calico and other thin products of the looms of civilization. Indeed, if one did not see these things and rate them as at first the gifts to this people of those noble old Franciscan friars and their harder-handed less noble Spanish companions, infinitely more pathetic than it is would be the history of the otherwise vain effort I have above outlined; for it is not to be forgotten that the principal of these gifts have been of incalculable value to the Zuñi. They have helped to preserve him, through an era of new external conditions, from the fate that met more than thirty other and less favored Pueblo tribes—annihilation by the better-armed, ceaselessly prowling Navajo and Apache. And for this alone, their almost sole accomplishment of lasting good to the Zuñi, not in vain were spent and given the lives of the early mission fathers.

It is intimated that aside from adding such resources to the tribe as enabled it to survive a time of fearful stress and danger, even the introduction of Spanish plants, animals, and products did not greatly change the Zuñis. This is truer than would at first seem possible. The Zuñi was already a tiller of the soil when wheat and peaches were given him. To this day he plants and irrigates his peach trees and wheat crops much as he anciently planted and watered his corn—in hills, hoeing all with equal assiduity; and he does not reap his wheat, but gathers it as he gathers his corn in the ear. Thus, only the kind of grain is new. The art of rearing it and ways of husbanding and using it remain unchanged. The Zuñi was already a herder when sheep and goats were given him. He had not only extensive preserves of rabbits and deer, but also herds—rather than flocks—of turkeys, which by day were driven out over the plains and mesas for feeding, and at night housed near the towns or in distant shelters and corrals. It is probable that his ancestry had even other domesticated animals. And he used the flesh of these animals as food, their feathers and fur as the materials for his wonderfully knitted, woven, and twilled garments and robes, as he now uses the mutton and goat meat for food, and the wool of the sheep for his equally well-knitted, woven, and twilled, though less beautiful, garments and robes. Thus, only the kinds (and degree of productivity) of the animals are new; the arts of caring for them and modes of using their products are unchanged. This is true even in detail. When I first went to live with the Zuñis, their sheep were plucked, not sheared, with flat strips of band iron in place of the bone spatulae originally used in plucking the turkeys; and the herders always scrupulously picked up stray flecks of wool—calling it "down," not hair, nor fur—and spinning it, knitting, too, at their long woolen leggings as they followed their sheep, all as their fore-fathers used ever to pick up and twirl the stray feathers and knit at their down kilts and tunics as they followed and herded their turkeys. Even the silversmiths of Zuñi today work coins over as their ancestors of the stone-using age worked up bits of copper, not only using tools of stone and bone for the purpose but using even the iron tools of the Spaniard mostly in stone-age fashion.

This applies equally to their handling of the hoes, hatchets, and knives of civilized man. They use their hoes—the heaviest they can get—as if weighted, like the wooden and bone hoes of antiquity, vertically, not horizontally. They use their hatchets or axes and knives more for hacking and scraping and chipping than for chopping, hewing, and whittling, and in such operations they prefer working toward themselves to working from themselves, as we work. Finally, their garments of calico and muslin are new only in material. They are cut after the old fashion of the ancestral buckskin breeches and shirts, poncho coats of feathers and fur or fiber, and down or cotton breech clouts, while in the silver rings and bracelets of today, not only the shapes but even the half-natural markings of the original shell rings and bracelets survive, and the silver buttons and bosses but perpetuate and multiply those once made of copper as well as of shell and white bone.

Thus, only one absolutely new practical element and activity was introduced by the Spaniards—beasts of burden and beast transportation and labor. But until the present century cattle were not used natively for drawing loads or plows, the latter of which, until recently being made of a convenient fork, are only enlarged harrowing-sticks pointed with a leaf of iron in place of the blade of flint; nor were carts employed. Burdens were transported in panniers adapted to the backs of burros instead of to the shoulders of men.

The Zuñi is a splendid rider, but even now his longest journeys are made on foot in the old way. He has for centuries lived a settled life, traveling but little, and the horse has therefore not played a very conspicuous part in his later life as in the lives of less sedentary peoples, and is consequently unheard of, as are all new things—including the greatest of all, the white man himself—in his tribal lore, or the folk tales, myths, and rituals of his sacred cult-societies. All this strengthens materially the claim heretofore made, that in mind, and especially in religious culture, the Zuñi is almost as strictly archaic as in the days ere his land was discovered.

From "Outlines of Zuñi Creation Myths," *Thirteenth Annual Report of the Bureau of American Ethnology, 1891–1892* (Washington, D.C., 1896), pp. 333–41.

Note

1. The church has now been restored, by the diocese, and is open as a tourist attraction. [Ed. note]

Outline of Zuñi Mytho-Sociologic Organization

THE Zuñi of today number scarcely 1,700 and, as is well known, they inhabit only a single large pueblo—single in more senses than one, for it is not a village of separate houses, but a village of six or seven separate parts in which the houses are mere apartments or divisions, so to say. This pueblo, however, is divided, not always clearly to the eye, but very clearly in the estimation of the people themselves, into seven parts, corresponding, not perhaps in arrangement topographically, but in sequence, to their subdivisions of the "worlds" or world-quarters of this world. Thus, one division of the town is supposed to be related to the north and to be centered in its kiva or estufa, which may or may not be, however, in its center; another division represents the west, another the south, another the east, yet another the upper world and another the lower world, while a final division represents the middle or mother and synthetic combination of them all in this world.

By reference to the early Spanish history of the pueblo it may be seen that when discovered, the Áshiwi or Zuñis were living in seven quite widely separated towns, the celebrated Seven Cities of Cibola, and that this theoretic subdivision of the only one of these towns now remaining is in some measure a survival of the original subdivision of the tribe into seven sub-tribes inhabiting as many separate towns. It is evident that in both cases, however, the arrangement was, and is, if we may call it such, a mythic organization; hence my use of the term the mytho-sociologic organization of the tribe. At any rate, this is the key to their sociology as well as to their mythic conceptions of space and the universe. In common with all other Indian tribes of North America thus far studied, the Zuñis are divided into clans, or artificial kinship groups, with inheritance in the female line. Of these clans there are, or until recently there were, nineteen, and these in turn, with the exception of one, are grouped in threes to correspond to the mythic subdivision I have above alluded to. These clans are also, as are those of all other Indians, totemic; that is, they bear the names and are supposed to have intimate relationship with various animals, plants, and objects or elements. Named by their totems they are as follows:

Kâ'lokta-kwe, Crane or Pelican people; *Póyi-kwe* (nearly extinct), Grouse or Sagecock people; *Ta'hluptsi-kwe* (nearly extinct), Yellow-wood or Evergreen-oak people; *Ain'shi-kwe,* Bear people; *Súski-kwe,* Coyote people; *Aiyaho-kwe,* Red-top plant or Spring-herb people; *Ána-kwe,* Tobacco people; *Tâ'a-kwe,* Maize-plant people; *Tónashi-kwe,* Badger people; *Shóhoita-kwe,* Deer people; *Máawi-kwe* (extinct), Antelope people; *Tóna-kwe,* Turkey people; *Yä'tok'ya-kwe,* Sun people; *Ápoya-kwe* (extinct), Sky people; *K'yä'k-yäli-kwe,* Eagle people; *Ták'ya-kwe,* Toad or Frog people; *K'yána-kwe* (extinct), Water people; *Chitola-kwe* (nearly extinct), Rattlesnake people; *Píchi-kwe,* Parrot-Macaw people.

Of these clans the first group of three appertains to the north, the second to the west, the third to the south, the fourth to the east, the fifth to the upper or zenith, and the sixth to the lower or nadir region; while the single clan of the Macaw is characterized as "midmost," or of the middle, and also as the all-containing or mother clan of the entire tribe, for in it the seed of the priesthood of the houses is supposed to be preserved. The Zuñi explanation of this very remarkable, yet when understood and comprehended, very simple and natural grouping of the clans or totems is exceedingly interesting, and also significant whether it throw light on the origin, or at least the native meaning, of totemic systems in general, as would at first seem to be the case, or whether, as is more probably the case in this instance, it indicates a native classification, so to say, or reclassification of clans which existed before the culture had been elaborated to its present point. Briefly, the clans of the north—that is, those of the Crane, the Grouse, and Evergreen-oak—are grouped together and are held to be related to the north because of their peculiar fitness for the region whence comes the cold and wherein the season of winter itself is supposed to be created, for the crane each autumn appears in the van of winter, the grouse does not flee from the approach of winter but puts on his coat of white and traverses the forests of the snow-clad mountains as freely as other birds traverse summer fields and woodlands, caring not for the cold, and the evergreen-oak grows as green and is as sturdy in winter as other trees are in spring or summer; hence these are totems and in a sense god-beings of the north and of winter, and the clanspeople named after them and considered as, mythically at least, their breath-children, are therefore grouped together and related to the north and winter as are their totems. And as the bear, whose coat is grizzly like the evening twilight or black like the darkness of night, and the gray coyote, who prowls amidst the sagebrush at evening and goes forth and cries in the night-time, and the spring herb or the red-top plant, which blooms earliest of all flowers in spring when first the moisture-laden winds from the west begin to blow—these and the people named after them are as appropriately grouped in the west. The badger, who digs his hole on the sunny sides of hills and in winter appears only when the sun shines warm above them, who excavates among the roots of the juniper and the cedar from which fire is kindled with the fire drill; the wild tobacco, which grows only where fires have burned, and the corn which anciently came from the south and is still supposed to get its birth from the southland, and its warmth—these are grouped in the south. The turkey, which wakes with the dawn and helps to awaken the dawn by his cries; the antelope and the deer, who traverse far mesas and valleys in the twilight of the dawn—these and their children are therefore grouped in the east. And it is not difficult to understand why the sun, the sky (or turkis), and the eagle appertain to the upper world; nor why the toad, the water, and the rattlesnake appertain to the lower world.

By this arrangement of the world into great quarters, or rather as the Zuñis conceive it, into several worlds corresponding to the four quarters and the zenith and the nadir, and by this grouping of the towns, or later of the wards (so to call them) in the town, according to such mythical division of the world, and finally the grouping of the totems in turn within the divisions thus made, not only the ceremonial life of the people, but all their governmental arrangements as well, are completely systemized. Something akin to written statutes results from this and similar related arrangements, for each region is given its appropriate color and number, according to its relation to one of the regions I have named or to others of those regions. Thus the north is designated as yellow with the Zuñis, because the light at morning and evening in winter time is yellow, as also is the auroral light. The west is known as the blue world, not only because of the blue or gray twilight at evening, but also because westward from Zuñiland lies the blue Pacific. The south is designated as red, it being the region of summer and of fire, which is red; and for an obvious reason the east is designated white (like dawn light); while the upper region is many-colored, like the sunlight on the clouds, and the lower region black, like the caves and deep springs of the world. Finally, the midmost, so often mentioned in the following outline, is colored of all these colors, because, being representative of this (which is the central world and of which in turn Zuñi is the very middle or navel), it contains all the other quarters or regions, or is at least divisible into them. Again each region—at least each of the four cardinal regions, namely, north, west, south, and east—is the home or center of a special element, as well as of one of the four seasons each element produces. Thus the north is the place of wind, breath, or air, the west of water, the south of fire, and the east of earth or the seeds of earth; correspondingly, the north is of course the place of winter or its origin, the west of spring, the south of summer, and the east of autumn. This is all because from the north and in winter blow the fiercest, the greatest winds or breaths, as these people esteem them; from the west early in spring come the moistened breaths of the waters in early rains; from the south comes the greatest heat that with dryness is followed by summer, and from the east blow the winds that bring the frosts that in turn mature the seeds and perfect the year in autumn. By means of this arrangement no ceremonial is ever performed and no council ever held in which there is the least doubt as to the position which a member of a given clan shall occupy in it, for according to the season in which the ceremonial

is held, or according to the reason for which a council is con-
vened, one or another of the clan groups of one or another of the
regions will take precedence for the time; the natural sequence
being, however, first the north, second the west, third the south,
fourth the east, fifth the upper, and sixth the lower; but first, as
well as last, the middle. But this, to the Zuñi, normal sequence of
the regions and clan groups, etc., has been determined by the
apparent sequence of the phenomena of the seasons, and of their
relations to one another; for the masterful, all conquering element, the first necessity of life itself, and to all activity, is the
wind, the breath, and its cold, the latter overmastering, in winter
all the other elements as well as all other existences save those
especially adapted to it or potent in it, like those of the totems
and gods and their children of the north. But in spring, when
with the first appearance of the bear and the first supposed
growls of his spirit masters in the thunders and winds of that time
their breaths begin to bring water from the ocean world, then the
strength of the winter is broken, and the snows thereby melted
away, and the earth is revivified with drink, in order that with the
warmth of summer from the south things may grow and be
cherished toward their old age or maturity and perfection, and
finally toward their death or sleeping in winter by the frost-laden
breaths of autumn and the east.

Believing, as the Zuñis do, in this arrangement of the universe and this distribution of elements and beings chiefly concerned in them, and finally in the relationship of their clans and
the members thereof to these elementary beings, it is but natural
that they should have societies or secret orders or cult institutions composed of the elders or leading members of each group
of their clans as above classified. The seriation of these secret
and occult medicine societies, or, better, perhaps, societies of
magic, is one of the greatest consequence and interest. Yet it can
but be touched upon here. In strict accordance with succession
of the four seasons and their elements, and with their supposed
relationship to these, are classified the four fundamental activities of primitive life, namely, as relating to the north and its
masterfulness and destructiveness in cold, is war and destruction; relating to the west is war cure and hunting; to the south,
husbandry and medicine; to the east, magic and religion; while

the above, the below, and the middle relate in one way or another to all these divisions. As a consequence, the societies of cold or winter are found to be grouped, not rigidly, but at least theoretically, in the northern clans, and they are, respectively: 'Hléwe-kwe, Ice-wand people or band; *Áchia-kwe*, Knife people or band; *Kâ'shi-kwe*, Cactus people or band; for the west: *Pí'hla-kwe*, Priesthood of the Bow or Bow people or band (*Ápi'hlan Shiwani*, Priests of the Bow); *Sániyak'ya-kwe*, Priesthood of the Hunt or Coyote people or band; for the south: *Máke'hlána-kwe*, Great fire (ember) people or band; *Máketsána-kwe*, Little fire (ember) people or band; of the east: *Shíwana-kwe*, Priests of the Priesthood people or band; *Úhuhu-kwe*, Cottonwood-down people or band; *Shúme-kwe*, or *Kâ'Kâ'hlána-kwe*, Bird-monster people or band, otherwise known as the Great Dance-drama people or band; for the upper region: *Néwe-kwe*, Galaxy people or band or the All-consumer or Scavenger people or band (or life preservers); and for the lower regions: *Chítola-kwe*, Rattlesnake people or band, generators (or life makers). Finally, as produced from all the clans and as representative alike of all the clans and through a tribal septuarchy of all the regions and divisions in the midmost, and finally as representative of all the cult societies above mentioned is the *Kâ'-kâ* or *Ákâkâ-kwe* or Mythic Dance drama people or organization. It may be seen of these mytho-sociologic organizations that they are a system within a system, and that it contains also systems within systems, all founded on this classification according to the six-fold division of things, and in turn the six-fold division of each of these divisions of things. To such an extent, indeed, is carried this tendency to classify according to the number of the six regions with its seventh synthesis of them all (the latter sometimes apparent, sometimes nonappearing) that not only are the subdivisions of the societies also again subdivided according to this arrangement, but each clan is subdivided both according to such a six-fold arrangement and according to the subsidiary relations of the six parts of its totem. The tribal division made up of the clans of the north takes precedence ceremonially, occupying the position of elder brother or the oldest ancestor, as the case might be. The west is the younger brother of this, and in turn, the south of the west, the east of the south, the upper of the east, the under of them all, while the middle division is supposed to be a representative being, the heart or navel of all the brothers of the regions first and last, as well as elder and younger. In each clan is to be found a set of names called the names of childhood. These names are more of titles than of cognomens. They are determined upon by sociologic and divinistic modes, and are bestowed in childhood as the "verity names" or titles of the children to whom given. But this body of names relating to any one totem—for instance, to one of the beast totems—will not be the name of the totem beast itself, but will be names both of the totem in its various conditions and of various parts of the totem, or of its functions, or of its attributes, actual or mythical. Now these parts or functions, or attributes of the parts or functions, are subdivided also in a six-fold manner, so that the name relating to one member of the totem—for example, like the right arm or leg of the animal thereof—would correspond to the north, and would be the first in honor in a clan (not itself of the northern group); then the name relating to another member—say to the left leg or arm and its powers, etc.—would pertain to the west and would be second in honor; and another member—say the right foot—to the south and would be third in honor; and of another member—say the left foot—to the east and would be fourth in honor; to another— say the head—to the upper regions and would be fifth in honor; and another—say the tail—to the lower region and would be sixth in honor; while the heart or the navel and center of the being would be first as well as last in honor. The studies of Major Powell among the Maskoki and other tribes have made it very clear that kinship terms, so called, among other Indian tribes (and the rule will apply no less or perhaps even more strictly to the Zuñis) are rather devices for determining relative rank or authority as signified by relative age, as elder or younger of the person addressed or spoken of by the term of relationship. So that it is quite impossible for a Zuñi speaking to another to say simply brother; it is always necessary to say elder brother or younger brother, by which the speaker himself affirms his relative age or rank; also it is customary for one clansman to address another clansman by the same kinship name of brother-elder or brother-younger, uncle or nephew, etc.; but according as the clan of the one addressed ranks higher or lower than the clan of the one using the term of address, the word-symbol for elder or younger relationship must be used.

With such a system of arrangement as all this may be seen to be, with such a facile device for symbolizing the arrangement (not only according to number of the regions and their subdivisions in their relative succession and the succession of their elements and seasons, but also in colors attributed to them, etc.), and, finally, with such an arrangement of names correspondingly classified and of terms of relationship significant of rank rather than of consanguinal connection, mistake in the order of a ceremonial, a procession or a council is simply impossible, and the people employing such devices may be said to have written and to be writing their statutes and laws in all their daily relationships and utterances. Finally, with much to add, I must be content with simply stating that the high degree of systemization which has been attained by the Zuñis in thus grouping their clans severally and serially about a midmost group, we may see the influence of the coming together of two diverse peoples acting upon each other favorably to the development of both in the application of such conceptions to the conduct of tribal affairs. It would seem that the conception of the midmost, or that group within all these groups which seems to be made up of parts of them all, is inherent in such a system of world division and tribal subdivision corresponding thereto; but it may also well be that this conception of the middle was made more prominent with the Zuñis than with any other of our southwestern peoples through the influence of the earthquakes, which obviously caused their ancestors from the west again and again to change their places of abode, thus emphasizing the notion of getting nearer to or upon the lap or navel of the earth mother, where all these terrific and destructive movements, it was thought, would naturally cease.

Be this as it may, this notion of the "middle" and its relation to the rest has become the central fact indeed of Zuñi organization. It has given rise to the septuarchy I have so often alluded to; to the office of the mortally immortal *K'yäk'lu*, keeper of the rituals of creation, from which so much sanction for these fathers of the people is drawn; to the consequent fixing in a series like a string of sacred epics, a sort of inchoate Bible, of these myths of creation and migration; and finally, through all this accumulated influence, it has served to give solidarity to the Zuñi tribe at the time of its division into separate tribes, making the outlying pueblos they inhabited subsidiary to the central one, and in the native acceptation of the matter, mere parts of it.

From "Outlines of Zuñi Creation Myths," *Thirteenth Annual Report of the Bureau of American Ethnology, 1891–1892* (Washington, D.C., 1896), pp. 367–73.

Zuñi Fetiches

THE *Á-shi-wi*, or Zuñis, suppose the sun, moon, and stars, the sky, earth, and sea, in all their phenomena and elements; and all inanimate objects, as well as plants, animals, and men, to belong to one great system of all-conscious and interrelated life, in which the degrees of relationship seem to be determined largely, if not wholly, by the degrees of resemblance. In this system of life the starting point is man, the most finished, yet the lowest organism; at least, the lowest because most dependent and least mysterious. In just so far as an organism, actual or imaginary, resembles his, is it believed to be related to him and correspondingly mortal; in just so far as it is mysterious, is it considered removed from him, further advanced, powerful, and immortal. It thus happens that the animals, because alike mortal and endowed with similar physical functions and organs, are considered more nearly related to man than are the gods; more nearly related to the gods than is man, because more mysterious, and characterized by specific instincts and powers which man does not of himself possess. Again, the elements and phenomena of nature, because more mysterious, powerful and immortal, seem more closely related to the higher gods than are the animals; more closely related to the animals than are the higher gods, because their manifestations often resemble the operations of the former.

In consequence of this, and through the confusion of the subjective with the objective, any element or phenomenon in nature which is believed to possess a personal existence, is endowed with a personality analogous to that of the animal whose operations most resemble its manifestation. For instance, lightning is often given the form of a serpent, with or without an arrow-pointed tongue, because its course through the sky is serpentine, its stroke instantaneous and destructive; yet it is named *Wí-lo-lo-a-ne*, a word derived not from the name of the serpent itself, but from that of its most obvious trait, its gliding, zigzag motion. For this reason, the serpent is supposed to be more nearly related to lightning than to man; more nearly related to man than is lightning, because mortal and less mysterious. As further illustrative of the interminable relationships which are established on resemblances fancied or actual, the flint arrow-point may be cited. Although fashioned by man, it is regarded as originally the gift or "flesh" of lightning, as made by the power of lightning, and rendered more effective by these connections with the dread element; pursuant of which idea, the zigzag or lightning marks are added to the shafts of arrows. A chapter might be written concerning this idea, which may possibly help to explain the Celtic, Scandinavian, and Japanese beliefs concerning "elf-shafts," and "thunder-stones," and "bolts."

In like manner, the supernatural beings of man's fancy—the "master existences"—are supposed to be more nearly related to the personalities with which the elements and phenomena of nature are endowed than to either animals or men; because, like those elements and phenomena, and unlike men and animals, they are connected with remote tradition in a manner identical with their supposed existence to-day, and therefore are considered immortal.

To the above descriptions of the supernatural beings of Zuñi Theology should be added the statement that all of these beings are given the forms either of animals, of monsters compounded of man and beast, or of man. The animal gods comprise by far the largest class.

In the Zuñi, no general name is equivalent to "the gods," unless it be the two expressions which relate only to the higher or creating and controlling beings—the "causes," Creators and Masters, *"Pí-kwain-á-hâ-i"* (Surpassing Beings), and *"Á-tä-tchu"* (All-fathers), the beings superior to all others in wonder and power, and the "Makers" as well as the "Finishers" of existence. These last are classed with the supernatural beings, personalities of nature, object beings, etc., under one term—

a. *Í-shothl-ti-mon-á-hâ-i*, from *í-shothl-ti-mo-na* = ever recurring, immortal, and *á-hâ-i* = beings.

Likewise, the animals and animal gods, and sometimes even the supernatural beings, having animal or combined animal and human personalities, are designated by one term only—

b. *K'ia-pin-á-hâ-i*, from *k'ia-pin-na* = raw, and *á-hâ-i* = beings. Of these, however, three divisions are made:

(1.) *K'ia-pin-á-hâ-i* = game animals, specifically applied to those animals furnishing flesh to man.

(2.) *K'iä-shem-á-hâ-i*, from *k'iä-we* = water, *she-man* = wanting, and *á-hâ-i* = beings, the water animals, specially applied not only to them, but also to all animals and animal gods supposed to be associated sacredly with water, and through which water is supplicated.

(3.) *Wé-ma-á-hâ-i*, from *we-ma* = prey, and *á-hâ-i* = beings, "Prey Beings," applied alike to the prey animals and their representatives among the gods. Finally we have the terms—

c. *Ak-na-á-hâ-i*, from *ák-na* = done, cooked, or baked, ripe, and *á-hâ-i* = beings, the "Done Beings," referring to mankind; and

d. *Äsh-i-k'ia-á-hâ-i*, from *ä'-sh-k'ia* = made, finished, and *á-hâ-i* = beings, "Finished Beings," including the *dead* of mankind.

That very little distinction is made between these orders of life, or that they are at least closely related, seems to be indicated by the absence from the entire language of any general term for *God*. True, there are many beings in Zuñi Mythology godlike in attributes, anthropomorphic, monstrous, and elemental, which are known as the "Finishers or makers of the paths of life," while the most superior of all is called the "Holder of the paths (of our lives)," *Hâ'-no-o-na wí-la-po-na*. Not only these gods, but all supernatural beings, men, animals, plants, and many objects in nature, are regarded as personal existences, and are included in the one term *á-hâ-i*, from *á*, the plural particle signifying "all," and *hâ-i*, being or life, = "Life," "the Beings." This again leads us to the important and interesting conclusion that all beings, whether deistic and supernatural, or animistic and mortal, are regarded as belonging to one system; and that they are likewise believed to be related by blood seems to be indicated by the fact that human beings are spoken of as the "children of men," while *all* other beings are referred to as "the Fathers," the "All-fathers," and "Our Fathers."

It naturally follows from the Zuñi's philosophy of life, that his worship, while directed to the more mysterious and remote powers of nature, or, as he regards them, existences, should relate more especially to the animals; that, in fact, the animals, as more nearly related to himself than are these existences, more nearly related to these existences than to himself, should be frequently made to serve as mediators between them and him. We find this to be the case. It follows likewise that in his inability to differentiate the objective from the subjective he should establish relationships between natural objects which resemble animals and the animals themselves; that he should even ultimately imitate these animals for the sake of establishing such relationships, using such accidental resemblances as his *motives*, and thus developing a conventionality in all art connected with his worship. It follows that the special requirements of his life or of the life of his ancestors should influence him to select as his favored mediators or aids those animals which seemed best fitted, through peculiar characteristics and powers, to meet these requirements. This, too, we find to be the case, for, pre-eminently a man of war and the chase, like all savages, the Zuñi has chosen above all other animals those which supply him with food and useful material, together with the animals which prey on them, giving preference to the latter. Hence, while the name of the former class is applied preferably as a *general* term to all animals and animal gods, as previously explained, the name of the latter is used with equal preference as a term for all fetiches (*Wé-ma-we*), whether of the prey animals themselves or of other animals and beings. Of course it is equally natural, since they are connected with man both in the scale of being and in the power to supply his physical wants more nearly than are the higher gods, that the animals or animal gods should greatly outnumber and even give character to all others. We find that the Fetiches of the Zuñis relate mostly to the animal gods, and principally to the prey gods.

This fetichism seems to have arisen from the relationships

heretofore alluded to, and to be founded on the myths which have been invented to account for those relationships. It is therefore not surprising that those fetiches most valued by the Zuñis should be either natural concretions, or objects in which the evident original resemblance to animals has been only heightened by artificial means.

Another highly prized class of fetiches are, on the contrary, those which are elaborately carved, but show evidence, in their polish and dark patina, of great antiquity. They are either such as have been found by the Zuñis about pueblos formerly inhabited by their ancestors or are tribal possessions which have been handed down from generation to generation, until their makers, and even the fact that they were made by any member of the tribe, have been forgotten. It is supposed by the priests (Á-shi-wa-ni) of Zuñi that not only these, but all true fetiches, are either actual petrifactions of the animals they represent, or were such originally. Upon this supposition is founded the following tradition, [regarding the "drying of the world" by the Twin Gods in the "days of the new"].

Now that the surface of the earth was hardened, even the animals of prey, powerful and like the fathers (gods) themselves, would have devoured the children of men; and the Two thought it was not well that they should all be permitted to live, "for," said they, "alike will the children of men and the children of the animals of prey multiply themselves. The animals of prey are provided with talons and teeth; men are but poor, the finished beings of earth, therefore the weaker."

Whenever they came across the pathway of one of these animals, were he great mountain lion or but a mere mole, they struck him with the fire of lightning which they carried in their magic shield. *Thlu!* and instantly he was shriveled and burnt into stone.

Then said they to the animals that they had thus changed to stone, "That ye may not be evil unto men, but that ye may be a great good unto them, have we changed you into rock everlasting. By the magic breath of prey, by the heart that shall endure forever within you, shall ye be made to serve instead of to devour mankind."

Thus was the surface of the earth hardened and scorched

and many of all kinds of beings changed to stone. Thus, too, it happens that we find, here and there throughout the world, their forms, sometimes large like the beings themselves, sometimes shriveled and distorted. And we often see among the rocks the forms of many beings that live no longer, which shows us that all was different in the "days of the new."

Of these petrifactions, which are of course mere concretions or strangely eroded rock-forms, the Zuñis say, "Whomsoever of us may be met with the light of such great good fortune may *see* (discover, find) them and should treasure them for the sake of the sacred (magic) power which was given them in the days of the new. For the spirits of the We-ma-á-hâ-i still live, and are pleased to receive from us the Sacred Plume (of the heart—*Lä-sho-a-ni*), and sacred necklace of treasure (*Thlâ-thle-a*); hence they turn their ears and the ears of their brothers in our direction that they may hearken to our prayers (sacred talks) and know our wants."

This tradition not only furnishes additional evidence relative to the preceding statements, but also, taken in connection with the following belief, shows quite clearly to the native wherein lies the power of his fetiches. It is supposed that the hearts of the great animals of prey are infused with a spirit or medicine of magic influence over the hearts of the animals they prey upon, or the game animals (*K'ia-pin-á-hâ-i*); that their breaths (the "Breath of Life"—*Hâ-i-an-pi-nan-ne*—and soul are synonymous in Zuñi Mythology), derived from their hearts, and breathed upon their prey, whether near or far, never fail to overcome them, piercing their hearts and causing their limbs to stiffen, and the animals themselves to lose their strength. Moreover, the roar or cry of a beast of prey is accounted its *Sá-wa-ni-k'ia*, or magic medicine of destruction, which, heard by the game animals, is fatal to them, because it charms their senses, as does the breath their hearts. Since the mountain lion, for example, lives by the blood ("life fluid") and flesh of the game animals, and by these alone, he is endowed not only with the above powers, but with peculiar powers in the senses of sight and smell. Moreover, these powers, as derived from his heart, are preserved in his fetich, since his heart still lives, even though his person be changed to stone. . . .

The relative value of these varieties of fetiches depends

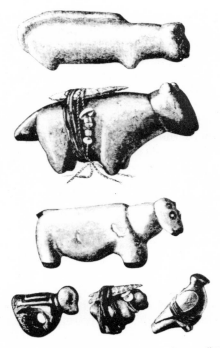

FIG. 32. Prey God Fetiches of the Six Regions. (From "Zuñi Fetiches")

largely upon the rank of the Animal god they represent. For instance, the Moutain Lion is not only master of the North, which takes precedence over all the other "ancient sacred spaces" (*Té-thlä-shi-na-we*), or regions, but is also the master of all the other Prey gods, if not of all other terrestrial animals. Notwithstanding the fact that the Coyote, in the Order of the Hunt (the Coyote society or the *Sá-ni-a-k'ia-kwe*), is given for traditional reasons higher *sacred* rank than the Mountain Lion, he is, as a Prey Being, one degree lower, being god of the West, which follows the North in order of importance. Hence we find the Mountain Lion and Coyote fetiches far more prized than any of the others, and correspondingly more numerous. The Coyote in rank is younger brother of the Mountain Lion, just as the Wild Cat is younger brother of the Coyote, the Wolf of the Wild Cat,

FIG. 33. Shield and Fetich of the Priesthood of the Bow. (From "Zuñi Fetiches")

and so on to the Mole, and less important Ground Owl. In relationship by blood, however, the yellow Mountain Lion is accounted older brother of the blue, red, white, spotted, and black Mountain Lions; the blue Coyote, older brother of the red, white, yellow, mottled or spotted, and black Coyotes.[1] So the Wild Cat of the South is regarded as the older brother of the Wild Cats of all the other five regions. And thus it is respectively with

FIG. 34. Shield and Fetich of the Priesthood of the Bow (From "Zuñi Fetiches")[2]

the Wolf, the Eagle, and the Mole. We find, therefore, that in the North all the gods of Prey are represented, as well as the Mountain Lion, only they are yellow. In the West all are represented, as well as the Coyote, only they are blue; and thus throughout the remaining four regions.

The Mountain Lion is further believed to be the special hunter of the Elk, Deer, and Bison (no longer an inhabitant of

New Mexico). His fetich is, therefore, preferred by the hunter of these animals. So, also, is the fetich of the Coyote preferred by the hunter of the Mountain Sheep; that of the Wild Cat, by the hunter of the Antelope; that of the Wolf, by the hunter of the rare and highly-valued *O-ho-li*; those of the Eagle and Falcon, by the hunter of Rabbits; and that of the Mole, by the hunter of other small game.

The exception to this rule is individual, and founded upon the belief that any one of the gods of Prey hunts to some extent the special game of all the other gods of Prey. Hence, any person who may discover either a concretion or natural object or an ancient fetich calling to mind or representing any one of the Prey gods will regard it as his special fetich, and almost invariably prefer it, since he believes it to have been "meted to" him (*añ-ik-tchi-a-k'ia*) by the gods.

· ·

From "Zuñi Fetiches," *Second Annual Report of the Bureau of American Ethnology, 1880–1881* (Washington, D.C., 1883), pp. 9–15, 30–31.

Notes

1. Each of the six species of prey animals—Mountain Lion (North), Bear (West), Badger (South), White Wolf (East), Eagle (Upper), and Prey Mole (Lower)—"is again divided into six varieties, according to color. . . . For instance, the Mountain Lion (Yellow) is primarily god of the North, but he is supposed to have a representative (younger brother) in the West (the Blue Mountain Lion), another in the South (the Red), in the East (the White), in the Upper regions (the Spotted), and in the lower regions (the Black). Hence, also, there are six varieties of the fetich representing any one of these divisions . . . "("Zuñi Fetiches," pp. 24–25). See figure 32 for fetich representations of these six species of prey animals. [Ed. note]

2. "The Priesthood of the Bow possesses three fetiches. These three beings are the Mountain Lion (fig. 33.2); the great White Bear *Ain-shi k'ó-ha-na*, god of the scalp-taking ceremonials (Fig. 34.2), and the Knife-feathered Monster, *Á-tchi-a lä-to-pa* (Fig. 33.1).

"This [latter] curious god, [who is] sometimes classed with [the prey animals], sometimes with the higher beings, [and who] may safely be said to form a connecting link between the idolatry proper of the Zuñis and their fetichism, . . . is the hero of hundreds of folklore tales, and the tutelar deity of several of the societies of Zuñi. He is represented as possessing a human form, furnished with flint-knife-feathered pinions, and tail. His dress consists of the conventional terraced cap (representative of his dwelling-place among the clouds), and ornaments, badge, and garments of the *Kâ'-kâ*. His weapons are the Great Flint-Knife of War, the Bow of the Skies (the Rain-bow), and the Arrow of Lightning, and his guardians or warriors are the Great Mountain Lion of the North and that of the Upper regions. He was doubtless the original War God of the Zuñis, although now secondary, in the order of war, to the two children of the Sun. Anciently he was inimical to man, stealing and carrying away to his city in the skies the women of all nations, until subdued by other gods and men of magic powers. At present he is friendly to them, rather in the sense of an animal whose food temporarily satisfies him than in the beneficent character of most of the gods of Zuñi.

"Both the Great White Bear and the Mountain Lion of the War Priesthood are, as well as the Knife-feathered Demon, beings of the skies. For this reason the fetich of the Mountain Lion of the skies (of aragonite) is preferred by a Priest of the Bow above all other kinds of colors." ["Zuñi Fetiches," p. 40]

Remarks on Shamanism

The account Dr. Morris has given us as to what Mr. Williams related to him concerning the life of an Indian youth of the Nez Percé tribe has interested me exceedingly by reason of its striking similarity to what I have myself heard, seen, and experienced among the Zuñi Pueblo Indians of New Mexico.

With these people, a child is not thought of, when first born, as quite yet a living *mortal* being. It is referred to as "it" or the "new being," nor is any name given to it until after the lapse of nine days. It is supposed to be *kái'-yu-na* and *ai'-ya-vwi*—unripe and tender, or soft and susceptible as are germinating seeds or unfinished clay vessels, until after one full day for each of the lunar months of its inter-uterine gestation has passed. During this period of nine days it is usually kept with its mother, secluded from the outer world and from sunlight, in order that it may gradually become hardened to, and so, safe in the "world of daylight"—as these people term the scene and condition of mortal life—that is, condensed to "middle being"—as they further term men's particular mortal existence.

At the close of this ceremonial period the umbilical cord, which has meanwhile sloughed off or has been removed and zealously cared for, is ceremoniously buried in the soil at some particular place, in order that thereat may be formed the "midmost shrine" of the child, and therein its connection with the earth mother—as formerly with its mortal mother—may be established, and that its vitality apart from her thenceforward, be maintained—by thus placing within the fertile bosom of the Universal Mother, that through which erstwhile the child received separately, or secondarily, its being, nourishment and growth, from its human mother.

Passing over many other ceremonials which attend the first naming of the child and its introduction to the Sun and to the tribe of its descent on the early morning of the tenth day (that is, at the end of these nine natal days), a few words relative to the meaning of the "midmost shrine" will serve to indicate what would likely be the symbolic significance to a people like the Nez Percé and the Zuñi Indians, of such an object (whether natural or artificial) as the one to which Dr. Morris has called our attention.

He has quite accurately stated, in the theory he has advanced regarding this object, the view one of these Indians would hold, as to the meaning of the *number* of its sides or faces and itself. To one of them, a cube would not be representative of six, its number of superfices, but of *seven*; and a dodecahedron, not of twelve, but of *thirteen*. For, when an untutored or primitive man like him contemplates or considers himself or any other distinct thing, in his or its relation to space or the surrounding directions, he notes that there is ever a front or face, a rear or back; two sides, or a right and a left; a head and a foot, or an above and a below; and that of and within all these, is himself or it; that the essence of all these aspects, in anything, is the thing-itself— that is, the thing that contains their numbers or sum, yet is one by itself.

This is indeed the very key to his conception of himself and of everything, in relation to space and the universe or cosmos. He observes that there are as many regions in the world as there are aspects of himself or sides to any equally separate thing; that there are as many directions from him or his place in the world (which is his "midmost" or place of attachment to the Earth-mother) or from anything in the world (which is *its* midmost or natural station) toward these corresponding regions. Hence to him a plane would be symbolized not by four, but by *five*, its four sides and directions thence, and its central self—as was actually the notion of the Prairie tribes; a cube, not by six, but by seven, as was the notion of the Valley-Pueblos and Navajos; a dodecahedron, not by twelve, but by thirteen, as was the notion of the Zuñis, the Aztecs, the Mayas, and apparently—from this example—of the Mound builders as well.

With all that I have thus far said, I cannot yet have made clear to you the relation this supposed connection of beings and things to their surroundings, to the regions in front, behind, at the right and left sides, and above, below and within them, can have to the subject under discussion. It will therefore be necessary for me to crave your patience while I enter a little more fully into a consideration of the beliefs of primitive man concerning *force, life,* and *form,* for it will be seen that these beliefs have a direct bearing on this apparently fantastic and mystic meaning of the numbers *seven* and *thirteen.*

To the primitive Shaman, all force necessarily seems to be derived from some kind of life, since he continually sees force as motion or stress originated in, or initiated as action by, life in some form—his own, or some other. Now the supreme characteristic or concomitant of his own or of any other form of life, is breath, which like force or stress, is invisible; hence he reasons that force is breath, and conversely that breath is the force of life. He sees that this breath enters into and issues from every living being, and since every such being has distinctive form, he further reasons that every separate form, whether animate in our sense or not, has life of some kind or degree. He has, for example, no knowledge of air—as a gas—no knowledge of it other than as wind, and no conception of wind other than as breath, as the sort of something that he feels when he blows upon his hand and knows absolutely that he or his own breath is blowing, and that this breath it is that is coexistent with his mortal existence.

Therefore, he thinks not only of all forms as living, but also of the wind as necessarily the breath of some living form or being. And since his own little breath is so intimately of himself, he naturally imagines that this other greater breath must needs be as intimately that of some other and correspondingly greater and more powerful—what though invisible—being. He also imagines that this great being of the wind resides in the direction whence comes prevailingly its wind or its breath. Now when he observes that there are prevailing or distinctive winds of the diverse directions,—that of the north which blows hardest of

them all and chiefly in winter; that of the west which blows more
temperately and chiefly in spring time; that of the south, which
blows softly and most frequently in summer; that of the east,
which is again more fierce and chilly, and blows mostly in autumn; he not only severally locates these winds in their various
quarters, but also differentiates them, and believes that the
wind-being of the north produces cold and winter; of the west,
moisture and spring; of the south, warmth, dryness and summer;
of the east, coolness again, frost, and therewith the aging or
maturing of all growing things, and autumn. And so to him the
element of the north world is wind (or air, breath) preëminently;
of the west world, water; of the south world, fire; and of the east
world, earth or its seeds; and that each of these elements is
produced by or is under the dominion of the special wind-god of
its quarter; yet all combine, in the regular succession of the
seasons, to make this World of the Middle what it is from year to
year. . . .

Now since the various animals are supposed, according to
their kinds, to be especially resident in one region or another, not
only is there attributed to the Great Being or God of Wind in a
particular region, a form more or less like to that of his supposed
kind of animal therein, but also, the clans are organized with
reference, in turn, to the supposed relation of their totems to
these various animals and animistic or mythic beings of the
special regions. And so, when, for example, a name is to be
conferred upon a child of one of these totems, some process of
divination must be entered into to determine what shall be his
relation to the creatures and the deific being of one region or
another, and correspondingly, of course, to his fellows among the
clans. For it is held to be essential that this sacred relationship be
symbolized, in some way or another, in the choice of his totemic
name, and thus—as well as for many reasons into a consideration
of which I cannot enter here—must be divined. Now in this
process of divination, various instrumentalities are employed.
For example, among the Zuñis, wands painted in diverse colors—each color being symbolic of a special region and plumed
with appropriate bird feathers—are sometimes set up in balls of
clay, each placed out on the floor in the direction of the region to
which the color of its wand relates it. Then it is noted which of

the plumes waves most actively in any wind (or breath) that may
be stirring. From this, the spiritual relation, so to say, or the
source or totemic origin of the child is divined, and he will be
named, and to a certain extent the course of his life will be
determined upon according to this divination. For example, the
Zuñi totem gods of the several regions are: the Gray Wolf for the
East or Dawn-Land; the Mountain Lion or Puma for the North or
fierce Winter-Land; the Black Bear for the Land of the West or
Night; the sun-loving Badger for the South or Summer-Land; the
Eagle for the Sky and Light, and the Burrowing Mole for the
Under-Land and Darkness. Let us suppose that the plume on
the white wand—the one that is set up toward the east—waves
most actively; then, what though the child belong to a clan or totem of one of the other regions, he will nevertheless be regarded
as *spiritually* related to the Gray Wolf of Dawn, and it will be
believed by his fellows—and with their belief he will himself
become, as he grows toward puberty, more and more impressed—that he is destined for membership in the sacred organization or Shamanistic Society or Lodge of the Medicine-men
of the East, or of the Wolf deity. Now when the age of puberty is
attained, and the boy is to be solemnly invested with the garment
or clout and the responsibilities of manhood, he is . . . required to
pass through various ordeals, such as a period of vigorous fasting
and purification (this both by means of emetics and purgatives);
and to retire to some lonely spot and there keep, day and night,
lengthy vigils, whereby it is sought to diminish for a time his
earthly grossness, interests and affections, to "still his heart" and
quicken his spiritual perception and hearing of the meaning of
the "Silent Surpassing Ones." This is in order that he may gain
sign from or actually behold one of the Beings who wield, in the
great quarters, the forces of nature, and who shall thereafter be
his special *Tamanawa* or spiritual guide. It is also in order to aid
him in seeking for some objective sign by which this relationship
to his Genius may be proven to himself and made manifest to his
people. In a condition of exaltation as he is—and I can attest to its
absorbing nature, through having myself endured such an ordeal—you can well understand that his perceptions will become
startlingly manifest in the various visions and signs he sees.
These will seem to him, I can again personally assure you, far

more real than the most absolutely actual things he has ever beheld or experienced. Perchance he gazes at the mist, or a cloud in the sky. The cloud will surely seem to take the form of a great gray wolf; and when he seeks for some token of that God of the Sky, a tooth-like fossil, a few hairs maybe, which he may find on the ground nearby or underneath the apparition, will be reverently accepted as potent amulets, and he will bear them to the tribal Fathers or Shamans, and by them they will be received as a sign of his Genius, and he will be relegated to the phratral division or lodge of the Wolf. Or again, it may be that he will find a crystal, and because this crystal shines clearly and therein resembles the light by which we see and the eye through which we see—and hence is regarded as helpful in seeing—it will be regarded as a token of seership, as a sign of the Seeing Spirit, and fortunate the youth who is thus supposed to be endowed with the power of penetration into the unseen. To give yet one more example, let us suppose that he finds a concretion exhibiting spiral or concentric lines. He will regard this as a symbol of the Midmost itself, a token of his relation thereto also—no matter to what totem he may belong, or to what region he may be related by birth. For the spiral lines perceived in this crystal resemble those of the marks upon the sand produced by the whirling about of objects like red-topped grass by the whirlwind, yet which are regarded as the tracks of the whirlwind god, whose breath is the midmost of all the winds of the world.

Permit me to here give parenthetically a striking illustration of the way in which these primitive Shamans personify phenomena of nature, by instancing their personification of this god of the whirlwind. Of all the winds of heaven, the whirlwind alone is upright—progresses as man does, by *walking* over the plains. The whirlwind god is therefore endowed in part, with the personality of a man; but like the eagle, also, the whirlwind flies aloft and circles widely in the sky; therefore he is endowed with the wings and tail, the head, beak and talons of an eagle. Since the sand which he, the whirlwind, casts about pricks the face as would minute arrows, the dreadful wings of the god are supposed to be flinty, and his character warlike or destructive, as is that of the eagle; yet of all the Beings of Wind, he is the most potent, for he twists about or banishes utterly from his trail, either the north wind or the south, the east wind or the west, and overcomes even gravity—the pulling-breath of the earth or under world—and therefore is the god of the midmost among all the six gods of wind. Thus, lucky in a purely practical way, is he who finds under given auspicious circumstances, his name-token in the shape of a little concentric concretion, for he will be in the line of ordination thereby, to the Central Council or Priesthood of his people. . . .

Now I have gone a long way around the subject in hand, in order to measurably substantiate my reasons for thinking that Dr. Morris is correct in his hypothesis as to the sacred and symbolic character and origin of the pentagonal dodecahedron which he has exhibited and commented upon here to-night. A figure even as elaborate and difficult of production in stone as is this, could readily have been formed by Indian artisans. Its shape might have been suggested in the process, perfectly familiar to them, of knapping a block or cube of stone, and afterwards breaking away its angles by battering, to form a sphere; or, better still, by the shapes of balls of clay—naturally formed round in the hands—and used as by the Zuñis in their processes of name-divination just described; or again, by the shapes of pentagonal or other like—ever sacred—crystals. The scratchings or figures observed upon the various faces of this stone are quite such as might well have been drawn to differentiate them as being related to one region or another, and in all probability the figures thus scratched were further marked with pigments symbolic of the different regions, when this stone was used in such processes of divination. Close observation of the more distinct lines of these figures on the faces of the stone, shows that they were made by a flint point, not a metal instrument; for they are double,—that is within each one is a minute bead such as would be produced by the fracturing of a fine point of flint or other hard concoidal stone when drawn over the surface of another stone like this,—and not simply V-shaped as would have been the case had a metal instrument been used.

Some question may arise in the minds of those who have listened to Dr. Morris' paper, and to my comments thereon, as to the meaning of the twelve faces in this particular specimen; since, as I have explained there are only *six* regions, the north, west, south, east, upper and lower, that the midmost is at once surrounded by and contains within, itself. But I failed to say earlier and in the proper connection, that to the primitive-minded man, as there is no form without life, so there is no life-form, without due duality of origin—the father and the mother. Consequently we find that in relation to all things, (with tribes of primitive peoples like the Zuñis of to-day, and like the mound builders of long ago, who possessed and reverenced this object), the sexenary divison is duplicated; but since there can be only one middle or content, the sexenary division is with them symbolized by the number seven, and when duplicated, we have, not fourteen, but thirteen; that is, six pairs which are visible, but only one for the concentric or synthetic middle, since there can be but one actual centre or middle to anything, even to the great world.

From "Discussion of J. Cheston Morris' Address ['The Relation of the Pentagonal Do-decahedron Found near Marietta, Ohio, to Shamanism'] and Remarks on Shamanism," *Proceedings of the American Philosophical Society* 36 (1897): 184–92.

Form

As every living thing they observe, every animal, has form, and acts or functions according to its form—the feathered and winged bird flying, because of its feathered form; the furry and four-footed animal running and leaping, because of its four-footed form, and the scaly and finny fish swimming, because also of its fins and scales and form appropriate thereto—so these things made or born into special forms [through] the hands of man also have life and function variously, according to their various forms.

As this idea of animals, and of things [as animals of another sort] is carried out to the minutest particular, so that even the differences in the claws of beasts, for example, are supposed to make the difference between their powers of foot (as between the hugging of the bear and the clutching of the panther), it follows that form in all its details is considered of the utmost importance to special kinds of articles made and used, even of structures of any much used or permanent type. Another phase of this curious but perfectly natural attribution of life and form-personality to material things is the belief that the forms of these things not only give them power, but also restrict their power, so that if properly made, that is, made and shaped strictly as other things of their kind have been made and shaped, they will perform only such safe uses as their prototypes have been found to serve in performing before them. As the fish, with scales and fins only, can not fly as the duck does, and as the duck can not swim under the water except so far as his feathers, somewhat resembling scales, and his scaly, webbed feet, somewhat resembling fins, enable him to do, thus also is it with things. In this way may be explained better than in any other way, I think, the excessive persistency of form survival, including the survival of details in conventional ornamentation in the art products of primitive peoples—the repetitions, for instance, in pottery, of the forms and even the ornaments of the vessels, basketry, or what not, which preceded it in development and use and on which it was first modeled. This tendency to persist in the making of well-tried forms, whether of utensil or domicile, is so great that some other than the reason usually assigned, namely, that of mere accustomedness, is necessary to account for it, and the reason I have given is fully warranted by what I know of the mood in which the Zuñis still regard the things they make and use, and which is so clearly manifest in their names of such things.

From "Outlines of Zuñi Creation Myths," *Thirteenth Annual Report of the Bureau of American Ethnology, 1891–1892* (Washington, D.C., 1896), p. 362.

Form and the
Dance-Drama

Wɪᴛʜ other primitive peoples as with the Zuñis, there seems
to be no bent of their minds so strong or pervasive of and influential upon their lives as the dramaturgic tendency—that tendency
to suppose that even the phenomena of nature can be controlled
and made to act more or less by men, if symbolically they do first
what they wish the elements to do, according to the ways in
which, as taught by their mystic lore, they suppose these things
were done or made to be done by the ancestral gods of creation
time. And this may be seen not only in a searching analysis of the
incidents and symbolisms in folk-tales as well as myths of such
primitive peoples, but also in a study of the moods in which they
do the ordinary things of life; as in believing that because a stone
often struck wears away faster than when first struck it is therefore helpful in overcoming its obduracy to strike it—work it—by
a preliminary dramatic and ritualistic striking, whereupon it will
work as though already actually worked over, and will be less
liable to breakage, etc. . . .

At this point it seems desirable that the sense in which the
terms "drama," "dramatic," and "dramaturgic" are employed in
relation to these ceremonials be explained. This may best be
done, perhaps, by contrasting the drama of primitive peoples, as
I conceive it, with that of civilized peoples. While the latter is
essentially spectacular, the former has for its chief motive the
absolute and faithful reproduction of creative episodes—one
may almost say, indeed, the revivification of the ancient.

That this is attempted and is regarded as possible by primitive man is not to be wondered at when we consider his peculiar

modes of conception. I have said of the Zuñis that theirs is a science of appearances and a philosophy of analogies. The primitive man, no less than the child, is the most comprehensive of observers, because his looking at and into things is not self-conscious, but instinctive and undirected, therefore comprehensive and searching. Unacquainted as he is with rational explanations of the things he sees, he is given, as has been the case throughout all time, to symbolic interpretation and mystic expression thereof, as even today are those who deal with the domain of the purely speculative. It follows that his organizations are symbolic; that his actions within these organizations are also symbolic. Consequently, as a child at play on the floor finds sticks all-sufficient for the personages of his play-drama, chairs for his houses, and lines of the floor for the rivers that none but his eyes can see, so does the primitive man regard the mute, but to him personified, appliances of his dance and the actions thereof, other than they seem to us.

I can perhaps make my meaning more clear by analyzing such a conception common to the Zuñi mind. The Zuñi has observed that the corn plant is jointed; that its leaves spring from these joints not regularly, but spirally; that stripped of the leaves the stalk is found to be indented, not regularly at opposite sides, but also spirally; that the matured plant is characterized, as no other plant is, by two sets of seeds, the ears of corn springing out from it two-thirds down and the tassels of seeds, sometimes earlets, at the top; also that these tassels resemble the seed-spikes of the spring-grass or pigeon-grass; that the leaves themselves while like broad blades of grass are fluted like plumes, and that amongst the ears of corn ever and anon are found bunches of soot; and, finally, that the colors of the corn are as the colors of the world—seven in number. Later on it may be seen to what extent he has legendized these characteristics, thus accounting for them, and to what extent, also, he has dramatized this, his natural philosophy of the corn and its origin. Nothing in this world or universe having occurred by accident—so it seems to the Zuñi mind—but everything having been started by a personal agency or supernal, he immediately begins to see in these characteristics of the corn plant the traces of the actions of the peoples in his myths of the olden time. Lo! men lived on grass seeds at first, but, as related in the course of the legends which follow, there came a time when, by the potencies of the gods and the magic of his own priests or shamans, man modified the food of first men into the food of men's children. It needed only a youth and a maiden, continent and pure, to grasp at opposite sides and successively the blades of grass planted with plumes of supplication, and walking or dancing around them, holding them firmly to draw them upward until they had rapidly grown to the tallness of themselves, then to embrace them together. Behold! the grasses were jointed where grasped four times or six according to their tallness; yea, and marked with the thumb-marks of those who grasped them; twisted by their grasp while circling around them and leaved with plume-like blades and tasseled with grass-like spikes at the tops. More wonderful than all, where their persons had touched the plants at their middles, behold! new seed of human origin and productive of continued life had sprung forth in semblance of their parentage and draped with the very pile of their generation. For lo! when the world was new all things in it were *k'yai'-una,* or formative, as now is the child in the mother's womb or the clay by the thoughts of the potter. That the seed of seeds thus made be not lost it needed that Pai-a-tu-ma, the God of Dew and the Dawn, freshen these new-made plants with his breath; that Te-na-tsa-li, the God of Time and the Seasons, mature them instantly with his touch and breath; that Kwe'-le-le, the God of Heat, ripen them with the touch of his Fire-brother's torch and confirm to them the warmth of a life of their own. Nevertheless, with the coming of each season, the creation is ever repeated, for the philosophy of ecclesiasticism is far older than ecclesiastics or their writings, and since man aided in the creation of corn, so must he now ever aid in each new creation of the seed of seeds. Whence the drama of the origin of corn is not merely reenacted, but is revived and reproduced in all its many details with scrupulous fidelity each summer as the new seed is ripening. And now I may add intelligibly that the drama of primitive man is performed in an equally dramaturgic spirit, whether seen, as in its merely culminating or final enactment, or unseen and often secret, as in its long-continued preparations. In this a given piece of it may be likened to a piece of Oriental carving or of Japanese joinery, in which the parts not to be seen are as scrupulously finished as are the parts seen, the which is likewise characteristic of our theme, for it is due to the like dramaturgic spirit which dominates even the works, no less than the ceremonials, of all primitive and semi-primitive peoples.

So also it seems to the Zuñi that no less essential is it that all the long periods of creation up to the time when corn itself was created from the grasses must be reproduced, even though hastily and by mere signs, as are the forms through which a given species in animal life has been evolved, rapidly repeated in each embryo.

The significance of such studies as these of a little tribe like the Zuñis, and especially of such fuller studies as will, it is hoped, follow in due course, is not restricted to their bearing on the tribe itself. They bear on the history of man the world over. I have become convinced that they thus bear on human history, especially on that of human culture growth, very directly too, for the Zuñis, say, with all their strange, apparently local customs and institutions and the lore thereof, are representative in a more than merely general way of a phase of culture through which all desert peoples, in the Old World as well as in the New, must sometime have passed. Thus my researches among these Zuñis and my experimental researches upon myself, with my own hands, under strictly primitive conditions, have together given me insight and power to interpret their myths and old arts, as I could never otherwise have hoped to do; and it has also enlarged my understanding of the earliest conditions of man everywhere as nothing else could have done.

From "Outlines of Zuñi Creation Myths," *Thirteenth Annual Report of the Bureau of American Ethnology, 1891–1892* (Washington, D.C., 1896), pp. 374–77.

A Case of
Primitive Surgery

DURING the first period of my residence among Zuñi Indians, in the autumn of 1880, I was called in to assist two medicine men or priests in the performance of a peculiarly interesting surgical operation.

A man belonging to the clan into which I had been adopted had for several months been suffering from the effects of either a contusion or a strain of the right foot, caused by a throw from his horse. This had at first given little trouble, then had appeared as an ordinary stone-bruise on the right side of the foot just below the instep. The inflammation had, however, extended until the whole foot and the lower part of the leg had become excessively swollen, so much so as to cause the skin to glisten from stretching, save at a point over and around the original injury, at which point a malignant and putrid sore had developed, the odor of which was extremely offensive, and both the foot and the leg were now of livid, purplish-red hue in places, suggestive of actual decay. As a layman in medicine I should have said that the case was now one of advanced mortification, and from the general condition of the patient I should have inferred that blood poisoning was likely soon to ensue.

I gathered from the conversation of the two old surgeons who had been called in, and who had in return requested my attendance in order that I might give "ease medicine" and "add with (my) breath strength and endurance to (my) clan-brother," that it was these appearances, this apparently *"decaying* condition" of the man's extremity, that had determined them to perform the operation.

When I entered the room the patient was lying on the floor and, although in extreme agony, turned his face toward me expectantly and with a smile, uttering the customary words of welcome. His head was pillowed in the lap of his little old white-haired mother, who was gently stroking his forehead and talking to him in the endearing phrases of mothers to little children. At his side was a small bowl containing a clear but bright red liquid (made, I afterwards learned, from an infusion of willow-root bark) in which half floated, half stood, a cane sucking-tube about six inches long. The old surgeons were removing certain bandages from the foot and washing off a yellow powder made from pollen and a certain bitter root, with which the sore had been dressed. They bade me sit at the right side of the man, so as to lay my hands on his left breast and to occasionally breathe into his face and administer to him my "white medicine" (which contained an opiate).

Then they produced, from a buckskin pouch and a roll of rags, a much shattered bottom of a dark-colored glass bottle and two or three broken nodules of obsidian, also several neat splints of cedar and masses of freshly gathered, clean yellow piñon gum, as well as a carefully tied bundle of willow-root bark and some of the yellow roots and pollen I have before mentioned. With a blunt-pointed knife, used vertically, one of them detached, by tapping, a number of small, thin, sharp flakes or chips from the bottle-glass and obsidian. Six or eight of these diminutive flakes were now selected and mounted, each in the cleft end of one of the cedar splints; some so as to form straight lancets, but others at right angles to the splint handles. The blades of one or two of these latter were wrapped round and round with sinew near the point of insertion in the splint, so that only a limited portion of the edge or tip of each protruded. These and the other improvised surgical instruments were laid out in due order on the floor. A quantity of shredded cedar-bark, buckskin scrapings, and old, soft rags were provided; also a large bowl of fresh water, and another filled with the red liquid and containing a small gourd dipper.

Everything being in readiness, the two priests closed their hands over their mouths and breathed into them, as does a man on a cold day, uttering, meanwhile, short invocations, for strength of wind or breath for the patient, and for power of wind or breath of guidance for themselves; literally the supplication was: "Their [The Beings'] wind of life, by its power may his will be strengthened and he quieted be, and likewise by it may our methods and good fortune straight be made!" Bidding the man "Stay himself with endurance," since "Things must be as they must, poor child," and telling me also to "Stay him," with my "Breath of relationship and sympathy," they set to work without further delay.

First, they bathed his foot to clear it of the astringent yellow powder, and to cleanse the sore in order that they might be the better able to inspect it. Then, very deliberately, they diagnosed the case, frequently comparing notes. It was from this diagnosis that I learned their reasons for attempting the operation They believed that the flesh of certain muscles in the foot had died or were dying from the violence done them, and were therefore *"wi-wi-yo-a"* (worm-becoming, worm-turning) in the depths of the foot. According to this theory, their plan was to make a double, or inverted T-shape, incision so that the integument could be lifted up from the affected parts in two flaps, the "dead flesh" removed, the "decayed" or "black blood" fully extracted, the worms and the "seed of their kind" found and utterly uprooted. They thereupon mapped out with their fingers the lines of the incisions they proposed to make. One of them gently bade their patient anew to "Stay himself," while the other seized his foot with both hands and turned it up, stretching the skin by pressure; then the first grasped one of the obsidian lancets (mounted sidewise and wrapped with sinew so that the point protruded just sufficiently to sever the skin) and deliberately, but with deft and even stroke, slashed down from the ankle about two and a-half inches, along a line corresponding in direction with that of the tendon of the little toe. He then quickly made another slash from the instep straight down to the middle of the first cut. Catching up one of the other kind of lancets, he deepened both incisions, avoiding with the utmost skill the crooked vein that descended over this portion of the foot, and also the tendon lying over the tarsal and metatarsal bones. The wound was then squeezed strongly by the assistant, while, with water poured over it and with wads of the cedar bark used as sponges, he washed away the pus and serum that gushed forth, and then with the scraped buckskin stanched the flow of blood.

Having at the outset tenderly admonished their patient, these men seemed thereafter to be oblivious of his agony, to hold in view only his ultimate betterment. And the patient himself seemed almost as oblivious of them, although from suffering his face was drawn and ashen in color, and great drops of perspiration stood on his forehead while his breath came in short quick gasps. Yet he no more changed his grimly set but acquiescent expression than would one of the totem-animals of his ancestry, whose stoicism—as under all circumstances his kind ever do—he sought to emulate. The old surgeons took up one after another of the straight lancets, and with them dissected away the proud flesh and other diseased tissue, removing it cleanly, without severing vein or artery or tendon, until they had fairly exposed the bone itself. Here they found a swollen and diseased bit of nerve or tendon. They ruthlessly cut it out and examined it critically; stuffing some cedar-bark into the wound, they laid their lancets down and discussed thoroughly, and in an interested, leisurely manner, the question as to whether it was already a worm or only a "becoming" worm. After deciding that whether worm or "becoming-worm" it was not the chief or sole source of the disease, they laid it carefully aside on some ashes in a hollow potsherd. Then removing the bark and calling upon me to squeeze water into the wound they proceeded until the bone was plainly exposed. They found the periosteum inflamed and discolored, and, therefore, with evident satisfaction, they proceeded to scrape it until every particle of the discoloration was removed. It was claimed that in the substance of the material thus scraped away the deepest source of the disease and "seat worms" was found. This was also placed on the ashes with the fragment of nerve or tendon. Then one of them took a small fetish, or medicine-stone, from his wallet. It was an ovoid object of banded aragonite, much resembling a ringed worm or maggot. He laid it in the wound. He presently took it out, lifted it aloft with an air of triumph, and carefully placed it on the ashes with the ligament and bone-scrapings. The incision was now held open and thoroughly washed out, and then the chief operator, dipping up gourdfuls of the red liquid, filled his mouth therewith, and repeatedly sprayed the wound by vigorously blowing the fluid into it. All dissected surfaces were then washed, dried with the scraped buckskin, washed and dried again, until it not only became, but actually looked, clean, and was sprayed yet again with the red fluid. Finally, the openings were filled up, or rather stuffed, with the piñon-gum softened by warmth of the breath and in the hands, that were the while kept constantly wet with the red fluid. More of this gum was spread on narrow strips of cloth, and with these the wound was neatly closed as with adhesive plaster. The entire foot was sprinkled or thickly dusted over with the yellow pollen and root-powder, and then bandaged with long strips of the old rags as neatly as it would have been bandaged by a surgeon among ourselves.

The procedure of these primitive surgeons, if we consider the antiseptic treatment involved in their copious sprayings with the willow-bark infusion, in the filling of the wound with purifying piñon gum and the remarkably effective closure of the incisions thereby, and in the surface-coating with the astringent yellow powder, would certainly seem to have been, almost from beginning to end, as strictly rational also as would have been those of one of our own surgeons. But in reality they were nothing of the sort. If we except the exceeding ingenuity and courage and the anatomic knowlege and skill displayed by these surgeons in their operations, the theories upon which they based their procedure were, from our point of view, irrational in the highest degree. They were a combination of empiric and thaumaturgic modes, chiefly the latter.

These men believed, according to the general philosophy of their people, founded on the superficial appearance of things, that blood—good, fresh, red blood—was the source of "new flesh." They believed that when the blood became thinned and black it was weakened and spoiled and must therefore be removed and replaced with fresh blood; that as blood is the source of new flesh, so is water the first source of new blood, of life itself, since nothing can live without water, howsoever abundant sustenance of other sort may be. Therefore, since the willow never lives apart from springs or other continuous sources of water, it must contain within its roots, its sources, the very essence, the very source of life. An infusion of its roots and bark becomes brightly red. It is imagined, therefore, to be the source of new life-blood, of flesh-forming blood itself, and to be effective for the renewal of decaying or "worm-turning" flesh. The employment of the "fire-feeding" and, therefore, "purifying and maturing" piñon gum, and of the cooling and hardening yellow (or "winter" root) powder and sustaining pollen, also quite accorded to like ways of reasoning, was as strictly sustained by practical results, and therefore seemed, in turn, to prove the propriety of such reasoning.

They also believed that the violence of the man's injury had so weakened the part injured that it was infested with worms or else was killed and turning to worms. This belief was also based on appearances. Dead flesh putrifies, is filled with pus, or with thin, fluid, black or dead blood, stinks, and is always likely to be, with these people, infested with worms (maggots). A festering sore arising from violence, real or imaginary, done to the part in which it occurs, exhibits all these characteristics, and, if unchecked, leads to death. Such a sore, if malignant and deep, causes pain as of the bones. Its seed, then, must be deep-seated or in the bones themselves; this seed must be removed, else it will grow and cause death. Any pain like that arising from such a sore, though no sore be apparent, must be caused also by unseen worms or some worm born of violent injury, as by a magical or ghostly arrow.

There remain to be explained two or three of the manifestly irrational operations involved in the procedure. One was the treatment of the pain-causing worm-filament—or diseased nerve—and the ultimate "source of worm-turning" in the bone they scraped; the other was the use of the maggot-fetish or medicine-stone. The supposedly incipient maggot and the infectious seed-substance of his kind in the bone were placed on the ashes, because fire-ashes are considered, in themselves, to be dissolving and destructive, and (among other quaint reasons) tend toward "clogging" or "hindering escape"; for no worm or insect can progress through, or escape from, fine ashes. With the scraping of the bone everything had been done that was humanly possible to remove the infection; but something more must be done, some potency applied, to absorb any remaining infection. Therefore the fetish-stone, as a sort of spiritual sponge, was introduced.

And I would here enter a plea for the primitive medicine man. He is not usually the arrant knave or juggler so frequently pictured by travellers. His so-called "tricks" are not attempts at deception. They are solemn operations by which he is himself as much deceived as are any of his witnesses. We are told that these earliest practitioners suck, knead or cut their patients, and end by pretending to find and extract, and by triumphantly holding aloft, some grub, insect or other small object—frequently a minute fetish-stone like the one I have described, that "they claim" to have actually extracted from the diseased part. We aliens are the only ones of their witnesses who are deceived by them in the way we accuse them of deceiving, for what they really attempt to do is either to expose, or otherwise make as uncomfortable as possible, the animate seat of the disease, and then to furnish it with a decoy, as it were, a vehicle or body of escape, as a killed and squeezed-out body of one of its own kind, or else in the form of its kind as seen in some ancient and more potent and nearly natural object resembling it. Sometimes, again, living insects or worms, or fetishes that are supposed to be living, ravenous and inimical to the worms of disease, are introduced, that they may prey upon and destroy these worms and the seed-substance of their kind. This is especially apt to be the case when thick pus is abundant and parasites are forming; for the squeezed-out pus itself resembles worms more or less, portions of it even in mass, being streaked, seeming to contain their forms in embryo. It, also, is therefore held to be the seed-plasm or substance of worms, and the proof of this is alleged to lie in the fact that, if exposed, like dead flesh, it speedily turns to worms.

The subsequent treatment received by the man whose case I have described, at the hands of his primitive doctors, was quite as much in keeping with this sort of philosophy as had been their operation. His wound was, of course, dressed, cleaned, copiously sprayed, and, I may add, "Spiritually disinfected," every day. But, in addition to this, he was put on diet—the freshest or "newest" possible corn food—and was, for the first four days, deprived of salt (this, too, being abundant in pus-like excreta) and all flesh-food, and was thereafter until perfectly cured—for he recovered with amazing rapidity—denied all meat containing fat and other non-muscular tissue, since these, as well as old and so-to-say "decrepit" seeds, are supposed to be, of themselves, peculiarly liable to "worm-turning."

"A Case of Primitive Surgery," *Science*, June 25, 1897, pp. 977–81.

Origins of
Pueblo Pottery

Pottery and Basketry

THERE is no other section of the United States where the potter's art was so extensively practiced, or where it reached such a degree of perfection, as within the limits of these ancient Pueblo regions. To this statement not even the prolific valleys of the Mississippi and its tributaries form an exception.

On examining a large and varied collection of this pottery, one would naturally regard it either as the product of four distinct peoples or as belonging to four different eras, with an inclination to the chronologic division.

When we see the reasonable probability that the architecture, the primeval arts and industries, and the culture of the Pueblos are mainly indigenous to the desert and semi-desert regions of North Amierca, we are in the way towards an understanding of the origin and remarkable degree of development in the ceramic art.

In these regions water not only occurs in small quantities, but is obtainable only at points separated by great distances; hence to the Pueblos the first necessity of life is the transportation and preservation of water. The skins and paunches of animals could be used in the effort to meet this want with but small success, as the heat and aridity of the atmosphere would in a short time render water thus kept unfit for use, and the membranes once empty would be liable to destruction by drying. So far as language indicates the character of the earliest water vessels which to any extent met the requirements of the Zuñi ancestry, they were tubes of wood or sections of canes. The latter, in ritualistic recitation, are said to have been the receptacles that the creation-priests filled with the sacred water from the ocean of the cave-wombs of earth, whence men and creatures were born, and the name for one of these cane water vessels is *shó-tom-me*, from *shó-e*, cane or canes, and *tóm-me*, a wooden tube. Yet, although in the extreme western borders of the deserts, which were probably the first penetrated by the Pueblos, the cane grows to great size and in abundance along the two rivers of that country, its use, if ever extensive, must have speedily given way to the use of gourds, which grew luxuriantly at these places and were of better shapes and of larger capacity. The name of the gourd as a vessel is *shop'-tom-me*, from *shó-e*, canes, *pó-pon-nai-e*, bladder-shaped, and *tóm-me*, a wooden tube; a seeming derivation (with the exception of the interpolated sound significant of form) from *shó-tom-me*. The gourd itself is called *mó-thlâ-â*, "hard fruit." The inference is that when used as a vessel, and called *shop'-tom-me*, it must have been named after an older form of vessel, instead of after the plant or fruit which produced it.

While the gourd was large and convenient in form, it was difficult of transportation owing to its fragility. To overcome this it was encased in a course sort of wicker-work, composed of fibrous yucca leaves or of flexible splints. Of this we have evidence in a series of gourd-vessels among the Zuñis, into which the sacred water is said to have been transferred from the tubes, and a pair of which one of the priests, who came east with me two years ago, brought from New Mexico to Boston in his hands—so precious were they considered as relics—for the purpose of replenishing them with water from the Altantic. These vessels are encased rudely but strongly in a meshing of splints (see fig. 35), and while I do not positively claim that they have been piously preserved since the time of the universal use of gourds as water-vessels by the ancestry of this people, they are nevertheless of considerable antiquity. Their origin is attributed to the priest-gods, and they show that it must have once been a common practice to encase gourds, as above described, in osiery.

This crude beginning of the wicker-art in connection with water-vessels points toward the development of the wonderful water-tight basketry of the Southwest, explaining, too, the resemblance of many of its typical forms to the shapes of gourd-

FIG. 35. Gourd Vessel Enclosed in Wicker

vessels. Were we uncertain of this, we might again turn to language, which designates the impervious wicker water-receptacle of whatever outline as *tóm ma*, an evident derivation from the restricted use of the word *tóm-me* in connection with the gourd or cane vessels, since a basket of any other kind is called *tsi'-i-le*.

It is readily conceivable that water-tight osiery, once known, however difficult of manufacture, would displace the general use of gourd-vessels. While the growth of the gourd was restricted to limited areas, the materials for basketry were everywhere at hand. Not only so, but basket vessels were far stronger and more durable, hence more readily transported full of water, to any distance. By virtue of their rough surfaces, any leakage in such vessels was instantly stopped by a daubing of pitch or mineral asphaltum, coated externally with sand or coarse clay to harden it and overcome its adhesiveness.

We may conclude, then, that so long as the Pueblo ancestry were semi nomadic, basketry supplied the place of pottery, as it still does for the less advanced tribes of the Southwest, except in cookery. Possibly for a time basketry of this kind served in place of pottery even for cookery, as with one of the above-mentioned tribes, the Havasupai or Coconinos, of Cataract Cañon, Arizona. These people, until recently, were cut off from the rest of the world by their almost impenetrable cañon, nearly half a mile in depth at the point where they inhabit it. For example, when I visited them in 1881, they still hafted sharpened bits of iron, like celts, in wood. They had not yet forgotten how to boil food in

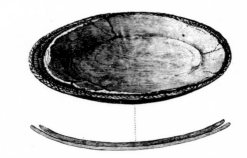

FIG. 36. Havasupai Clay-Lined Roasting-Tray

FIG. 37. Zuñi Earthenware Roasting-Tray

water-tight basketry, by means of hot stones, and continued to roast seeds, crickets, and bits of meat in wicker-trays, coated inside with gritty clay. (See fig. 36.) The method of preparing and using these roasting-trays has an important bearing on several questions to which reference will be made further on. A round basket-tray, either loosely or closely woven, is evenly coated inside with clay, into which has been kneaded a very large proportion of sand, to prevent contraction and consequent cracking from drying. This lining of clay is pressed, while still soft, into the basket as closely as possible with the hands and then allowed to dry. The tray is thus made ready for use. The seeds or other substances to be parched are placed inside of it, together with a quantity of glowing wood-coals. The operator, quickly squatting, grasps the tray at opposite edges, and, by a rapid spiral motion up and down, succeeds in keeping the coals and seeds constantly shifting places and turning over as they dance after one another around and around the tray, meanwhile blowing or

FIG. 38. Havasupai Boiling-Basket

puffing the embers with every breath to keep them free from ashes and glowing at their hottest.

That this clay lining should grow hard from continual heating, and in some instances separate from its matrix of osiers, is apparent. The clay form thus detached would itself be a perfect roasting-vessel.

This would suggest the agency of gradual heat in rendering clay fit for use in cookery and preferable to any previous makeshift. The modern Zuñi name for a parching-pan, which is a shallow bowl of black-ware, is *thlé-mon-ne*, the name for a basket-tray being *thlä'-lin-ne*. The latter name signifies a shallow vessel of twigs, or *thlá-we*; the former etymologically interpreted, although of earthenware, is a hemispherical vessel of the same kind and *material*. All this would indicate that the *thlä'-lin-ne*, coated with clay for roasting, had given birth to the *thlé-mon-ne*, or parching-pan of earthenware. (See fig. 37.)

Among the Havasupai, still surviving as a sort of bucket, is the basket-pot or boiling-basket, for use with hot stones, which form I have also found in some of the cave deposits throughout the ancient Zuñi country. These vessels (see fig. 38) were bottle-shaped and provided near the rims of their rather narrow mouths with a sort of cord or strap-handle, attached to two loops or eyes (fig. 38a) woven into the basket, to facilitate handling when the vessel was filled with hot water. In the manufacture of one of these vessels, which are good examples of the helix or spirally-coiled type of basket, the beginning was made at the center of the bottom. A small wisp of fine, flexible grass stems or

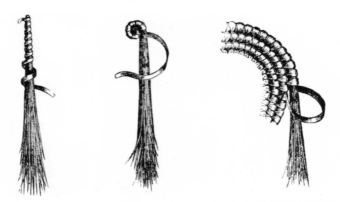

FIG. 39. Sketches Illustrating Manufacture of Spirally Coiled Basketry

osiers softened in water was first spirally wrapped a little at one end with a flat, limber splint of tough wood, usually willow. This wrapped portion was then wound upon itself; the outer coil thus formed being firmly fastened as it progressed to the one already made by passing the splint wrapping of the wisp each time it was wound around the latter through some strands of the contiguous inner coil, with the aid of a bodkin. (See fig. 39.) The bottom was rounded upward and the sides were made by coiling the wisp higher and higher, first outward, to produce the bulge of the vessel, then inward, to form the tapering upper part and neck, into which the two little twigs or splint loop-eyes were firmly woven. (See again fig. 38a.)

These and especially kindred forms of basket-vessels were often quite elaborately ornamented, either by the insertion at proper points of dyed wrapping-splints, singly, in pairs, or in sets, or by the alternate painting of pairs, sets, or series of stitches. Thus were produced angular devices, like serrated bands, diagonal or zigzag lines, chevrons, even terraces and frets. (See fig. 40.) There can be no doubt that these styles and ways of decoration were developed, along with the weaving of baskets, simply by elaborating on suggestions of the lines and figures unavoidably produced in wicker-work of any kind when strands of different colors happened to be employed together. Even slight discolorations in occasional splints would result in

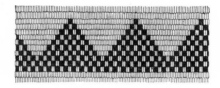

FIG. 40. Typical Basket Decorations

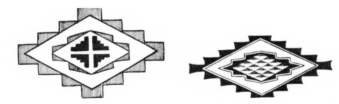

FIG. 41. Terraced Lozenge Decoration, or "Double Splint-Stitch Forms"

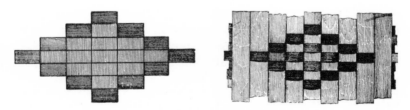

FIG. 42. Double Splint-Stitch

such suggestions, for the stitches would here show, there disappear. The probability of this view of the accidental origin of basket-ornamentation may be enhanced by a consideration of

FIG. 43. Diagonal Parallel-Line Decoration

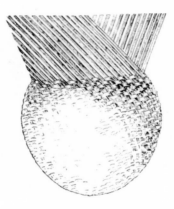

FIG. 44. Splints at Neck of Unfinished Basket

the etymology of a few Zuñi decorative terms, more of which might be given did space admit. A terraced lozenge (see fig. 41), instead of being named after the abstract word *a-wi-thlui-ap-i-pä-tchi-na*, which signifies a double terrace or two terraces joined together at the base, is designated *shu-k'u-tu-li-a-tsi'-nan*, from *shu-e*, splints or fibers; *k'u-tsu*, a double fold, space, or stitch (see fig. 42); *li-a*, an interpolation referring to form; and *tsi'-nan*, mark; in other words, the "double splint-stitch-form mark." Likewise, a pattern, composed principally of a series of diagonal or oblique parallel lines *en masse* (see fig. 43), is called *shu'-k'ish-pa-tsi-nan*, from *shú-e*, splints; *k'i'sh-pai-e*, tapering *(k'ish-pon-ne,* neck or smaller part of anything); and *tsi'-nan,* mark; that is, "tapering" or "neck-splint mark." Curiously enough, in a bottle-shaped basket as it approaches completion the splints of the tapering part or neck all lean spirally side by side of one another (see fig. 44), and a term descriptive of this has come to be used as that applied to lines resembling it, instead of a derivative from *ä's-sël-lai-e,* signifying an oblique or leaning line. Where splints variously arranged, or stitches, have given names to decorations—applied even to painted and embroidered designs—it is not difficult for us to see that these same combinations, at first unintentional, must have suggested the forms to which they gave names as decorations.

Pueblo Coiled Pottery Developed from Basketry

Seizing the suggestion afforded by the rude tray-molded parching-bowls, particularly after it was discovered that if well burned they resisted the effects of water as well as of heat, the ancient potter would naturally attempt in time to reproduce the boiling-basket in clay. She would find that to accomplish this she could not use as a mold the inside of the boiling-basket, as she had the inside of the tray, because its neck was smaller than its body. Nor could she form the vase by plastering the clay outside of the vessel, not only for the same reason, but also because the clay in drying would contract so much that it would crack or scale off. Naturally, then, she pursued the process she was accustomed to in the manufacture of the basket-bottle. That is, she formed a thin rope of soft clay, which, like the wisp of the basket, she coiled around and around a center to form the bottom, then spirally upon itself, now widening the diameter of each coil more and more, then contracting as she progressed upward until the desired height and form were attained. As the clay was adhesive, each coil was attached to the one already formed by pinching or pressing together the connecting edges at short intervals as the winding went on. This produced corrugations or indentations marvelously resembling the stitches of basket-work. Hence accidentally the vessel thus built up appeared so similar to the basket which had served as its model that evidently it did not seem complete until this feature had been heightened by art. At any rate, the majority of specimens belonging to this type of

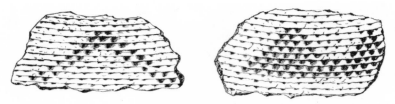

FIG. 45. Examples of Indented Decoration on Corrugated Ware

FIG. 46. Cooking Pot of Corrugated Ware, Showing Conical Projections near Rim

pottery—especially those of the older periods during which it was predominant—are distinguished by an indented or incised decoration exactly reproducing the zigzags, serrations, chevrons, terraces, and other characteristic devices of water-tight basketry. (Compare fig. 45 with fig. 40.) Evidently with a like intention two little cone-like projections were attached to the neck near the rim of the vessel (see fig. 46) which may hence be regarded as survivals of the loops whereby it has been seen the ends of the strap-handle were attached to the boiling-basket. (See again fig. 38a.) Although varied in later times to form scrolls, rosettes, and other ornate figures (see fig. 47), they continued ever after quite faithful features of the spiral type of pot, and may even some-times be seen on the cooking-vessels of modern Zuñi. To add yet another link to this chain of connection between the coiled boiling-basket and the spirally-built cooking-pot, the names of

FIG. 47. Cooking Pot of Corrugated Ware, Showing Modified Projections near Rim

FIG. 48. Wicker Water-Bottle, Showing Double Loops for Suspension

the two kinds of vessels may be given. The boiling-basket was known as *wó-li-a-k'ia-ní-tu-li-a-tom-me*, the corrugated cooking pot as *wo-li-a-k'ia-te'-ni-tu-li-a-ton-ne*, the former signifying "coiled cooking-basket," the latter "coiled earthenware cooking-basket."

Other very important types of vessels were made in a similar way. I refer especially to canteens and water-bottles. The water-bottle of wicker differed little from the boiling-basket. It was generally rounder-bodied, longer and narrower necked, and provided at one side near the shoulders or rim with two loops of hair or strong fiber, usually braided. (See fig. 48.) The ends of the burden-strap passed through these loops made suspension of the

FIG. 49. Water-Bottle of Corrugated Ware, Showing Double Handle

FIG. 50. Water-Bottle of Corrugated Ware, Showing Plain Bottom

vessel easy, or when the latter was used simply as a receptacle, the pair of loops served as a handle. Sometimes these basket-bottles were strengthened at the bottom with rawhide or buckskin, stuck on with gum. When, in the evolution of the pitcher, this type of basket was reproduced in clay, not only was the general form preserved, but also the details above described. That is, without reference to usefulness—in fact at no small expense of trouble—the handles were almost always made double (see fig. 49); indeed, often braided, although of clay. Frequently, especially as time went on, the bottoms were left plain, as if to simulate the smooth skin-bottoming of the basket-bottles. (See fig. 50.) At first it seems odd that with all these points

FIG. 51. Food-Bowl and Water-Jar, Showing Open or Unjoined Space in Line near Rim

of similarity the two kinds of water-vessel should have totally dissimilar names; the basket-bottle being known as the *k'iá-pu-k'ia-tom-me*; from *k'iá-pu-kia*, "for carrying or placing water in," and *tóm-me*; the handled earthen receptacle, as the *i'-mush-ton-ne*. Yet when we consider that the latter was designed not for transporting water, for which it was less suited than the former, but for holding it, for which it was even preferable, the discrepancy is explained, since the name *i'-mush-ton-ne* is from *i'-mu*, to sit, and *tóm-me*, a tube. This indicates, too, why the basket-bottle was not displaced by the earthen bottle. While the former continued in use for bringing water from a distance, the latter was employed for storing it. As the fragile earthen vessels were much more readily made and less liable to become tainted, they were exclusively used as receptacles, removing the necessity of the tedious manufacture of a large number of the basket-bottles. Again, as the pitcher was thus used exclusively as a receptacle, to be set aside in household or camp, the name *i'-mush-ton-ne* sufficed without the interpolation *te*—"earthenware"—to distinguish it as of *terra cotta* instead of osiery.

. . . .

Decorative Symbolism

On every class of food- and water-vessels, in collections of both ancient and modern Pueblo pottery (except, it is important to note, on pitchers and some sacred receptacles), it may be observed as a singular, yet almost constant feature, that encircling lines, often even ornamental zones, are left open or not, as it were, closed at the ends. (See fig. 51a.) This is clearly a conventional quality and seemingly of intentional significance. An explanation must be sought in various directions, and once found will be useful in guiding to an understanding of the symbolic element in Pueblo ceramic art. I asked the Indian women, when I saw them making these little spaces with great care, why they took so much pains to leave them open. They replied that to close them was *a'k-ta-ni*, "fearful!"—that this little space through the line or zone on a vessel was the "exit trail of life or being," *o' ne-yäthl-kwái-na*, and this was all. How it came to be first left open and why regarded as the "exit trail," they could not tell. If one studies the mythology of this people and their ways of thinking, then watches them closely, he will, however, get other clews. When a woman has made a vessel, dried, polished, and painted it, she will tell you with an air of relief that it is a "Made Being." Her statement is confirmed as a sort of article of faith, when you observe that as she places the vessel in the kiln, she also places in and beside it food. Evidently she vaguely gives something about the vessel a personal existence. The question arises how did these people come to regard food-receptacles or water-receptacles as possessed of or accompanied by conscious existences. I have found that the Zuñi argues actual and essential relationship from similarity in the appearance, function, or other attributes of even generically diverse things.

I here allude to this mental bias because it has both influenced the decoration of pottery and has been itself influenced by it. In the first place, the noise made by a pot when struck or when simmering on the fire is supposed to be the voice of its associated being. The clang of a pot when it breaks or suddenly cracks in burning is the cry of this being as it escapes or separates from the vessel. That it has departed is argued from the fact that the vase when cracked or fragmentary never resounds as it did when whole. This vague existence never cries out violently unprovoked, but it is supposed to acquire the power of doing so by imitation; hence, no one sings, whistles, or makes other strange or musical sounds resembling those of earthenware under the circumstances above described during the smoothing, polishing, painting, or other processes of finishing. The being thus incited, they think, would surely strive to come out, and would break the vessel in so doing. In this we find a partial explanation of the native belief that a pot is accompanied by a conscious existence. The rest of the solution of this problem in belief is involved in the native philosophy and worship of water. Water contains the source of continued life. The vessel holds the water; the source of life *accompanies* the water; hence its dwelling place is in the vessel with the water. Finally, the vessel is supposed to contain the treasured source, irrespective of the water—as do wells and springs, or even the places where they have been. If the encircling lines inside of the eating bowl, *outside* of the water jar, were closed, there would be no exit trail for this invisible source of life or for its influence or breath. Yet, why, it may be asked, must the source of life or its influence be provided with a trail by which to pass out from the vessel? In reply to this I will submit two considerations. It has been stated that on the earliest South-western potteries decoration was effected by incised or raised ornamentation. Any one who has often attempted to make vessels according to primitive methods as I have has found how difficult it is to smoothly join a line incised around a still soft clay pot, and that this difficulty is even greater when the ornamental band is laid on in relief. It would be a natural outgrowth of this predicament to leave the ends unjoined, which indeed the savage often did. When paint instead of incision or relief came to be the decorative agent, the lines or bands would be left unjoined in imitation. As those acquainted with Tylor's "Early History" will realize, a "myth of observation" like the above would come to be assigned in after ages. This may or may not be true of the case in question; for, as before observed, some classes of sacred receptacles, as well as the most ancient painted bowls, are not characterized by the unjoined lines. Whether true or not, it is an insufficient solution of the problem.

It is natural for the Pueblo to consider water as the prime source of life, or as accompanied by it, for without the presence of living water very few things grow in his desert land. During many a drought chronicled in his oral annals, plants, animals, and men have died as of a contagious scourge. Naturally, there-

FIG. 52. Conical or Flat-Bellied Canteen

fore, he has come to regard water as the milk of adults, to speak of it as such, and as the all-sufficient nourishment which the earth (in his conception of it as the mother of men) yields. In the times when his was a race of cliff and mesa dwellers, the most common vessel appertaining to his daily life was the flat-bellied canteen or water carrier. (See fig. 52.) This was suspended by a band across the forehead, so as to hang against the back, thus leaving the hands as well as the feet free for assistance in climbing. It now survives only for use on long journeys or at camps distant from water. The original suggestion of its form seems to have been that of the human mammary gland, or perhaps its peculiar form may have suggested a relationship between the two. (See fig. 53.) At any rate, its name in Zuñi is *me'-he-ton-ne*, while *me'-ha-na* is the name of the human mammary gland. *Me'-he-ton-ne* is from *me'-ha-na*, mamma, *e'-ton-nai-e*, containing within, and *to'm-me*. From *me'-ha-na-* comes *wo'-ha-na*, hanging or placed against anything, obviously because the mammaries hang or are placed against the breast; or possibly, *me'-ha-na* may be derived from *wo'-ha-na* by a reversal of reasoning, which view does not affect the argument in question. It is probable that the *me'-he-ton* was at first left open at the apex (fig. 53a) instead of at the top (fig. 53b); but, being found liable to leak when furnished with the aperture so low, this was closed. A surviving superstition inclines me to this view. When a Zuñi woman has completed

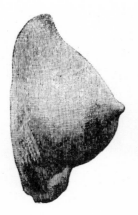
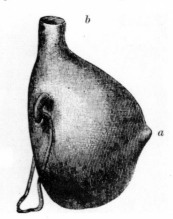

FIG. 53. Conical Canteen Compared with Human Mammary Gland

the *me'-he-ton* nearly to the apex, by the coiling-process, and before she has inserted the nozzle (fig. 53b), she prepares a little wedge of clay, and, as she closes the apex with it, she turns her eyes away. If you ask her why she does this, she will tell you that it is *a'k-ta-ni* (fearful) to look at the vessel while closing it at this point; that, if she look at it during this operation, she will be liable to become barren; or that, if children be born to her, they will die during infancy; or that she may be stricken with blindness; or those who drink from the vessel will be afflicted with disease and wasting away! My impression is that, reasoning from analogy (which with these people means actual relationship or connection, it will be remembered), the Zuñi woman supposes that by closing the apex of this *artificial* mamma she closes the exit-way for the "source of life"; further, that the woman who closes this exit-way knowingly (in her own sight, that is) voluntarily closes the exit-way for the source of life in her *own* mammae; further still, that for this reason the privilege of bearing infants may be taken away from her, or at any rate (experience showing the fallacy of this philosophy) she deserves the loss of the sense (sight) which enabled her to *"knowingly"* close the exit-way of the source of life.

By that tenacity of conservative reasoning which is a marked mental characteristic of the sedentary Pueblo, other types of the

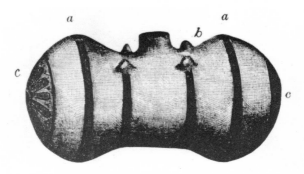

FIG. 54. Double-Lobed or Hunter Canteen

canteen, of later origin, not only retained the name-root of this primeval form, but also its attributed functions. For example, the *me'-wi-k'i-lik-ton-ne* (see fig. 54) is named thus from *me-we*, mammaries, *i-ki-lïk-toï-e'*, joined together by a neck, and *to'm-me*.

Now, when closing the ends (fig. 54c, c) of this curious vessel in molding it, the women are as careful to turn the eyes away as in closing the apex of the older form. As the resemblance of either of the ends of this vessel to the mamma is not striking, they place on either side of the nozzle a pair of little conical projections, resembling the teats, and so called. (Fig. 54b.) There are four of these, instead of, as we might reasonably expect, two. The reason for this seems to be that the *me'-wi-k'i-lik-ton-ne* is the canteen designed for use by the hunter in preference to all other vessels, because it may be easily wrapped in a blanket and tied to the back. Other forms would not do, as the hunter must have the free use not only of his hands but also of his head, that he may turn quickly this way or that in looking for or watching game. The proper nourishment of the hunter is the game he kills; hence, the source of his life, like that of the young of this game, is symbolized in the canteen by the mammaries, not of human beings, but of game-animals. A feature in these canteens dependent upon all this brings us nearer to an understanding of the question under discussion. When ornamental bands are painted around either end of the neck of one of them (fig. 54b), they are inter-

FIG. 55. Paintings of Deer and Sea-Serpent

rupted at the little projections (fig. 54b). Indeed, I have observed specimens on which these lines, if placed farther out, were interrupted at the top (fig. 54a, a) opposite the little projections. So, by analogy, it would seem the Pueblos came to regard paint, like clay, a barrier to the exit of the source of life. This idea of the source of life once associated with the canteen would readily become connected with the water-jar, which, if not the offspring of the canteen, at least usurped its place in the household economy of these people. From the water-jar it would pass naturally to drinking-vessels and eating-bowls, explaining the absence of the interrupted lines on the oldest of these and their constant occurrence on recent and modern examples; for the painted lines being left open at the apexes, or near the projections on the canteens, they should also be unjoined on other vessels with which the same ideas were associated.

So, also, it will be observed that in paintings of animals there is not only a line drawn from the mouth of the plainly depicted heart, but a little space is left down the center or either side of this line (see fig. 55), which is called the *o-ne-yäthl-kwa' to-na*, or the "entrance-trail" (of the source or breath of life).

By this long and involved examination of *one* element in the symbolism of Pueblo ceramic decoration, we gain some idea how many others not quite so striking, yet equally curious, grew up; how, also, they might be explained.

From "A Study of Pueblo Pottery as Illustrative of Zuñi Cultural Growth," *Fourth Annual Report of the Bureau of American Ethnology, 1882–1883* (Washington, D.C., 1886), pp. 482–93, 510–15.

Pottery in the Making

THE clay which served for their wares was seldom taken from the native quarries without prayers and propitiatory offerings. Dependently upon the kind of vessel to be made, it was the subject of careful choice. It was brought from the distant sources of supply in the form of dry lumps, which, as needed, were pulverized on the metates, and mixed with crushed quartz, sand or pot shards, then moistened and kneaded until in condition to be easily dented with the tip of the tongue.

For cooking-vessels red clay was selected and tempered with a larger allowance of sand or grit than was used for the finer wares. This not only kept the clay from cracking as it dried, but rendered the ware tougher and better able to withstand the effects of fire. Either a semi-circular bowl or basket was used as a mold for the bottoms of the vessels, the clay being pressed evenly into the inside and drawn up half an inch above the margin of this impromptu form. Around on the raised border, then around and around on itself, shortened here to form the contraction of the neck, there lengthened to flare the rim, a little strip or flattened rope of clay was spirally wound and cemented, smoothed down outside and in with scoop-shaped trowels of gourd-rind or old pottery, and the vessel was shaped; after which it was set away in a shady place to partially dry, thereby contracting so much that it could easily be removed from the mold at the bottom. It was then additionally smoothed outside with pieces of sandstone and again set away in a safe nook until thoroughly dry, when it was taken out and placed in a little underground kiln or else surrounded top and sides, above

FIG. 56. Pottery Firing. (From "My Adventures in Zuñi")

ground, with a dome of turf and grease-weed or other light fuel.
Just before the summit of this dome was completed the women,
muttering a short prayer, threw inside a few crumbs or bits of
dried bread or dough, which ceremonial was pronounced the
"Feeding." The whole mass was then fired, and blankets held up
to intercept drafts. Within a few minutes all was aglow with heat.
As soon as the turf or wood had been reduced to cinders, the
red-hot vessel was removed with a long poker and gently laid on
hot ashes hastily drawn to one side of the fire for the purpose.
Here it was thoroughly coated inside and out with the
mucilaginous juice of crushed cactus leaves, piñon gum being
liberally applied in addition, to the interior. Another dome, this
time of coarser fuel was quickly erected, the vessel placed inside

and again fired. The effect of the catus juice and piñon gum under the second burning, was to close all pores in the pot and cover the inside with a shining, hard black glaze. So perfectly fireproof and compact were these vessels thus rendered that they might be placed over a bed of embers empty, heated almost to redness, and cold water dashed into them without causing breakage or even cracking. I have often with fear and vain re-monstrances seen this done, yet never witnessed an accident as the result therefrom. The women make in the same way, only with the addition of a larger proportion of sand, the crucibles with which the native jewelers melt their silver.

In some details the process of manufacturing water jars, eating bowls and other receptacles was different. It is true they were built up in much the same way, and when nearly dry, scoured smooth with sandstone, but the clay of which they were made was either of a blue variety, or a kind of carbonaceous shale or marl. When the wares had been smoothed, they were coated with a thin wash of whatever argillaceous earth was found to produce the desired body-color—white, yellow, red or pink—and highly polished with little water-worn pebbles. The paints were usually ochres and jasper for red and yellow; hematite with a sizing of prairie-dog urine or the syrup of the datila fruit, for black; the simple iron ore ground with water for brown; kaolin for white, or various combinations of these pigments for inter-mediate hues. The designs were laid on with little brushes made by chewing the ends of sections cut from fibrous yucca-leaves split beforehand to the desired degree of coarseness or fineness. As I have said before, throughout all of these operations atten-dant upon the finishing and decorating of these vessels, no laughing, music, whistling or any other unnecessary noises were indulged in, and conversation was carried on in faint whispers or by signs; for it was feared that the "voice" would enter into the vessels, and that when the latter were fired, would escape with a loud noise and such violence as to shiver the ware into shards. That this should not in any event happen, the voice-spirit in the vessels—especially those designed for water and food, was fed during the burning. Thus not only was it propitiated but also rendered beneficent . . .

From "Zuñi Breadstuff," *Millstone* 9, no. 10 (1884): 175–76.

Zuñi Farming:
Starting a New Field

W HEN a young Zuñi wishes to add to his landed possessions, he goes out over the country, caring, to all appearance, nothing at all for distance. He selects the mouth of some *arroyo* which winds up from the plain into the hills or mountains, and seeking, where it merges into the plain, some flat stretch of ground, his first care is to "lift the sand." This is done by striking the hoe into the earth at intervals of five or six yards, and hauling out little heaps of soil until a line of tiny boundary mounds has been formed all around the proposed field. Next to this space he cuts away the sage brushes with his heavy hoe, and clods of grass, weeds, etc., all of which he heaps in the middle of the field and burns. He then throws up long banks of sand on the line first indicated by the heaps of soil. Each embankment is called a *so'-pit-thlan* (sand string). At every corner he sets a rock, if possible columnar, sometimes rudely sculptured with his tokens. It is rare he does anything more to the piece in a single year. Not unfrequently even years before the land is actually required for cultivation, the "sand is lifted" and a stone of peculiar shape is placed at one corner as a mark of ownership. Ever after, the place is, unless relinquished, the exclusive property of the one who lifted the sand, or, in case of his death, of the clan he belonged to.

In riding over the ancient country of the Zuñis I have sometimes found these rows of little soil heaps as many as forty miles away from the central valley. Even after the lapse of years, overgrown with grasses, each the bases of a diminutive sand-drift, these marks of savage preëmption are distinct. Thus too, for ages they will remain to serve the archaeologist when the Zuñi

and his theme shall have passed away, as material for specula-
tion. Distance could not have been the sole cause for the abandonment of these pieces, as some fields, still under the hoe, are
equally as far away, yet give evidence of having been cultivated,
probably in consequence of great fertility, for several generations.

With the Zuñis one-half the months in the year are "Nameless;" the others are "Named." The year is called "A Passage of
Time," the seasons "The Steps" (of the year), and the months
"Crescents"—probably because each begins with the new
moon. New year is called the "Mid-journey of the Sun"—that is,
the middle of the solar trip between one summer solstice and
another—and, occurring invariably about the nineteenth of December, usually initiates a short season of great religious activity.
The first month after this is now called *I'-koh-pu-yä-tchun*,
"Growing White Crescent," as with it begins the Southwestern
winter. The origin of the name is evident. The *ancient* name of
the month seems to have been different in meaning, although
strikingly similar in sound, *I-shoh-k o' a-pu-yä-tchun* or "Crescent of the Conception," doubtless a reference to the kindling of
the sacred fire by drilling with an arrow shaft into a piece of soft
dry wood-root, a ceremony still strictly observed. Interesting
evidence of this meaning may be found on the old notched
calendar-sticks of the tribe, the first month of the new year being
indicated by a little fire socket at one end.

The second month is *Ta'-yäm-tchu-yä-tchun*, so named from
the fact that it is the time when boughs are broken by the weight
of descending snow.

Then follows *O-nan-úl-ak-k'ia-kwum-yä-tchun*, or the
month during which "Snow lies not in the pathways," with
which ends winter or the "Sway of Cold."

Spring, called the "Starting Time," opens with *Thli'-te-
kwa-na-k' ia-tsa-na-yä-tchun*, or the month of the "Lesser Sand
Storms," followed by *Thli'-te-kwa-na-k' ia-thla'-na-yä-tchun*, or
the month of the "Greater Sand Storms," and this, the ugliest
season of the Zuñi year, is closed by *Yä-tchun-kwa-shi'-am-o-na*,
"The Crescent of No Name." Summer and Autumn, the period of
the "Months Nameless," are together called *O'-lo-i-k' ia*, the
season "Bringing Flour-like Clouds." In priestly or ritualistic

language these six months, although called nameless, are designated successively the "Yellow, Blue, Red, White, Variegated or Iridescent, and Black," after the colors of the plumed prayersticks sacrificed in rotation at the full of each moon to the gods of the North, West, South, East, the Skies and the Lower Regions.

In common parlance these months and the minute division of the seasons they embrace are referred to by the terms descriptive of the growth of corn-plants and the development and naturescence of their grain—[illustrating] the tendency of the Zuñis to make corn the standard of measurement for time [as well as] for many other things.

Early in the month of the "Lesser Sand Storms" the same Zuñi, we will say, who preëmpted, a year since, a distant arroyo-field goes forth hoe and axe in hand, to resume the work of clearing, etc. Within the same embankment he now selects that portion which the arroyo enters from above, and cutting many forked cedar branches, drives them firmly into the dry streambed, in a line crossing its course, and extending a considerable distance beyond either bank. Against this row of stakes he places boughs, clods, rocks, sticks and earth, so as to form a strong barrier or dry-dam; open, however, at either end. Some rods below this on either side of the stream-course, he constructs, less carefully, other and longer barriers. Still further down, he seeks in the "Tracks" of some former torrent, a ball of clay, which having been detached from its native bank, far above, has been rolled and washed, down and down, ever growing rounder and smaller and tougher, until in these lower plains it lies embedded in and baked by the burning sands. This he carefully takes up, breathing reverently from it, and places it on one side of the stream-bed, where it is desirable to have the rain-freshets overflow. He buries it with a brief supplication in the soil and then proceeds to heap over it a solid bank of earth which he extends obliquely across, and to some distance beyond the arroyo. Returning, he continues the embankment past the clay ball either in line of, or at whatever angle with the completed portion seems to his practiced eye most suited to the topography.

To those not acquainted with savage ways of thought, this proceeding will gain interest from explanation. The national game of the Zuñi is *Ti⸴kwa-we*, or The Race of the Kicked Stick.

Two little cylindrical sticks of hard wood are cut, each the length of the middle finger. These, distinguished one from the other by bands of red paint, are laid across the toes of either leader and kicked in the direction the race is to be run. At full speed of the runners these sticks are dexterously shoveled up on the toes, and kicked on and on. The party which gets its stick over the goal first is counted the winning side. This race is usually run by no fewer than twelve men, six opposed to an equal number. The distance ordinarily accomplished without rest or even abatement, is twenty-five miles. Now the time taken in running this race is marvelously short, never exceeding three hours; yet, were you to ask one of the runners to undertake the race without his stick, he would flatly tell you he could not possibly do it. So imbued with this idea are the Zuñis that frequently, when coming in from distant fields, and wishing to make haste, they cut a stick, and kick it on ahead of them, running to catch up with it and so on. The interesting feature about all this is that the Indian in this, as in most things else, confounds the cause with the effect, thinks the stick helps him, instead of himself being the sole motive power of the stick. The lump of clay before mentioned is supposed to be the *Ti'-kwa* of the water gods, fashioned by their invisible hands and pushed along by their resistless feet, *not* hindering, but adding to the force and speed of the waters. The field-maker fancies that the waters, when they run down this trail again, will be as anxious to catch up with their *Ti'-kwa* as he would be. So he takes this way of tempting the otherwise tameless, *he* thinks, torrents out of their course. Yet, to make doubly sure, he has thrown a dam across their proper pathway. On the outskirts of the field thus planned, little inclosures of soil, like earthen bins are thrown up wherever the ground slopes how little-soever from a central point, these inclosures being either irregularly square or in conformity to the lines of the slope. (See fig. 57.)

My hope has been in so minutely describing these beginnings of a Zuñi farm to give a most precious hint to any reader interested in agriculture, or who may possess a field some portions of which are barren because too dry. We may smile at the superstitious observances of the Indian agriculturist, but when we come to learn what he accomplishes, we shall admire and I

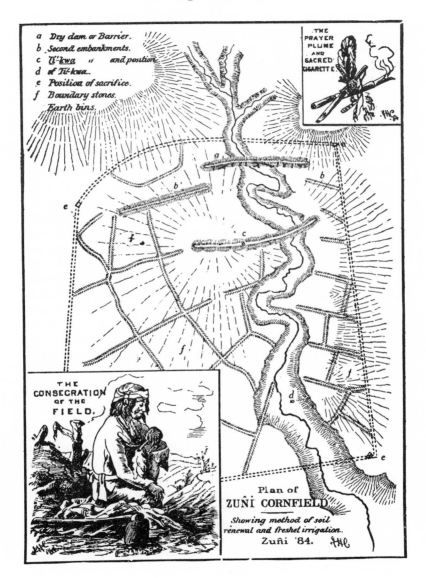

a   Dry dam or Barrier.
b   Second embankments.
c   Ti-kwa   "   and position
d   of Ti-kwa.
e   Position of sacrifice.
f   Boundary stones.
    Earth bins.

THE
PRAYER
PLUME
AND
SACRED
CIGARETTE

THE
CONSECRATION
OF THE
FIELD.

Plan of
ZUÑI CORNFIELD
Showing method of soil
renewal and freshet irrigation.
Zuñi '84.

FIG. 57. Plan of Zuñi Cornfield

hope find occasion to imitate his hereditary ingenuity. The country of the Zuñis is so desert and dry, that times out of number within even the fickle memory of tradition, the possession of water for drinking and cooking purposes alone, has been counted a blessing. Yet, by his system of earth banking the Zuñi Indian and a few of his western brothers and pupils—the Moquis—have heretofore been the only human beings who could, without irrigation from living streams, raise to maturity a crop of corn within its parched limits.

The use of the principal barriers and embankments may be inferred from the terms of the invocation with which the field is consecrated after the completion of all the earthworks. The owner then applies to whatever corn-priest is keeper of the sacred "medicine" of his clan or order. This priest cuts and decorates a little stick of red willow with plumes from the legs and hips of the eagle, turkey and duck, and with the tail-feathers from the Maximilian's jay, night-hawk, yellow-finch and ground-sparrow, fastening them on, one over the other, with cords of fine cotton. From the store of paint which native tradition claims was brought from the original birth-place of the nation (a kind of plumbago) he takes a tiny particle, leavening with it a quantity of black mineral powder. To a sufficient measure of rain water, he adds a drop of ocean water with which he moistens the pigment, and with a brush made by chewing the end of a yucca-leaf, applies the paint to the stick. With the same paint he also decorates a section of cane filled with wild tobacco supposed to have been planted by rain, hence sacred. These two objects, sanctified by his breath, he gives to the applicant. Taking them carefully in his left hand, the latter goes forth to his new field. Seeking a point in the middle of the arroyo below all his earthworks, he kneels, or sits down on his blanket facing east. He then lights his cane cigarette and blows smoke toward the North, West, South, East, the Upper and the Lower regions. Then, holding the smoking stump and the plumed stick near his breast, he says a prayer. From the substance of his prayer, which, remarkably curious though it be, is too long for literal reproduction here, we learn the important facts relative to his intentions and his faith. We find he believes: that he has infused the consciousness of his prayer into the plumed stick; that with his sacred cigarette he has prepared a way "Like the trails of the winds and rains" (clouds) for the wafting of that prayer to the gods of all regions. Having taken the cloud-inspiring down of the turkey, the strength-giving plume of the eagle, the water-loving feather of the duck, the path-finding tails of the birds who counsel and guide Summer, having moreover severed and brought hither the flesh of the water-attracting tree, which he has dipped in the god-denizened ocean, beautified with the very cinders of creation, bound with strands from the dress of the sky-born goddess of cotton—he beseeches the god-priests of earth, sky and cavern, the beloved gods whose dwelling places are in the great embracing waters of the world, not to withhold their mist-laden breaths, but to canopy the earth with cloud banners, and let fly their shafts little and mighty of rain, to send forth the fiery spirits of lightning, lift up the voice of thunder whose echoes shall step from mountain to mountain bidding the *mesas* shake down streamlets. The streamlets shall yield torrents; the torrents, foam-capped, soil-laden, shall boil toward the shrine he is making, drop hither and thither the soil they are bearing, leap over his barricades unburdened and stronger, and in place of their lading, bear out toward the ocean as payment and faith-gift the smoke-cane and the prayer-plume. Thus thinking, thus believing, thus yearning, thus beseeching, (in order that the seeds of earth shall not want food for their growing, that from their growth he may not lack food for his living, means for his fortune) he this day plants, standing in the trail of the waters, the smoke-cane and prayer-plume.[1]

The effect of the net-work of barriers is what the Indian prayed for—attributes, furthermore, as much to his prayer as to his labors—namely, that with every shower, although the stream go dry three hours afterward, water has been carried to every portion of the field, has deposited a fine loam over it all and moistened from one end to the other, the substratum. Not only this, but also, all rainfall on the actual space is retained and absorbed within the system of minor embankments.

At the stage of operations above last described, the field is again left for a year, that it may become thoroughly enriched. Meanwhile, during the same month (the first of spring) each planter repairs the banks in his old fields, and proceeds to adopt quite a different method for renewing or enriching the soil.

Along the western sides of his field, as well as of such spots throughout it as are worn out or barren, he thickly plants rows of sage-brush, leaving them standing from six inches to a foot above the surface. As the prevailing winds of the Zuñi plains hail from the southwest, and as during the succeeding month ("the Crescent of the Greater Sand Storms") these winds are laden many tens of feet high in the air with fine dust and sand, behind each row of the sage-brush a long level, deep deposit of soil is drifted. With the coming of the first—and as a rule, only—rain-storm of the spring-time, the water, carried about by the embankments, and retained lower down by the "earth bins" redistributes this "soil sown by the winds" and fixes it with moisture to the surface it has usurped.

Thus, with the aid of nature's hand, without plow or harrow, the Zuñi fits and fertilizes his lands, for the planting of May-time, or the Nameless month.

From "Zuñi Breadstuff," *Millstone* 9, no. 4 (1884): 58–59.

Note

1. The kind of philosophy which can give rise to faith in this remarkable reversal of nature's order—making the growth of willows the explanation of the presence of waters, instead of the consequence; making summer birds the *bringers* of summer instead of summer the incentive of their yearly migration—is, strange as it may seem, the teaching of nature by her appearances, for natural philosophy is hidden under natural phenomena. Therefore, wonder not, ridicule not the retrogressive reasoning of savages. Rather, look to this, this one great dissimilarity between child-mind and civilized mind, as the fruitful cause of misunderstanding between the American and the Indian—a misunderstanding which will end, moreover, only with the death of this peculiar philosophy or the doom of its devoted adherents. [F.H.C.]

Corn Raising:
The Decay of the Seed

THE reader of this chapter will at the end, like a man lost in the woods, find himself only where he started; but unlike such a man he will be, for all that, much nearer home. That is to say, a description of the last ceremonial of Harvest must begin an account of Zuñi Corn-Planting and Rearing.

In each corn-room or granary of Zuñi, are preserved carefully, four objects: an ear of yellow corn full to the very tip of perfect kernels, called a *yä'-po-to*; an ear of white corn which has resulted from the intergrowth of two or more ears within a single husk-fold, called, from its disproportionate breadth and flatness, a *mi'-k'iap-pan-ne*; a moderately large normal ear of corn which has been dipped by a Seed-Priest in the waters of the great sacred Salt Lake far south of Zuñi (*"Las Salinas"* of New Mexico), and a bunch of unbroken corn-soot. The latter two objects are laid side by side on the floor in the middle of the corn-room, and upon them also side by side, usually connected by a bandage of cotton filaments, the *yä'-po-to* and the *mi'-k'iap-pan-ne*. (See fig. 58.1.)

The significance of all this is both interesting and poetic. The corn soot is held to symbolize the "generation of life," the salted and sanctified ear of corn, the material given by the gods and prepared by man, as the means whereby generated life is sustained, and finally, both these are regarded as the "resting place" or "couch" of the "Father and Mother of corn-crops" or seed; the *yä'-po-to* being the "male," the *mi'-k'iap-pan-ne*, the "female."

In a field of growing maize, the owner selects such hills as

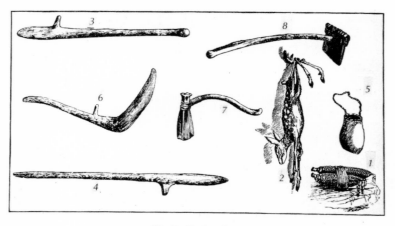

FIG. 58. Zuñi Implements

give promise of speediest maturity. These receive his special
care. No sooner have a few ears ripened on them than he picks
the most perfect, as well as a bunch of soot from some neighboring stalk, and tenderly carries them home in his arms. Arrived at
the entrance-way of his house he calls to the women within:
"We come!"
"Ah? How come ye?" say they.
"Together, happily," he replies.
"Then enter ye!" calls out the chorus of women's voices,
whereupon the man goes slowly in. One of the women beckons
his attention to the "sitting place," which, in this instance, is a
decorated basket-tray in the center of the room. Thither he proceeds and places, one by one, the ears of corn in the tray—using
care that they shall all point eastward—and lays the bunch of
soot over them. The women of the house flock to the mantel
whereon stands the family bowl of prayer-meal, each taking a
pinch of the sacred substance, while one of their number, the
"corn-matron," hastens away to the granary, and carefully lifting
the *yä'-po-to* and *mi'-k'iap-pan-ne*, brings them forth. As she
nears the tray, she says, across the objects in her hands (addressing the new corn), "My children, how be ye these many days?"
Then the new corn is supposed to reply through the voices of the

other women, now gathered near, "Happily, our old ones, happily!" With this the corn-matron deposits her burden on the new bunch of soot, and all present say little prayers significant of the occasion and setting forth their wishes for "age of life, happy fortune and the health of strength born of the food of maize." This ceremonial is called the "Meeting of the Children" and is performed in commemoration of the return of the lost corn maidens under the guidance of Pai-a-tu-ma, and their welcome by the Seed-Priests of ancient Zuñi.[1]

With the closing of the prayers, the right hand of each worshiper is passed gently over the tray—while scattering prayer-meal—and breathed from. The corn-matron then returns to the granary, bearing both the old corn and the new. She replaces the old bunch of soot with the new, laying the former away with the fresh ears of corn and returning the *yä⸍-po-to* and *mi⸍-k'iap-pa-ne* to their resting place.

When all the harvest has been gathered, dried, sorted and corded up, around and over the "Father and Mother" in the corn-room, the ceremonial interrupted at the beginning is resumed. While the corn is being classified as to color and grade, the finest ears of each kind are selected and laid aside. These, and the ears of "new corn" are together laid along the outer edge of the corn-pile. Next morning the "corn-matron" takes a basket-tray—perhaps the same one used before, or at least one like it—and goes to the door of the corn-room. Here she slips off her left moccasin, then enters. As she passes the threshold she looks around as though she were about to address a group of waiting friends, and exclaims:

"My mothers and children, how be ye, and how have you come unto the morning?" and after a moment herself replies:

"Happily!"

Reverently, for she is in the presence of the conscious and the benign—so it seems to her—she approaches the cord of corn and with her left hand takes of the selected ears along the top, an ear for each finger (that is, four,) then with the right hand an equal number, placing them in the tray. She brings these forth and assisted by the male head of the household, shells them with such care that not a kernel is lost. Dust from the old bunch of soot is scattered over the shelled corn, and a curious sacred pigment is prepared, in an earthen ladle, of yellow paint and a kernel of salt, from the mountain near the lake of the dead, and the salt lake in the South. To these ingredients are added two or three kinds of little yellow flowers, the principal variety being precious in the eyes of the Zuñi, as that which was "left over of the seed stores of the gods." All this is mixed with pollen and water, and the whole tray of kernels is thoroughly sprinkled and annointed by stirring. The corn grains thus treated are bright yellow in color and pleasantly odoriferous. All this is done that the "seed" may have the power of reproduction, rapid growth and strength, and that it may bear fruit possessed of the properties of food, which fruit shall mature with the season when thrive most and bloom the little yellow flowers—early autumn. We are at first surprised when we learn that to a remarkable degree the corn thus treated has vigor and the quality of ripening early; but our wonder may be lessened when we reflect that these seeds are the most perfect of the whole harvest, selected mostly from among those ears which soonest reached maturity. Still, with the Zuñi all these things are living testaments of faith, proving the infallibility of his theory of "Medicine," or Fetichism and of his practice of religion.

The corn, now fully prepared, is poured into a pouch made from the whole skin of a fawn. (See fig. 58.2.) Most fantastic in appearance is this spotted, life-like corn-bag, as it hangs, at night-time, against the wall, gilded by the fire-light, head down-ward, the incessantly flickering shadows of its broad ears and dangling fore-legs giving it the appearance of struggling to get free from the strong antlers which seem as actively trying to cast it off. And there, notwithstanding these illusionary struggles, it hangs until late springtime.

I have told how, during the months of the sand storms the banks in the old cornfields are newly built up. Little more need be done, and some fine morning in May, the voice, low, mourn-ful, yet strangely penetrating and tuneful, of the Sun Priest is heard from the house-tops. As you listen in the shadow of some tall terrace, you think that voice must come from a spirit of the Heroic age of Zuñi, returned on the night-wind and hastening to call his wayward game-becrazed children to the fields, so old fashioned, so hidden in meaning seem the words it is uttering.

However little the sleepy-eyed devotee of "cane-weeds" and "stick-shuffling" may understand of that archaeic monologue, he knows its one principal meaning, and if he be the head of the household who assisted in the shelling of the seed-corn last autumn, he bethinks himself of the planting stick and bestirs himself to sharpen (against a slab of sandstone) that useful, simple, yet ingenious instrument of husbandry. This planting stick (see fig. 58.3) is a kind of prod made from a straight-grained juniper sapling, the base flattened and sharpened to a round-nosed blade-like point, and possessed of one ear formed by a fortuitous branch cut off and scraped until just enough is left to be useful as a brace for the right foot. The utensil our friend has just finished sharpening, glistens from long use. The blade is worn short, ground shorter, and the whole thing has an air of antiquity; was, likely as not made long ago by the man's grandfather on the mother's side or by some other equally pristine potterer early in this century or late in the last. He will not use this venerable relic, let us hope, for planting the whole field; but at any rate he prefers it, short though it be, for the work presently in hand. He has leaned it against the wall near the doorway now, and has gone in to get his feather-box and paint-pots. With these and a piece of willow (cut *this* time at the "Lake of the Dead") he makes a plumed prayer-stick. He then chooses from the fawn-skin pouch six kernels of corn, each, of course, of a different color, and in a broad husk wraps them with the plumed wand. Slinging the pouch over his shoulder, he takes up the old planting-stick and says ceremoniously to the women:

"We go!"

As he steps out of the doorway, the corn-matron hustles after him with a bowl of fresh, cold water, with which she lavishly sprinkles him and his pouch, laughingly telling "them" to go. Thoroughly be-drenched, he shuffles down the hill, across the river, and out to his field.

I need not stop to explain that a Zuñi would by no means miss this sprinkling process, as—jokingly performed though it may be—it is symbolic of rain, believed to be provocative of that blessing, without which the seed-corn would be powerless to grow. Arrived at the field, he goes to a well-known spot near the center. Here he digs in the soft sandy soil by pushing his prod

down with his foot, and turning it around and around—four deep
holes equally distant from a central space; the first to the North,
the second to the West, the third to the South and the fourth to the
East. By the left side of the northern hole he digs another to
represent the Sky-regions, and by the right side of the southern
hole still another relating it to the Lower regions. In the central
space he kneels facing the East, and drawing forth the plumed
prayer-wand first marks by sprinkling prayer-meal, a cross on the
ground—to symbolize not only the four cardinal points, but also,
the stars which shall watch over his field by night-time. Then
with prayer, he plants the plumed stick at the intersection of the
cross, sprinkles it with more prayer-meal—as the corn-matron
had sprinkled him with water—and withdraws. From his pouch
he selects three grains of each of the six colors—yellow, blue,
red, white, speckled and black—and places them respectively
with the six grains of like colors which had been wrapped in the
shuck. He now goes back and kneeling down, holds the four
grains of yellow color in his left hand, and facing toward the
northern hole crones the following first verse of a planting chant:

"U—ai——o-a—ho——o
U—ai——o-a—ho——o
U—ai——o-a—ho——o
Li wa ma ha'ni,
Pish le a ha'n kwi,
Ho-lon e-te, hom thlup-tsi-kwa
Mi-a na-kia, an hai'te na kia.
U—ai——a—i—o—a——o ho."

U——ai, etc.
"Off over yonder,
Toward the North-land.
Will it but prove that my *yellow* corn grains
Shall grow and bear fruit asking which I now sing."
U——ai, etc.

And just as he sings the refrain he drops the yellow kernels into
the hole toward the North. Continuing the refrain so that it runs
into the prelude of the next stanza, he shifts about so as to face
westward and taking up the four blue grains, repeats as before,
except that he sings to the "West-land" and of the "blue corn

grains," and when he comes to the refrain, drops the blue grains into the hole toward the West. Thus he proceeds, not once interrupting his droning chant, until all the sets of grains have been dropped into the holes which their colors respectively relate them to; the red into the Southern, the white into the Eastern, the speckled into the Upper and the black into the Lower. Ceremonial is now abandoned. He covers the grains he has dropped, and in lines corresponding to the directions of the four hills, plants rows far out into the field until the corn in the fawn-skin pouch is exhausted. Then he returns home, not again to plant until four days shall have passed by, during which time (let me add) he dutiously fasts, prays regularly at sunrise by the riverside, and abstains from all unbecoming pleasures.

It will not be held against me that I forgot to tell how the rest of the seed corn was provided. Those ears from among which the first eight were selected by the corn-matron, have been brought out, last autumn, from the place of storage, and shelled in the most matter-of-fact way. Part of the grains are laid by as seed for the *Kâ⸱kâ*, or sacred dance, while the remainder are stored in large buckskin bags to serve as the "common-seed" for the planting of the fields.

At the end of the fourth day after the first planting the householder quite likely makes a new planting-stick (fig. 58.4), laying the old one aside. He also gets out his seed bags. These (see fig. 58.5) are curious; usually of rawhide, they have been so puckered and sewed that they form egg-shaped receptacles, cut off at the smaller end. They are ingeniously made to remain open and otherwise retain their shape by being moistened, filled first with damp, then with moderately hot, dry sand, and hung up to harden by desiccation, which of course takes place in a short time. A little hoop of wood is, moreover, fitted around the upper edge, much as is the large wire rim of a tin bucket, and like the latter, the seed-pouch is also furnished with a bail—of twisted buckskin.

Taking a luncheon of paper-bread—substantial in quantity at least—and a bag of common seed-corn, together with the various appliances above described, and followed by a discontented urchin, staggering under a big, earthen canteen of water, the planter now proceeds to his field. Along the eastern side of the rows of last year's broken stalks (or corn butts), four or five inches from each bunch, he digs holes with his wooden prod, to the depth of from four to seven inches. The boy comes along after him dropping into each hole from twelve to twenty kernels, and pushing sand in with his foot until it is filled. Wherever the stalk-butts happen to be thin, they reinforce them with bunches of grease-wood or sage-bush sprigs. The consequence is that not only is the crop not planted twice successively in the same spots, but a long drift of fresh soil is blown by the still prevailing west winds directly over each new hill of corn, forming without labor, neat little mounds of earth. The country of the Zuñis is so dry that the seeds have to be planted to great depths—even at the expense of great delay in their growth—and the little drifts of sandy soil protect the underlying loam in which the kernels are embedded from the fierce south-western sun. Not only on account of this dryness but because some of the plants die in their efforts to reach daylight, the large number of kernels for each hill is required.

Now comes the time when young Zuñi and his elder brother may indulge in fanciful creations which would astound the most talented scare-crow makers of New England. The glossy large south-western crow or raven is abroad. He sits on every rock, soars through every cloud-shadow, laughs and cackles in every corn-arroyo at safe, nevertheless impertinent distances from the busy planter. He as much as says to his companions—in the language of Zuñi crow lore—"Ah! you just wait until those little green spikes come up! They grow solely for our benefit that we may have signs whereby to find the good things those long-legged fearful fellows are hiding so deep in the sand; why, that's what our heavy noses are provided for!" Alas, poor birds! Have they forgotten last season? What a shock is in store for them! What disappointment shall soon be attested by the most discordant kaw croaks of anguish!

The old man is busy setting up cedar poles at intervals of a few rods, all over the field. Not knowing what these poles were for, you would think an eastern bean-patch or hop-field had been transferred to Zuñi-land. But if you carefully look, you will see that each pole is furnished at the top with a bunch of its own or some other prickly leaves, so that the crows may not light on it.

FIG. 59. Zuñi Cornfield with Crow-Traps

Moreover, the busy planter is now stringing from one pole to another, cords of split yucca leaves, which but for their knottiness, would remind you of the telegraph wires of New York City, so thick they are. A sort of network is thus formed all over the field. To make this more imposing, tattered rags, pieces of dog and coyote skins, old shoulder blades strung two or three together, streamers of moss, in fact streamers of every conceivable thing which has the property of swaying in the wind, are thickly attached to these numerous cords making them appear much as I fancy a clothes-line would left by a hurricane.

Meanwhile the youngsters are busy. They have pilfered from the old storeroom everything in the shape of off-duty clothing they could lay hands on. You must know, my reader, that this is quite what their fathers and uncles want; but not so their mothers, aunts and grandmothers. These representatives of Zuñi consanguinity are the stingiest creatures human breath was ever vouchsafed to. If a dress be too dirty and ragged to be kept comfortably on, it will do, backed by straw, to stop up sky-holes with; if too far gone for this, still, it is serviceable baby bedding, and yet more; if even not good enough for this, it is most gracious in their eyes for the manufacture of "holders of hot things." Therefore, it is stored away in common with numerous predecessors for the "wanting time." Yet, young Zuñi is quite as sharp as any other boy. He gets what he covets, be assured, and that too without the knowledge of even his younger sister! Off to the deep arroyo near his father's field he goes with his plunder. His older brother is "in with him." Both of them have been deprived all their lives long of slates and pencils. They have found no vent for their caricaturistic capacities, which are great, and they take it out on occasions like the present. They are prolific of invention, bold, and of ready execution. Twenty-four hours hence behold the result! As you ride along some outward-bound trail your feelings would be mirthful but for the effect on your shaky Indian nag. He will *not* be convinced that those things standing or sitting around so frequently are inanimate! Yonder on the hillside is an old woman limping (*not* along). She carries a basket on her back and a rib-scapula-tin-can-and-stick-rattle in her hand. Does it rattle? Yes; it is safe to say that you can hear it—if the wind be blowing—even before you see the stuffed old woman. This way further *expressively* tearing right along, is a being with outstretched hands, streaming shocks of gray hair (pulled from a dead horse's tail), a black *black* rawhide face, eyes made of husk-balls popping out of his head and painted yellow, teeth of corn-stalks from jaw-rim to jaw-rim, and a great red tongue which lolls in and out from side to side, with every breeze-gust. He seems to be frightened by the frog-legged character behind him. Now all these *shé-tu-na-kwe* ("watchers of corn sprouts") have the desired effect! The *old* crows let the field most faithfully alone!

Not so with the new generation of "kernel diggers"—which gets feathers and finds wings about this time. Before growth has made the corn invulnerable, these guileless young creatures come along. They are no more fearful of the extravagant effigies than of the embracing boughs of their paternal rookery. Many of them, therefore, get caught in little hair nooses plentifully attached to convenient cobbles. Others commit suicide in pairs by swallowing the tempting kernels at either end of a hair thread and then winding one another up and choking. They seem to prefer this to being "Siamese twins" all their lives!

The captives are, in due course of time, taken up. They are carried home and treated with the utmost tenderness, but they are *not* fed! If one of them happens to find something to eat or drink (rarely the case) his beak is promptly cut off in order that he shall not be tempted a second time. Of course, the wretched birds "die young," and are then crucified on two flexible twigs and hung, head downward, to one or another of the numerous yucca lines. This course of action is, it seems, prompted by the belief that the souls of these dead crows will warn their mortal companions that man is "very painful," and in order that these souls may not lack for witnesses they are furnished with their own bodies, hung up in conspicuous places.[2]

The scarecrow and the bird it scares are subjects of such grave interest to the Zuñi, such an element of agitation during its brief season in his industrial life, so undoubtedly the chief root of evil to his bread material—on which subject he is as touchy as a miser—that a little anecdote relative to the bird in particular, would not be, it seems to me, out of the way.

The corn had just sprouted in the spring of 1881, and my "Older Brother's" scarecrows (fault of his own) had not been so successful as those of his neighbors. That those of his neighbors were better than his own was not in itself an aggravation, but certainly a nuisance, for it caused the crows to leave their fields and fairly flock to his. He came to my "little house" one morning wearing a weary look.

"What's inside of you?" I asked.

"Crows!"

"Why do you not make scarecrows?" said I.

"Scarecrows? ho! *Nothing* will remedy the folly of our ancients, *nothing*, I say, Younger Brother!"

"Why? What did they do?" said I, feeling for a pencil.

"Now look here!" exclaimed the old man. "You little fool, put away that writing stick. I'm in earnest very, this morning, and I want to ask you two questions."

"Go on then," said I.

"Well, you know when our ancients came out of the four caves? There was a priest with them—he belonged to *my* clan too!" (added the old man with a look of injury and exceeding disgust.) "Well, from under the world this priest had brought a wonderful and beautiful wand, but no one had seen it in the dark. Now, they all asked 'What is it? what is it?'

"'It is a baton,' said the priest, 'given by the Makers of Life.'

"'What is it for?' said some, and 'How pretty it is!' said others, for it was covered with many colored feathers in bright patterns and bands.

"'It is a baton,' said the priest, 'given to test children's understandings,' saying which he spoke a charm, struck the wand against a rock and behold! Four eggs issued from one end and rolled out in front of the lookers. One pair was dull; the other beautiful like pale turquoise—with little marks all over.

"'My children,' said the priest, 'listen! These are the seed of living things. Two of them are to become more beautiful than my wand, and precious—the blessing of those whom they accompany; for wheresoever they dwell, there will be everlasting summer and beautiful growing things. But the others will become beasts who, every year's end will fight the summer birds away and bring back winter; and every summer-dawn will tear up growing things, leaving hunger and perplexing thoughts to those they live with. Be wise, now, my children, and, above all, choose not with greed,' said the priest.

"Now what do you suppose those fools did?"

"I don't know."

"*Well*! They took the pretty *blue* eggs of *course*, 'because,' said they, 'these are of the color of precious stones; therefore they must surely be the seed of precious things!' So they carried them with great gentleness to a place on the sunny side of a cliff and laid them in soft down, and watched them day by day. By and by the eggs cracked and two little worms came out, which presently became birds with pin-feathers under their skins and open eyes. They never seemed satisfied with their food—always wanted more, you see! But the pin-feathers looked blue, green and yellow (under their skins), and the people chuckled, saying 'Ha-ha, wa-ha! We have *understandings*, for look! If their dresses be pretty *under* their skins think what they will be when they come out and *cover* them!' So they fed the greedy little wretches all they could stuff. When the birds feathered out they were *black,* and they flew away laughing Ka-ha, Ka-ha, as they've laughed ever since—the pesky corn-pullers!

"But the priest sent the dull eggs to summer-land in a rain-cloud, and they became the fathers of macaws, and wherever they dwell, like the color of their plumage are the flowers, fruits and leaves, and summer abides there forever.[3]

"Younger Brother, there are just two things I want!"

"What are they?"

"Some tail-feathers of the macaw for my medicine-wand, and some of that 'white wizard-powder' that Americans make and that they say 'will kill even a Zuñi *dog*' if you can only get him to eat it."

My Older Brother looked considerably happier when I told him I would get some of the white powder; but when I added that it would not be so easy to find the macaw feathers, he fell to cursing his grandfathers as heartily as ever.

From "Zuñi Breadstuff," *Millstone* 9, no. 5 (1884) 75–78.

Notes

1. See "Creation and the Origin of Corn," below. [Ed. note]

2. Peculiarly gentle in his relations to fellow-men, never or rarely punishing his children for even the worst behavior, the Zuñi is, as a measure of self-defense, the embodiment of cruelty to crows, sneak-curs, coyotes, and other pestiverous animals. . . . [F.H.C.]

3. "Thus first was our nation divided into the People of Winter and the People of Summer," we are told in another version of this story, "in such wise as are their children today, into *anotiwe* (clans or kinties) of brothers and sisters who may not marry one another" ("Outlines of Zuñi Creation Myths," pp. 386–387). Fred Eggan suggests that the dual division here referred to may have existed before the consolidation of the Zuñi villages around 1700, at which point a multiple phratry type of organization developed (*Social Organization of the Western Pueblos,* pp. 212–13). [Ed. note]

Corn Raising:
The Regeneration of the Seed

W HEN the kernels have sprouted all through the field described in the last chapter, we find the planter busy inspecting
the hills near the prayer-stick. Upon this inspection hangs the
fate—so *he* thinks—of his cornfield; for if every kernel in each of
the six sacred hills has "come out," the crop will be productive.
If, on the contrary, one or two of the grains in, for example, the
southern hill have not sprouted forth, "Alas!" part of his crop of
red corn will be a failure; will not get ripe before frost time.

Toward noon he is joined by two or three of the women and
some of the children of the household, and perhaps by as many
neighbors. Wherever a sprout looks yellow, they dig down and
kill the little white worm they are sure to find near the root. This
is called "grub-finishing." Wherever the plants are very vigorous,
they pull up all except four or five of the best, and this is called
"leafing" or "leaf-lifting."

The occasion which follows soon and is recurrent twice or
thrice during the warm season is perhaps the jolliest of the
summer. It is the "hoeing" or "staving time" as the Zuñis call it in
well remembrance of the instruments with which their ancestors
hoed, away back in the age of stone. These were crooked, sharp-
edged staves of hard wood, shaped not unlike sickles, or better
still, short scythes. (See fig. 58.6.) Rude as they were, they seem
to have been wonderfully efficacious in the removal of weeds, for
the operator, progressing on his knees, swept the scythe-hoe
from side to side between the rows of corn, cutting off wide
swathes of weeds, just below the surface of the soft yielding soil.
The principal drawback to this implement was that it proved

equally efficacious in wearying the man who wielded it. Therefore, while with the introduction of iron the heavy hand-wrought
hoes affected to-day by the Zuñis displaced the ancient wooden
instrument, not so with the name the latter gave to hoeing.

Every night at staving time you will hear women calling in at
the doorways as they go the rounds of their husbands' clans,
"She! Tomorrow we stave," for only the poorest Zuñis hoe their
fields unaided. Next morning a goodly number of the men thus
summoned gather at whatever house was represented by the
woman who summoned them. Without breakfast they betake
themselves to the field and·hoe with might and main until about
eleven o'clock, then stop to eat luncheon and joke with the girls
who brought it down, and who are, true to nature, dressed in
regular holiday costume. They have been "grinding" all the
morning, in time to the shrill chant of the mistress, or of some old
aunt whose back is too stiff for the mealing trough (or who
pretends it is) but whose voice is, if possible, shriller than ever. If
you look at these giggling, droop-eyed girls, you will see that
they are a degree whiter than they were yesterday. They've
actually been powdering! Just before starting out with the luncheon each one, warmed and perspiring from the violent exercise at the metate, grabbed up a handful of white meal, rubbed it
well between her palms, and applied it evenly all over her face
and neck.

When the girls have returned to help cook for the "stavers,"
the latter resume the work, but now more moderately. Laughing, joking, telling stories of the olden time (*not* folklore, *that*
is forbidden, for the rattlesnake is abroad!), racing at their
task, playing pranks, they are the lightest-hearted laborers you
ever saw.

According to these stories, it was not like this in the olden
time of which they tell. Many of the laborers of primitive pueb-
lodom were given their tasks which they had to finish under a
priest's inspection. Later on (and even *that* was a long time ago)
war originated these hoeing bees (or "staving councils"). They
were not then as now light-hearted crowds. Each member of
them was like a deer on an open plain, fearful lest every puff of
wind should bring sounds or sight of some enemy. Full often the
enemy did come. Daring not to attack the terraced town, he hung

about the distant fields, seeking vengeance for those of his tribe who had fallen under the knotty clubs of Zuñi. And woe to the workers if they proved but few! Armed even as they worked, brave with desperation, it was rare they ever saw Zuñi again; for the cowardly Navajos rarely came but in swarms. Some of the most thrilling traditions of Zuñi tongue concern these and the harvest days of long ago; and it is with regret that I pass my notes of many a long recital by for the short and perhaps less interesting tale below.

Below the pueblo of Zuñi westward, in one of the long arms of the valley, there stands, perched upon the summit of a high rock, an ancient tower of stone. You reach the doorway of this solitary little citadel by means of an old log notched at intervals to form rude steps. Entering, you find a neat little room, well plastered, in one corner a tiny fire-place, and opposite a single mealing-slab, while above hangs a blanket-pole. The cinders yet lie on the hearth-stone, the pole glistens still brightly from its shadowy recess, the meal clings even now to the roughened face of the mill-stone.

It seems as though only yesterday the fire was kindled, as though its light still lingered along the polished pole, as though the women had but just ceased to ply the *molina* in the mealing trough and had gone out to watch the wide cornfields or bring water. But it is fifty years since the flames died away on that hearthstone; fifty years a little streak of sunlight has played along the blanket-pole, replacing the fire's ruddy glow; and for fifty years the story has been related at each hoeing, how the woman went out one morning—never to return.

And the half of this tale is already told if you but climb another notched log leading through the trap-door by the chimney into an upper room. There are double port-holes here, which from without seem like the sightless sockets of a crumbling skull. By the light they let in you see that the plaster is broken and stained here and there with dark patches. Splintered shafts and shivered stones lie strewn about—ungathered by those who anxiously searched there fifty summers ago at sunset.

For the little house on the rock once belonged to Um'-thla-na—"He of large muscles." He was living there with his family to tend the cornfields. The women went out early one morning to get water. No sooner had they neared the distant pool than they heard the tread of many horse-hoofs. Then they saw, sweeping down the valley, a crowd of mounted warriors. They dropped their water-jars and fled, one to the neighboring rocks, hours after to appear breathless and fainting at Zuñi; but the younger toward the little tower, the steps of which she never ascended, for, caught up by some wrangling horsemen, wrangling for her possession, she was borne away into years of captivity.

Um⌐-thla-na heard the rush of the riders, grasped up his war-club, bow and arrows, and not pausing to close the doorway, clambered the step-log in the corner and barricaded the trap-door. Soon the Navajos thronged into the lower room. They snatched the serapes from the blanket-pole, they stole the basket of corn cakes and paper bread. Wild with glee over these delicacies so rare to their roving life, they never noticed the trap-door, but ran out and sat down about the doorway to feast. Alas, Um⌐-thla-na! why did he not keep quiet? Peering out through a port-hole, he saw a big Navajo calmly sitting near the step-log eating a roll of paper bread. He drew an arrow to the head, let fly, and struck so fairly the feasting raider that he uttered never a groan but fell over against the ladder still grasping his roll of *guyave*. Another, sitting near, saw him fall, but ere he could call an alarm he too was pinned with one of Um⌐-thla-na's arrows. As this one fell, Um⌐-thla-na raised a yell of victory, "changing his key that the Navajos might think him many." At first the enemy fell back, but when they found there was only one man, they rushed toward the house again. For awhile Um⌐-thla-na's arrows fell so thickly that the hazard of near approach kept the Navajos from charging. Even when his shafts were spent he pulled stones from the wall and broke them against one another, casting them down at the enemy. The port-holes were small and he had to stand quite close to them. Soon an arrow whizzed through one, sticking him in the arm. Um⌐-thla-na clinched his teeth and plucked it out, shooting it back.

Ere long he was wounded in many places and weak from loss of blood; still he stood bravely at bay by the port-holes. One of the Navajos more distant than the rest, saw Um⌐-thla-na's face at the hole. Taking careful aim he let go so cleverly that Um⌐-thla-na, dodging, was shot through the neck. He staggered back, falling heavily, then roused himself and sat up against the wall, clutching his war-club. *Now* the Navajos rushed toward the doorway. Suddenly they fled away, for, behold! coming swiftly across the valley in a cloud of dust was a band of Zuñi horsemen. The Zuñis pursued the flying Navajos, never thinking of Um'-thla-na. At last the poor old man, hearing no sound, pulled some of the arrows from his wounds, broke others off, and slowly, painfully clambered down the step-log, and staggered out into the plain toward Zuñi. Fainter and fainter he grew, until he swooned by the trailside. Toward sunset they found him there, those who came to seek. Some staid to tenderly care for him, while others went to search for the young woman. They did not find *her*, but lying dead on the rocks near the tower were five Navajos. One of them was leaning against the step-log still grasping in his hand a roll of paper bread. Um'-thla-na lived to tell the story, but grew worse as the arrow wounds rancored, and "killed himself that he might be divided from pain."

Nobody lives in the little house now. "It is a place of painful thoughts," say the narrators; but it stands always the same, for its builder was "He of large muscles."

At sunset the men file in from the field. The women have spread or rather strung the feast out on the lowest roof. Ten or twelve great bowls in a row, smoking hot with stew, every one as red with chili as its rising vapors are with the touches of sunset. There is a row of breadstuff, thin as paper, flaky as crackers, red, yellow, blue and white, piled up in baskets down either side of the meat bowls. Outside these, two other rows, this time of blankets and stool blocks. The first man whose head appears up the ladder is besieged with polite invitations to "Sit and eat, sit and eat," from as many pairs of lips as there are women on the house-top. When all are seated, a sacrifice is made to the household fire; up to this time the talking has been rife; now it ceases altogether. Everything except eating seems *tabu* until the feast has disappeared, and the cigarettes are rolled and lighted. Then talking resumes and long into the night continues.

At the second or third hoeing, which takes place usually after one of the late summer rains, they "hill" the corn much as our eastern farmers do. In ancient times a sort of broad pick-axe or hoe made from the scapula of an elk and bound with rawhide

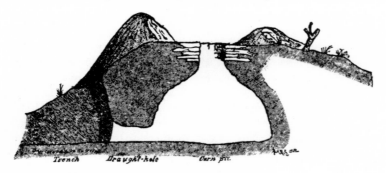

FIG. 60. Corn Roasting Pit

to a wooden handle (see fig. 58.7) or a hoe of hard wood similarly fastened to the handle and surmounted by a heavy stone (fig. 58.8) were used for this purpose.

Autumn comes and the "corn children" have been taken in to meet their "Father and Mother," the *yä'-po-to* and the *mi'-k'iap-pan-ne*. A while later, another search is made through the field, this time for such corn as gives no promise of ripening. Blanketful after blanketful is picked, husks and all, and carried to some distant wooded hill where the soil is solid. Here, with sharp sticks, and hoes, a hole is dug resembling a well (see fig. 60). At the top, it is cut larger around, to the depth of a foot or more and walled up neatly and solidly with sandstone. Below this wall, say a foot, the hole is gradually enlarged toward the bottom, until it embraces a room several feet in diameter and cone-shaped, the apex as it were, being the walled, circular opening. From the windward side of the hill, a trench is dug to a level with the bottom of the excavation. A hole or passage, about two feet in diameter is cut from the end of the trench to the interior. Dry grass, old leaves, pitchy sticks, are thrown in from above, and arranged by a man who has entered through the trench. On top of these wood is piled until the hole is full. The mass is now fired. As soon as the night-wind rises, flames dart upward through the circular hole, many feet into the air, straight, lurid, setting the woodlands around and the skies above, fairly aglow with ruddy splendor. All night long, a merry group of young people dance, sing and romp around this volcano-like oven. Wood, whenever needful, is piled in until late next morning. At last the embers have burned low, and smoke has ceased to rise from their glaring red depths. Corn-stalks, green and plentiful are thrown in, more are tucked into the large draught-hole, and preparations are made for artificially ripening that which nature has procrastinated over. A beautiful, long, fresh stalk is chosen, leaves, tassels and roots complete. Two fine ears of corn are stripped of their husks. One of them is laid against the stalk, the other cleansed of its silk as though for boiling. The chief of ceremonials bites off from this all the milky kernels mouthful by mouthful, chews them to pulp, and blows their substance into fine mist over the heaps of plucked corn. He then places the cob by the side of the other ear, and binds both firmly to the stalk. This, in the brief prayer he presently makes, is called the *shi'-wa-ni* or priest. It is cast into the still glowing pit, and then, men, women, young and old, begin to hurl in the unhusked corn from all sides until no more is left. Most likely space remains at the top. If so, it is quickly filled with green stalks, more of which are bundled up and used as a cork for the circular opening. A mound of damp soil is heaped to a considerable height above this impromptu stopper. As night again comes on, campfires, bright enough it is true, but pale compared with the flames of last night, are built at convenient distances. Muffled sounds come all night from the buried oven. Sometimes, though rarely, the top is blown off, but usually next morning the mound is found unchanged and the sounds have ceased.

Now comes a sight which would surprise a stranger, miles away though he might be. The earthen mound is removed and the stopper of corn-stalks, with great trepidation, most gingerly pulled out. Instantly, hissing and seething, the steam from the heated corn and stalks below, shoots hundreds of feet into the air. On a clear day in green-corn time dozens of these white columns may be seen rising from the wooded slopes around the vale of Zuñi. It is not until toward afternoon that the mass is sufficiently cooled to admit of approach. As soon as possible the corn is handed out through the draught hole (which has been enlarged for the purpose) sewed up in blankets, strapped across burros and transported to the town. Every member of the party, as it approaches Zuñi, may be seen gorging this—really delicious—

FIG. 61. Zuñi Farm Hut

baked corn. When it is unloaded into the spare room, the heat has not yet left it. With all possible haste, the husks are stripped down, and the ears, now brown and plump, are braided into long bunches, and the whole is hung up to dry in an upper room.

Many of the leaves in the field still remain green. These are gathered, carefully dried and folded into large long bundles, for winter kitchen use. Quantities of late squash and pumpkin flowers are stored away in jars to serve a similar end.

As the corn ripens, you may see fires burning at almost any of the quaint little farm huts (see fig. 61), for children or very old men watch there day and night, to keep crows, coyotes, and burros away. The crows are worse than they were last spring. The coyotes are not outdone by the crows at either time, but the burros are worse than both together. They are, to quote Zuñi, *Mi'-wi-hâ* or "adopted of corn." You may put them in the corrals, tie their fore-feet close together, or herd them as you will, but *some* of them will "leave tracks and love corn in every field." The remedies are many and ingenious, but all more or less fatally short of happy results. Each man in Zuñi knows every other man, and equally as well, he knows every other man's burros. If a burro is found in a cornfield some morning, the field owner counts the exact number of missing or injured ears, and drives the burro home. Forthwith he seeks out the animal's owner. If the latter prove obdurate, the sufferer informs the chief and bides his time. Woe to that burro if he get into the cornfield again. He may consider himself fortunate if he lose but one or even both ears. Sometimes he is gagged with a big stick, a cord being passed from either end of the stick up over the shoulders and back, and under the tail. The burro is then welcome to remain in the cornfield as long as he chooses. At other times, the luckless animal is thrown and a few of his teeth pulled Zuñi fashion; which is to say, a thread of sinew is looped to each, a heavy stone is tied to the sinew, and hurled into the air. I remember a lawsuit of three nights' duration over one of these animals. Ever after, he was called the "short-horn," and little wonder! For his ears had been shaved close to his head, his tail cut off short, the tip of his tongue and part of his teeth amputated, his left eye put out, and his back so stiffened by castigation that a five-foot straight-edge laid lengthwise along the very acute angle of his vertebra, would have touched at every point. Two years I knew that burro personally. His working days were over. He used to get deplorably hungry, and I sometimes fed him; for, winter or summer, he dared not stir from the protecting although inhospitable shadows of the walls of Zuñi. He preferred picking cedar bark from the fire-wood, anything he preferred, to going abroad. In fact, had he been able to run he would certainly have done so at the sight of a field of corn.

In pity both for crows and burros, I have sometimes pleaded mitigation of the customary severe measures. My experiences at such times lead me to advise all aspiring ethnologists to mind their own business when corn is in the question. As I have said before, the Zuñis, and probably most other Indians, are touchy on the subject of their breadstuff.

Frost comes, changing the green of the stalks to yellow gold, the leaf-like shucks to feathers. In every field are corn pickers and huskers. Such corn as is not husked in the field, is packed with consummate method on burros or in carts and a few second-hand wagons, and brought to the town. Husking bees are formed by the women, and at three o'clock any afternoon you can see around a corner, mountains of cast-away shucks, and many a black, frouzzly head sticking up from their flaky slopes, bobbing bodilessly with the severance of every ear from its rattling wrappings. At such times husks in great numbers are selected, bundled into neat bunches and strung several feet long on threads of yucca fiber. They will be needed before the month is gone, particularly in the council chambers, where every night brings the weary law-givers of Zuñi fresh cases of trespass for consideration.

How the roofs groan under the weight of drying corn; how the walls gleam and glory with the festoons of chili or red pepper! But in time the corn is dry, the peppers ripened enough for storage, and the work of "corn-sorting" begins. The different colors, yellow, blue, red, white, speckled and black are separated. The "nubbin-ears" are put in a cellar by themselves for sale or for burros, and as described before, the corn is corded up in the granary around the tutelar divinities of the place—the "Father and Mother of corn crops."

Patient reader, forgive me for having lingered so long in Zuñi cornfields. However closely we may have scrutinized these crops growing green, golden grown as they may have been, we have but barely glanced at them according to the rules and practices of their dusky owners. In illustration of *his* watchfulness—quite as well as in memory of a former promise—I repeat below a song of the growth of corn plants. Let me begin, however, by saying that I shall give only in the first verse the prelude and refrain which opens and closes each stanza of the song.

I.

"A-hee-e'-iu, a-he-e'-iu!
A-hee-e'-iu, a-he-e'-iu!
Sa-ni-hi' akia tchu etai'-e
Te-tchi-nai-u-le, te-tchi-nai-iu-le'e'e."
"Soil shorn and spread by storms!
Soil shorn and spread by storms!
Band of Hunters, their corn grains planted
There may now be seen, there may now be seen."

II.

Sa-ni-hi'-akia, ke'-mu-toi'-ye,—
Band of hunters, their corn grains sprouted.

III.

Sa-ni-hi'-akia, thia-kwi-moi'-ye,—
Band of hunters, their corn grains rooted.

IV.

Sa-ni-hi'-akia, k'e-tsithl-pol'-ye,—
Band of hunters, their corn leaves fluted.

V.

Sa-ni-hi'-akia, la she yai' ye,—
Band of hunters, their corn leaves feathered.

VI.

Sa-ni-hi'-akia, ta-a-nai-ye,—
Band of hunters, their corn stalks tasseled.

VII.

Sa-ni-hi'-akia, u-te-ai'-ye,—
Band of hunters, their corn plants blooming.

VIII.

Sa-ni-hi'-akia, te-k'u-ai'-ye,—
Band of hunters, their corn ears started.—
[i.e. enfolded within the leaves.]

IX.

Sa-ni-hi'-akia, thia-k'u-nai'-ye, etc.,
Band of hunters, their corn ears shooting,—
[i.e. starting forth from the leaves.]

X.

Sa-ni-hi'-akia, mi-i-ai'-ye,—
Band of hunters, their corn ears kerneled.

XI.

Sa-ni-hi'-akia, sho-ho-nai-ye,—
Band of hunters, their corn ears silkened.

XII.

Sa-ni-hi'-akia, o-sho-nai-yo,—
Band of hunters, their corn plants sooted.

XIII.

Sa-ni-hi'-akia, thla-shi-nai-ye, —
Band of hunters, their corn grown aged.

This song, although beautiful in the original language and music (possessed as it is of perfect metre, fair rhythm and considerable poetic sentiment) defies exact translation. Not only is it framed in archaic syllables, but the terms in Zuñi for every phenomenon connected with corn and its growth are so numerous and technical that it is as difficult to render them into English as it would be to translate into Zuñi the terminology of an exact science. I have, however, introduced this approximation as illustrative not only of Indian powers of observation but also as giving a fair example of the terms wherewith from planting time to harvesting time may be designated any given period; for the Zuñi, simply adding to any of the above expressions a syllable expressive of time, thus divides the quarters of the "Nameless Months."

From "Zuñi Breadstuff," *Millstone* 9, no. 6 (1884): 93–95.

Corn and the Early Kitchen

In order that the preparation of the more elaborate kinds of corn food, in which the *metate* and *molina* bore a conspicuous part, may be the better referred to and understood, I must risk a little repetition by giving below the Zuñi classification of their materials as introductory to some following more descriptive paragraphs.

As the reader is already aware, the generic term for corn in Zuñi is *Tâ'-a*, or *A'-tâ-a*, the approximate English of which is "the seed of seeds," yet which applies not only to the grain itself in the abstract, but also to the green plants which produce it. Corn on the ear is termed *Mi'-we*, in the grain *Tchu'-we*. When the corn grains have been simply cracked on the coarse grinding-stones, they are called *Tchu'-thlä-tsa-we*. When skinned through the agency of ashes and water, as above described, or by boiling in water alone, and careful rubbing on the mealing-stone, it is termed *Tchu'-tsi-kwah-na-we*. Broken under the muller into very coarse meal or samp, it is called *Sa'-k'o-we*; reduced to meal, *O'-we*; and when ground to exceedingly fine flour, *O'-lu-tsi-na*.

Passing over the various dishes which answer to our hasty-pudding, mushes, and the like, which were all well known, we may be interested to find out how the settled, semi-civilized [early] pueblo Zuñi improved on the baked things of his farming or cliff-dwelling predecessor. His most notable advance was perhaps the introduction of ashes, or of very finely ground lime, called *A'-lu-we*, mingled with salt into fermented mush-yeast to overcome its acidity. The most prized leaven of his time, however, was chewed *Sa'-k'o-we* mixed with moderately fine meal and warm water and placed in little narrow-necked pots over or near the hearth until fermentation took place, when lime flour and a little salt were added. Thus a yeast in nowise inferior to some of our own was compounded. In addition to its leavening qualities, this yeast had the remarkable property, when added to the meal of the blue corn or black, to change the color during cookery to a beautiful green hue, or, mingled with yellow-corn flour, to render it light blue.

The greater variety and nicety of cookery which this yeast made possible to the pueblo Zuñi required also vastly improved culinary methods and appliances, giving origin undoubtedly to a special apartment for cookery which we may without exaggeration term the kitchen. I will be pardoned for pausing to describe one of these rooms, using those I am familiar with in modern Zuñi at least as my model. Behind the "sitting place," as it was called (or the dining-room and living-room combined), entered by a narrow doorway, and unilluminated save by the gray light which struggled down its broad chimney or eddied forth from the flicker of its almost constant fires, was the diminutive cookery of these ancient days. In the dim twilight of this place the uninitiated would have stumbled almost at every step upon its furnishings; for scattered over the floor, dependent from the rafters—which the shortest could almost reach by stretching—and hanging against the walls, were the rude appliances which we may dignify by this title—sieves made of coarsely woven yucca (see fig. 62.5), meal trays (fig. 62.6), bread plaques (fig. 62.4), enormous cooking pots, some with prong-like, irregular legs (fig. 62.1), pigmy water boilers (fig. 62.2) with their round stone covers, polished baking stones blackened by a thousand heatings, bread bowls (fig. 62.3), carved pudding sticks, numerous hard wood pokers charred to all degrees of shortness, and, finally, bundles of grease-wood or faggots of finely splintered piñon-wood suspended in the chimney for drying—were some of the objects which would meet the eye as it grew accustomed to the place. A more specific description must be given to the fire-place. This extended entirely across the end of the room, down from the ceiling of which, like one side of an elongated hopper, descended the flange or flue made of staves slantingly set side by side upon a pole—either end of which was inserted in

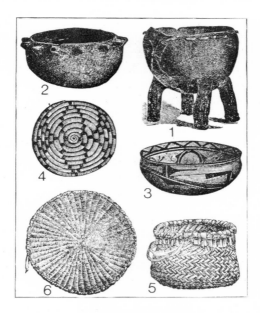

FIG. 62. Kitchen Appliances

either wall—and smoothly plastered with mud. Below this pole, exactly on a line with it, was a row of thick stones set on edge to divide the hearth from the floor of the room. In one corner of this commodious hearth a baking stone, large and thick, rested upon four rough pillars of mud masonry. In the middle, sunken deep down into the ground, was a square stone cist, not unlike the excavated ovens described on a former page; and in the corner opposite to the baking stone one might see four or five rudely hollow columns or upright cylinders of masonry open in front and behind for the draft, on at least one or two of which rested, as though permanently placed there, cooking pots of more than ordinary size and thickness. Within this dark retiring place the women concocted many strange dishes. . . .

From "Zuñi Breadstuff," *Millstone* 9, no. 10 (1884); 173–74.

And Some Recipes

Doubtless survivals of [earlier] efforts to thoroughly effect the cooking of mushes, gruels, etc., by the immerson of heated stones was a series of boiled breads or dumplings, of which the simplest were the *Mu'-k'iä-li-we* and *Mu'-k'iä-pa-we.* The first of these was made by mixing fine meal or flour with an equal quantity of coarse meal of *Sa'-k'o-we*, salting, and by the addition of cold water and the intervention of excessive kneading to form a stiff dough. This was divided into little pieces which were rolled into hard balls between the hands. A pot of water was set over one of the columnar receptacles and, as soon as this was made to boil violently, the little balls were poured in. Instead of disintegrating, they became harder and harder with the progress of the cooking, yet enough of their substance mingled with the water to cause it to become pasty, no sooner than which the pot was lifted from the fire, and the balls, fluid and all were poured into a large eating trencher or bowl of pottery. While still hot these "water balls," as they were called, were eaten with brine sauce. . . .

Perhaps belonging to this same class of food, although counted among the delicacies of the Zuñis, was the *Ä'-tea-mu-we*, a kind of sweet pudding. It was made of yellow cornmeal, a portion of the batter of which was sweetened either by previous mastication and fermentation or by the admixture of dried flowers. This batter was most dexterously enwrapped in green corn leaves preserved for the purpose by drying and rendered flexible as occasion required by immersion in hot water. Of necessity these little masses of paste or dough took the form of crescents.

They were usually boiled, rarely baked, but in either case were perhaps the sweetest cooked food known to the Zuñis, which heightened sweetness doubtless owed not a little to the succulent corn leaves. Perhaps more complex than any of the hitherto described products of the ancient Zuñi kitchen were the *Tchu'-tsi-kwah-na-mu'-we*. These were made by hulling corn, then grinding it with water, precisely as colors are ground by artists with oil. This batter, fine and sticky, well seasoned with lime yeast, was wrapped in broad shucks carefully folded over and tied at the ends, then boiled. The batter was solidified by the boiling and when done resembled to a great extent well-cooked gristle or tough gelatine. Great quantities of these rubber-like dumplings were made at a time as the process of their manufacture was tedious and laborious. When cold, they were freshened by roasting on the embers or by baking in the little hearth-cists of the kitchen.

A crude kind of batter-cake, yet much of an improvement on the variety before described, the forerunner, doubtless, of the most important breadstuff known to the Zuñis to-day, was made from the corn flour. This and lime-yeast were mixed together in liberal quantities, hot water enough being added to make a stiff batter, which was boiled until adhesive and pasted or spread over the well-greased, polished baking-stone in the corner of the hearth. . . . This same dough minus the yeast, and thinner, like batter, was used to make "Johnny-cakes" or "corn-dodgers," which were baked on little flat stones at first well heated, then placed very near a hot fire.

The rudest forms of true *bread* were made by placing in a bowl fine flour, into which enough cold water was poured to make of it dough, and sufficient lime-yeast to leaven it. This was then kneaded and molded into thick cakes, which were set away a short time to rise, after which they were cooked on hot coals by frequent turning, in which form they were called *Mui-ä-ti-we* (fire loaves); or baked, buried deep under hot ashes. In this shape they were known as *Lu-pan-mu'-lo-ko-na* or ash-bread, which differed as much from the former as though made from entirely foreign materials. It is needless to say that this bread was also frequently baked, especially for feasts, when it assumed under the artistic treatment of the Zuñi women most extraordinary shapes in the large dome-shaped ovens or in the little fire-boxes on the tops of the houses.

We now come to the greatest delicacy in the way of bread known either to the older or the recent Zuñis. In its simplest form it was known as *K'os-he-pa-lo-kia*, or "salty buried-bread." It was made by the mixture of *Sa-ko k'o'-ha-na*, or the samp of white corn in water to which enough fine flour of the same corn was added to render the batter very sticky. Broad husks, made pliable with hot water, were then laid on a flat stone; the paste spread over them to the thickness of about an inch, covered with more husks folded at the edges to keep the batter in place, covered over with another stone, and so on until a sandwich like that described for "stone-cakes" was built up. Instead of being in-closed in a casing of thicker stones, this was buried in the hearth-cist—which had been previously heated almost to red-ness—then sealed up with mud and baked by a night-long fire. Leaving salt out of this recipe and adding to it dried flowers, licorice-root, wild honey, or, more frequently than any of these, masticated and fermented meal, this buried bread was made sweet like our own Indian pudding, which it exactly resembled in taste. The latter variety was baked, however, even more slowly, and quite as often cooked in a small mush-pot of earth-enware, well lined with husks to keep the batter from adhering to its sides, as between flat stones. . . .

Of all substances known to the Zuñis, however, none ap-proach in nutritive quality the *tchu'-k'i-na*, or "moistening flour." White or yellow corn is boiled with cob-ashes until the hull may be removed. It is then dried a day or two and well toasted in the parching pot, ground to coarse samp, toasted again, ground to very fine flour, and once more toasted, then carefully sifted. Thus manipulated, what with waste and excessive reduction, a bushel of corn makes but a few quarts of flour. A single teaspoonful of this powder when stirred into a pint of water will make a tolera-bly thick batter of it; in which condition it is drunk, a few sips sufficing to satisfy the most hungry appetite. When combined with meat-meal or jerked venison toasted and well ground up with red pepper and salt, it embraces all the elements necessary for man's sustenance. Very rarely, all this, too, is made the basis of a kind of *hé-we*; but as, in the former condition, it may be preserved year in and out, is very ready for consumption without the intervention of fire, and may be transported in small compass yet in sufficient quantity for a long campaign—it rarely gets further than its first stages.

Many a time have I subsisted alone on this meal and the game I shot, nor did I ever long for other foods the while. Tracts of barren country otherwise impassable, are made, by this food, the easiest routes of traders; and in times of war when a fire, however slight, might doom the party who kindled its flames, it becomes absolutely indispensable.

From "Zuñi Breadstuff," *Millstone* 9, no. 10 (1884): 174–75, and 9, no. 11 (1884): 199.

Wafer Bread and the Baking Stone

FOR no art or industry within the range of the domestic duties of
Zuñi is so much care and instruction bestowed by the old women
on the young, as for every process in the making of the *he'-we*, or
wafer breads. Year in and year out, too, while these lessons are
being plied, it is told how the famed and beloved "Goddess of
the White Shells" taught not a few of her graces—and some
secrets—in connection with the daily occupation which forms
their theme. Of these secrets, a chosen few old women of the
tribe are the keepers. With many a mysterious rite and severe
penance, they quarry and manufacture the enormous baking-
stones on which the flaky, toothsome *he'-we* is made. . . .

The setting up of these baking-stones in the kitchen fire-
place is a matter quite ranking with our own old "hanging of the
crane," though in nature a very different ceremonial. When all
has been made ready in the household for which one of them was
designed, it is solemnly ushered in by one or a couple of the
ancient dames who hewed and tempered it. By the latter it is
leaned, face to the East, against the wall, and "made acquainted"
with selected ears of corn which are placed on either side of it. It,
or something about it, is then exorcised with rituals, and abundantly "invested" with prayer-meal, and drinking-water presented by sprinkling. Finally, it is taken to its bed or "sitting
place" in the kitchen (four strongly built columns of mud
masonry in the corner of the wide hearth), laid out, and a fire of
splintered cedar built under it. As it gradually heats—so that it
would hiss if moistened with the mouth through the messenger-
ship of the fingers—a pot of thin paste, composed of hot water

FIG. 63. Making Hé-we (Paper Bread). (From "My Adventures in Zuñi")

and fine flour of all the six varieties of corn, is set to cook, while a bread-bowl is nearly filled with a similar though thicker paste or batter made in cold water, and placed near the left end of the stone. The latter is now "tried for heat" as above suggested, and, if found right, is scoured with salt, greased and well rubbed with an old rag. A small bowl of the sticky, well stewed paste is set also near the left end of the stone (some drops from each dish being dashed into the fire underneath as a sacrifice), and the first baking begins! The anxiety which attends this trial is by no means trivial when viewed, as it is by the assembled women, in the light of an oracle. One of the "chosen" ancients officiates. She squats on her heels in front of the baking-stone, dips her closed fingers first into the hot, then into the cold paste, scooping up just the requisite quantity of each, and then with a graceful, skimming sweep of the hand along the surface of the stone, applies thinly and evenly to it the fluid batter. Instantly a cloud of steam rises, hovers a moment over all, then joins the smoke of the fire in its upward flight. No sooner this, than the edges of the large sheet of paste now slightly toasted, begin to roll up; then they are grasped at one side, slightly pulled and lifted, when lo! the whole huge, almost transparent wafer is triumphantly laid on a square plaited mat near by. Sad would be the occasion if this first effort should fail—which it rarely does—for it would signify that the stone was inimical to some of the six kinds of corn-food to be cooked on it by and by—or they to it!

Leaving out all ceremonial except the little sacrifice to the fire, yet adding much coquetry and grace to all motions accompanying this frequent occupation—especially among the younger women during preparations for feasts—the above description will apply in all cases. Since the successful *he'-we*, or wafer-bread, maker may aspire to almost any match outside of her own clan, no matter how high; since also, she is esteemed of the greatest importance in her household to the very last of her working days, no wonder this apparently simple art is practiced by young maidens more assiduously than any other. Blankets may be purchased, embroideries for the sacred dance paid for, pottery-making in any quantity and quality hired, but the inferior *he'-we*-baker dooms her family to tough, uneven, ill-cooked shreds and bundles in place of crisp sheets and lightsome rolls, [and she] is herself doomed to the stinging ridicule of her more fortunate sisters, and unending envy of their ability.

From "Zuñi Breadstuff," *Millstone* 9, no. 11 (1884): 197–98.

Wheat Farming

I have before alluded to the farming towns of *Tai'-ya* or Las Nutrias, *Ojo del Pescado*, and *Los Ojos Calientes*. The first named of these pueblos and springs, now, alas! somewhat infamously famous in newspaper controversy,[1] is situated at the foot of the Zuñi mountains some twenty-five miles by trail northeast of Zuñi; and in a magnificent valley of its own. Forth from the heart of the mountains, through a cañon scarce twenty feet across yet hundreds deep, bursts into the light of day, a clear impetuous little stream; fed ever and set forth like the truant that it is, by the combined efforts of six or eight small-sized springs, to feed in its turn the crops and mingle with the sweat of men. Twisting this way and that through a mountain-girt plain, and rushing at last into the narrow portal of a perpendicular wall of strangely eroded red-sandstone strata, it disappears under a dense bed of rushes and cane-grass. When again looked for half a mile below, there is nothing to remind you of it but a feeble brook, lazily sliding along past the base of the worn, ancient town of *Tâi'-ya*, or "Place of Planting." Up among these rushes, one may soon discover why the life of the stream has departed. No sooner does it rush into the open gateway than it is imprisoned by the strong arms of an Indian dam and driven, slave to the will of its savage masters, directly over its own deep-worn trails of former ages, in viaducts made of enormous hollow logs. These conduct it—as it now thinks to escape—through straight ditches two miles in length into certain numerous earth-walled pens, where, trying to stretch itself for a leap, it instantly disappears and gets stuck in the loose loam which has been laid for it, only to be rescued by catching at the straws of sundry green-growing wheat-stems which forthwith adopt it as sap. You should see these earth-pens, laid out for irrigation (I am speaking plainly now), from the topmost house in *Tâi⸍-ya* just at the close of an April day. Although the sun is setting, his rays are reflected by the mountain-ridge close to your left and the red rock-wall behind you; so that there is a subdued glimmer of spectacular light over everything. Far enough south to make them artistic in tone, lie the earth-pens. Side by side, end to end, there they lie, ridged like waffle-irons and regular as a checker board. Down through the middle of each set runs the straight ditch, the water in it every bit as bright at this time of day as the sun himself, and far more gorgeous. A few Indians, rather undersized in the distance, but perfectly distinct, linger to water the wheat they have been planting. As they slowly stride along the sides of the ditches chopping the clods with their sand-burnished hoes, they seem to be flinging the sunlight out of the water.

Each of these square inclosures is ten by twelve feet, rarely larger. Fifteen or twenty of them make up the patch of a poor man; those of the wealthy who can afford feasts for many laborers being several times larger. The soil within them is like that of a garden, and the wheat is planted in rows, cross-wise so that it may be easily watered and hoed in mid-summer. The cultivated area extends a mile and a half up and down the valley, and is nearly as wide as it is long. Within it forty families raise their wheat for the winter. So limited is the supply of water during the dry months, that every householder keeps an account-stick hanging somewhere near the sky-hole. Every time he waters a set of his "earth-bins," he has to cut a notch in this account-stick; and as the latter is liable to inspection by the sub-chiefs any morning, he dares not, or rather does not, use more than his proper allowance of the water. As summer wanes and the wheat, grown tall and heavy with grain under so much kind treatment begins to ripen, the villagers, who have mostly departed several weeks ago, return in full force. The harvesting is accomplished by means of knives, short, crude sickles. If a man be fortunate enough to get hold of an American sickle, he forthwith breaks off one-half of the blade and makes two of it. The wheat is cut off near the head. Huge blanket-bags full of the ears are transported

FIG. 64. A Zuñi Bread-Making Scene

to one of the several threshing-floors of the village. These are simply cleared circular spaces on argillaceous soil well beaten down, sprinkled, beaten again until level, and baked in the sun until as hard as brick. There is usually a post in the center; more rarely an enarching palisade. The wheat ears are tumbled pretty evenly over the extent of one of these floors, and a motley throng of urchins, horses and donkeys let in upon it. The horses go in against their will; the burros for business—part of which is eating (but illegitimate); the urchins go to goad all the other beasts! There is plenty of shouting and cursing among the elders of the party, a deal of laughter and romping among the younger—as is always apt to be the case when both sexes are represented. During temporary lulls in the activity of the beasts, the women rush in, clear off the straw, gather up the chaff and grain at the bottom, and carry it in blankets to the other clear spaces where they winnow it in the wind, which considerately fans nearly every afternoon in late summer or early autumn.

After being cleaned, the grain is packed in bags and either

dragged home by cattle in lumber-wagons and lumbering carts, or else stacked on burros and thus taken through. Burros being plentiful, the latter is the popular method—except with themselves. You should see a family *en voyage* at the end of harvest. Leading the van, is the sub-youth of the household. He is discontented because his eldest brother has gone to the Pescado races; but on the whole, takes it out quite silently—on the shanks and other visible parts of the two grain-submerged burros he is driving. A rod or two rearward follows the matron—astride. A baby, eloquent with the mystery and milk-famine of the occasion, is tightly muffled to her back in a blanket, whence the ample folds of which, its unarticulated protestations but faintly issue. Clinging behind are the little boy and girl, bearing with compressed lips and heroic half-gasps the pain of their unaccustomed sitting place—for they are "The little man and woman of the family," you know! In her left hand this lady carries an old parasol; in her right, a well-sharpened prod of hard wood with which she nickingly touches up a sore place on the burro's right shoulder. Her feet are tied into the straps of the saddle—the stirrups being too long—and with her heavy, buckskin-bandaged shanks—which show short and are so—she fearlessly thumps the sides of the burro until he groans and staggers—but patiently keeps his accustomed pace. Next—the old man! His burro is loaded with household paraphernalia. Among these, a cat, sewn up skin-tight in a cotton bag, head protruding, ears laid and eye-whites active, yowls and hisses as she swings along, balancing the family eagle on the other side. This gentleman, like the cat, is "done up" and resentful. He continually pecks and snaps his beak at his own reflection in the brass kettle overhead, transferring these attentions to the old man when the latter approaches to maul the burro, or varying them with nipping his animate but thick-skinned conveyance. The old man is the liveliest member of the party. Listen to him for a moment.

"Tsuk-tsuk suk-suk" (that means get along lively). "Sha a a" (mind now). "Stop eating, will you? No? Very well then!" Whack! "Suk-suk—what are you about *now*? O yes; very well!" Whack-bang—"*there* now!" "What, at it again? *Wa na ni!*" (just wait). Whack-bang, whack—"aha! hum!" The old man, still jogging along, breathes himself, having whack-banged with all his muscle. Of this lull the burro takes advantage, which shortly reanimates the old boy. "So-ho!" he exclaims, "*You* cause of cogitation!" Whack—"You slave of faggots"—whack—"You anger of the gods"—bang,—"Insect—long-eared turtle,—take *that!*"—whackity-whack—"and that!!" Bang. The last blow, hitting the gambol joint of the jack, causes him to twist out of the trail with his hind feet and progress sidewise. "Here now!" shouts his persecutor, as he skips around—quite nimble for his age—toward the head of the brute, "get in there, you one-eyed, worm-paced breeder of vermin, get in, I say!" and cuffity-cuff goes the stick down on the long flopping ears of the donkey. And thus things go on to the end of the twenty-five miles.

The story is told of one old fellow who, in administering condign (?) punishment to his burro, missed his aim and knocked out the brains of his favorite eagle. He then and there made a clean sweep of the business. In his excitement he killed the cat, broke a couple of water-jars, and ended up by murdering the donkey.

From "Zuñi Breadstuff," *Millstone* 9, no. 12 (1884): 225–26.

Note

1. The controversy to which Cushing alludes here is that concerning the attempted land grab mentioned in the Introduction—the controversy which eventuated in Cushing's recall to Washington. [Ed. note]

Zuñi Etiquette

Zuñi hospitality, if it were more generally known, would become proverbial. Among the neighboring tribes it is so. The Navajos, for example, were, until recently, the oldest and worst enemies of the Zuñis (and mutual hatred has by no means ceased); yet if one but poke his frouzzly head inside of any port-hole or doorway of Zuñi, the instant greeting—often indeed the sole one—will be: "Enter; sit and eat!"

In order that this national trait may be appreciated at its true worth, I must speak of another native characteristic so at variance with the first that a return to the latter topic will be essential presently, to reconcile us to the belief that both may pertain at the same time to a single people. The stinginess of the Zuñis—to put it mildly—is quite as celebrated as their profuse hospitality. In trade it is, like most main things of their daily life, a matter of religion. The hostess of a sumptuous meal, where *he'-we* has been piled before the guests as high as their knees, and the major part of a sheep has been seethed into a homogenous stew for their delectation, will glean from the floor (thriftily swept with a view to this process beforehand) every flake and crumb of the feast, and scrutinize critically each bone that has been dropped, to see if perchance it may be cracked for the marrow! Any man, woman or child of the tribe is as welcome as frogs are to water, to a place at the family trencher; but let an unlucky wight find his corn-bin low or his pepper-string naked, and he will have to pay doubly and dearly in service or chattels for each corn grain or red pod!

When I sauntered into the great eating-room of my "Elder

Brother's" house one morning three winters ago, I found the old man affectingly giving welcome to a handsomely dressed Navajo chief, from the far Northern country. As I listened to the elaborately phrased flatteries which passed between the two smiling worthies, I inferred that there must have been something extraordinary in their past associations. The sequel proved that I was quite right! "This," said Pa-lo-wah-ti-wa, turning to me with a strange beam in his eye, "is my friend and brother. He is a great chief whose wives are as the fingers of his hand. Has he not come all the way from *Cañon de Chelly* to renew the breath of friendship?" At this juncture, as if to force the sincerity of his protestations upon my benighted and unfeeling American mind, the old man picked up a costly silver necklace and with reckless liberality bestowed it upon the grinning Navajo. By this time the guest's pack-horses were unladen and several fat buckskin bags—shiny with grease and wear—to say nothing of blankets, silver-decked bridles, saddles, and weapons, were neatly stacked up in a near corner. The Navajo strode over to the pile, jerked a fat sheep-carcass from the rear of his saddle and threw it down on an upturned goat-pelt—spurning it in depreciation of his liberality, as he beckoned one of the women to come and take it away. Then he pulled a costly serape and snowy buckskin from one of the bags and ostentatiously unfolding them, dropped the twain over the shoulders of my Elder Brother. Mutual thanks and renewed embraces ensued! Then came the women with the breakfast. To say that they brought enough extra provender for ten men would state but plain truth.

"Let us eat!" exclaimed they.

"Yes, loosen your belt and lessen your hunger," briskly added my brother, waving his hand toward the steaming bowls and baskets. Four times that day did I see this guest "loosen his belt"—literally—to the ample good things placed before him. Next morning all was still effusive and more presents were exchanged; but as the forenoon waned away and the Navajo's horses were brought up to be given their last nip of corn, I thought a kind of coldness settled on the faces of the two friends.

When nearly everything had been packed, the Navajo laid an empty bag on the floor with the remark that one of his wives—who was in a bad way—had asked him to bring some of the "toothsome" *he⸍-we* and "honied" *he⸍-pa-lo-k'ia* so abundant in his "cherished" friend's home.

The old Governor turned to his wife. "Give him some *he⸍-we* and *he⸍-pa-lo-k'ia:*" said he, sententiously, "pick out the *dryest*—it will be lighter for him to carry, you know!"

K'ia-u, with set face and lowering spirits, hobbled away and presently returned with a tray of old *he⸍-we* (well shaken up to look big) in one hand, and a basket bowl of very dry, somewhat musty *he⸍-pa-lo-k'ia* in the other. She poured them into the bag. The Navajo packed them well home and suggestively weighed the still lank pouch.

"Friend," he began,—

"Give him a little more!" commanded the governor. K'ia-u darted an unhealthy glance toward the Navajo, but went back to the storeroom, bringing this time the smallest quantity that would suffice to cover the bottom of the baskets. The Navajo again packed the bag, and after scanning it a moment, held the mouth of it open—and looked up meaningly—for more.

"Humph!" ejaculated K'ia-u, shaking her head. "Gone; *all* gone."

"Alas!" exclaimed the Navajo. Then a thought seemed to strike him. He went up to his pack, fumbled around a good deal, and finally brought in a fairly large buckskin. K'ia-u brightened up; for buckskins are the pride of a woman's heart in Zuñi. She made a pretense of talking sharply to her brother's wife, then nodded her head to the Navajo, and hurried back to the storeroom. Forthwith she re-appeared laden with two big heaping trays. The Navajo leaned his chin on his hand and contemplated them. After a long time, he said:

"A little more, friend, only a little."

"The skin is miserable and small," said K'ia-u.

"No! it is thick and large," retorted the Navajo. "What sort of *he⸍-pa-lo-k'ia* do you call *that*?" he added, rapping a lump of it on the stone floor. "Red sandstone were more easily milled."

"Stop up his blabbering mouth with a little more," chipped in the Governor, beginning to lose temper. K'ia-u dived into the storeroom still again, and came back, after a long absence, with an old tin plate I had given her about two-thirds full.

"There," said she, dusting her hands, "*all* gone *now*."

"I think that's a lie!" pleasantly remarked the Navajo. "Fill it up, friend, and I'll be satisfied."

"Ho! Navajos are born without shame," remarked K'ia-u.

"The Zuñi women are regular chip-munks," mused the Navajo in his own language, referring to their habit of chewing *he'-pa-lo-k'ia* and storing it away.

"She has given you enough," grumbled the Governor, who understood the Navajo tongue. "*Enough* for that rag of a buckskin."

"Well, didn't I give her a *sheep*?" queried the Navajo.

"And who gave you a silver necklace?" snapped the Governor.

"Who gave you a fine serape and a buckskin as big as a buffalo hide?" yelled the Navajo.

"Who killed my uncle?" hissed the Governor.

"My father!" shouted the Navajo, with a triumphant look. "*And* you killed *him!*" he added with a darker look—at the same time snatching at the buckskin as though to reject the bargain. This was too much for K'ia-u; she filled the plate! They parted rather coolly, but as "friends," yet I conjectured from the facial expressions of the two men that it would be bad for one if the other chanced to catch him napping in the mountains some fine lonely night.

Afterward the Governor told me one day with a grin that the father of his "friend" had been a silversmith. "That's why *I'm* one now," explained the old man. "The punches and dies I pound out buttons with cost me nothing but a little work, and I got even with him for killing my uncle besides." Then he went through the whole dialogue again, and gleefully affirmed with a blink of his black eye, "*We* understand each other; my friend will come back again the next time he hungers for corn-food, and I'll give him some buttons made on his father's die-plate!"

I am aware that I shall be accused of having romanced in telling this almost incredible anecdote, but those who are familiar with Indians and their ever-changing tribal relations, will not find it hard to believe that I erred only in greatly condensing the above conversation. It can be easily understood how Zuñi and Navajos who have murdered into one another's families during war times, may "forgive" one another with the return of peace. They do it as a matter of policy, knowing full well the unstable quality of their inter-tribal relations. . . .

Toward one another, the Zuñis—as has been already hinted—still more studiously exercise these rites [of hospitality]. A Zuñi may not be on speaking terms with another, may even go so far as to refuse to eat with him, but if by chance that other should happen inside his door he will certainly have a bread-tray placed before him and be bidden in a matter-of-course kind of a way to eat.

Enter any house at whatever time of day or night, and unless you be on the most familiar footing with the inmates, the invariable tray of *he⸍-we* will be brought forth, also parched corn, or, if in their seasons, peaches, melons or piñon nuts, nor once having taken to the sitting-block, or bench, may you state your errand without first making a fair show of eating. Should you visit several such houses, in each the proceedings will be the same, until the oft-taken morsel of politeness though small individually—has aggregated to uncomfortable proportions. Yet at the next fire-side, though your brow be bathed in sweat of former striving, you must not falter, but tuck up your blanket and fall to with as evident a grace as at the outset.

Another feature of Zuñi etiquette is rather a tax on the will-power and digestion. It is the desirability of showing your appreciation of the skill and fare of your hostess by consuming a liberal and relatively equal amount of every article she places in front of you. I used to observe that with a native diner-out this was actually a severer task than with me. There were sure to be some special dishes which he preferred above others. Now the chief difference between him and me was not that I cared for none of the dishes—though I confess to having eaten all more or less under protest; the fact is, I was—what with my hopeless longing for the food of better days, and the dyspepsia which I speedily acquired by battling for approval with the *cuisine* of Zuñi—perpetually hungry, so I liked, for instance, the stewed peaches and baked squash, primarily because they were of excellent quality, and secondarily because they could not be spoiled in cooking, and tertiarily because they were *clean*. Then, too, I liked the double-done *he'we* and certain strips of tender fresh meat, coiled and skewered on the end of a long rod and toasted, with much basting, over a slow fire; yet it goes without saying that there were certain to be many things I did *not* like. Thus it will be seen, the native feaster and I were at first fairly mated. In matters of eating, his was a positive, mine a negative nature. While his resolution was staunch in the direction of quantity to the extreme of his viscerial capacity—or as he would have worded it, "to the joint of his jaw"—his power to eschew was relatively weak. Hence he was naturally certain, on sitting down, to move in the "line of least resistance" and eat within an ace of his fill, of the things he esteemed most. I always pursued the opposite course and usually had the satisfaction of winning with ease and tolerable comfort, while it cost my neighbor frightful absorptive effort, no little time and many shiftings of position, and left him—the victorious—protuberant of eye, short of breath, and rigidly erect.

Goaded on by both their liking for American food and their sense of duty toward a class of hosts they held in reverent respect, five of the six Indians I brought East in the spring of 1882, suffered, literally, miseries untold, for they rarely complained save to sadly depreciate their own abilities.

"What is it?" exclaimed one of them after a prolonged tussle with the courses of a Palmer House dinner, each one of which he would persist in regarding as a separate meal and eat the desired quota of each article composing it—condiments and all!—"what is it in American food, my son, that fills the insides with much fighting?"

"Would you have me cover my nation with shame?" indignantly asked another, as he reached his hand for a lemon which a generous-minded man on board a Chicago, Burlington & Quincy railroad train offered him. "What though we be wafted in this swift wagon as on the wings of the wind!" continued he, taking and flourishing the lemon, "Is it not a house with many sitters?" He was in the dawn of his hundredth summer and had never, during his long life, tasted a spoonful of acid, save such a mild suggestion of it as might have lodged in a green peach or resulted from the fermentation of a meat stew. So I protested, but in vain. He whipped out his hunting knife and severed the lemon. "It must be some kind of little melon," speculated the old man, as he buried his toothless gums in the major half of it—but the next instant the lemon was rolling on the floor, and he off his seat! He seized his chops with both hands; tears oozed from his close-shut eyes, he wriggled, groaned, hawked, bent far over the aisle, retched, heaved—and one of his companions remarked:

"Well, he has covered his nation with shame after all!" But the old man did not hear.

It was this same old man who afterwards avoided the suffering of the other five at the Palmer House by refusing to be convinced that he need not pay the penalty of eating sour things were he to touch anything else; so he dined on *tchu-k'ia-na-owe*. He, in common with the two other elders of the party, had prudently provided a liberal supply of this favorite lunch-material, in the belief that where such armies of Americans dwelt as they had been told inhabited the "Land of Sun-rise" one *might* find a scarcity of provisions.

One day after we had been in Washington a long time, I went to make my customary visit at the lodgings of my Zuñi companions. The old man was stretched out on the floor groaning piteously and writhing under the bony hands of Lai⌐-iu-ah-tsai-lunkia—the medicine man of the party. The others were sitting around looking dark and out of sorts.

"What's the matter?" I exclaimed.

"Ah," was the answer, "Another '*some kind of little melon!*'"

"How so?" said I. "Has he been eating anything, green apples or grapes?"

"No," replied my informant. "He knows better, but you told him yesterday that he was too feeble, and must not climb up to the top of that 'Standing White Rock' of Was-sin-tona [The Washington Monument]. Well, last night he said you were a mere youngster, anyway, and had no business to forbid his praying to the Sun-father whencesoever he pleased. This morning before we were open-eyed, he sneaked out—may the old burro be reduced to the eating of cedar-bark!—and climbed up the inside of that 'Standing White Rock.' A little while ago some

Me-li-kana-kwe in blue breeches and yellow buttons [policemen] brought him home and said much, but we could not understand them."

. . . .

On few points are the Zuñis more particular than on that of humanity in eating. They concern themselves less about the *cultivation* of punctuality than we do, because their excellent appetites and the natural alacrity with which they fall to whenever the women announce that things are ready, make the exercise of this grace almost instinctive, and therefore nearly universal. If, by accident, but one adult male member of the family be delayed at meal-time, [however,] the women—merely by refraining from saying the word—will keep the rest waiting as long as the slightest moisture remains in the body of the meat stew. And although these mistresses of the occasion will themselves go about, scratching their heads, poking the fire, and absent-mindedly sweeping the floor over and over to make ready, or rather to make themselves and the rest believe they are *not* ready, nevertheless the men are expected to—and do—sit through it all with exemplary manifestations of patience—considering their "natural alacrity!" Seeing them, one would think they were quite glad of the excuse to idly lie about and talk, which this delay affords them. Thinking thus, however, one would be mistaken. All this seeming indifference is the triumph of traditional enjoinder and its acceptance; not—like the habit of punctuality—a constitutional tendency.

Often have I watched an old gray-head crawl stiffly and complainingly out from his bundle of blankets, and hobble over to the hearth-side, at the earliest peep of daylight through the sky-hole. That he did this with the express purpose of lying in wait for the infantile members of the family, I verily believe. At any rate, no sooner would one of the members in question move uneasily in its sleep than the old man would assume the alert. Let this movement be followed by the more evident and invariable sign of a waking child in Zuñi—the scratching of the head—and the old fellow would instantly open up a fire of instructions on duty and politeness. It might be barely sunrise and he at the moment crouching over the still weak blaze; nevertheless,

FIG. 65. Sit and Eat

scorning the illustration of precept by example, he would immediately exclaim: "Here now, young one, get up! For shame that you should be lying here, still nesting, and the day already grown aged and *warm!*" No matter either, if his own eyes were masty, his own bodily consciousness of parasitical activity so acute as to cause his constant prosecution of vengeance on its perpetrators—all the same he would continue:

"Up, up, I say! Run out to the river and wash your winkers in cold water; it will brighten your vision and lighten the footfalls of the itch-makers, whom you only encourage to travel by lying in bed so long!"

By this time the child would doubtless be wakeful enough—though still yawning and plying his scratchers—to observe the old man's jaw wagging to the tune of parched corn or a meat-scrap, saved—like an unfinished end of tobacco—over night. This would naturally make him hungry; but his first whimper would be met by:

"There now, never lie around longing for food; never whine

for it—*dogs* do *that*! Wait till the heat of day; it will enliven your sense of the taste of good things. Food whistles on the spit and sings in the cooking-pot when it is ready, and only women know its music or understand its language; *little children* should wait for *them* to interpret!"

And after such style would he continue, utterly unmindful of the bewilderment with which his too mature harangue would be greeted, until the women came around with breakfast parapher-nalia and bade him get out of the way. I do not exaggerate when I say that I have repeatedly seen one of these old men get his *two-year old* grandson on his knee and talk to the little fellow about the amenities of eating time, as though he were a well-grown youth about to enter the solemn precincts of a sacred feast.

However unpromising all this may seem, its long con-tinuance has due effect. Such seasonable and salutary effect, indeed, that the youth are generally better behaved than their elders, and the children look upon these oracular ancients as the latter look upon the gods themselves. The result of this is that admirable self-control under even the trying circumstances above alluded to.

The motive which has given origin to this custom of ob-serving entire unanimity in the eating of a meal is obviously of a generous nature; for, where food is served in bulk, as it is in Zuñi, each dish being common property, only such a custom could insure equal choice and fair division for all concerned. So, not only will a meal be unmurmuringly waited for, but no person will begin the eating of one—certainly not if himself a guest, or if guests be present —until all are gathered around. Then he, and every other, independently selects a bit of each food, breathes on it and says:

"*I-sa'!* Na^1-na-kwe, i^1-tâ-na-we; yam-i^1-ke-na, yam-án-i-kwa-nan, a-k'ia, te-li-ana-we; yam-k'id^1-she-ma, yam-tâ^1-sho-nan-ne, yam-thla^1-shi-a-k'ia, ha-no-än^1-ik-tchi-a-nap-tu'!"

"Receive! (Oh, souls of) my ancestry, and eat; resuscitate by means of your wondrous knowledge, your hearts; return unto us of yours the water we need, of yours the seeds of earth, of yours the means of attaining great age."

As the last phrase of this grace dies away, the food is cast into the fire. Whether at home or abroad, I have never seen a Zuñi, young or old, taste food, even though but the merest hasty morsel, without first going through this invocation or abbreviated modification of it. Among the first words a child is taught to lisp are some of the above; and until, with his own hand, and his own lips guided and prompted by the mother's, he can make this offering and mutter this grace, no child is ever regularly weaned in Zuñi.

From "Zuñi Breadstuff," *Millstone* 10, no. 6 (1885): 98–100, and no. 7 (1885); 120–21.

On the Trail

THERE are few among ourselves who can realize how simply
the Southwestern Indian is able to travel the wilds which sur-
round his desert home. On the war-path, or on his far-reaching
expeditions in quest of game, his requirements are insignificant
compared with what we have learned to regard as essential to the
traveler's barest needs; his appliances for the preparation of
meals *en route*, wonderfully limited in number, but of surpassing
ingenuity in method. So, too, are the food materials themselves
which he carries, as few as the things with which he cooks them.
A bag of *tchu'-k'i-na-owe*, another of coarse meal and a saddle-
wallet of dried *he'-we*, complete, if we but add salt, red pepper
and tobacco in smaller sacks to the list, his provendery. These,
together with a small bowl and a little cooking pot, he rolls up in a
blanket and mounts, on the rear of his saddle, to the bow of which
he also slings a bottle of water-tight wicker-ware. Underneath
that saddle as a sort of padding, are a thick cloth and a half of a
deerskin dressed soft with the hair on. Over his shoulders is
strapped a quiver and bow-case, slung to his side a hunting knife,
and about his waist is ingeniously twirled his heavy serape—
overcoat, waterproof and bed-covering combined; for the skin
and cloth under the saddle, and the blanket in which are enwrapped his utensils and provisions, serve with cedar twigs or a
few handfuls of grass, for his bed.

Thus accoutred have I joined my adopted Indian brethren
on many a trip—nor suffered severely, winter or summer, for
want of ample comfort. More as an exhibition of their manner of
cookery and food service while traveling than as a distinct narra-

tive, I will give a hasty itinerary of a part of one of these expeditions:

It was in the early years of my life at Zuñi that Pa-lo-wah-ti-wa, a young half-brother named Kesh-pa-he, and I set out one sandy morning for the far away southern mesas. I say a "*sandy morning*," for the wind was blowing through the mountain funnels west of Zuñi such a terrific gale that not the least particle of landscape—except such as was flying through the air in the shape of sand—could be seen two rods ahead of us. Earth, sky, and the little river along which our trail ran, were equally invisible; for far above the tops of mesas, themselves a thousand feet high, sail the sand-clouds at Zuñi during the fierce winds of springtime, nor do their trailing feet ever lift themselves from the ground. Through this, shouting songs which strangely blended [with the] storm-voices around us, rode the two Indians—unconcerned as ever; for their serapes, unrolled but not untied from their waists and elevated to the heads, became huge hoods, effectually keeping out the flinty blasts which would have almost skinned the face of an American.

Soon we left the river and climbed the foot-hills to the boundary plateaus of the valley. Once upon the latter the wind alone swept past us, singing through the piñon trees and tall, lank winter grass; for the "legs of the sand-storm," so said the Indians, "were tangled in the tree-tops and mesas." All day long, never stopping for rest or refreshment, we kept on our course. Growing thirsty, I was advised to pick gum from the pine shrubs we passed under, and by chewing it allay my longing for water; for my Zuñi companions had not yet done "hardening my meat," and steadily refused to uncork their one basket bottle of water. Toward evening as we were picking our way through a thick copse of evergreens Kesh-pa-he gave a shout, and dismounting, pointed to a little twig which, from the look of things, must have been broken years before. Under the tree it depended from, hidden by a lichen-covered piece of bark, was a cake of yellow pine-gum, placed there no doubt by some former hunter and so marked to be discoverable to others of his class. The gum was somewhat bitter at first, but after awhile grew sweet in the mouth and served admirably the purpose for which it is used by Zuñi hunters—the quenching or staying of thirst.

From the wooded, hilly mesa-tops, we descended, just as the sun was setting, into one of those long, low white-walled cañons south of Zuñi which, running westward and treeless, seem as they are passed one by one, like great wandering rivers of light, flowing out flame-like from the fiery sunset world. No sooner were we well down before an exclamation from Pa-lo-wah-ti-wa caused me to look around. "Supper is ready!" he cried, pointing to a little "cotton-tail" rabbit which was just scudding into a hole in the rocks. Forthwith Kesh-pa-he dismounted, and cutting a slender twig, so trimmed the branches from it as to leave one or two hooks or barbs at the lower end. He then pushed the twig into the hole, prodded about until he suddenly exclaimed, "There he is!" then began to twist the twig until it would no longer turn about, when, giving it a cautious pull, behold! out came the rabbit, as thoroughly fastened to the end of the rod as though transfixed by a spear. The rabbit kicked and screamed in vain. His loose furry coat was too securely wound about the end of the stick to admit of much movement, or escape, and he was soon grasped by the hind legs, hit a sharp blow with the open hand just behind the ears, and instantly his struggles ceased. Before he was fairly dead the Indians drew his face up to their own and breathed from his nostrils the last faint sighs of his expiring breath.

Thus they killed no fewer than three or four rabbits, then abandoning the sport, made haste to seek a place for camping. Although spring had come the weather was by no means mild, and here and there in deep chasms, still lingered patches of melting snow. To my surprise the Indians turned from the little walled valley we had been traveling in, and sought the leeward side of an apparently exposed hill near at hand. Here, midway up, under a wide-spreading little cedar, they pitched their camp. Wisely, too, as I have since learned; for in such situations only can one find full protection from the wind and smoke of a camp in the wilds. Very close to the tree they built a fire; then, while one went about collecting snow, the other led our tired horses away to a little water pocket not far down the valley we had just abandoned. When the horses had been brought back and hobbled, the snow collected on a blanket out of range of the heat, one of the Indians found a flat stone and three or four lesser ones,

FIG. 66. A Bivouac in the Valley of the Pines (From "My Adventures in Zuñi")

while the other moved the fire considerably outward. The flat stone was mounted on the others as a table on very short legs, so propped up at one end, however, that it sloped gently from the fire near which it was stationed. Under the end opposite the fire our one bowl was placed, and on the flat rock the snow was heaped like a huge sugar-loaf as high as it could be packed. Then great sticks and logs of piñon were piled on the fire which soon shot upward and swirled about far above the lowermost branches of the trees by which we were surrounded. In a few moments the snow began to melt very rapidly, and the water soaking its way down the sloping stone, ran a constant stream into the bowl.

The Indians now began to prepare our first meal. One of the rabbits they threw into the middle of the blazing fire where almost instantly the hair and parts of the skin were singed off. When the carcass looked more like a cinder than the body of an animal it was hauled forth, and with a few dextrous turns of Kesh-pa-he's hand divested of its charred skin as a nut would be of its shuck—then dressed, spread out on a skewer, spitted and set up slantingly—to take care of itself for a while, before a thick bed of embers.

From the basket-bottle some water was poured into our cooking-pot and when it had begun to boil violently, some coarse meal was briskly stirred in. Before this had quite become mush, while still sticky and quite thin, that is, some of it was poured out on a stone, some dry meal thoroughly kneaded into it, and the whole ingeniously wrapped or plastered around the end of a long stick. This stick, like the rabbit spit, was then set up slant-ingly over the coals and occasionally turned until considerably swollen, and browned to a nicety. Behold a fine loaf of exceed-ingly well-done—and as I afterward found—also exceedingly good-tasting corn-bread!

The bowl of snow-water was removed from its place under the stone, and into it was stirred some *tchu'-k'i-na-owe*—just enough to make a cream-like fluid to serve as our beverage, and on the upturned sides of our saddle skins, in the light and warmth of our genial fire, our meal was at last spread out. The rabbit carcass, delicately cooked as ever was game at Delmonico's, the mush in the kettle it had been boiled in, the bread on the stick it had been baked around, and the one good sized bowl of *tchu'-k'i-na-owe* broth in our midst, we all sat down, made our sac-rifices to the gods, and ate as only hungry travelers *can* eat, enjoying our food as only hunters and husbandmen are privileged to enjoy the fruits of their labors.

And now, after the food was disposed of, the ashes were raked away from where our first fire had been built—"too close to the tree"(!). The sand underneath was dry as dust and hot, but not enough so to scorch the thin layer of cedar twigs with which each of our hastily scooped-out hip-holes was speedily lined.

Over the cedar leaves we spread the saddle-cloths and skins, over these our wrapping-blankets and serapes. A few more logs were brought in and placed near the fire, a little shelter of cedar branches built up to keep the wind off our heads, then we stretched out to smoke our cigarettes, listen to the hunter tales of our Elder Brother, and to make plans for the morrow's hunting.

I have already wandered so far and often from my parent theme in this discursive series, that no longer is there space for telling of the wild tales we heard that night. This summer, under the broad oaks and in sight of the dancing waters of Shelter Island, my old brother Pa-lo-wah-ti-wa will be with me again; again in some mimic camp which we shall make will I listen to those ever-wondrous tales, and may be, write them somewhere that my readers may learn with what romances the Zuñis replace the novels of our own less active hours.

That night, though the wind whistled by and cast sparks into the darkness around, until fair morning, we slept nor once were wakened by cold or discomfort; for our sand-bath beds, under their covering of fragrant, springy cedar leaves, kept warm as long as we kept our places on them, and supplied, with the heat of our camp-fire, the lack of more abundant covering.

In the morning, while Kesh-pa-he went to find our horses, old Pa-lo-wah-ti-wa remained to get breakfast. He fell to talking of expeditions he had accompanied in which provisions had failed, and was telling me how an Indian, though almost destitute, might travel for days in the most forbidding of countries without starving.

"If he thirst," continued Pa-lo-wah-ti-wa, "let him get up when the antelopes do and drink what they drink—dew from the inner leaves of the yucca, or the juices of cactus-pods, and other plants. If he hunger, and his arrow sees crooked, or not at all, let him catch prairie-dogs with nooses made from his own hair, or twist out a few vermin from the roots of juniper-trees and make 'rat brine.'"

Just as he was proceeding to tell me how this was done, Kesh-pa-he appeared, leading the horses.

"There's a *'nest'* just outside of camp!" said he.

"Where?" exclaimed Pa-lo-wah-ti-wa, catching up his hunting knife and cutting a twig like the one with which the rabbits had been captured the evening before. "I've been telling Little Brother how hunters make *'rat-brine,'*" said he, with a grin, and a stirring motion of the knife he was whittling with. "He is so hungry for some that his breath is hot and his eyes moist with anxiety!—look at him!"

Thereupon both rushed to find the "nest" in question. It was composed of sticks, stalks, and abundant cactus spines—with which the Southwestern wood-rats cleverly protect the approaches to their houses—all piled compactly about the roots of a large juniper tree. With a prod all this was soon demolished, and the holes in one of the roots examined.

"They're in!" called out Kesh-pa-he excitedly, and forthwith the flexible sapling probe was introduced, twirled a few times, and withdrawn, *two* squirming, staring-eyed rats well twisted to its end, and another prodding brought out one more. The rats were choked *en route* to our camp, and perhaps a little too soon for their own comfort, thrown into a bed of embers, where, after roasting a few moments, they bloated up into oblong balls, became divested of their tails, legs, ears, winkers, and all other irregularities, and when pulled from the fire, looked like roasted potatoes overdone. They were "shucked" in a twinkling—came out clean and white except for a greenish tendency of what were once their under-sides—and were forthwith mashed into a pulp between two stones—meat, bones, visceral contents and all, and stirred into about a pint of salt and water. Thus concocted was the "rat-brine;" green in color, semi-fluid, and meaty in taste—for they made me eat some of it, I do *not* regret to say—and very aromatic in flavor; a quality which the rats derive from the trees in which they live and on the berries and leaves of which they feed. Disgusting indeed would this delicacy of the hunter be, were the wood-rat of the Southwest anything like his various Eastern representatives and congeners; but he is not. He lives on but one or two kinds of food all his life, and the peculiar flavor of the sauce made from him is due to the way in which—visceral contents and all—he is worked up into "rat-brine."

From "Zuñi Breadstuff," *Millstone* 10, no. 8 (1885): 140–41.

Clowns, Priests,
and Festivals of the *Kâ'-kâ*

PERHAPS the most sacred, though least secret of [Zuñi] esoteric societies, is the *Kâ'-kâ*, or great dance organization—truly the church of these pagan worshipers, if church they may be said to possess, for in it are included priests, laymen and song-leaders. The public celebrations of this *Kâ'-kâ* consist of wonderfully fantastic dances, in which gods, demons and the men of ancient times are dramatically represented by costumed actors. Inside one of the estufas, or subterranean council chambers, which, on occasions of great moment are embellished with fringed and plumed bows strung across their entrance-ladders, rituals are repeated, prayers and sacrifices offered during a whole night preceding the public appearance of the actors. But during the day the worship consists almost wholly of dances to the time of loud invocation chants and wild metric music. To describe the various features of this worship would be to give a history of the whole Zuñi mythology and delineate a hundred diverse and striking costumes and maskings. In each celebration, however, certain elements are constant. Such are the clowns—priests annually elected from the membership of the *Kâ'-kâ*, and disguised as monsters, with warty, wen-eyed, pucker-mouthed pink masks [see fig. 67] and mud-bedaubed equally pink bodies.

First appear the dancers, some fifty of them, costumed and masked with such similarity that individuals are as indistinguishable as the birds or the animals they conventionally represent are from each other. Large-jawed and staring-eyed demons of one kind or another marshal them into the open plaza of the

FIG. 67. Clowns' Heads

village under the guidance of a sedate unmasked priest bearing
sacred relics and prayer-meal. One of the demons sounds a rattle
and howls the first clause in the song stanza; then all fall into line,
all in equal time sing the weird song, and go through the pan-
tomime and dance which invariably illustrate its theme. When
four verses have been completed, the actors, bathed in perspiration, retire to their estufa to rest and pray, while the priest-clowns
appear with drum, cabalistic prayer-plumes and the paraphernalia of guess-games. They begin the absurdest, most ingenious
and witty of buffoonery and raillery, generally managing,
nevertheless, to explain during their apparently nonsensical
dialogues, the full meanings of the dance and song—the latter
being often couched in archaic or jargonistic terms utterly incomprehensible to others than the initiated among the audience
which throngs the terrace-tops. To merely see these clowns,
without understanding a word of their incessant and really most
humorous jabber, is to laugh immoderately. To understand ev-

erything, withal, is to sometimes wish from sheer excess of laughing, that the dancers would file in and thus put an end to their jibes and antics.

If these clowns accompany certain most beautiful corn-dances of late autumn, then each bears a bundle of beautifully painted and feathered toy bows and arrows, or hideous dolls, with all sorts of bread-loaves and cakes depending from them. The bread tied to the bows has usually the forms of deer, antelope, rabbits, turkeys or other game animals, while that attached to the dolls—unless these be of a certain kind—has the shape of delicately-made cakes of all forms other than such as above described, with sometimes the effigies of infants or men and women interspersed. Toward evening when all the spectators are gathered in full force, the clowns take up their burdens of toys, and go searching cautiously and grotesquely amid the children as though afraid of the person they sought. When one of them finds the object of his search, he stares, wiggles, cuts capers and dodges about, approaching nearer and nearer the wondering child and extending the toy he has selected. Finally the half-frightened little one is induced by its mother to reach for the treasure; as it clutches the proffered gift the clown suddenly straightens up and becomes grave, and delivers a long loud-toned harangue. If the toy he has just handed be a bow and arrows, it is given to a boy; if a doll, to either a very *little* boy, or a girl. The bow and arrows symbolize the hunt whereby the little man shall in later life provide the food rudely represented by the eatable effigies tied to it. The doll with its fanciful loaves is emblematic of housewifely dexterity and, with the addition of the little human effigies, of the duties and cares of maternity. So, too, the lectures delivered with the presents correspond to the functional character of the toys represented.

It is with these dolls, carved in imitation of the personae of the sacred dance, that the Zuñi child is first taught the simpler of the myriad weary prayer formulae which, as a member of the Kâ'-kâ he will have to become familiar with by and by. With them, also, the little maiden is first initiated into the mysteries of the matron-life she will some day presumably lead, as well as into the less profound rites of food consecration and hospitality.

As the Zuñi New Year approaches, the dances increase in

number and variety. The ten clowns appear at night eight days before the grand festival, for the last time in their yearly service. They tell the people who assemble by torchlight to listen to their final ludicrosities, that the great feast day is at hand; that the men must make new garments for the women, and the women renew their houses with whitewash and cleaning for the men; their larders with fresh *he'-we*, *he'-pa-lo-k'ia* and other breadstuffs, for the strangers who are sure to flock in from the neighboring tribes to participate in the lavish festivities, witness the elaborate ceremonials and barter for the products of the Zuñi looms and kitchens.

With a few not very delicate jokes (for the New Year is of all others the marrying time in Zuñi) the clowns retire to their secret lodgings, there to remain until sun-rise eight days later, initiating the ten newly-chosen priests into the mysteries of their humor-laden vocation and severe ritualistic duties.

Thousands of sheep are driven in during the ensuing days, hundreds of them and dozens of cattle slaughtered, dissected and piled up in the corner of the newly plastered rooms. Hunters come in from the southern wilds bringing game, messengers speed away to surrounding tribes, bearing invitations to all who may wish to feast from Zuñi plenty or witness Zuñi dancing and beauty. Fires burn all over the house-tops each night cooking *he'-pa-lo-k'ia*, and all day in the little cooking rooms the *he'-we* stones are kept hot for the busy bakings. I have seen in one house at such times, twenty sheep carcasses, two quartered cattle, enough *he'-we* to fill a wagon box, and numerous other dishes of the kinds already so specifically described.

On the seventh evening the cry of the Sun-Priest is heard announcing the approach of "The Gods and the Ancients." At midnight, south of the town near the foot-hills, watch-fires are built to guide these coming personations—the chiefs and priests of the *Kâ'-kâ*, whose shrill flutes pipe dolefully in the night wind, and the rattles of whose masked attendants sound sharply on the frosty air. All night long, Navajos, Moquis, Pueblos and not a few Apaches, decked out in their finest costumes, and painted with ochre, vermillion, blue powder and marrow until their faces shine like those of Mediaeval Madonnas, ride in from the surrounding country and take up their quarters with welcoming hosts on every hand.

But in the midst of all these busy preparations, the "Meal with the Fathers" is not forgotten. I have said before that husbands abandon their own homes when they marry, to dwell in the houses of their wives. Early on the morning of New Year, however, old men may be seen tottering from place to place, gathering up their married sons and conducting them to homes of their nativity. Arrived there, the mother welcomes them as though returned from a long journey, and the first bread broken on that day of all days in the Zuñi year, is sacrificed in their honor on the hearth around which she has seen these sons, mostly grown middle-aged, frolic or play at the games they now scarce remember.

As the day wears away the Sun-Priest of the *Kâ'-kâ*—a god *pro tem* and treated as such—[and] the priests of a lesser degree, bird-like, beast-like, monster-like in apparel and disguise, come from where the fires burned last night, in solemn procession. Amid the showers of prayer meal with which they are reverently received, they consecrate the pueblo, the ladders of new houses and the plazas of the dances they are the leaders of. Later on they are followed by the *Sha'-la-k'o*, or giant war-priests of the *Kâ'-kâ*. These demoniac monsters tower far above the new clowns, flute players, and armed Priests of the Bow who herald and conduct their approach. They are ingeniously made effigies, long-haired, bearded, great-eyed, and long-snouted, so managed by means of strings and sticks by a person concealed under their ample, embroidered skirts that they seem alive, and strike terror to the uninitiated.

On entering the new houses they come to consecrate, they crouch low beside the sun-altar and glare out with gaping, clapping beaks and rolling eyes from the dark corner they are ensconced in, or fitfully start up at certain signals from the singer and drummers, like gigantic "Jacks" till their head-plumes fairly brush the rafters and their resounding clappers wake every sleepy child in the assemblage with nightmares of Zuñi devils and perdition. . . .

At about midnight, when fires glare fiercest and brightest in every sacred house in Zuñi, in each of them are stretched out like huge strings of beads across the immaculate floors, the rows and rows of round bowls, baskets and little black cooking-pots which make up the service of a great Zuñi feast.

Yet for long stand these many vessels of tempting viands untouched; for the Sun-Priest, the hereditary Priest of the House, the chief Priest of the Bow, all in turn have to pronounce long-winded rituals over them. Then the black-masked youth personating the god of fire, sweeps in bearing his burning brand of cedar bark, and gracefully swinging it over each kind of food, brushes away, as it were, the impure influences. The Priest of the Bow once more pronounces an invocation, takes a few bits of food from each dish, hands it to attendant juniors, who disappear to sacrifice it, then turns with a smile to the great crowd and calls out:

"Thus many have the days been numbered,
"The days of our anxious awaiting,
"That we might EAT WITH THE BELOVED!"

Whereupon the women echo his last clause and the hungry crowd gathers about the bowls and baskets. Eating is then the main business. Except for the shouts—"Approach with salt!"— "The favor of more meat this way."—"The *he'-we* is wasted down here"—"I am satisfied, thanks."—and the various appropriate responses, nothing is heard but the clatter of bones on the floor and the *subdued* smacking of lips; for the feasts of ceremonials are most decorous, and few of the rules for showing one's appro- bation at ordinary dinners are deemed in place at these, where the gods themselves are supposed to be the hosts and hostesses.

There is one other great festival, greater even than this. It is the "Initiation of Children" into the *Kâ'-kâ*. Occurring only once in four years, it is prepared for months beforehand, follows a fast of eight days, and lasts two days and two nights. The supply for it is provided with liberal hand by the parents of the little ones for whom it is instituted. Indeed, prodigality in everything seems to be the order of the day.

I cannot pause to describe separately the many fanciful personages which take part in this observance. There are the six-colored *Sa-la-mo-pi-as*, the Gods of the Dance, the Ancient

"Long-horned-Demons" of war, the light-footed Tablet-dancers, and the Bird-beasts of the Mountains and Oceans, represented. The novitiates having been duly dieted almost to starvation, are ranged in a circular row about the main plaza, their backs covered with robes and blankets. To prepare them for the passage under the fringed bow of [the] mystic estufa, they are soundly drubbed with long wands by each one of the forty-eight dancers, four times, four blows each time. Although the paddings on their backs be thick, they howl piteously before the several hundred blows they have to crouch under be meted out to them; and the more they howl the harder descend the blows. When this flagellation is completed, they are led into the estufa, there to be divested of most of their coverings, and again most soundly flogged, though this time a less number of times. Then, indeed, their cries resound and they wriggle to free themselves from the firm hands of their weird captors. After this comes a grand baptism, and a breathing into the nostrils of the still whimpering urchins, of the sacred breath of the *Kâ'-kâ*. No sooner is this done then the great effigy of the sea serpent, managed by means of invisible cords, wriggles into their midst through a curtained port-hole, and vomits with unearthly groanings a quantity of green medicine-water, with the drinking of which the poor frightened little wretches are freed from the probation of the estufa.

Meanwhile, outside, the two white-bodied, gray-headed tribute-bearers of the gods—whose faces are grim and ghastly with their great deep eyes and black hand-marks over the mask-mouths—appear on the scene. They are followed by the *Sa-la-mo-pi-a* crew and the little god of fire. From house-top to house-top they go, throughout the pueblo, casting down the rarest vessels—set out to await them—and breaking up baskets and all other food vessels not hidden before their approach. As each vessel strikes the ground the *Sa-la-mo-pi-as* rush upon it and dance it into the ground—while the baskets as they fall are lighted by the torch of the fire god, and soon nothing but cinders remain of their bright colors and involved pattern-work. When it is considered that over each bowl, basket and water-jar or cooking pot a series of passes have to be made by the tribute collectors with their plumed wands, a prayer said, and a low, long dirge-moan uttered, it may be conceived that, naked as they are in the cold winter afternoon, theirs is no enviable task; but the end of it signalizes the cessation of ceremonials, and the beginning of the joyous feasting. In the abandoned estufa, however, all through that boisterous night, a strange crowd of priests is gathered. The leaders of the *Kâ'-kâ* are assembled to listen to the great epic of creation, delivered by a masked and beautifully appareled priest. This epic, or ritual, is the Iliad of Zuñi. It is kept and handed down word for word by four priests, one of whom no sooner dies than another member of the *Kâ'-kâ* is installed in his place. One of these priests repeats every word of the ritual once in each of the six estufas, every fourth year. Each repetition requries six hours for its delivery—thirty-six hours in all—during which time the solemn-toned, rapid-speeched priest is not allowed to taste food other than *O'ki'dis-lu* water. Not once is his mask raised. None save those of the innermost circle of the *Kâ'-kâ* are supposed to know whom they are listening to, and the people at large so reverence the office, that to touch this priest's garments with the finger-tips as he is borne along from estufa to estufa by the ten clowns, is deemed a sacred, favor-laden grace.

Opposed to these, and the many other festivals I might tell of, are the Fasts, not less abundant in Zuñi. The most important of these, because almost universally observed, is the fast following the New Year festival. When the war-gods have been set up in their shrines on Thunder Mountain and the Mount of the Beloved, and the great "Last Fire" has been kindled as a signal by the Priests of the Bow, then only certain kinds of vegetable food are eaten by man, woman or child in Zuñi. All meat, all fatty matter, even vessels which have been contaminated by the touch of flesh, are abstained from. No fire is built out of doors during ten days, nor are many other things, allowable at other times, indulged in. The last night of the ten, however, is again full of ceremonial. Again the cooking-fires are busy. At daylight, however, they are all put out, and the cinders and ashes thrown to the winds of the open valley. Two nearly nude maskers of the dance may be seen in the twilight swiftly wending their way to a distant, lonely cañon, where the God of Fire is supposed to have once dwelt. There, with an ancient stick and shaft, they kindle tinder by drilling the two sticks together, and lighting a torch hurry it back to the great central estufa, where matrons, maidens and young men anxiously await the gift of New Fire. No sooner are the new flames kindled from this on the hearths of the households, than great baskets of food are cast into them, that the imperishable substance of life may be wafted upward into the outer world as food for the spirits of the ancestry and those who have died during the year just past. By no means unbeautiful is the sight of a gentle matron standing in prayer before the fireplace, dressed as if to meet beloved friends, and weeping softly to herself as she casts loaf after loaf unsparingly into the flames. Then, by all save the hereditary priests, who must continue their mortification of appetite six days longer, the great fast is broken.

Whenever a man is initiated into the Priesthood or one of the sacred Medicine Societies of the tribe, severe fastings are required. Never shall I forget the wretched existence I led during the four days of my probation when it had been decided I should become a "Priest of the Bow." In the council chamber of that priesthood I was confined. All meat, cooked food, salt, warmth and other comforts, including the cigarette, were denied me. Every morning, at the rising of the sun, I was conducted to an enormous bowl of dark, greenish-yellow medicine-water. By the side of this bowl stood another equally ample, but empty, and laid conveniently near, a *turkey-quill*. The offices of the extra bowl and the turkey-quill may be better implied than described when I say that I had to drink every drop—four gallons in all—of the tepid, nauseating draught before me. It left me weak and *very* empty each of those painful mornings, and after a pilgrimage to a distant shrine under the guardianship of a matron of my clan and two stalwart warriors, my breakfast, what though raw and stale, seemed most tempting—until I essayed to become satisfied of it! By the third day the habit of indigestion—artificially induced as has been described—became quite easy and natural; and although the "rising-water," turkey-quill and extra bowl were just as vigorously forced on my notice by my guardians, there really was no other than a purely chimerical reason for their use.

There is one secret order of the tribe wherein initiatory rules, though severe, are of quite an opposite nature. It is an esoteric society, of which I spoke in a foot-note of the first chapter of this series—the *Neʼ-we-kwe,* or "Gluttons." [1] Like the ten mud-priests, they are the most ridiculous of clowns when they appear in public, the most serious of sacred personages when gathered into the secret councils. They are the medicine-men *par excellence* of the tribe, whose special province is the cure of all diseases of the stomach—the elimination of poisons from the systems of the victims of sorcery or imprudence. They are exempt from all fasts, though denied for life the use of two or three kinds of delicacies, such as water-cress, and the flesh of the birds sacred to their order. But the penalty they have to pay is a dear one. No foods aside from the latter taboos are unwholesome or, whatever their conditions, are considered harmful to them. Nude to the waist, grotesquely painted about the eyes and mouth, there is no chance for deception when, in broad daylight, they sit down to a "demonstration" in the middle of the dance plaza. I have seen one of them gather about him his melons, green and ripe, raw peppers, bits of stick and refuse, unmentionable water, live puppies—or dead, no matter—peaches, stones and all, in fact everything soft enough or small enough to be forced down his gullet, including wood-ashes and pebbles, and, with the greatest apparent gusto, consume them all at a single sitting. Once after such a repast, two of these *Neʼ-wes* pretended, though their stomachs were bloated to distortion, to still be hungry. They fixed their staring eyes on me, and motioned me to give them *something else to eat!* I pitied them profoundly, but as it is considered the height of indecency to refuse a *Neʼ-we* anything, I ran home, caught up some crackers, threw them into a paper, and in order to make them relish the better, poured a pint or two of molasses over them. I wrapped an old woolen army jacket around this as a present to the enterprising clowns, and hurried back. There they were anxiously waiting—the people watching them to see how much more they could get away with. I cast the bundle into the plaza. The pair immediately fell to fighting for its possession, consequently broke the paper, scattered some of the crackers about the ground and daubed the back of the coat thoroughly with the molasses. They gathered up the fragments of crackers and ate them—with their whole burden of adhesions, then fought over the paper and ate that, finally tore pieces out of the back of the coat with their teeth and ate *them* (though it nearly choked them to do so), after which the victor put the coat on and triumphantly wore it, his painted skin showing like white patches through the holes he had bitten in the back of the coat. I observed that ere long—one at a time—they disappeared. When either returned he was fairly *lank* and pretended to be woefully hungry—and manifested, moreover, quite as much readiness to devour everything as before.

Whatever the "medicine" is that these *Neʹ-wes* possess, it must be superlatively good; for I have never yet known one to die from the effect of his extraordinary gourmandizing, and but one to grow sick during my long stay in the Pueblo—*he* only for a little while.

I hesitate to record in this, my last article on Breadstuff, the many other seemingly super-gastral exploits of these inimitably funny doctor-clowns. The most amusing chapter within the scope of my pen would be such a record; but not only would it be too often disgusting to one unaware of its almost heroic motive, it would be wholly disbelieved by such of my readers as never chanced to visit me in Zuñi and personally witness the performances of these *Neʹ-wes*. When it is considered, however, that the *Neʹ-we* never appears in public as a *demonstrator* of the power of his medicine until after years of arduous training, even then only after elaborate preparation, it will be conceded that the above narration transcends in no wise mere sober truth.

The *Neʹ-wes* may frequently be seen in seasons of scarcity, going from house to house in company with the *Keoʹ-yi-mo-shi*, or Priest-clowns, and in the service of certain strange *mendicants*. These mendicants usually travel in pairs. They are powerful men disguised as saurian monsters. Their heads are entirely encased in enormous long-jawed masks precisely resembling—what with their teeth of plaited corn-husk or shining squash-seeds—the heads of crocodiles. Out of the foreheads of these masks, stare eyes composed of balls of buckskin painted white and dotted with black, so adjusted that like the eyes of wax dolls they roll about or seem to wink with the upward, downward or side-wise motion of the man they disguise. The masks, cloths fastened to them to conceal the neck and bodies of the performers, are painted black, and a streamer of dark colored cloth hangs down the back and trails behind, covered with a row of eagle

FIG. 68. Zuñi Mendicants

plumes which stand erect like the spines in a sea-monster's dorsal fin. All over the head and body of these figures are little patches of snowy eagle down—stuck on with wild honey—to represent scales. The mendicants are dressed in the armlets, wristlets, sashes and badges of war to proclaim their bloodthirsty proclivities. They are armed with bows and long arrows tipped with corn-cobs. This latter circumstance is fortunate for the *Ne'-wes* and *Keo'-yi-mo-shi*; for no sooner does one of the latter succeed in gathering up a blanket-load of *he'-we*, corn or other provender, than he is unmercifully plugged by the howling monsters [see illustration] and compelled to make a deposit of his precious cargo, or else goaded on to beg for more. If any woman to whom application is made by a *Keo'-yi-mo-shi*, be hardy enough to refuse him alms, the clown rushes bawling and whimpering back to his monster-master who, uttering low, hoarse gutteral bellows, very becoming to his appearance, proceeds to shoot out a few window-lights in her house, or sends—not very gently, either—two or three arrows at the woman herself, or her children, until she is fain to hand over any kind of breadstuff she may have at hand.

But ere we complete this series on ZUNI BREADSTUFF, let us see how, once in four years or eight, the ovens whence it issues in such abundant variety are cleaned (ceremonially speaking) of

FIG. 69. Demon Inspector of Ovens

the last vestiges of old bakings and the "bad influences" which are accounted as having accumulated in them.

On a certain summer evening of the fourth or, as the case may be, eighth year, a curious figure—a veritable ideal chimney-sweep appears. Black as the soot with which he is painted can make him, is he; bristling at many points with tufts of hair and cedar brushes. His head is round like an oven; round too his eyes, like flue-holes, with yellow ladders painted over them for brows. A bunch of stiff hair surmounts his crown, out of which issues like a flame a red eagle plume to symbolize fire. His mouth is almost square like an oven-door, but with red lips—the light gleaming out when the stone door is closed—with a stiff thin beard shooting forth from its under side which makes it look, despite its parallelogramic proportions, like a cyclopean eye with heavy winkers—placed too low down. On either cheek is painted in glaring yellow the paw of a badger or some other famous burrower—also symbolic of function. The creature carries in one hand a wand of yucca leaves with which to scourge away dogs; and in the other a little broom of hemlock. To his rump is fastened a long cord of fiber like the tail of a kite. As he travels along he staggers, crooks his thighs, crawls eccentrically from side to side and plunges this way and that as though seeking for or trying to enter ovens; for in everything he sees nothing but ovens—sometimes mistakes ladders or even burros for such and strives to get into them. When at last he espies a veritable oven, he leaps wildly toward it with a low growl of satisfaction, and eagerly disappears through its dark doorway. Presently out come crumbs and fragments of bread or bits of *he'-we* (left there, of course, in anticipation of his visit) which scarcely strike the ground before they are grabbed up by the ever attendant *Keo'-yi-mo-shi*, or *Ne'-wes*. Dust and cinders follow—as though the oven had never been cleaned!—nor do the exertions of the Oven-demons cease short of mischief to the masonry of the structure, unless one of his companions, with great to-do, snakes him forth by means of the long rope of fiber. No sooner is he out than he turns on his captor with his yucca weapon, and breaks away and goes plunging along to another oven, and so on until every dome-shaped bread receptacle in the village has been duly visited and purified.

Thus, O, patient reader, with thanks indeed for your long-suffering kindness in the reading of these hasty sketches, let us leave these ovens, nor pollute them again with fresh bakings, or the mention of them!

From "Zuñi Breadstuff, *Millstone* 10, no. 8 (1885): 141–44.

Note

1. See p. 363, n. 6

III. TRANSLATIONS

Translations

When at the dead of a night in mid-winter the talk of the men, like the smoke of the pine-knots, lulls and blends with the roar in the chimney, and the women doze over their spinning along the farthest wall, then the aged Zuñi story teller squats cross-legged on a skin beside the fire and begins his olden tale.

"*Són-ah-tchi!*" he exclaims; "shall we bide this night with the ancients?" And from all around him come the responses "*E'-so E'-so,*" "Yea, so let it be!"

"Well then," he resumes with a smile, "Sit ye straight; if ye droop ere my story be ended, stooped with age will ye be ere by age ye be bended."

He pauses, puffs his cigarette to the gods of the six regions and with half closed eyes and dreamy, distant manner, continues. . . .
—"The Discovery of Zuñi"[1]

In the oral literature of Zuñi, as in that of various other American Indian cultures, there are basically two kinds of stories: the myths of the first origins and migrations, set in a time when the world was still "soft," and the tales, pertaining to a not quite so distant but still ancient time when the world had assumed its present and familiar form (except for some last few features, to be "hardened" in the narrative) and the people were settled in the old *Shi-wona* towns—now long deserted and fallen in ruins.[2] Traditionally (if not always in practice), this latter kind of story is told, as in the scene recalled in the passage above, "at the dead of night in mid-winter"; whereas origin stories, at least nowadays, can apparently be told at any time, though their recitation in ritual form seems to have been far more strictly circumscribed. In Cushing's account, the priests in charge of this ritual were enjoined, because of the sacred character of the material, from reciting any part separately; once begun, the entire cycle had to be completed. An "epic-ritual," as he describes it, "of great length, metrical, even rhythmical in parts, and filled with archaic expressions nowhere to be found in the modern Zuñi, . . . this piece of aboriginal literature is jealously guarded by the priests who are its keepers and is publicly repeated by them only once in four years, and then only in the presence of the priests of the various orders."[3]

In Cushing's words, the origin stories constitute a kind of unwritten Bible or Iliad, accounting for the main characteristics of Zuñi "sociologic organization" as well as informing nearly every one of the myriad religious observances which dominate the life of the community. The subject of prayer, song, and dramatic reenactment in dance throughout the ceremonial calendar both of the community as a whole and of the various cults, priesthoods, and kiva groups, this body of sacred story, according to recent report, is still "regarded as literally true, even by some white-collar Zuñis with Christian leanings."[4] The tales, on the other hand, while frequently overlapping into myth, are generally regarded as fiction, in the sense that literal truth is not expected in their every detail.

The selections to follow, with one exception, are tales—chosen from the collection of Cushing translations published by his wife in 1901 under the title *Zuñi Folk Tales*. To read the tales without the origin myth, however, as Mary Austin puts it in her introduction to the 1931 reprint of this volume, "would be like trying to understand English literature without a knowledge of the King James Bible."[5] Hence the selections here are introduced by a review or "outline" of that myth which appears in the first chapter of *Zuñi Breadstuff*. Cushing of course never completed his translation of the "epic-ritual" itself, portions of which are included in the "Outlines of Zuñi Creation Myths," and even if he had, its bulk (to say nothing of its merits as poetry) would prohibit inclusion here. The version chosen is essentially a brisker abridgment of the same story that is reviewed at greater length in the "Outlines."

The version of the "epic-ritual" described by Cushing above

is that which he heard performed in the meetings of the cult society of the *Kâ'-kâ* rain gods. As he understood, however, and as Ruth L. Bunzel in her "Introduction to Zuñi Ceremonialism" rightly credits him for understanding, "the true character of Zuñi mythology [is such that] there is no single origin myth but a long series of separate myths. Each ceremonial group has a myth which contains, in addition to a general synopsis of early history, the mythological sanction for its own organization and rituals." [6] (Cushing's theory was that a grand collection of all these versions existed in the minds of a "midmost" group, but he did not remain in Zuñi long enough to test that theory, and it has not survived subsequent investigation.)

As suggested earlier, Cushing also understood another factor precluding the acquisition of "the" single, authoritative version of any such material—the fact, as Bunzel puts it, that "all ethnological information comes to us through the medium of another mind." [7] Two other minds, in fact, when it comes to the matter of mythology, since, as Cushing points out, the stories themselves really do not exist separate or discrete from the vast range of interconnected lore from which they emanate, and each telling, including what and how much is told, varies according to the teller, the occasion, and the eligibility of the listener to hear. "If these primitive myth tellers deem you a stranger," he writes in an unpublished note, "there are parts—always the most vital—which no bribe will induce them to relax their hold on." On the other hand, a story which ordinarily might occupy an hour in the telling may instead, "related with abundant parentheses and saws," take up most of the night. "If the myth be serious (a *thla-she-awa* of the ancients), then this constant enlargement of the theme is the more certain to result, and to be interrupted with practical demonstrations from, for example, mutual experiences."

"In view of all this," he continues, evidently referring to his "Outlines of Zuñi Creation Myths" but in words equally applicable to *Zuñi Folk Tales*,

> it has seemed good to me to tell these tales as I do—not always withholding little touches which do not belong strictly in the places where they occur, yet which are, in the way of understandings, always implied as understood. . . . [The pieces] are not to be

considered as literally translated, yet nevertheless they are true in word as well as in ideas to the originals. As I have presented them, each is a composite of the various accounts I have heard of it and of the large amount of information of one kind and another always vouchsafed me with each repetition or separate telling of it and related myths.

"In a riper time of research," he concludes hopefully, his work may be looked on as better the way it is than if "more categorically and 'accurately' presented." [8]

It is in this same note that he speaks of the unavoidability of the "personal equation" in the transmission of ethnological information of any kind and argues indeed that there is no substitute for "subjective saturation" on the part of the would-be transmitter. Predictably, however, Cushing's translations have attracted criticism from the scientific community on account of those "little touches" and other expressions of "subjective saturation" that his note sought to defend. The problem is a knotty one. On the one hand, the translator whose concern is all for scientific purity and literal accuracy is likely to miss the spirit, and the artfulness, of the narrative he has heard—and thus distort in his treatment of it. On the other, the translator who approaches his task as a spirited participant and an artful storyteller himself, drawing, as would his tribal counterpart, not alone on one telling of a tale but on a cumulated lore—such a translator is in peril of intruding into the tale colorations derived from his own tastes and cultural background and thus compromising in this other way the authenticity of his work as translation.

For his sins of this latter order in *Zuñi Folk Tales*—"embroider[ing] the tales with devices, lines, and even whole passages which are clearly of his own invention and not mere distortions"—Cushing is treated with considerable severity by Dennis Tedlock in his recent important essay "On the Translation of Style in Oral Narrative." Specifically, he charges Cushing with (a) making up quaint oaths ("By the delight of death!" "Demons and corpses!") to "translate" various interjections which have no denotation at all in the Zuñi, (b) dressing up the narrative with similes, which do not exist in the Zuñi, (c) inserting explanatory material, whereas "a Zuñi narrator would take his audience's knowledge for granted," and, "most distressing of all," (d) introducing explicit statements of what he takes to be the moral of the story, whereas, as Tedlock points out, "the didactic content of Zuñi tales is usually either implicit or addressed by one tale character to another [but] never addressed by the narrator directly to his audience."[9]

Aside from noting that some are more grievous than others, it would be pointless to try to defend Cushing against these charges. He is guilty of them all, and of other faults as well, no doubt—mostly accounted for, as Tedlock seems to recognize, by variances of taste, standards, and expectations (perhaps especially in the translation of "primitive" literature) between our own time and that of Queen Victoria. Cushing's work does date from the end of the nineteenth century, and his style now and then betrays this fact. Tedlock's criticism is reassuring, however, for having heard it, one has heard the worst that can judiciously be said about Cushing's translations, and while the sorts of flaws Tedlock points out are occasionally serious enough to make one wince in the reading of a Cushing tale, neither these flaws nor the merits of Tedlock's own impressive translations in his book *Finding the Center: Narrative Poetry of the Zuñi Indians* are likely to render Cushing's work obsolete.[10]

Cushing and Tedlock have, in fact, something in common as translators, each seeking to convey not merely the letter of the narrative dutifully dictated and transcribed but the experience of the tale itself in the communal moment of its telling, the one with the advantage of modern recording equipment, the other with only his ear and the combined narrative skills he and his storytelling Zuñi friends could bring to bear. In Cushing's case, moreover, the translating itself was in substantial degree an oral process. According to a review of *Zuñi Folk Tales* by his friend Washington Matthews, "many of the tales were taken directly from stenographic notes of Cushing's spontaneous recital [translating] to Mrs. Hemenway in the autumn of 1886," when his friends Waihusiwa, Palowahtiwa, and Heluta were staying with him on her estate.[11] Waihusiwa was the teller of most of the tales. Cushing of course used prose in translating them, whereas Tedlock's special achievement—likely to open a whole new phase in the translating of Indian oral narrative—is to have shown what can be accomplished treating this kind of literature as dramatic poetry. Here again, however, we are dealing with a fact of history as well as a difference in talents. Unlike the contemporary poetry Tedlock heard performed in the late 1960s, the kind of poetry to which Cushing was evidently accustomed had less to offer—and was more "Victorian"—than prose as a vehicle for translating American Indian oral narrative. Cushing did attempt verse translation of bits of the great "epic-ritual" in his "Outlines of Zuñi Creation Myths," but judging by the results in this case and in various other fugitive efforts, we may be grateful that he stuck to prose in translating the tales.

From the scholarly standpoint, of course, such work as *Zuñi Folk Tales* cannot become obsolete, for the simple reason that it is unique and irreplaceable. As the first recording of a large number of Zuñi tales, preceding by some ten years the work of his nearest follower and by almost half a century the nearest comparably large-scale collections of Parsons, Bunzel, and Benedict, Cushing's *Zuñi Folk Tales* is likely to remain in the future, as it has been in the past, a major resource for students of the genre and of the ethnology of the Southwest.[12] Moreover, the virtues of Cushing's translations as literature—virtues of which the "impurities" may be the defect—give them a perennially fresh interest that goes well beyond that merely of source material for anthropological study. It is not surprising that Mary Austin should have put down in 1931 as "the sole reason" for reprinting *Zuñi Folk Tales*, "after a complete lapse from public attention," that among the then extant translators of American Indian myth or song Cushing was "the only American who notably brought to bear on that field adequate literary understanding."[13] Defects notwithstanding, *Zuñi Folk Tales* is still a classic.

In the matter of selection, personal preference joins with the intent to be representative so far as very limited space allows. The stories chosen offer glimpses of several ubiquitous characters and a variety of frequently encountered themes and story situations in Zuñi folklore. Two favorite figures who appear are the twin war gods, Ahaiyuta and Matsailema, otherwise known as "Our Beloved," the "Terrible Two," and the "Boy-gods of War." Fathered by the Sun and brought forth out of a patch of foam floating on the waters of the world, these two figure in the origin myth as the guardians and guides who lead the people out of the underworld wombs into the light and later protect them in their struggles and wanderings. Armed "with the rainbow for their weapon and thunderbolts for their arrows—swift lightning-shafts pointed with turquoise—, they were the greatest warriors of all in the days of the new." Their role as invincible protectors of the Corn People carries over as well into the tales in the form of their services in killing off various monsters. Here, however, another side of their character becomes equally important: the side of pure impulse, impishly playful and frequently destructive even of the humans who chance to get in their way. Olympian-like, or childlike, or like a natural force, on this side they are quite without judgment or feeling with respect to their impact; they simply act.

Another favorite character is Coyote, matched in one of the stories here in a losing competition with a pair of ravens. Like the twin gods, Coyote is one of the primal figures who appear not only in the tales but in the origin myth; also like the twin gods—and like the ritual clowns of the *Kâʼ-kâ* rites—Coyote is a kind of double character, a container of oppositions, at once one of the most hallowed of the animal spirits and the most foolish, the meddling trickster who is forever being tricked.

In keeping with Cushing's observation (in the essay on fetishes) of the special role of animals in Zuñi experience, nearly every one of the tales has its animal characters—a number of whom, by stepping out of their skins and appearing as "fine little old men," illustrate the Indian view of animal forms as inhabited by spirit beings closely kin to the humans themselves. This form changing is itself a recurrent theme—a reverse version of which is the changing, by witchcraft, of humans into animal forms. While no longer "soft," the world of the tales—and for that matter of the Zuñi tradition in general—has by no means settled into fixed categories.

Here, too, there is "another side," however, for if the "fine little old man" inside the animal skin looks human, he nevertheless belongs to a different order, just as do the beings of all sorts in the world who have their origins and homes in the various directional "spirit quarters." One may pass back and forth between one's own quarter, or form, and another; but the passage itself is as often or as much an experience of otherness as of relationship. This experience of other worlds, ubiquitous in *Zuñi Folk Tales*, figures in at least one of the stories selected: "The Trial of Lovers," which involves an Orpheus-like journey to the Land of Spirits. Among other examples in *Zuñi Folk Tales* one might mention "The Youth and His Eagle," which involves ascent into the sky domain of the eagles and marriage to an eagle being, and "The Foster Child of the Deer," which involves the change of identity undergone when a boy who has grown up thinking of himself as a deer is confronted by his human kin.

A variant of this theme may also be seen in the various stories in which Coyote comes to grief attempting to take on the forms of other creatures—as, for example, the one in which, with borrowed feathers, he attempts to fly with the blackbirds, or, for that matter, the one included here, in which he tries to do with his eyes what he sees the ravens doing with theirs. The lesson in these stories about Coyote seems to be that one should stick to one's own form. Still another variant or related theme concerns the sexual form—or, as we would say, sex roles. In "The Rabbit Huntress" a girl who tries to step over into the man's world as a hunter of game loses her way, her clothes, her game, and nearly her life, before she is rescued by the Divine Twins and set on the right path toward marriage and a husband who will do her hunting for her.

Interestingly enough, it happens that in the case of "The Rabbit Huntress" different versions of the story have been obtained from male and female informants. In the women's version, according to Ruth Benedict, the girl kills many rabbits and marries her supernatural savior; in the men's, she kills only two, marries a human, and soon dies.[14] (Cushing's version seems to be a compromise; she kills many rabbits and marries a human.) A more general sense of otherness, as experienced from at least one side of the boundary between the men's world and women's, may be inferred from the fact (again according to Ruth Benedict) that all witch tales involving sex (e.g., stories of the toothed-vagina woman) and all tales of sex fetishism and intercourse with beasts are told by men.[15] What this tells us about the male attitudes with respect to sex will be left to the psychological analysts of the tales to explain.

Like all folk tales, or all literature for that matter, the Zuñi stories are products combining tradition and individual talent. The formal opening, for example, as described by Cushing in the passage at the head of this introduction, is the standard one required by tradition, though it is not usually included in full in the stories as translated. There is also a regulation pattern for the closing of a story, observed in most of the selections, which includes a sentence beginning "That is why," the statement that "Thus it was in the days of the ancients," and finally an archaic phrase which Cushing renders in the sentence "Thus shortens my story." What has been observed already about the rules governing the recitation of the origin ritual suggests that behind such rules here too are considerations not of aesthetics but of magic powers which inhere in the stories and must be "tied off" or put to rest properly rather than left loose. Also traditional, of course, and common in European oral literature as well, are the routines demanded by occasions such as the arrival of a visitor— the set phrase of greeting, food offering, etc., and then, if the visitor is a suitor, the invitation to state his business: "It is not thinking of nothing that a stranger comes to the house of a stranger." [16]

The incidents of which the tales are composed are likewise drawn, as are those of European (and perhaps all) folk tales, from a collective stock, the same incidents turning up, in different combinations, in a variety of tales. For instance, in one of the versions of the rabbit huntress story which includes her death, the mourning husband makes the same Orpheus type of journey to the land of the dead that is featured in the version of "The Trial of Lovers" reprinted here. Such incidents may be strung together in sequence, worked in as more or less decorative details, or expanded to include other incidents as subordinate elements.

The storyteller's art lies in what is done with these stock elements in an individual narrative—how the themes and incidents are elaborated and combined. Two main stylistic objectives, according to Ruth Benedict, are to incorporate as much cultural detail as possible and to build into the plot as many incidents as possible. In this process of inclusion, however, a test of the narrator's skill is his success in maintaining a coherent focus, adapting to his own themes the elements he has borrowed from other tales and "following out the implications of the new sequence he has chosen."[17]

In Cushing's version of "The Trial of Lovers" (to let one illustration stand for several) the narrator has woven in some seven incidents listed in Benedict's index, including the reluctant bride, the marriage test, the false bride, conflict with a witch, the Orpheus journey, encounter of obstacles, and help given by animals. Favored themes also appear, such as the reward of modest virtue and the consequences of failing to resist temptation. And throughout the story, the narrator works in details of his extensive knowledge of local geography, history, technology, and the manners and customs of the people, as when we are told of the flint knives and wooden hoes used "in the days of the ancients" and the whole series of formal courtesies exchanged upon the visits of the young men to the house of the maiden of Matsaki.

Such details, as Dennis Tedlock points out in his article "Pueblo Literature: Style and Verisimilitude," are "one of the most important devices a Zuñi narrator has for giving the appearance of reality to a tale . . . embedded in fantasy"[18] —somewhat as in "The Ancient Mariner" we are propelled along routes that are known into an unknown sea. An example cited by Tedlock: the realistic context provided by elaborate information about hunting clothes and rabbit hunting techniques in a tale featuring a girl who hunts (fantasy) and encounters an ogre. In "The Trial of Lovers" we enter the realm of fantasy when the maiden opens her jar of pet gnats and mosquitoes, but there is great realism in the description of what these troublesome insects do to her suitors and how the fourth young man (such things always happen in fours) provides against them.

As for the incidents, the "marriage test" segment of "The Trial of Lovers" is virtually a tale in itself, complete with "that's why" flourish explaining the subsequent behavior of gnats and mosquitoes. The progression of suitors, which opens with one who is rich and overconfident, ends, with satisfying moral symmetry, in the victory of one who is poor and devout and has a loving heart and a crafty grandmother.[19] Also satisfying, both to her parents and to the audience, is the girl's conversion from reluctance to eagerness for marriage. Consummation at this point is of course prevented by introduction of the incident of the witch, in the form of the false bride. This time, resolution is delayed by interrupting the story, thus converting what might have been an end into what appears rather to be only the nadir. The second part of the story takes in a succession of fours: the four days between the girl's death and her departure for the land of the dead, the four days of journeying thither (into which are incorporated the incidents of the obstacles and the helpful animals), and finally, foreshortened in the telling, the four days of the return journey and its fatal issue.

How, other than through the continued presence of the same two characters, does this series of incidents cohere as a single, unified tale? We have the beginning of an answer to this question when we recognize that in the second part of the story the narrator has carried forward and repeated the pattern of the first: twice, after the overcoming of obstacles and at the very moment of achievement, success and happiness are converted to defeat and death. In truth, continuity of character counts for a good deal in the story, since in both instances it is by his own foolish act that the young man, after his faithful labors, loses the object of his love. Perhaps there is even the hint of connection between the extremity of his love and of his grief, beyond the norm, and the headlong way in which he leaps into the fray to kill the wrong girl, as well as his inability to resist embracing her at the end. For all his endearing and admirable qualities, there is wanting in him a certain steadiness of judgment and self-control. He has his flaw.

Just as Aristotle observes of the Greek tragedies, however, it is not merely the hero's flaw that brings about the catastrophe. Here, instead of fate, the extra-personal force is magic—so central to the Zuñi experience that it is to be encountered everywhere in the tales. In its malevolent form as witchcraft, magic in this story serves the fatal purpose of the wicked elder sister, effecting the bride's death and the despair of the youth. It is not merely in this one episode, moreover, that the play of magic is felt in the story. From the beginning the young man is moving in deep waters, for the desired girl herself, as enchantress of the insects, is identified as a "Passing Being." While her magic is overcome in the first part of the story, through the craft of the old grandmother, she seems more than ordinarily at home when she arrives in the second part of the story at the Land of Spirits and is seen "there in the midst of the *Kâʻ-kâ* sitting at the head of the dancers." Even at the end, when, having journeyed back to within sight of Matsaki, she stops to sleep, there is the half-suggestion that her sleep is feigned—as a deliberate temptation. So that when she awakes and flies off to the westward in the form of an owl, paralleling the sister's flight in the form of a crow at the end of the first part, she may be seen not only as receding again into death but as liberated to return to her real home.

"It is not well with my beautiful child," the old priest-chief, her father, says, shaking his head, when he hears of her death in the first part of the story; "but as They (the gods) say, thus must all things be." Such, essentially, is also the conclusion drawn at the end of the second part, when we are told that the young man's kiss may have been the cause ("that's why") of all subsequent death and mourning: "But then, it is well!" In this larger view of how all things must be, even the evil of the elder sister falls into perspective. For the Land of Spirits is not the home only of the bride of Matsaki. As the origin myth tells us, it is the sacred abode of the rain gods, to which all the waters of the world and all the souls of men travel when they are "finished," and whence, as from the original womb-caves, new moistures and new life must recurrently emerge. In the Zuñi tale, as in the classic tragedy, there is evoked a sense of this larger life which goes on even as the figures of the story fade from the scene. Registering through the kinds of parallels noticed, moreover, this sense of things serves as a unifying force within the tale itself.

There is of course no way of knowing exactly how much and what sort of credit for the stories in *Zuñi Folk Tales* should go respectively to Cushing and to his informant(s). By now these stories belong to a pool which includes variants contributed by a host of anthropologists, and differences among them may be attributed as much to the informants, and to what time has wrought in Zuñi, as to the style of the translators. Cushing's tales in any case belong in a class by themselves. "All the color and gesture of the time so delightfully rendered," as Mary Austin puts it, "more than compensate for the occasional lapses of the translator, not a practiced *littérateur*, but instinctively familiar with the rhythms that subtend all literatures and make them akin."[20]

Notes

1. "The Discovery of Zuñi, or the Ancient Provinces of Cibola and the Seven Lost Cities," a lecture given before the Geographic Society of Boston in 1885 (MS, Box no. 1, Hodge-Cushing Collection, Southwest Museum).

2. See Tedlock, "Pueblo Literature: Style and Verisimilitude," pp. 221–22, for an exposition of this distinction of Zuñi narrative. For a parallel distinction in Winnebago narrative, see Paul Radin, *The Evolution of an American Indian Prose Epic: A Study in Comparative Literature*, p. 15.

3. "Zuñi Fetiches," p. 12. Ruth Benedict states, however, that "in Zuñi, tales fall into no clearly distinguishable categories. . . . Even the Emergence story, which is the Zuñi scripture, is not reserved for the priests nor owned by them. It is freely repeated by any fireside by any layman, and all versions differ markedly, not so much in order of incidents as in the details introduced. Incidents of it, moreover, can be lifted and used as the basis of entertaining stories" (*Zuñi Mythology*, 1:xxx).

4. Tedlock, "Pueblo Literature," p. 222.

5. *Zuñi Folk Tales* (1931), p. xxvii.

6. Ruth L. Bunzel, "Zuñi Origin Myths," p. 547.

7. Ibid., p. 547.

8. "Notes on Myth and Folklore," pp. 1b–6b and 6c, Box no. 1, Hodge-Cushing Collection, Southwest Museum.

9. Dennis Tedlock, "On the Translation of Style in Oral Narrative," pp. 116–17.

10. Dennis Tedlock, *Finding the Center: Narrative Poetry of the Zuñi Indians*.

11. Washington Matthews, review of *Zuñi Folk Tales*, p. 144.

12. Cushing was in Zuñi from 1879 to 1884, but he seems to have done much of the work on *Zuñi Folk Tales* in 1886 during a visit east of several of his main informants. Matilda Coxe Stevenson's "The Zuñi Indians" includes both a summary of the origin story, comparable to Cushing's presentation in "Outlines of Zuñi Creation Myths," and a translation of one tale (see "The Zuñi Indians," pp. 23–61, 135–37). The

next wave of translations consists of those produced by Boas and his followers in the 1920s and 1930s, including: Franz Boas, "Tales of Spanish Provenience from Zuñi," *Journal of American Folklore* 35 (1922): 62–98; Elsie Clews Parsons and Franz Boas, "Spanish Tales from Laguna and Zuñi, New Mexico," *Journal of American Folklore* 33 (1920): 47–72; Elsie Clews Parsons, "Notes on Zuñi, Part II," *Memoirs of the American Anthropological Association* 4 (1917): 302–27; idem, "Pueblo Indian Folk Tales, Probably of Spanish Provenience," *Journal of American Folklore* 31 (1918): 216–55; idem, "The Origin Myth of Zuñi," *Journal of American Folklore* 36 (1923): 135–62; idem, "The Scalp Ceremonial of Zuñi," *Memoirs of the American Anthropological Association* 31 (1924): 28–34; idem, "Zuñi Tales," *Journal of American Folklore* 43 (1930): 1–58; Edward L. Handy, "Zuñi Tales," *Journal of American Folklore* 31 (1918): 451–71; Ruth L. Bunzel, "Zuñi Origin Myths," "Zuñi Ritual Poetry," and "Zuñi Texts"; and Benedict, *Zuñi Mythology.*

13. *Zuñi Folk Tales*, p. xx.

14. Benedict, *Zuñi Mythology*, p. xli.

15. Ibid., p. xlii.

16. See Bunzel, "Zuñi Ritual Poetry," p. 618, for discussion of such "formulas," or what she calls "regular stereotyped phrases," in Zuñi prayers.

17. Benedict, *Zuñi Mythology*, p. xxxiv.

18. Tedlock, "Pueblo Literature: Style and Verisimilitude," p. 234.

19. A particularly popular theme in Zuñi tales, according to Benedict, is the triumph of the underdog—someone who has been despised and weak and previously worsted. Hence it is, probably, that the suitor who finally succeeds in withstanding the insects in "The Trial of Lovers" is, if not despised or weak, at least poor. Also consistent with this ideal are the juvenile age and diminutive size usually associated with the invincible twin war gods, usually pitted (as in the two selections in which they appear here) against foes much larger than themselves. This theme figures as well, along with its obverse side—the downfall which comes to those who display hubris—in two other tales, not included here: "How the Gopher Raced with the Runner of K'iakime" and "The Cock and the Mouse." In the former the runners of K'iakime, grown contemptuous of their challengers, having beaten them so often, are put to shame with the help of a crafty gopher. In the latter—that is, in the Zuñi adaptation of the story, a European folk tale originally told to his Indian friends by Cushing himself—it is on the theme of avenged humiliation and humbled haughtiness that the Zuñi storyteller who introduces it builds his variations. For a discussion of

"The Cock and the Mouse" as an adaptation, see Benedict, *Zuñi Mythology*, p. xxi; Alan Dundes, *The Study of Folklore* (Englewood Cliffs, N.J.: Prentice Hall, Inc., 1965), p. 274; and Tedlock, "On the Translation of Style in Oral Narrative," p. 116.

    20. *Zuñi Folk Tales*, p. xxviii.

Creation and the Origin of Corn

I once heard a Zuñi priest say: "Five things alone are necessary to the sustenance and comfort of the 'dark ones' [Indians] among the children of earth."

"The sun, who is the Father of all.

"The earth, who is the Mother of men.

"The water, who is the Grandfather.

"The fire, who is the Grandmother.

"Our brothers and sisters the Corn, and seeds of growing things."

This Indian philosopher explained himself somewhat after the following fashion:

"Who among men and the creatures could live without the Sun-father? for his light brings day, warms and gladdens the Earth-mother with rain which flows forth in the water we drink and that causes the flesh of the Earth-mother to yield abundantly seeds, while these—are they not cooked by the brand of fire which warms us in winter?"

That he reasoned well, may be the better understood if we follow for a while the teachings which instructed his logic. These relate that:

First, there was sublime darkness, which vanished not until came the "Ancient Father of the Sun," revealing universal waters. These were, save him, all that were.

The Sun-father thought to change the face of the waters and cause life to replace their desolation.

He rubbed the surface of his flesh, thus drawing forth *yep'-na*.[1]

The *yep'-na* he rolled into two balls. From his high and "ancient place among the spaces," (*Te'-thlä-shi-na-kwin*) he cast forth one of these balls and it fell upon the surface of the waters. There, as a drop of deer suet on hot broth, so this ball melted and spread far and wide like scum over the great waters, ever growing, until it sank into them.

Then the Sun-father cast forth the other ball, and it fell, spreading out and growing even larger than had the first, and dispelling so much of the waters that it rested upon the first. In time, the first became a great being—our Mother, the Earth; and the second became another great being—our Father, the Sky. Thus was divided the universal fluid into the "embracing waters of the World" below, and the "embracing waters of the Sky" above. Behold! this is why the Sky-father is blue as the ocean which is the home of the Earth-mother, blue even his flesh, as seem the far-away mountains—though they be the flesh of the Earth-mother.

Now while the Sky-father and the Earth-mother were together, the Earth-mother conceived in her ample wombs— which were the four great underworlds or caves—the first of men and creatures. Then the two entered into council that they might provide for the birth of their children.

"How shall it be?" said the one to the other. "How, when born forth, shall our children subsist, and who shall guide them?"

"Behold!" said the Sky-father. He spread his hand high and abroad with the hollow palm downward. Yellow grains like corn he stuck into all the lines and wrinkles of his palm and fingers. "Thus," said he, "shall I, as it were, hold my hand ever above thee and thy children, and the yellow grains shall represent so many shining points which shall guide and light these, our children, when the Sun-father is not nigh."

Gaze on the sky at night-time! Is it not the palm of the Great Father, and are the stars not in many lines of his hand yet to be seen?

"Ah yes!" said the Earth-mother, "yet my tiny children may not wander over my lap and bosom without guidance, even in the light of the Sun-father; therefore, behold!"

She took a great terraced bowl into which she poured water;

upon the water she spat, and whipping it rapidly with her fingers it was soon beaten into foam as froths the soap-weed, and the foam rose high up around the rim of the bowl. The Earth-mother blew the foam. Flake after flake broke off, and bursting, cast spray downward into the bowl.

"See," said she, "this bowl is, as it were, the world, the rim its farthest limits, and the foam-bounden terraces round about, my features, which they shall call mountains whereby they shall name countries and be guided from place to place, and whence white clouds shall rise, float away, and, bursting, shed spray, that my children may drink of the water of life, and from my substance add unto the flesh of their being. Thou has said thou wilt watch over them when the Sun-father is absent, but thou art the cold being; I am the warm. Therefore, at night, when thou watchest, my children shall nestle in my bosom and find there warmth, strength and length of life from one day light to another."

Is not the bowl the emblem of the Earth, our mother? for from it we draw both food and drink, as a babe draws nourishment from the breast of its mother, and round, as is the rim of a bowl, so is the horizon, terraced with mountains, whence rise the clouds. Is not woman the warm, man the cold being? For while woman sits shivering as she cooks by the fire in the house-room, man goes forth little heeding the storms of winter, to hunt the feed and gather pine-faggots.

Yet alas! men and the creatures remained bounden in the lowermost womb of the Earth-mother, for she and the Sky-father feared to deliver them as a mother fears for the fate of her first offspring.

Then the Ancient Sun pitied the children of Earth. That they might speedily see his light, he cast a glance upon a foam cap floating abroad on the great waters. Forthwith the foam cap became instilled with life, and bore twin children, brothers one to the other, older and younger, for one was born before the other. To these he gave the *k'ia'-al-lan*, or "water-shield," that on it they might fly over the waters as the clouds—from which it was spun and woven—float over the ocean; that they might blind with its mists the sight of the enemy as the clouds darken the earth with rain-drops. He gave them for their bow, the rainbow, that with it they might clear men's trails of enemies, as the rain-bow clears away the storm-shadows; and for their arrows gave he them the thunder-bolts, that they might rive open the mountains, as the lightning cleaves asunder the pine trees; and then he sent them abroad to deliver, guide and protect the children of earth and the Sky-father. With their bow they lifted from his embraces the Sky-father from the bosom of the Earth-mother, "for," said they, "if he remain near, his cold will cause men to be stunted and stooped with shivering and to grovel in the earth," as stunted trees in the mountains delve under the snow to hide from the cold of the Sky-father. With their thunder-bolts they broke open the mountain which gave entrance to the cave-wombs of the Earth-mother, and upon their water-shields they descended into the lowermost of the caves, where dwelt the children of earth—men and all creatures.

Alas! It was dark as had been the world before the coming of the Sun, and the brothers found men and the beings sadly bewailing their lot. When one moved it was but to jostle another, whose complaints wearied the ears of yet others; hence the brothers called a council of the priest-chiefs—even ere the coming forth of men such lived—and they made a ladder of tall canes which they placed against the roof of the cavern. Up this rushed the children of earth. Some, climbing out before of their own wills, found deliverance from the caves above and, wandering away, became the ancestors of nations unknown to us; but our fathers followed in the footsteps of the older and younger brothers. Does not the cane grow jointed to-day, showing thus the notches which men traversed to day-light?

In the second cave all was still dark, but like starlight through cloud rifts, through the cleft above showed the twilight. After a time the people murmured again, until the two delivered them into the third world where they found light like that of early dawn. Again they grew discontented, again were guided upward, this time into the open light of the Sun—which was the light of this world. But some remained behind, not escaping until afterward; and these were the fathers of the Western nations whom our ancients knew not.

Then indeed for a time the people complained bitterly, for it was then that they *first* saw the light of the Sun-father, which, in its brilliancy, smote them so that they fell grasping their eye-balls and moaning. But when they became used to the light they looked around in joy and wonderment; yet they saw that the earth seemed but small, for everywhere rolled about the great misty waters.

The two brothers spread open the limbs of the Earth-mother, and cleft the western mountains with their shafts of lightning and the waters flowed down and away from the bosom of the Earth-mother, cutting great cañons and valleys which remain to this day. Thus was widened the land, yet the earth remained damp. Then they guided the people eastward.

Already before men came forth from the lower worlds with the priest-chiefs, there were many gods and strange beings. The gods gave to the priests many treasures and instructions, but the people knew not yet the meaning of either. Thus were first taught our ancients incantations, rituals and sacred talks (prayer), each band of them according to its usefulness. These bands were the "Priesthood"—*Shi'-wa-na-kwe*; the "Hunter-band"—*Sa'-ni-a-k'ia-kwe*; the "Knife-band"—*A'tchi-a-k'ia-kwe* or Warrior, and the *Ne'-we-kwe*, or Band of Wise Medicine Men. The leaders of each band thus came to have wonderful knowledge and power—even as that of the gods! They summoned a great council of their children—for they were called the 'Fathers of the People'—and asked them to choose such things as they would have for special ownership or use. Some chose the macaw, the eagle, or the turkey; others chose the deer, bear, or coyote; others the seeds of earth, or *a'-tâ-a*, the spring vine, tobacco, and the plants of medicine, the yellow-wood and many other things. Thus it came about that they and their brothers and sisters and their children, even unto the present day, were named after the things they chose in the days when all was new, and thus was divided our nation into many clans, or gentes (*A'-no-ti-we*) of brothers and sisters who may not marry one another but from one to the other. To some of the elders of these bands and clans was given some thing which should be, above all other things, precious. For instance, the clans of the Bear and Crane were given the *Mu'-et-ton-ne*, or medicine seed of hail and snow. For does not the bear go into his den, and appears not the crane when come storms of hail and snow?

When more than one clan possessed one of these magic medicines they formed a secret society—like the first four—for its keeping and use. Thus the Bear and Crane peoples became the "Holders of the Wand"—who bring the snow of winter and are potent to cure the diseases which come with them. In time they let into their secret council others, whom they had cured, that the precious secrets of their band might not be wasted. Thus it was that one after another were formed the rest of our medicine bands, who were and are called the finishers of men's trails, because, despite disease and evil, they guard and lengthen our lives; but in the "days of the new" there were only four bands.[2]

To the Eagle, Deer and Coyote peoples was given the *Nal'-e-ton*, or "Deer Medicine Seed," which the Hunter-band still guards; and to the Macaw, Sun and Frog peoples the *Kia'-et-ton*, or the "Medicine Seed of Water," which the priesthood and the Sacred Dance, or *Kâ'-kâ*, still hold—without the administration of which the world would dry up and even the insects of the mountains and hollows of earth grow thirsty and perish. Yet, not less precious was the gift to the "Seed-people," or *Ta'-a-kwe*. This was the *Tchu'-et-ton*, or the "Medicine Seed of Corn"—for from this came the parents of flesh and beauty, the solace of hunger, the emblems of birth, mortal life, death and immortality. To the Badger people was given the knowledge of Fire, for in the roots of all trees, great and little—which the badger best knows how to find—dwells the essence of fire.[3]

To all of these peoples it was told that they should wander for many generations toward the land whence the Sun brings the day-light (Eastward) until at last they would reach the "middle of the world," where their children should dwell forever over the heart of our Earth-mother until their days should be numbered and the light of Zuñi grow dark.

Toward this unknown country the "twin brothers of light" guided them. In those times a day meant a year, and a night another, so that four days and nights meant eight years. Many days the people wandered eastward, slaying game for their flesh-food, gathering seeds from grasses and weeds for their bread-food, and binding rushes about their loins for their clothing; they knew not until afterward, the flesh of the cotton and yucca-mothers.

The earth was still damp. Dig a hole in a hill-side, quickly it filled with water. Drop a seed on the highest table-land and it without waiting shot forth green sprouts. So moist, indeed, was the soil, that even foot-prints of men and all creatures might be traced whithersoever they tended. The beings and strange creatures increased with men, and spread over the world. Many monsters lived, by whose ferocity men perished.

Then said the twin brothers: "Men, our children, are poorer than the beasts, their enemies; for each creature has a special gift of strength or sagacity, while to men has been given only the power of guessing. Nor would we that our children be web-footed like the beings that live over the waters and damp places."

Therefore, they sent all men and harmless beings to a place of security; then laid their water shield on the ground. Upon it they placed four thunder-bolts, one pointed north, another west, another south, and the other eastward. When all was ready they let fly the thunder-bolts. Instantly the world was covered with lurid fire and shaken with rolling thunders, as is a forest to-day burned and blasted where the lightning has fallen. Thus as the clay of vessels is burned to rock, and the mud of the hearth crackled and reddened by fire, so the earth was mottled and crackled and hardened where now we see mountains and masses of rock. Many of the great monsters and prey-beings were changed in a twinkling to enduring rock or shriveled into twisted idols which the hunter and priest-warrior know best how to prize. Behold, their forms along every mountain side and ravine, and in the far western valleys and plains, still endure the tracks of the fathers of men and beings, the children of earth. Yet some of the beings of prey were spared, that the world might not become over-filled with life, and starvation follow, and that men might breathe of their spirits and be inspired with the hearts of warriors and hunters.

Often the people rested from their wanderings, building great houses of stone which may even now be seen, until the Conch of the Gods sounded, which lashed the ocean to fury and beat the earth to trembling.[4] Then the people started up, and gathering the few things they could, again commenced their wanderings; yet often those who slept or lingered were buried beneath their own walls, where yet their bones may sometimes be found.

Marvelous both of good and evil were the works of the ancients. Alas! there came forth with others, those impregnated with the seed of sorcery. Their evil works caused discord among men, and, through fear and anger, men were divided from one another. Born before our ancients, had been other men, and these our fathers sometimes overtook and looked not peacefully upon them, but challenged them—though were they not their older brothers? It thus happened when our ancients came to their fourth resting place on their eastward journey, that which they named *Shi-po-lo-lon-K'ai-a*, or "The Place of Misty Waters," there already dwelt a clan of people called the *A'-ta-a*, or Seed People, and the seed clan of our ancients challenged them to know by what right they assumed the name and attributes of their own clan. "Behold," said these stranger-beings, "we have power with the gods above yours, yet can we not exert it without your aid. Try, therefore, your own power first, then we will show you ours." At last, after much wrangling, the Seed clan agreed to this, and set apart eight days for prayer and sacred labors. First they worked together cutting sticks, to which they bound the plumes of summer birds which fly in the clouds or sail over the waters. "Therefore," thought our fathers, "why should not their plumes waft our beseechings to the waters and clouds?" These plumes, with prayers and offerings, they planted in the valleys, and there, also, they placed their *Tchu'-e-ton-ne*. Lo! for eight days and nights it rained and there were thick mists; and the waters from the mountains poured down bringing new soil and spreading it over the valleys where the plumed sticks had been planted. "See!" said the fathers of the seed clan, "water and new earth bring we by our supplications."

"It is well," replied the strangers, "yet *life* ye did not bring. Behold!" and they too set apart eight days, during which they danced and sang a beautiful dance and prayer song, and at the end of that time they took the people of the seed clan to the valleys. Behold, indeed! Where the plumes had been planted and the *tchu'-e-ton* placed grew seven corn-plants, their tassels waving in the wind, their stalks laden with ripened grain.

"These," said the strangers, "are the severed flesh of seven maidens, our own sisters and children. The eldest sister's is the yellow corn; the next, the blue; the next, the red; the next, the white; the next, the speckled; the next, the black, and the last and youngest is the sweet-corn, for see! even ripe, she is soft like the young of the others. The first is of the North-land, yellow like the light of winter; the second is of the West, blue like the great world of waters; the third is of the South, red like the Land of Everlasting Summer; the fourth is of the East, white like the land whence the sun brings the daylight; the fifth is of the upper regions, many-colored as are the clouds of morning and evening, and the sixth is of the lower regions, black as are the caves whence came we, your older, and ye, our younger brothers." "Brothers indeed be we, each one to the other," said the people to the strangers, "and may we not journey together seeking the middle of the world?" "Aye, we may," replied the strangers, "and of the flesh of our maidens ye may eat, no more seeking the seeds of the grasses and of your water we may drink, no more wondering whither we shall find it; thus shall each help the other to life and contentment. Ye shall pray and cut prayer-plumes, we shall sing, and dance shall our maidens that all may be delighted and that it may be for the best. But beware! no mortal must approach the persons of our maidens."

Thenceforward, many of the A'-ta-a and the seed clan journeyed together, until at last the Sun, Macaw, and some other clans-people found the middle of the world; while others yet wandered in search of it, not for many generations to join their brothers, over the heart of the Earth-mother, which is Shi-wi-na-kwin, or the "Land of the Zuñis."

Day after day, season after season, year after year, the people of the seed clan and the A'-ta-a, who were named together the Corn-clan, or people, prepared, and their maidens danced the dance of the thla-he-kwe,[5] or "Beautiful Corn Wands," until their children grew weary and yearned for other amusements.

Sometimes the people saw over Thunder-mountain thick mists floating and lowering. At such times, near the Cave of the Rainbow, a beautiful halo would spring forth, amidst which the many-colored garments of the rainbow himself could be seen, and soft, sweet music, stranger than that of the whistling winds in a mountain of pines, floated fitfully down the valley. At last the priests and elders gathered in council and determined to send their two chief warriors (Priests of the Bow) to the cavern of the rainbow, that it might be determined what strange people made the sights and sounds. "Mayhap it will prove some new dancers, who will throw the light of their favor on our weary hearts and come to cheer us and delight our children." Thus said they to the warriors when they were departing.

No sooner had the warriors reached the cave-entrance than the mists enshrouded them and the music ceased. They entered and were received by a splendid group of beings, bearing long brightly-painted flutes, amongst whom the leader was Pai⌐-a-tu-ma, the father of the *Ne⌐-we* band, and the God of Dew.

"Enter, my children," said he, "and sit. We have commanded our dancers to cease and our players to draw breath from their flutes, that we might listen to your messages; for 'not for nothing does one stranger visit the house of another.'"

"True," replied the warriors. "Our fathers have sent us that we might greet you, and the light of your favor ask for our children. Day after day the maidens of the corn-people dance one dance which, from oft repeating, has grown undelightful, and our fathers thought you might come to vary this dance with your own, for that you knew one we were taught by your music, which we sometimes heard."

"Aha!" replied Pai⌐-a-tu-ma, "it is well! We will follow; but not in the day-time—in the night-time we will follow. My children," said he, turning to the flute-players, "show to the strangers our custom."

The drum sounded till it shook the cavern; the music shrieked and pealed in softly surging unison, as the wind does in a wooded cañon after the storm is distant, and the mists played over the medicine bowl around which the musicians were gathered, until the rainbow fluttered his bright garments among the painted flutes. Maidens filed out brandishing wands whence issued tiny clouds white as the down of eagles, and as the sounds died away between the songs the two warriors in silent wonder and admiration departed for their home.

When they returned to their fathers in Zuñi, they told what they had seen and heard. Forthwith the fathers (priest-chiefs and elders) prepared the dance of the corn-maidens. A great bower was placed in the court of the pueblo, whither went the mothers and priests of the Seed-clan. The priests of the Macaw, Sun and Water clans were there. A terrace of sacred meal was marked on the ground, an altar set up over its base, and along its middle were placed the *E'-ta-e* or Medicine Seeds of corn and water. Along the outer edges were planted the sticks of prayer, plumed with the feathers of summer birds, and down in front of the altar and terrace were set basket-bowls covered with sacred mantles made of the flesh of the Cotton-mother (Goddess of Cotton), whose down grows from the earth and floats in the skies (cotton and the clouds are one in the Zuñi mythology). By the side of each basket-bowl sat a mother of the clan, silent in prayer and meditation. To the right were the singers, to the left the corn maidens. Night was coming on. The dance began and a fire was built in front of the bower beyond where the maidens danced. More beautiful than all human maidens were those maidens of the corn, but as are human maidens, so were they, irresistibly beautiful.

As the night deepened, the sound of music and flutes was heard up the river, and then followed the players of the rainbow-cave with their sisters, led by the God of Dew. When the players entered and saw the maidens their music ceased and they were impassioned. And when their turn came for leading the dance, they played their softest strains over their medicine bowl—the terraced bowl of the world—whence arose the rainbow. The people were delighted, but the corn maidens were sad; for no sooner had the dancing ceased a little than the flute players sought their hands and persons. In vain the corn maidens pleaded they were immortal virgins and the mothers of men! The flute players continually renewed their suits 'till the next day, and into the night which followed, while the dance went on. At last the people grew weary. The guardian warrior-priests nodded, and no longer wakened them. Silently the corn maidens stole up between the basket-trays and the sleeping people. There, passing their hands over their persons they placed something under the mantles, vanishing instantly as do the spirits of the dying, leaving only their flesh behind. Still the people slept, and ere long even the flute-players and dancers ceased. When the sun came out the people awoke. Then every one cried to the others "Where are our maiden mothers, our daughters?" Yet not even the warriors knew; for only of the flesh of the maidens (corn) could be found a little in the trays under the mantles. Then the place was filled with moaning among the women and up-braidings among the men, each blaming every other loudly until the priests cried out to silence their wranglings, and called a council. Then said they:

"Alas, we have laden our hearts with guilt, and sad thoughts have we prepared to weigh down our minds. We must send to seek the maidens, that they desert us not. Who shall undertake the journey?"

"Send for the eagle," it was said. The two warrior-priests were commanded to go and seek him.

Be it known that while yet the earth was young her children, both men and the creatures, spoke as men alone now speak, any one with any other. This the aged among all nations agree in saying, and are not those who grow not foolish with great age the wisest of men? Their words we speak!

Therefore, when the two warriors climbed the mountain whereon the eagle dwelt, and found only his eaglets at home, the little birds were frightened and tried to hide themselves in the hole where the nest was built. But when the warriors came nearer they screamed: "Oh do not pull our feathers; wait 'till we are older and we will drop them for you."

"Hush," said the warriors, "we seek your father."

But just then the old eagle, with a frown on his eyebrow, rushed in and asked why the warriors were frightening his "pin-feathers."

"We came for you, our father. Listen. Our mothers, the beautiful corn maidens, have vanished, leaving no trace save of their flesh. We come to beseech that you shall seek them for us."

"Go before!" said the eagle, smoothing his feathers, which meant that he would follow. So the warriors returned.

Then the eagle launched forth into the sky, circling higher

and higher up, until he was smaller than a thistle-down in a whirlwind. At last he flew lower, then into the bower of the dancers where the council awaited him.

"Ah, thou comest!" exclaimed the people.

"Yes," replied the eagle. "Neither a blue-bird nor a wood-rat can escape my eye," said he, snapping his beak, "unless they hide under rocks or bushes. Send for my younger brother; he flies nearer the ground than I do."

So the warriors went to seek the sparrow-hawk. They found him sitting on an ant hill, but when he saw them he would have flown away had they not called out that they had words for him and meant him no harm.

"What is it?" said he. "For if you have any snare-strings with you I'll be off."

"No, no! we wish you to go and hunt for our maidens—the corn maidens," said the warriors,—"your old brother, the eagle, cannot find them."

"Oh, that's it; well, go before—of course he can't find them! He climbs up to the clouds and thinks he can see under every tree and shadow as the Sun, who sees not with eyes, does."

The sparrow-hawk flew away to the north and the east and the west, looking behind every cliff and copsewood, but he found no trace of the maidens, and returned, declaring as he flew into the bower, "they can not be found. They are hiding more snugly than I ever knew a sparrow to hide," said he, ruffling his feathers and gripping the stick he settled on as though it were feathers and blood.

"Oh, alas! alas! our beautiful maidens!" cried the old women; "we shall never see them again!"

"Hold your feet with patience, there's old heavy nose out there; go and see if he can hunt for them. He knows well enough to find their flesh, however so little that may be," said an old priest, pointing to a crow who was scratching an ash-heap sidewise with his beak, trying to find something for a morning meal. So the warriors ran down and accosted him.

"O caw!" exclaimed the crow, probing a fresh place, "I am too hungry to go flying around for you stingy fellows. Here I've been ever since perching-time, trying to get a mouthful; but you pick your bones and bowls too clean, be sure for that!"

"Come in, then, grandfather, and we'll give you a smoke and something to eat," said the two warriors.

"Caw, haw!" said the old crow, ruffling up his collar and opening his mouth wide enough to swallow his own head. "Go before!" and he followed them into the dance-court.

"Come in, sit and smoke," said the chief priest, handing the crow a cigarette.

At once the old crow took the cigarette and drew such a big whiff into his throat that the smoke completely filled his feathers, and ever since then crows have been black all over, although before that time they had white shoulder-bands and very blue beaks, which made them look quite fine.

Then the crow suddenly espied an ear of corn under one of the mantles, for this was all the maidens had left; so he made for the corn and flew off with it, saying as he skipped over the houses, "I guess this is all you'll see of the maidens for many a day," and ever since then crows have been so fond of corn that they steal even that which is buried. But bye and bye the old crow came back, saying that he had a "sharp eye for the *flesh* of the maidens, but he could not find any trace of the maidens themselves."

Then the people were very sad with thought, when they suddenly heard Pai⸜-a-tu-ma joking[6] along the streets as though the whole pueblo were listening to him. "Call him," cried the priests to the warriors, and the warriors ran out to summon Pai⸜-a-tu-ma.

Pai⸜-a-tu-ma sat down on a heap of refuse, saying he was about to make a breakfast of it. The warriors greeted him.

"Why and wherefore do you two cowards come not after me?" inquired Pai⸜-a-tu-ma.

"We do come for you."

"No, you do not."

"Yes, we do."

"Well! I won't go with you," said he, forthwith following them to the dance-court.

"My little children," said he, to the gray-haired priests and mothers, "good evening;"—it was not yet mid-day—"you are all very happy, I see."

"Thou comest," said the chief priest.

"I do not," replied Pai-̱a-tu-ma.

"Father," said the chief priest, "we are very sad and we have sought you that we might ask the light of your wisdom.

"Ah, quite as I had supposed; I am very glad to find you all so happy. Being thus you do not need my advice. What may I not do for you?"

"We would that you seek for the corn-maidens, our mothers, whom we have offended, and who have exchanged themselves for nothing in our gaze."

"Oh, *that's all*, is it? The corn maidens are not lost, and if they were I would not go to seek them, and if I went to seek for them I could not find them, and if I found them I would not bring them, but I would tell them you 'did not wish to see them' and leave them where they are not—in the Land of Everlasting Summer, which is not their home. Ha! you have no prayer-plumes here, I observe," said he, picking up one each of the yellow, blue and white kinds, and starting out with the remark—

"I come."

With rapid strides he set forth toward the south. When he came to the mouth of the "Cañon of the Woods," whence blows the wind of summer in spring-time, he planted the yellow-plumed stick. Then he knelt to watch the eagle down, and presently the down moved gently toward the north, as though some one were breathing on it. Then he went yet farther, and planted the blue stick. Again the eagle down moved. So he went on planting the sticks, until very far away he placed the last one. Now the eagle plume waved constantly toward the north.

"Aha!" said Pai-̱a-tu-ma to himself, "It is the breath of the corn maidens, and thus shall it ever be, for when *they* breathe toward the northland, thither shall warmth, showers, fertility and health be wafted, and the summer birds shall chase the butterfly out of Summer-land and summer itself, with my own beads and treasures shall follow after." Then he journeyed on, no longer a dirty clown, but an aged, grand god, with a colored flute, flying softly and swiftly as the wind he sought for.

Soon he came to the home of the maidens, whom he greeted, bidding them, as he waved his flute over them, to follow him to the home of their children.

The maidens arose, and each taking a tray covered with

embroidered cotton, followed him as he strode with folded arms, swiftly before them.

At last they reached the home of our fathers. Then Paiᴸ-a-tu-ma gravely spoke to the council.

"Behold, I have returned with the lost maidens, yet may they not remain or come again, for you have not loved their beautiful custom—the source of your lives—and men would seek to change the blessings of their flesh itself into suffering humanity were they to remain amongst you.

"As a mother of her own blood and being gives life to her offspring, so have these given of their own flesh to you. Once more their flesh they give to you, as it were their children. From the beginning of the new Sun each year, ye shall treasure their gift, during the moon of the sacred fire, during the moon of the snow-broken boughs, during the moon of the great sand-driving winds, during the moon of the lesser sand-driving winds, ye shall treasure their flesh. Then, in the new soil which the winter winds and water have brought, ye shall bury their flesh as ye bury the flesh of the dead, and as the flesh of the dead decays so shall their flesh decay, and as from the flesh of the dead springs the other being (the soul), so from their flesh shall spring new being, like to the first, yet in eight-fold plenitude. Of this shall ye eat and be bereft of hunger. Behold these maidens, beautiful and perfect are they, and as this, their flesh, is derived from them, so shall it confer on those whom it feeds perfection of person and beauty, as of those whence it was derived." He lifted the tray from the head of the maiden nearest him. She smiled and was seen no more; yet when the people opened the tray it was filled with yellow seed-corn. And so Paiᴸ-a-tu-ma lifted the trays, each in turn, from the heads of the other maidens, and, as he did so, each faded from view. In the second tray the people found blue corn; in the third, red; in the fourth, white; in the fifth, varie-gated; and in the sixth, black. These they saved, and in the spring-time they carefully planted the seeds in separate places. The breaths of the corn maidens blew rain-clouds from their homes in Summer-land, and when the rains had passed away green corn plants grew everywhere the grains had been planted. And when the plants had grown tall and blossomed, they were laden with ears of corn, yellow, blue, red, white, speckled and black. Thus to this day grows the corn, always eight-fold more than is planted, and of six colors, which our women preserve separately during the moons of the sacred fire, snow-broken boughs, great sand-driving winds and lesser sand-driving winds.

It was Pai'-a-tu-ma who found the corn maidens and brought them back. He took the trays from their heads and gave them to the people; hence, when in winter, during the moon of the sacred fire, the priests gather to bless the seed-corn for the coming year, the chief-priest of the *Ne'-we-kwe* hands the trays of corn-seed into the estufa.

Ever since these days, the beautiful corn maidens have dwelt in the Land of Everlasting Summer. This we know. For does not their sweet-smelling breath come from that flowery country, bringing life to their children, the corn-plants? It is the south wind which we feel in spring-time.

Thus was born *Tâ-a*, or the "Seed of Seeds."

From "Zuñi Breadstuff," *Millstone* 9, no. 1 (1884): 1–3.

Notes

1. Or the "substance of living flesh." This is exemplified as well as may be by the little cylinders of cuticle and fatty-matter that may be rubbed from the person after bathing. [F.H.C.]

2. It may be seen that the Zuñis have here their own way of accounting for their primitive social organization into *Gentes* and *Phratries*—organizations well nigh universal in the ancient world, as with the society of the early Greeks and Romans, and still prevalent amongst savage tribes of today. [F.H.C.]

3. In ancient times when desirous of making fire, and even today when kindling the sacred flame, the Zuñis produced and still produce, the first spark by drilling with a hard stick like an arrow-shaft into a dry piece of soft root. An arrow-shaft is now used by preference, as it is the emblem of lightning. [F.H.C.]

4. Doubtless this refers to the earthquake. Ruins may sometimes be found in the Southwest, buried like Pompeii beneath the ashes and lava of ancient eruptions, thus pointing either to a remote origin of the Pueblo or a recent cessation of volcanic action in New Mexico and Arizona. [F.H.C.]

5. Unexceptionably this is one of the most beautiful of the native ceremonials, and is one of the few sacred dances of the Zuñis in which women assume the leading part. It is still performed with untiring zeal,

usually during each summer, although accompanied by exhausting fasts and abstinences from sleep. Curiously enough, it was observed and admirably, though too briefly described, by Coronado . . . nearly three hundred and fifty years ago.

It was with this ceremonial that the delighted nation welcomed the water which my party brought in 1882 from the "Ocean of Sunrise." As I was then compelled to join the watch of the priests and elders, I had ample leisure during two sleepless days and nights to gather the above and following story from the song which celebrates the origin of the custom, but which both in length and poetic beauty far surpasses the limits and style of the present paper. [F.H.C.]

6. The *Ne'-we-kwe*, of whom the God of Dew, or Pai'-a-tu-ma, was the first Great Father, are a band of medicine priests belonging, as explained heretofore, to one of the most ancient organizations of the Zuñis. Their medical skill is supposed to be very great—in many cases—and their traditional wisdom is counted even greater. Yet they are clowns whose grotesque and quick-witted remarks amuse most public assemblies of the Pueblo holiday. One of their customs is to speak the opposite of their meaning; hence too, their assumptions of the clown's part at public ceremonials, when really their office and powers are to be reversed. Their grotesque costuming and face-painting are quite in keeping with their assumed characters, and would, were it possible, justify the belief that our own circus clowns were their lineal descendants or copyists. Often so like are human things, though geographically widely severed. [F.H.C.]

FIG. 70. Waihusiwa, Zuñi Storyteller

The Trial of Lovers; or, the Maiden of Mátsaki and the Red Feather

(*Told the First Night*)

In the days of the ancients, when Mátsaki was the home of the children of men, there lived, in that town, which is called "Salt City," because the Goddess of Salt made a white lake there in the days of the New, a beautiful maiden. She was passing beautiful, and the daughter of the priest-chief, who owned more buckskins and blankets than he could hang on his poles, and whose port-holes were covered with turquoises and precious shells from the ocean—so many were the sacrifices he made to the gods. His house was the largest in Mátsaki, and his ladder-poles were tall and decorated with slabs of carved wood—which you know was a great thing, for our grandfathers cut with the *tímush* or flint knife, and even tilled their corn-fields with wooden hoes sharpened with stone and weighted with granite. That's the reason why all the young men in the towns round about were in love with the beautiful maiden of Salt City.

Now, there was one very fine young man who lived across the western plains, in the Pueblo of the Winds. He was so filled with thoughts of the maiden of Mátsaki that he labored long to gather presents for her, and looked not with favor on any girl of his own pueblo.

One morning he said to his fathers: "I have seen the maiden of Mátsaki; what think ye?"

"Be it well," said the old ones. So toward night the young man made a bundle of mantles and necklaces, which he rolled up in the best and whitest buckskin he had. When the sun was setting he started toward Mátsaki, and just as the old man's children had gathered in to smoke and talk he reached the house

of the maiden's father and climbed the ladder. He lifted the corner of the mat door and shouted to the people below—*"Shé!"*
"Hai!" answered more than a pair of voices from below.

"Pull me down," cried the young man, at the same time showing his bundle through the sky-hole.

The maiden's mother rose and helped the young man down the ladder, and as he entered the fire-light he laid the bundle down.

"My fathers and mothers, my sisters and friends, how be ye these many days?" said he, very carefully, as though he were speaking to a council.

"Happy! Happy!" they all responded, and they said also: "Sit down; sit down on this stool," which they placed for him in the fire-light.

"My daughter," remarked the old man, who was smoking his cigarette by the opposite side of the hearth-place, "when a stranger enters the house of a stranger, the girl should place before him food and cooked things." So the girl brought from the great vessel in the corner fresh rolls of *héwe*, or bread of corn-flour, thin as papers, and placed them in a tray before the young man, where the light would fall on them.

"Eat!" said she, and he replied, "It is well." Whereupon he sat up very straight, and placing his left hand across his breast, very slowly took a roll of the wafer bread with his right hand and ate ever so little; for you know it is not well or polite to eat much when you go to see a strange girl, especially if you want to ask her if she will let you live in the same house with her. So the young man ate ever so little, and said, "Thank you."

"Eat more," said the old ones; but when he replied that he was "past the naming of want," they said, "Have eaten," and the girl carried the tray away and swept away the crumbs.

"Well," said the old man, after a short time, "when a stranger enters the house of a stranger, it is not thinking of nothing that he enters."

"Why, that is quite true," said the youth, and then he waited.

"Then what may it be that thou hast come thinking of?" added the old man.

"I have heard," said the young man, "of your daughter, and have seen her, and it was with thoughts of her that I came."

Just then the grown-up sons of the old man, who had come to smoke and chat, rose and said to one another: "Is it not about time we should be going home? The stars must be all out." Thus saying, they bade the old ones to "wait happily until the morning," and shook hands with the young man who had come, and went to the homes of their wives' mothers.

"Listen, my child!" said the old man after they had gone away, turning toward his daughter, who was sitting near the wall and looking down at the beads on her belt fringe. "Listen! You have heard what the young man has said. What think you?"

"Why! I know not; but what should I say but 'Be it well,'" said the girl, "if thus think my old ones?"

"As you may," said the old man; and then he made a cigarette and smoked with the young man. When he had thrown away his cigarette he said to the mother: "Old one, is it not time to stretch out?"

So when the old ones were asleep in the corner, the girl said to the youth, but in a low voice: "Only possibly you love me. True, I have said 'Be it well'; but before I take your bundle and say 'thanks,' I would that you, to prove that you verily love me, should go down into my corn-field, among the lands of the priest-chief, by the side of the river, and hoe all the corn in a single morning. If you will do this, then shall I know you love me; then shall I take of your presents, and happy we will be together."

"Very well," replied the young man; "I am willing."

Then the young girl lighted a bundle of cedar splints and showed him a room which contained a bed of soft robes and blankets, and, placing her father's hoe near the door, bade the young man "wait happily unto the morning."

So when she had gone he looked at the hoe and thought: "Ha! if that be all, she shall see in the morning that I am a man."

At the peep of day over the eastern mesa he roused himself, and, shouldering the wooden hoe, ran down to the corn-fields; and when, as the sun was coming out, the young girl awoke and looked down from her house-top, "Aha!" thought she, "he is doing well, but my children and I shall see how he gets on somewhat later. I doubt if he loves me as much as he thinks he does."

So she went into a closed room. Down in the corner stood a water jar, beautifully painted and as bright as new. It looked like other water jars, but it was not. It was wonderful, wonderful! for it was covered with a stone lid which held down many may-flies and gnats and mosquitoes. The maiden lifted the lid and began to speak to the little animals as though she were praying.

"Now, then, my children, this day fly ye forth all, and in the corn-fields by the river there shall ye see a young man hoeing. So hard is he working that he is stripped as for a race. Go forth and seek him."

"*Tsu-nu-nu-nu*," said the flies, and "*Tsi-ni-ni-ni*," sang the gnats and mosquitoes; which meant "Yes," you know.

"And," further said the girl, "when ye find him, bite him, his body all over, and eat ye freely of his blood; spare not his armpits, neither his neck nor his eyelids, and fill his ears with humming."

And again the flies said, "*Tsu-nu-nu-nu*," and the mosquitoes and gnats, "*Tsi-ni-ni-ni*." Then, *nu-u-u*, away they all flew like a cloud of sand on a windy morning.

"Blood!" exclaimed the young man. He wiped the sweat from his face and said, "The gods be angry!" Then he dropped his hoe and rubbed his shins with sand and slapped his sides. "*Atu!*" he yelled; "what matters—what in the name of the Moon Mother matters with these little beasts that cause thoughts?" Whereupon, crazed and restless as a spider on hot ashes, he rolled in the dust, but to no purpose, for the flies and gnats and mosquitoes sang "*hu-n-n*" and "*tsi-ni-ni*" about his ears until he grabbed up his blanket and breakfast, and ran toward the home of his fathers.

"*Wa-ha ha! Ho o!*" laughed a young man in the Tented Pueblo to the north, when he heard how the lover had fared. "*Shoom!*" he sneered. "Much of a man he must have been to give up the maid of Mátsaki for may-flies and gnats and mosquitoes!" So on the very next morning, he, too, said to his old ones: "What a fool that little *boy* must have been. I will visit the maiden of Mátsaki. I'll show the people of Pínawa what a Hámpasawan man can do. Courage!"—and, as the old ones said "Be it well," he went as the other had gone; but, pshaw! he fared no better.

After some time, a young man who lived in the River Town heard about it and laughed as hard as the youth of the Tented

Pueblo had. He called the two others fools, and said that "girls were not in the habit of asking much when one's bundle was large." And as he was a young man who had everything, he made a bundle of presents as large as he could carry; but it did him no good. He, too, ran away from the may-flies and gnats and mosquitoes.

Many days passed before any one else would try again to woo the maiden of Mátsaki. They did not know, it is true, that she was a Passing Being; but others had failed all on account of mosquitoes and may-flies and little black gnats, and had been more satisfied with shame than a full hungry man with food. "That is sick satisfaction," they would say to one another, the fear of which made them wait to see what others would do.

Now, in the Ant Hill, which was named Hálonawan, lived a handsome young man, but he was poor, although the son of the priest-chief of Hálonawan. He thought many days, and at last said to his grandmother, who was very old and crafty, *"Hó-ta?"*

"What sayest my *nána?*" said the old woman; for, like grandmothers nowadays, she was very soft and gentle to her grandson.

"I have seen the maiden of Mátsaki and my thoughts kill me with longing, for she is passing beautiful and wisely slow. I do not wonder that she asks hard tasks of her lovers; for it is not of their bundles that she thinks, but of themselves. Now, I strengthen my thoughts with my manliness. My heart is hard against weariness, and I would go and speak to the beautiful maiden."

"*Yo á!* my poor boy," said the grandmother. "She is as wonderful as she is wise and beautiful. She thinks not of men save as brothers and friends; and she it is, I bethink me, who sends the may-flies and gnats and mosquitoes, therefore, to drive them away. They are but disguised beings, and beware, my grandson, you will only cover yourself with shame as a man is covered with water who walks through a rain-storm! I would not go, my poor grandchild. I would not go," she added, shaking her head and biting her lips till her chin touched her nose-tip.

"Yes, but I must go, my grandmother. Why should I live only to breathe hard with longing? Perhaps she will better her thoughts toward me."

"Ah, yes, but all the same, she will test thee. Well, go to the mountains and scrape bitter bark from the finger-root; make a little loaf of the bark and hide it in your belt, and when the maiden sends you down to the corn-field, work hard at the hoeing until sunrise. Then, when your body is covered with sweat-drops, rub every part with the root-bark. The finger-root bark, it is bitter as bad salt mixed in with bad water, and the 'horn-wings' and 'long-beaks' and 'blue-backs' fly far from the salt that is bitter."

"Then, my gentle grandmother, I will try your words and thank you,"—for he was as gentle and good as his grandmother was knowing and crafty. Even that day he went to the mountains and gathered a ball of finger-root. Then, toward evening, he took a little bundle and went up the trail by the river-side to Mátsaki. When he climbed the ladder and shouted down the mat door: "*Shé!* Are ye within?" the people did not answer at once, for the old ones were angry with their daughter that she had sent off so many fine lovers. But when he shouted again they answered:

"*Hai,* and *Ée,* we are within. Be yourself within."

Then without help he went down the ladder, but he didn't mind, for he felt himself poor and his bundle was small. As he entered the fire-light he greeted the people pleasantly and gravely, and with thanks took the seat that was laid for him.

Now, you see, the old man was angry with the girl, so he did not tell her to place cooked things before him, but turned to his old wife.

"Old one," he began—but before he had finished the maiden arose and brought rich venison stew and flaky *héwe,* which she placed before the youth where the fire's brightness would fall upon it, with meat broth for drink; then she sat down opposite him and said, "Eat and drink!" Whereupon the young man took a roll of the wafer-bread and, breaking it in two, gave the girl the larger piece, which she bashfully accepted.

The old man raised his eyebrows and upper lids, looked at his old wife, spat in the fireplace, and smoked hard at his cigarette, joining the girl in her invitation by saying, "Yes, have to eat well."

Soon the young man said, "Thanks," and the maiden quickly responded, "Eat more," and "Have eaten."

After brushing the crumbs away the girl sat down by her mother, and the father rolled a cigarette for the young man and talked longer with him than he had with the others.

After the old ones had stretched out in the corner and begun to "scrape their nostrils with their breath," the maiden turned to the young man and said: "I have a corn-field in the lands of the priest-chief, down by the river, and if you truly love me, I would that you should hoe the whole in a single morning. Thus may you prove yourself a man, and to love me truly; and if you will do this, happily, as day follows day, will we live each with the other."

"*Hai-í!*" replied the young man, who smiled as he listened; and as the young maiden looked at him, sitting in the fading fire-light with smile on his face, she thought: "Only possibly. But oh! how I wish his heart might be strong, even though his bundle be not heavy or large.

"Come with me, young man, and I will show you where you are to await the morning. Early take my father's hoe, which stands by the doorway, and go down to the corn-field long before the night shadows have run away from Thunder Mountain"— with which she bade him pass a night of contentment and sought her own place.

When all was still, the young man climbed to the sky-hole and in the starlight asked the gods of the woodlands and waters to give strength to his hands and power to his prayer-medicine, and to meet and bless him with the light of their favor; and he threw to the night-wind meal of the seeds of earth and the waters of the world with which those who are wise fail not to make smooth their trails of life. Then he slept till the sky of the day-land grew gray, and then shouldered his hoe and went down to the corn-field. His task was not great, for the others had hoed much. Where they left off, there he fell to digging right and left with all his strength and haste, till the hard soil mellowed and the earth flew before his strokes as out of the burrows of the strongest-willed gophers and other digging creatures.

When the sun rose the maiden looked forth and saw that his task was already half done. But still she waited. As the sun warmed the day and the youth worked on, the dewdrops of flesh stood all over his body and he cast away, one after the other, his blanket and sash and even his leggings and moccasins. Then he stopped to look around. By the side of the field grew tall yellow-tops. He ran into the thicket and rubbed every part of his body, yea, even the hair of his head and his ear-tips and nostrils, with the bark of the finger-root. Again he fell to work as though he had only been resting, and wondered why the may-flies and gnats and mosquitoes came not to cause him thoughts as they had the others. Yet still the girl lingered; but at last she went slowly to the room where the jar stood.

"It is absurd," thought she, "that I should hope it or even care for it; it would indeed be great if it were well true that a young man should love me so verily as to hold his face to the front through such a testing." Nevertheless, she drew the lid off and bade her strange children to spare him no more than they had the others.

All hasty to feast themselves on the "waters of life," as our old grandfathers would say for blood, again they rushed out and hummed along over the corn-fields in such numbers that they looked more like a wind-driven sandstorm than ever, and "tsi-ni-ni-i, tso-no-o" they hummed and buzzed about the ears of the young man when they came to him, so noisily that the poor fellow, who kept at work all the while, thought they were already biting him. But it was only fancy, for the first may-fly that did bite him danced in the air with disgust and exclaimed to his companions, "Sho-o-o-m-m!" and "Us-á!" which meant that he had eaten something nasty, that tasted as badly as vile odors smell. So not another may-fly in the throng would bite, although they all kept singing their song about his ears. And to this day may-flies are careful whom they bite, and dance a long time in the air before they do it.

Then a gnat tried it and gasped, "Weh!" which meant that his stomach had turned over, and he had such a sick headache that he reeled round and round in the air, and for that reason gnats always bite very quickly, for fear their stomachs will turn over, and they will reel and reel round and round in the air before doing it.

Finally, long-beak himself tried it, and, as long-beak hangs on, you know, longer than most other little beasts, he kept hold until his two hindlegs were warped out of shape; but at last he had to let go, too, and flew straight away, crying, "Yá kotchi!"

which meant that something bitter had burned his snout. Now, for these reasons mosquitoes always have bent-up hindlegs, which they keep lifting up and down while biting, as though they were standing on something hot, and they are apt to sing and smell around very cautiously before spearing us, and they fly straight away, you will notice, as soon as they are done.

Now, when the rest of the gnats and mosquitoes heard the words of their elder brothers, they did as the may-flies had done—did not venture, no, not one of them, to bite the young lover. They all flew away and settled down on the yellow-tops, where they had a council, and decided to go and find some prairie-dogs to bite. Therefore you will almost always find may-flies, gnats, and mosquitoes around prairie-dog holes in summer time when the corn is growing.

So the young man breathed easily as he hoed hard to finish his task ere the noonday, and when the maiden looked down and saw that he still labored there, she said to herself: "Ah, indeed he must love me, for still he is there! Well, it *may be*, for only a little longer and they will leave him in peace." Hastily she placed venison in the cooking-pot and prepared fresh *héwe* and sweetened bread, "for *maybe*," she still thought, "and then I will have it ready for him."

Now, alas! you do not know that this good and beautiful maiden had a sister, alas!—a sister as beautiful as herself, but bad and double-hearted; and you know when people have double hearts they are wizards or witches, and have double tongues and paired thoughts—such a sister elder had the maiden of Mátsaki, alas!

When the sun had climbed almost to the middle of the sky, the maiden, still doubtful, looked down once more. He was there, and was working among the last hills of corn.

"Ah, truly indeed he loves me," she thought, and she hastened to put on her necklaces and bracelets of shells, her earrings as long as your fingers—of turquoises—and her fine cotton mantles with borders of stitched butterflies of summer-land, and flowers of the autumn. Then she took a new bowl from the stick-rack in the corner, and a large many-colored tray that she had woven herself, and she filled the one with meat broth, and the other with the *héwe* and sweet-bread, and placing the bowl of meat broth on her head, she took the tray of *héwe* in her hand, and started down toward the corn-field by the river-side to meet her lover and to thank him.

Witches are always jealous of the happiness and good fortune of others. So was the sister of the beautiful maiden jealous when she saw the smile on her *hani's* face as she tripped toward the river.

"*Ho há!*" said the two-hearted sister. "*Témithlokwa thlokwá! Wananí!*" which are words of defiance and hatred, used so long ago by demons and wizards that no one knows nowadays what they mean except the last one, which plainly says, "Just wait a bit!" and she hastened to dress herself, through her wicked knowledge, exactly as the beautiful maiden was dressed. She even carried just such a bowl and tray; and as she was beautiful, like her younger sister, nobody could have known the one from the other, or the other from the one. Then she passed herself through a hoop of magic yucca, which made her seem not to be where she was, for no one could see her unless she willed it.

Now, just as the sun was resting in the middle of the sky, the young man finished the field and ran down to the river to wash. Before he was done, he saw the maiden coming down the trail with the bowl on her head and the tray in her hand; so he made haste, and ran back to dress himself and to sit down to wait for her. As she approached, he said: "Thou comest, and may it be happily,"—when lo! there appeared two maidens exactly alike; so he quickly said, "Ye come."

"*E,*" said the maidens, so nearly together that it sounded like one voice; but when they both placed the same food before him, the poor young man looked from one to the other, and asked:

"Alas! of which am I to eat!"

Then it was that the maiden suddenly saw her sister, and became hot with anger, for she knew her wicked plans. "Ah, thou foolish sister, why didst thou come?" she said. But the other only replied:

"Ah, thou foolish sister, why didst *thou* come?"

"Go back, for he is mine-to-be," said the maiden, beginning to cry.

"Go back, for he is mine-to-be," said the bad one, pretending to cry.

And thus they quarrelled until they had given one another smarting words four times, when they fell to fighting—as women always fight, by pulling each other's hair, and scratching, and grappling until they rolled over each other in the sand.

The poor young man started forward to part them, but he knew not one from the other, so thinking that the bad one must know how to fight better than his beautiful maiden wife, he suddenly caught up his stone-weighted hoe, and furiously struck the one that was uppermost on the head, again and again, until she let go her hold, and fell back, murmuring and moaning: "Alas! that thus it should be after all, after all!" Then she forgot, and her eyes ceased to see.

While yet the young man looked, lo! there was only the dying maiden before him; but in the air above circled an ugly black Crow, that laughed *"kawkaw, kawkaw, kawkaw!"* and flew away to its cave in Thunder Mountain.

Then the young man knew. He cried aloud and beat his breast; then he ran to the river and brought water and bathed the blood away from the maiden's temples; but alas! she only smiled and talked with her lips, then grew still and cold.

Alone, as the sun travelled toward the land of evening, wept the young man over the body of his beautiful wife. He knew naught but his sad thoughts. He took her in his arms, and placed his face close to hers, and again and again, he called to her: "Alas, alas! my beautiful wife; I loved thee, I love thee. Alas, alas! Ah, my beautiful wife, my beautiful wife!"

When the people returned from their fields in the evening, they missed the beautiful maiden of Mátsaki; and they saw the young man, bending low and alone over something down in the lands of the priest-chief by the river, and when they told the old father, he shook his head and said:

"It is not well with my beautiful child; but as They (the gods) say, thus must all things be." Then he smiled—for the heart of a priest-chief never cries,—and told them to go and bring her to the plaza of Mátsaki and bury her before the House of the Sun; for he knew what had happened.

So the people did as their father had told them. They went down at sunset and took the beautiful maiden away, and wrapped her in mantles, and buried her near the House of the Sun.

But the poor young man knew naught but his sad thoughts. He followed them; and when he had made her grave, he sat down by her earth bed and would not leave her. No, not even when the sun set, but moaned and called to her: "Alas, alas! my beautiful wife; I loved thee, I love thee; even though I knew not thee and killed thee. Alas! Ah, my beautiful wife!"

"*Shonetchi!*" ("There is left of my story.") And what there is left, I will tell you some other night.

(Told the Second Night)

"*Sonahtchi!*"

"*Sons shonetchi!*" ("There is left of my story";) but I will tell you not alone of the Maid of Mátsaki, because the young man killed her, for he knew not his wife from the other. It is of the Red Feather, or the Wife of Mátsaki that I will tell you this sitting.

Even when the sun set, and the hills and houses grew black in the shadows, still the young man sat by the grave-side, his hands rested upon his knees and his face buried in them. And the people no longer tried to steal his sad thoughts from him; but, instead, left him, as one whose mind errs, to wail out with weeping: "Alas, alas! my beautiful wife; I loved thee, I love thee; even though I knew not thee and killed thee! Alas! Ah, my beautiful wife!"

But when the moon set on the western hills, and the great snowdrift streaked across the mid-sky, and the night was half gone, the sad watcher saw a light in the grave-sands like the light of the embers that die in the ashes. As he watched, his sad thoughts became bright thoughts, for the light grew and brightened till it burned the dark grave-sands as sunlight the shadows. Lo! the bride lay beneath. She tore off her mantles and raised up in her grave-bed. Then she looked at the eager lover so coldly and sadly that his bright thoughts all darkened, for she mournfully told him: "Alas! Ah, my lover, my husband knew not me from the other; loved me not, therefore killed me; even though I had hoped for love, loved me not, therefore killed me!"

Again the young man buried his face in his hands and shook his head mournfully; and like one whose thoughts erred, again he wailed his lament: "Alas, alas! my beautiful bride! I do love thee; I loved thee, but I did not know thee and killed thee! Alas! Ah, my beautiful bride, my beautiful bride!"

At last, as the great star rose from the sky-land, the dead maiden spoke softly to the mourning lover, yet her voice was sad and strange: "Young man, mourn thou not, but go back to the home of thy fathers. Knowest thou not that I am another being? When the sky of the day-land grows yellow and the houses come out of the shadows, then will the light whereby thou sawest me, fade away in the morn-light, as the blazes of late councils pale their red in the sunlight." Then her voice grew sadder as she said: "I am only a spirit; for remember, alas! ah, my lover, my husband knew not me from the other—loved me not, therefore killed me; even though I had hoped for love, loved me not, therefore killed me."

But the young man would not go until, in the gray of the morning, he saw nothing where the light had appeared but the dark sand of the grave as it had been. Then he arose and went away in sorrow. Nor would he all day speak to men, but gazed only whither his feet stepped and shook his head sadly like one whose thoughts wandered. And when again the houses and hills grew black with the shadows, he sought anew the fresh grave and sat down by its side, bowed his head and still murmured: "Alas, alas! my beautiful wife, I loved thee, though I knew not thee, and killed thee. Alas! Ah, my beautiful wife!"

Even brighter glowed the light in the grave-sands when the night was divided, and the maiden's spirit arose and sat in her grave-bed, but she only reproached him and bade him go. "For," said she, "I am only a spirit; remember, alas! ah, my lover, my husband knew not me from the other; loved me not, therefore killed me; even though I had hoped for love, loved me not, therefore killed me!"

But he left only in the morning, and again when the dark came, returned to the grave-side.

When the light shone that night, the maiden, more beautiful than ever, came out of the grave-bed and sat by her lover. Once more she urged him to return to his fathers; but when she saw that he would not, she said: "Thou hadst better, for I go a long journey. As light as the wind is, so light will my feet be; as long as the day is, thou canst not my form see. Know thou not that the spirits are seen but in darkness? for, alas! ah, my lover, my husband knew not me from the other; loved me not, therefore killed me; even though I had hoped for love, loved me not, therefore killed me!"

Then the young man ceased bemoaning his beautiful bride. He looked at her sadly, and said: "I do love thee, my beautiful wife! I do love thee, and whither thou goest let me therefore go with thee! I care not how long is the journey, nor how hard is the way. If I can but see thee, even only at night time, then will I be happy and cease to bemoan thee. It was because I loved thee and would have saved thee; but alas, my beautiful wife! I knew not thee, therefore killed thee!"

"Alas! Ah, my lover; and Ah! how I loved thee; but I am a spirit, and thou art unfinished. But if thou thus love me, go back when I leave thee and plume many prayer-sticks. Choose a light, downy feather and dye it with ocher. Wrap up in thy blanket a lunch for four daylights; bring with thee much prayer-meal; come to me at midnight and sit by my grave-side, and when in the eastward the dayland is lighting, tie over my forehead the reddened light feather, and when with the morning I fade from thy vision, follow only the feather until it is evening, and then thou shalt see me and sit down beside me."

So at sunrise the young man went away and gathered feathers of the summer birds, and cut many prayer-sticks, whereon he bound them with cotton, as gifts to the Fathers. Then he found a beautiful downy feather plucked from the eagle, and dyed it red with ocher, and tied to it a string of cotton wherewith to fasten it over the forehead of the spirit maiden. When night came, he took meal made from parched corn and burnt sweet-bread, and once more went down to the plaza and sat by the grave-side.

When midnight came and the light glowed forth through the grave-sands, lo! the maiden-spirit came out and stood by his side. She seemed no longer sad, but happy, like one going home after long absence. Nor was the young man sad or single-thoughted like one whose mind errs; so they sat together and talked of their journey till the day-land grew yellow and the black shadows gray, and the houses and hills came out of the darkness.

"Once more would I tell thee to go back," said the maiden's spirit to the young man; "but I know why thou goest with me, and it is well. Only watch me when the day comes, and thou wilt see me no more; but look whither the plume goeth, and follow, for thou knowest that thou must tie it to the hair above my forehead."

Then the young man took the bright red plume out from among the feathers of sacrifice, and gently tied it above the maiden-spirit's forehead.

As the light waved up from behind the great mountain the red glow faded out from the grave-sands and the youth looked in vain for the spirit of the maiden; but before him, at the height of one's hands when standing, waved the light downy feather in the wind of the morning. Then the plume, not the wife, rose before him, like the plumes on the head of a dancer, and moved through the streets that led westward, and down through the fields to the river. And out through the streets that led westward, and down on the trail by the river, and on over the plains always toward the land of evening, the young man followed close the red feather; but at last he began to grow weary, for the plume glided swiftly before him, until at last it left him far behind, and even now and then lost him entirely. Then, as he hastened on, he called in anguish:

"My beautiful bride! My beautiful bride! Oh, where art thou?"

But the plume, not the wife, stopped and waited. And thus the plume and the young man journeyed until, toward evening, they came to the forests of sweet-smelling piñons and cedars. As the night hid the hills in the shadows, alas! the plume disappeared, but the young man pressed onward, for he knew that the plume still journeyed westward. Yet at times he was so weary that he almost lost the strength of his thoughts; for he ran into trees by the trail-side and stumbled over dry roots and branches. So again and again he would call out in anguish: "My beautiful wife! My beautiful bride! Oh, where art thou?"

At last, when the night was divided, to his joy he saw, far away on the hill-top, a light that was red and grew brighter like the light of a camp-fire's red embers when fanned by the wind of the night-time. And like a star that is rising or setting, the red light sat still on the hill-top. So he ran hastily forward, until, as he neared the red light, lo! there sat the spirit of the beautiful maiden; and as he neared her, she said:

"Comest thou?" and "How hast thou come to the evening?"

As she spoke she smiled, and motioned him to sit down beside her. He was so weary that he slept while he talked to her; but, remember, she was a spirit, therefore she slept not.

Just as the morning star came up from the dayland, the maiden rose to journey on, and the young man, awaking, followed her. But as the hills came out of the shadows, the form of the maiden before him grew fainter and fainter, until it faded entirely, and only the red plume floated before him, like the plume on the head of a dancer. Far ahead and fast floated the plume, until it entered a plain of lava filled with sharp crags; yet still it went on, for the maiden's spirit moved over the barriers as lightly as the down of dead flowers in autumn. But alas! the young man had to seek his way, and the plume again left him far behind, until he was forced to cry out: "Ah, my beautiful bride, do wait for me, for I love thee, and will not turn from thee!" Then the plume stopped on the other side of the crags and waited until the poor young man came nearer, his feet and legs cut and bleeding, and his wind almost out. Then the trail was more even, and led through wide plains; but even thus the young man could scarce keep the red plume in sight. But at night the maiden awaited him in a sheltered place, and they rested together beneath the cedars until daylight. Then again she faded out in the daylight, and the red plume led the way.

For a long time the trail was pleasant, but toward evening they came to a wide bed of cactus, and the plume passed over as swiftly as ever, but the young man's moccasins were soon torn and his feet and legs cruelly lacerated with the cactus spines; yet still he pursued the red plume until the pain seemed to sting his whole body, and he gasped and wailed: "Ah, my beautiful wife, wait for me; do wait, for I love thee and will not leave thee!" Then the plume stopped beyond the plain of cactus and waited until he had passed through, but not longer, for ere he had plucked all the needles of the cactus from his bleeding feet, it floated on, and he lifted himself up and followed until at evening the maiden again waited and bade him "Sit down and rest."

That night she seemed to pity him, and once more spoke to him: "*Yo á!* My lover, my husband, turn back, oh, turn back! for the way is long and untrodden, and thy heart is but weak and is mortal. I go to the Council of Dead Ones, and how can the living there enter?"

But the youth only wept, and begged that she let him go with her. "For, ah," said he, "my beautiful wife, my beautiful bride, I love thee and cannot turn from thee!"

And she smiled only and shook her head sadly as she replied: "*Yo á!* It shall be as thou willest. It may be thy heart will not wither, for tomorrow is one more day onward, and then down the trail to the waters wherein stands the ladder of others, shall I lead thee to wait me forever."

At mid-sun on the day after, the plume led the way straight to a deep cañon, the walls of which were so steep that no man could pass them alive. For a moment the red plume paused above the chasm, and the youth pressed on and stretched his hand forth to detain it; but ere he had gained the spot, it floated on straight over the dark cañon, as though no ravine had been there at all; for to spirits the trails that once have been, even though the waters have worn them away, still are.

Wildly the young man rushed up and down the steep brink, and despairingly he called across to the plume: "Alas! ah, my beautiful wife! Wait, only wait for me, for I love thee and cannot turn from thee!" Then, like one whose thoughts wandered, he threw himself over the brink and hung by his hands as if to drop, when a jolly little striped Squirrel, who was playing at the bottom of the cañon, happened to see him, and called out: "*Tsithl! Tsithl!*" and much more, which meant "*Ah hai! Wananí!*" "You crazy fool of a being! You have not the wings of a falcon, nor the hands of a Squirrel, nor the feet of a spirit, and if you drop you will be broken to pieces and the moles will eat up the fragments! Wait! Hold hard, and I will help you, for, though I am but a Squirrel, I know how to think!"

Whereupon the little chit ran chattering away and called his mate out of their house in a rock-nook: "Wife! Wife! Come quickly; run to our corn room and bring me a hemlock, and hurry!

hurry! Ask me no questions; for a crazy fool of a man over here will break himself to pieces if we don't quickly make him a ladder."

So the little wife flirted her brush in his face and skipped over the rocks to their store-house, where she chose a fat hemlock and hurried to her husband who was digging a hole in the sand underneath where the young man was hanging. Then they spat on the seed, and buried it in the hole, and began to dance round it and sing,—

> "Kiäthlä tsilu,
>> Silokwe, silokwe, silokwe;
> Ki'ai silu silu,
>> Tsithl! Tsithl!"

Which meant, as far as any one can tell now (for it was a long time ago, and partly squirrel talk),

> "Hemlock of the
>> Tall kind, tall kind, tall kind,
> Sprout up hemlock, hemlock,
>> Chit! Chit!"

And every time they danced around and sang the song through, the ground moved, until the fourth time they said "Tsithl! Tsithl!" the tree sprouted forth and kept growing until the little Squirrel could jump into it, and by grabbing the topmost bough and bracing himself against the branches below, could stretch and pull it, so that in a short time he made it grow as high as the young man's feet, and he had all he could do to keep the poor youth from jumping right into it before it was strong enough to hold him. Presently he said "Tsithl! Tsithl!" and whisked away before the young man had time to thank him. Then the sad lover climbed down and quickly gained the other side, which was not so steep; before he could rest from his climb, however, the plume floated on, and he had to get up and follow it.

Just as the sun went into the west, the plume hastened down into a valley between the mountains, where lay a beautiful lake; and around the borders of the lake a very ugly old man and woman, who were always walking back and forth across the trails, came forward and laughed loudly and greeted the beautiful maiden pleasantly. Then they told her to enter; and she fearlessly walked into the water, and a ladder of flags came up out of the middle of the lake to receive her, down which she stepped without stopping until she passed under the waters. For a little—and then all was over—a bright light shone out of the water, and the sound of many glad voices and soft merry music came also from beneath it; then the stars of the sky and the stars of the waters looked the same at each other as they had done before.

"Alas!" cried the young man as he ran to the lake-side. "Ah, my beautiful wife, my beautiful wife, only wait, only wait, that I may go with thee!" But only the smooth waters and the old man and woman were before him; nor did the ladder come out or the old ones greet him. So he sat down on the lake-side wringing his hands and weeping, and ever his mind wandered back to his old lament: "Alas! alas! my beautiful bride, my beautiful wife, I love thee; I loved thee, but I knew not thee and killed thee!"

Toward the middle of the night once more he heard strange, happy voices. The doorway to the Land of Spirits opened, and the light shot up through the dark green waters from many windows, like sparks from a chimney on a dark, windless night. Then the ladder again ascended, and he saw the forms of the dead pass out and in, and heard the sounds of the *Kâ'-kâ*, as it danced for the gods. The comers and goers were bright and beautiful, but their garments were snow-white cotton, stitched with many-colored threads, and their necklaces and bracelets were of dazzling white shells and turquoises unnumbered. Once he ventured to gain the bright entrance, but the water grew deep and chilled him till he trembled with fear and cold. Yet he looked in at the entrances, and lo! as he gazed he caught sight of his beautiful bride all covered with garments and bright things. And there in the midst of the *Kâ'-kâ* she sat at the head of the dancers. She seemed happy and smiled as she watched, and youths as bright and as happy came around her, and she seemed to forget her lone lover.

Then with a cry of despair and anguish he crawled to the lake-shore and buried his face in the sands and rank grasses. Suddenly he heard a low screech, and then a hoarse voice seemed to call him. He looked, and a great Owl flew over him, saying: "*Muhaí! Hu hu! Hu hu!*"

"What wilt thou?" he cried, in vexed anguish.

Then the Owl flew closer, and, lighting, asked: "Why weepest thou, my child?"

He turned and looked at the Owl and told it part of his trouble, when the Owl suddenly twisted its head quite around—as owls do—to see if anyone were near; then came closer and said: "I know all about it, young man. Come with me to my house in the mountain, and if thou wilt but follow my counsel, all will yet be well." Then the Owl led the way to a cave far above and bade him step in. As he placed his foot inside the opening, behold! it widened into a bright room, and many Owl-men and Owl-women around greeted him happily, and bade him sit down and eat.

The old Owl who had brought him, changed himself in a twinkling, as he entered the room, and hung his owl-coat on an antler. Then he went away, but presently returned, bringing a little bag of medicine. "Before I give thee this, let me tell thee what to do, and what thou must promise," said he of the owl-coat.

The young man eagerly reached forth his hand for the magic medicine.

"Fool!" cried the being; "were it not well, for that would I not help thee. Thou art too eager, and I will not trust thee with my medicine of sleep. Thou shalt sleep here, and when thou awakest thou shalt find the morning star in the sky, and thy dead wife before thee on the trail toward the Middle Ant Hill. With the rising sun she will wake and smile on thee. Be not foolish, but journey preciously with her, and not until ye reach the home of thy fathers shalt thou approach her or kiss her; for if thou doest this, all will be as nothing again. But if thou doest as I counsel thee, all will be well, and happily may ye live one with the other."

He ceased, and, taking a tiny pinch of the medicine, blew it in the face of the youth. Instantly the young man sank with sleep where he had been sitting, and the beings, putting on their owl-coats, flew away with him under some trees by the trail that led to Mátsaki and the Ant Hill of the Middle.

Then they flew over the lake, and threw the medicine of sleep in at the windows, and taking the plumed prayer-sticks which the young man had brought with him, they chose some red plumes for themselves, and with the others entered the home of the *Kâ'-kâ*. Softly they flew over the sleeping fathers and their children (the gods of the *Kâ'-kâ* and the spirits) and, laying the prayer-plumes before the great altar, caught up the beautiful maiden and bore her over the waters and woodlands to where the young man was still sleeping. Then they hooted and flew off to their mountain.

As the great star came out of the dayland, the young man awoke, and lo! there before him lay his own beautiful wife. Then he turned his face away that he might not be tempted, and waited with joy and longing for the coming out of the sun. When at last the sun came out, with the first ray that brightened the beautiful maiden's face, she opened her eyes and gazed wildly around at first, but seeing her lonely lover, smiled, and said: "Truly, thou lovest me!"

Then they arose and journeyed apart toward the home of their fathers, and the young man forgot not the counsel of the Owl, but journeyed wisely, till on the fourth day they came in sight of the Mountain of Thunder and saw the river that flows by Salt City.

As they began to go down into the valley, the maiden stopped and said: "*Hahuá*, I am weary, for the journey is long and the day is warm." Then she sat down in the shadow of a cedar and said: "Watch, my husband, while I sleep a little; only a little, and then we will journey together again." And he said: "Be it well."

Then she lay down and seemed to sleep. She smiled and looked so beautiful to the longing lover that he softly rose and crept close to her. Then, alas! he laid his hand upon her and kissed her.

Quickly the beautiful maiden started. Her face was all covered with sadness, and she said, hastily and angrily: "Ah, thou shameless fool! I now know! Thou lovest me not! How vain that I should have hoped for thy love!"

With shame, indeed, and sorrow, he bent his head low and covered his face with his hands. Then he started to speak, when an Owl flew up and hooted mournfully at him from a tree-top. Then the Owl winged her way to the westward, and ever after the young man's mind wandered.

Alas! alas! Thus it was in the days of the ancients. Maybe had the young man not kissed her yonder toward the Lake of the

Dead, we would never have journeyed nor ever have mourned for others lost. But then it is well! If men and women had never died, then the world long ago had overflown with children, starvation, and warring.

Thus shortens my story.

From *Zuñi Folk Tales* (New York: G. P. Putnam's Sons, 1901), pp. 1–33.

The Coyote
and the Ravens
Who Raced Their Eyes

Long, long ago, in the days of the ancients, there lived in Hómaiakwin, or the Cañon of the Cedars, a Coyote,—doubtless the same one I have told you of as having made friends with the Woodpounder bird. As you know, this cañon in which he lived is below the high eastern cliff of Face Mountain.

This Coyote was out walking one day. On leaving his house he had said that he was going hunting; but,—miserable fellow!—who ever knew a Coyote to catch anything, unless it were a prairie-dog or a wood-rat or a locust or something of the kind? So you may depend upon it he was out walking; that is, wandering around to see what he could see.

He crossed over the valley northward, with his tail dragging along in an indifferent sort of a way, until he came to the place on Thunder Mountain called Shoton-pia ("Where the Shell Breastplate Hangs"). He climbed up the foot-hills, and along the terraces at the base of the cliff, and thus happened to get toward the southeastern corner of the mountain. There is a little column of rock with a round top to it standing there, as you know, to this day.

Now, on the top of this standing rock sat two old Ravens, racing their eyes. One of them would settle himself down on the rock and point with his beak straight off across the valley to some pinnacle in the cliffs of the opposite mesa. Then he would say to his companion, without turning his head at all: "You see that rock yonder? Well, ahem! Standing rock yonder, round you, go ye my eyes and come back." Then he would lower his head, stiffen his neck, squeeze his eyelids, and *"Pop!"* he would say as his eyes flew out of their sockets, and sailed away toward the rock like two streaks of lightning, reaching which they would go round it, and come back toward the Raven; and as they were coming back, he would swell up his throat and say "*Whu-u-u-u-u-u-u*,"—whereupon his eyes would slide with a *k'othlo!* into their sockets again. Then he would turn toward his companion, and swelling up his throat still more, and ducking his head just as if he were trying to vomit his own neck, he would laugh inordinately; and the other would laugh with him, bristling up all the feathers on his body.

Then the other one would settle himself, and say: "Ah, I'll better you! You see that rock away yonder!" Then he would begin to squeeze his eyelids, and *thlut!* his eyes would fly out of their sockets and away across the mesa and round the rock he had named; and as they flew back, he would lower himself, and say "*Whu-u-u-u-u-u-u*," when *k'othlo!* the eyes would slide into their sockets again. Then, as much amused as ever, the Ravens would laugh at one another again.

Now, the Coyote heard the Ravens humming their eyes back into their sockets; and the sound they made, as well as the way they laughed so heartily, exceedingly pleased him, so that he stuck his tail up very straight and laughed merely from seeing them laugh. Presently he could contain himself no longer. "Friends," he cried, in a shrieky little voice, "I say, friends, how do you do, and what are you doing?"

The Ravens looked down, and when they saw the Coyote they laughed and punched one another with their wings and cried out to him: "Bless you! Glad to see you come!"

"What is it you are doing?" asked he. "By the daylight of the gods, it is funny, whatever it is!" And he whisked his tail and laughed, as he said this, drawing nearer to the Ravens.

"Why, we are racing our eyes," said the older of the two Ravens. "Didn't you ever see anyone race his eyes before?"

"Good demons, no!" exclaimed the Coyote. "Race your eyes! How in the world do you race your eyes?"

"Why, this way," said one of the Ravens. And he settled himself down. "Do you see that tall rock yonder? Ahem! Well, tall rock, yonder,—ye my eyes go round it and return to me!" *K'othlo! k'othlo!* the eyes slipped out of their sockets, and the

Raven, holding his head perfectly still, waited, with his upper lids hanging wrinkled on his lower, for the return of the eyes; and as they neared him, he crouched down, swelled up his neck, and exclaimed *"Whu-u-u-u-u-u-u."* *Tsoko!* the eyes flew into their sockets again. Then the Raven turned around and showed his two black bright eyes as good as ever. "There, now! what did I tell you?"

"By the moon!" squeaked the Coyote, and came up nearer still. "How in the world do you do that? It is one of the most wonderful and funny things I ever saw!"

"Well, here, come up close to me," said the Raven, "and I will show you how it is done." Then the other Raven settled himself down; and *pop!* went his eyes out of their sockets, round a rock still farther away. And as they returned, he exclaimed *"Whu-u-u-u-u-u-u-u-,"* when *tsoko!* in again they came. And he turned around laughing at the Coyote. "There, now!" said he, "didn't I tell you?"

"By the daylight of the gods! I wish I could do that," said the Coyote. "Suppose I try my eyes?"

"Why, yes, if you like, to be sure!" said the Ravens. "Well, now, do you want to try?"

"Humph! I should say I did," replied the Coyote.

"Well, then, settle down right here on this rock," said the Ravens, making way for him, "and hold your head out toward that rock and say: 'Yonder rock, these my eyes go round it and return to me.'"

"I know! I know! I know!" yelled the Coyote. And he settled himself down, and squeezed and groaned to force his eyes out of his sockets, but they would not go. "Goodness!" said the Coyote, "how can I get my eyes to go out of their sockets?"

"Why, don't you know how?" said the Ravens. "Well, just keep still, and we'll help you; we'll take them out for you."

"All right! all right!" cried the Coyote, unable to repress his impatience. "Quick! quick! here I am, all ready!" And crouching down, he laid his tail straight out, swelled up his neck and strained with every muscle to force his eyes out of his head. The Ravens picked them out with a dexterous twist of their beaks in no time, and sent them flying off over the valley. The Coyote yelped a little when they came out, but stood his ground manfully, and cringed down his neck and waited for his eyes to come back.

"Let the fool of a beast go without his eyes," said the Ravens. "He was so very anxious to get rid of them, and do something he had no business with; let him go without them!" Whereupon they flew off across the valley, and caught up his eyes and ate them, and flew on, laughing at the predicament in which they had left the Coyote.

Now, thus the Coyote sat there the proper length of time; then he opened his mouth, and said "*Whu-u-u-u-u-u-u!*" But he waited in vain for his eyes to come back. And "*Whu-u-u-u-u-u-u-u-u!*" he said again. No use. "Mercy!" exclaimed he, "what can have become of my eyes? Why don't they come back?" After he had waited and "*whu-u-u-u-u-d*" until he was tired, he concluded that his eyes had got lost, and laid his head on his breast, woefully thinking of his misfortune. "How in the world shall I hunt up my eyes?" he groaned, as he lifted himself cautiously (for it must be remembered that he stood on a narrow rock), and tried to look all around; but he couldn't see. Then he began to feel with his paws, one after another, to find the way down; and he slipped and fell, so that nearly all the breath was knocked out of his body. When he had recovered, he picked himself up, and felt and felt along, slowly descending until he got into the valley.

Now, it happened as he felt his way along with his toes that he came to a wet place in the valley, not far below where the spring of Shuntakaiya flows out from the cliffs above. In feeling his way, his foot happened to strike a yellow cranberry, ripe and soft, but very cold, of course. "Ha!" said he, "lucky fellow, I! Here is one of my eyes." So he picked it up and clapped it into one of his empty sockets; then he peered up to the sky, and the light struck through it. "Didn't I tell you so, old fellow? It is one of your eyes, by the souls of your ancestors!" Then he felt around until he found another cranberry. "Ha!" said he, "and this proves it! Here is the other!" And he clapped that into the other empty socket. He didn't seem to see quite as well as he had seen before, but still the cranberries answered the purpose of eyes exceedingly well, and the poor wretch of a Coyote never knew the difference; only it was observed when he returned to his companions in the Cañon of the Cedars that he had yellow eyes instead of black ones, which everybody knows Coyotes and all other creatures had at first.

Thus it was in the days of the ancients, and hence to this day coyotes have yellow eyes, and are not always quick to see things.

Thus shortens my story.

From *Zuñi Folk Tales* (New York: G. P. Putnam's Sons, 1901), pp. 262–68.

The Rabbit Huntress
and Her Adventures

It was long ago, in the days of the ancients, that a poor maiden lived at K'yawana Tehua-tsana ("Little Gateway of Zuñi River"). You know there are black stone walls of houses standing there on the tops of the cliffs of lava, above the narrow place through which the river runs, to this day.

In one of these houses there lived this poor maiden alone with her feeble old father and her aged mother. She was unmarried, and her brothers had all been killed in wars, or had died gently; so the family lived there helplessly, so far as many things were concerned, from the lack of men in their house.

It is true that in making the gardens—the little plantings of beans, pumpkins, squashes, melons, and corn—the maiden was able to do very well; and thus mainly on the products of these things the family were supported. But, as in those days of our ancients we had neither sheep nor cattle, the hunt was depended upon to supply the meat; or sometimes it was procured by barter of the products of the fields to those who hunted mostly. Of these things this little family had barely enough for their own subsistence; hence they could not procure their supplies of meat in this way.

Long before, it had been a great house, for many were the brave and strong young men who had lived in it; but the rooms were now empty, or at best contained only the leavings of those who had lived there, much used and worn out.

One autumn day, near winter-time, snow fell, and it became very cold. The maiden had gathered brush and firewood in abundance, and it was piled along the roof of the house and down underneath the ladder which descended from the top. She saw the young men issue forth the next morning in great numbers, their feet protected by long stockings of deerskin, the fur turned inward, and they carried on their shoulders and stuck in their belts stone axes and rabbit-sticks. As she gazed at them from the roof, she said to herself: "O that I were a man and could go forth, as do these young men, hunting rabbits! Then my poor old mother and father would not lack for flesh with which to duly season their food and nourish their lean bodies." Thus ran her thoughts, and before night, as she saw these same young men coming in, one after another, some of them bringing long strings of rabbits, others short ones, but none of them empty-handed, she decided that, woman though she was, she would set forth on the morrow to try what luck she might find in the killing of rabbits herself.

It may seem strange that, although this maiden was beautiful and young, the youths did not give her some of their rabbits. But their feelings were not friendly, for no one of them would she accept as a husband, although one after another of them had offered himself for marriage.

Fully resolved, the girl that evening sat down by the fireplace, and turning toward her aged parents, said: "O my mother and father, I see that the snow has fallen, whereby easily rabbits are tracked, and the young men who went out this morning returned long before evening heavily laden with strings of this game. Behind, in the other rooms of our house are many rabbit-sticks, and there hang on the walls stone axes, and with these I might perchance strike down a rabbit on his trail, or, if he run into a log, split the log and dig him out. So I have thought during the day, and have decided to go tomorrow and try my fortunes in the hunt, woman though I be."

"*Naiya*, my daughter," quavered the feeble old mother; "you would surely be very cold, or you would lose your way, or grow so tired that you could not return before night, and you must not go out to hunt rabbits, woman as you are."

"Why, certainly not," insisted the old man, rubbing his lean knees and shaking his head over the days that were gone. "No, no; let us live in poverty rather than that you should run such risks as these, O my daughter."

But say what they would, the girl was determined. And the old man said at last: "Very well! You will not be turned from your course. Therefore, O daughter, I will help you as best I may." He hobbled into another room, and found there some old deerskins covered thickly with fur; and drawing them out, he moistened and carefully softened them, and cut out for the maiden long stockings, which he sewed up with sinew and the fiber of the yucca leaf. Then he selected for her from among the old possessions of his brothers and sons, who had been killed or perished otherwise, a number of rabbit-sticks and a fine, heavy stone axe. Meanwhile, the old woman busied herself in preparing a lunch for the girl, which was composed of little cakes of corn-meal, spiced with pepper and wild onions, pierced through the middle, and baked in the ashes. When she had made a long string of these by threading them like beads on a rope of yucca fiber, she laid them down not far from the ladder on a little bench, with the rabbit-sticks, the stone axe, and the deerskin stockings.

That night the maiden planned and planned, and early on the following morning, even before the young men had gone out from the town, she had put on a warm, short-skirted dress, knotted a mantle over her shoulder and thrown another and larger one over her back, drawn on the deerskin stockings, had thrown the string of corn-cakes over her shoulder, stuck the rabbit-sticks in her belt, and carrying the stone axe in her hand sallied forth eastward through the Gateway of Zuñi and into the plain of the valley beyond, called the Plain of the Burnt River, on account of the black, roasted-looking rocks along some parts of its sides. Dazzlingly white the snow stretched out before her—not deep, but unbroken,—and when she came near the cliffs with many little cañons in them, along the northern side of the valley, she saw many a trail of rabbits running out and in among the rocks and between the bushes.

Warm and excited by her unwonted exercise, she did not heed a coming snow-storm, but ran about from one place to another, following the trails of the rabbits, sometimes up into the cañons, where the forests of piñon and cedar stood, and where here and there she had the good fortune sometimes to run two, three, or four rabbits into a single hollow log. It was little work to split these logs, for they were small, as you know, and to dig out the rabbits and slay them by a blow of the hand on the nape of the neck, back of the ears; and as she killed each rabbit she raised it reverently to her lips, and breathed from its nostrils its expiring breath, and, tying its legs together, placed it on the string, which after a while began to grow heavy on her shoulders. Still she kept on, little heeding the snow which was falling fast; nor did she notice that it was growing darker and darker, so intent was she on the hunt, and so glad was she to capture so many rabbits. Indeed, she followed the trails until they were no longer visible, as the snow fell all around her, thinking all the while: "How happy will be my poor old father and mother that they shall now have flesh to eat! How strong will they grow! And when this meat is gone, that which is dried and preserved of it also, lo! another snow-storm will no doubt come, and I can go out hunting again."

At last the twilight came, and looking around, she found that the snow had fallen deeply, there was no trail, and that she had lost her way. True, she turned about and started in the direction of her home, as she supposed, walking as fast as she could through the soft, deep snow. Yet she reckoned not rightly, for instead of going eastward along the valley, she went southward across it, and entering the mouth of the Descending Plain of the Pines, she went on and on, thinking she was going homeward, until at last it grew dark and she knew not which way to turn.

"What harm," thought she, "if I find a sheltered place among the rocks? What harm if I remain all night, and go home in the morning when the snow has ceased falling, and by the light I shall know my way?"

So she turned about to some rocks which appeared, black and dim, a short distance away. Fortunately, among these rocks is the cave which is known as Taiuma's Cave. This she came to, and peering into that black hole, she saw in it, back some distance, a little glowing light. "Ha, ha!" thought she; "perhaps some rabbit-hunters like myself, belated yesterday, passed the night here and left the fire burning. If so, this is greater good fortune than I could have looked for." So, lowering the string of rabbits which she carried on her shoulder, and throwing off her mantle, she crawled in, peering well into the darkness, for fear of wild beasts; then, returning, she drew in the string of rabbits and the mantle.

Behold! there was a bed of hot coals buried in the ashes in the very middle of the cave, and piled up on one side were fragments of broken wood. The girl, happy in her good fortune, issued forth and gathered more sticks from the cliff-side, where dead piñons are found in great numbers, and bringing them in little armfuls one after another, she finally succeeded in gathering a store sufficient to keep the fire burning brightly all the night through. Then she drew off her snow-covered stockings of deerskin and the bedraggled mantles, and, building a fire, hung them up to dry and sat down to rest herself. The fire burned up and glowed brightly, so that the whole cave was as light as a room at night when a dance is being celebrated. By-and-by, after her clothing had dried, she spread a mantle on the floor of the cave by the side of the fire, and, sitting down, dressed one of her rabbits and roasted it, and, untying the string of corn-cakes her mother had made for her, feasted on the roasted meat and cakes.

She had just finished her evening meal, and was about to recline and watch the fire for awhile, when she heard away off in the distance a long, low cry of distress—*"Ho-o-o-o thlaia-a!"*

"Ah!" thought the girl, "someone, more belated than myself, is lost; doubtless one of the rabbit-hunters." She got up, and went nearer to the entrance of the cavern.

"Ho-o-o-o thlaia-a!" sounded the cry, nearer this time. She ran out, and, as it was repeated again, she placed her hand to her mouth, and cried, woman though she was, as loudly as possible: *"Li-i thlaia-a!"* ("Here!")

The cry was repeated near at hand, and presently the maiden, listening first, and then shouting, and listening again, heard the clatter of an enormous rattle. In dismay and terror she threw her hands into the air, and, crouching down, rushed into the cave and retreated to its farthest limits, where she sat shuddering with fear, for she knew that one of the Cannibal Demons of those days, perhaps the renowned Átahsaia of the east, had seen the light of her fire through the cave entrance, with his terrible staring eyes, and assuming it to be a lost wanderer, had cried out, and so led her to guide him to her place of concealment.

On came the Demon, snapping the twigs under his feet and shouting in a hoarse, loud voice: *"Ho lithlsh tâ ime!"* ("Ho, there! So you are in here, are you?") *Kothl!* clanged his rattle, while, almost fainting with terror, closer to the rock crouched the maiden.

The old Demon came to the entrance of the cave and bawled out: "I am cold, I am hungry! Let me in!" Without further ado, he stooped and tried to get in; but, behold! the entrance was too small for his giant shoulders to pass. Then he pretended to be wonderfully civil, and said: "Come out, and bring me something to eat."

"I have nothing for you," cried the maiden. "I have eaten my food."

"Have you no rabbits?"

"Yes."

"Come out and bring me some of them."

But the maiden was so terrified that she dared not move toward the entrance.

"Throw me a rabbit!" shouted the old Demon. The maiden threw him one of her precious rabbits at last, when she could rise and go to it. He clutched it with his long, horny hand, gave one gulp and swallowed it. Then he cried out: "Throw me another!" She threw him another, which he also immediately swallowed; and so on until the poor maiden had thrown all the rabbits to the voracious old monster. Every one she threw him he caught in his huge, yellow-tusked mouth, and swallowed, hair and all, at one gulp.

"Throw me another!" cried he, when the last had already been thrown to him.

So the poor maiden was forced to say: "I have no more."

"Throw me your overshoes!" cried he.

She threw the overshoes of deerskin, and these like the rabbits he speedily devoured. Then he called for her moccasins, and she threw them; for her belt, and she threw it; and finally, wonderful to tell, she threw even her mantle, and blanket, and her overdress, until, behold, she had nothing left!

Now, with all he had eaten, the old Demon was swollen hugely at the stomach, and, though he tried and tried to squeeze himself through the mouth of the cave, he could not by any means succeed. Finally, lifting his great flint axe, he began to shatter the rock about the entrance to the cave, and slowly but surely he enlarged the hole and the maiden now knew that as soon as he could get in he would devour her also, and she almost fainted at the sickening thought. Pound, pound, pound, pound, went the great axe of the Demon as he struck the rocks.

In the distance the two War-gods were sitting in their home at Thla-uthla (the Shrine amid the Bushes) beyond Thunder Mountain, and though far off, they heard thus in the middle of the night the pounding of the Demon's hammer-axe against the rocks. And of course they knew at once that a poor maiden, for the sake of her father and mother, had been out hunting,—that she had lost her way and, finding a cave where there was a little fire, entered it, rebuilt the fire, and rested herself; that, attracted by the light of her fire, the Cannibal Demon had come and besieged her retreat, and only a little time hence would he so enlarge the entrance to the cave that he could squeeze even his great over-filled paunch through it and come at the maiden to destroy her. So, catching up their wonderful weapons, these two War-gods flew away into the darkness and in no time they were approaching the Descending Plain of the Pines.

Just as the Demon was about to enter the cavern, and the maiden had fainted at seeing his huge face and gray shock of hair and staring eyes, his yellow, protruding tusks, and his horny, taloned hand, they came upon the old beast, and, each one hitting him a welt with his war-club, they "ended his daylight," and then hauled him forth into the open space. They opened his huge paunch and withdrew from it the maiden's garments, and even the rabbits which had been slain. The rabbits they cast away amongst the soap-weed plants that grew on the slope at the foot of the cliff. The garments they spread out on the snow, and by their knowledge cleansed and made them perfect, even more perfect than they had been before. Then, flinging the huge body of the giant Demon down into the depths of the cañon, they turned them about and, calling out gentle words to the maiden, entered and restored her; and she, seeing in them not their usual ugly persons, but handsome youths (as like to one another as are two deer born of the same mother), was greatly comforted; and bending low, and breathing upon their hands, thanked them over and over for the rescue they had brought her. But she crouched herself low with shame that her garments were but few, when, behold! the youths went out and brought in to her the garments they had cleaned by their knowledge, restoring them to her.

Then, spreading, their mantles by the door of the cave, they slept there that night, in order to protect the maiden, and on the morrow wakened her. They told her many things, and showed her many things which she had not known before, and counselled her thus: "It is not fearful that a maiden should marry; therefore, O maiden, return unto thy people in the Village of the Gateway of the River of Zuñi. This morning we will slay rabbits unnumbered for you, and start you on your way, guarding you down the snow-covered valley, and when you are in sight of your home we will leave you, telling you our names."

So, early in the morning the two gods went forth; and flinging their sticks among the soap-weed plants, behold! as though the soap-weed plants were rabbits, so many lay killed on the snow before these mighty hunters. And they gathered together great numbers of these rabbits, a string for each one of the party; and when the Sun had risen clearer in the sky, and his light sparkled on the snow around them, they took the rabbits to the maiden and presented them, saying: "We will carry each one of us a string of these rabbits." Then taking her hand, they led her out of the cave and down the valley, until, beyond on the high black mesas at the Gateway of the River of Zuñi, she saw the smoke rise from the houses of her village. Then turned the two War-gods to her, and they told her their names. And again she bent low, and breathed on their hands. Then, dropping the strings of rabbits which they had carried close beside the maiden, they swiftly disappeared.

Thinking much of all she had learned, she continued her way to the home of her father and mother; and as she went into the town, staggering under her load of rabbits, the young men and the old men and women and children beheld her with wonder; and no hunter in that town thought of comparing himself with the Maiden Huntress of K'yawana Tehua-tsana. The old man and the old woman, who had mourned the night through and sat up anxiously watching, were overcome with happiness when they saw their daughter returning; and as she laid the rabbits at their feet, she said: "Behold! my father and my mother, foolish have I been, and much danger have I passed through, because I forgot the ways of a woman and assumed the ways of a man. But two wondrous youths have taught me that a woman may be a huntress and yet never leave her own fireside. Behold! I will marry, when some good youth comes to me, and he will hunt rabbits and deer for me, for my parents and my children."

So, one day, when one of those youths who had seen her come in laden with rabbits, and who had admired her time out of mind, presented himself with a bundle at the maiden's fireside, behold! she smilingly and delightedly accepted him. And from that day to this, when women would hunt rabbits or deer, they marry, and behold, the rabbits and deer are hunted.

Thus shortens my story.

From *Zuñi Folk Tales* (New York: G. P. Putnam's Sons, 1901), pp. 297–309.

Átahsaia, the Cannibal Demon

[*This story tells how the twin war gods, Áhaiyúta and Mátsailéma, rescue two girls and kill the last of the monsters who troubled the Corn People in the days of the new. Only the conclusion of the story is presented here, for the glimpse it provides of these two gods in their characteristic playful mood.—Ed.*]

Now, when the maidens disappeared among the rocks below, the brothers looked each at the other and laughed. Then they shouted, and Áhaiyúta kicked Átahsaia's ugly carcass till it gurgled, at which the two boys shouted again most hilariously and laughed. "That's what we proposed to do with you, old beast!" they cried out.

"But brother younger," said Áhaiyúta, "what shall be done with him now!"

"Let's skin him," said Mátsailéma.

So they set to work and skinned the body from foot to head, as one skins a fawn when one wishes to make a seed-bag. Then they put sticks into the legs and arms, and tied strings to them, and stuffed the body with dry grass and moss; and where they set the thing up against the cliff it looked verily like the living Átahsaia.

"Uhh! what an ugly beast he was!" said Mátsailéma. Then he shouted: "*Wahaha, hihiho!*" and almost doubled up with laughter. "Won't we have fun with old grandmother, though. Hurry up; let's take care of the rest of him!"

They cut off the head, and Áhaiyúta said to it: "*Thou hast been a liar, and told a falsehood for every life thou has taken in the world; therefore shalt thou become a lying star, and each night thy guilt shall be seen of all men throughout the wide world.*" He twirled the bloody head around once or twice, and cast it with all might into the air. *Wa muu!* it sped through the spaces into the middle of the sky like a spirt of blood, and now it is a great red star. It rises in summer-time and tells of the coming morning when it is only midnight; hence it is called *Mokwanosana* (Great Lying Star).

Then Mátsailéma seized the great knife and ripped open the abdomen with one stroke. Grasping the intestines, he tore them out and exclaimed:"*Ye have devoured and digested the flesh of men over the whole wide world; therefore he shall be stretched from one end of the earth to the other, and the children of those ye have wasted will look upon ye every night and will say to one another: 'Ah, the entrails of him who caused sad thoughts to our grandfathers shine well tonight!' and they will laugh and sneer at ye.*" Whereupon he slung the whole mass aloft, and *tsolo!* it stretched from one end of the world to the other, and became the Great Snow-drift of the Skies (Milky Way). Lifting the rest of the carcass, they threw it down into the chasm whither the old demon had thrown so many of his victims, and the rattlesnakes came out and ate of the flesh day after day till their fangs grew yellow with putrid meat, and even now their children's fangs are yellow and poisonous.

"Now, then, for some fun!" shouted Mátsailéma. "Do you catch the old bag up and prance around with it a little; and I will run off to see how it looks."

Áhaiyúta caught up the effigy, and, hiding himself behind, pulled at the strings till it looked, of all things thinkable, like the living Átahsaia himself starting out for a hunt, for they threw the lion skins over it and tied the bow in its hand.

"Excellent! Excellent!" exclaimed the boys, and they clapped their hands and *wa-ha-ha-ed* and *ho-ho-ho-ed* till they were sore. Then, dragging the skin along, they ran as fast as they could, down to the plain below Twin Mountain.

The Sun was climbing down the western ladder, and their old grandmother had been looking all over the mountains and valleys below to see if the two boys were coming. She had just climbed the ladder and was gazing and fretting and saying: "Oh! those two boys! terrible pests and as hard-hearted and as long-winded in having their own way as a turtle is in having his! Now, something has happened to them; I knew it would," when suddenly a frightened scream came up from below.

"*Ho-o-o-ta! Ho-o-o-ta!* Come quick! Help! Help!" the voice cried, as if in anguish.

"Uhh!" exclaimed the old woman, and she went so fast in her excitement that she tumbled through the trap-door, and then jumped up, scolding and groaning.

She grabbed a poker of piñon, and rushed out of the house. Sure enough, there was poor Mátsailéma running hard and calling again and again for her to hurry down. The old woman hobbled along over the rough path as fast as she could, and until her wind was blowing shorter and shorter, when, suddenly turning around the crags, she caught sight of Áhaiyúta struggling to get away from Átahsaia.

"*O ai o!* I knew it! I knew it!" cried the old woman; and she ran faster than ever until she came near enough to see that her poor grandson was almost tired out, and that Mátsailéma had lost even his war-club. "Stiffen your feet,—my boys,—wait—a bit," puffed the old women, and, flying into a passion, she rushed at the effigy and began to pound it with her poker, till the dust fairly smoked out of the dry grass, and the skin doubled up as if it were in pain.

Mátsailéma rolled and kicked in the grass, and Áhaiyúta soon had to let the stuffed demon fall down for sheer laughing. But the old woman never ceased. She belabored the demon and cursed his cannibal heart and told him that was what he got for chasing her grandsons, and that, and that, and that, whack! whack! without stopping, until she thought the monster surely must be dead. Then she was about to rest when suddenly the boys pulled the strings, and the demon sprang up before her, seemingly as well as ever. Again the old woman fell to, but her strokes kept getting feebler and feebler, her breath shorter and shorter, until her wind went out and she fell to the ground.

How the boys did laugh and roll on the ground when the old grandmother moaned: "Alas! alas! This day—my day—light is—cut off—and my wind of life—fast going."

The old woman covered her head with her tattered mantle; but when she found that Átahsaia did not move, she raised her eyes and looked through a rent. There were her two grandsons rolling and kicking on the grass and holding their mouths with both hands, their eyes swollen and faces red with laughter. Then she suddenly looked for the demon. There lay the skin, all torn and battered out of shape.

"So ho! you pesky wretches; that's the way you treat me, is it? Well! never again will I help you, never!" she snapped, "nor shall you ever live with me more!" Whereupon the old woman jumped up and hobbled away.

But little did the brothers care. They laughed till she was far away, and then said one to the other: "It is done!"

Since that time, the grandmother has gone, no one knows where. But Áhaiyúta and Mátsailéma are the bright stars of the morning and evening, just in front of and behind the Sun-father himself. Yet their spirits hover over their shrines on Thunder Mountain and the Mount of the Beloved, they say, or linger over the Middle of the World, forever to guide the games and to guard the warriors of the Land of Zuñi. Thus it was in the days of the ancients.

Thus shortens my story.

From *Zuñi Folk Tales* (New York: G. P. Putnam's Sons, 1901), pp. 379–84.

 IV. ZUÑI COMES EAST

Zuñi Comes East

In 1882, prompted both by reasons of his own and by the repeated urging of his Zuñi hosts, Cushing arranged a trip east with five Indian companions. The Indians were eager for the trip as an opportunity to bring back to Zuñi some of the sacred water of the "Ocean of Sunrise"; for Cushing it was a chance to perform a service that would promote his acceptance into the cult of the *Kâ'-kâ*. The tour, including public appearances in Washington, Boston, and elsewhere, a meeting with the president, and a visit to Wellesley College, attracted national attention and made Cushing a famous man.[1] The selection following, however, concerns a second Zuñi visit in the East.

In his letter to Professor Baird proposing the original tour, Cushing mentions the enthusiasm for this project expressed by certain "ladies of Boston." Such a lady of Boston was Mrs. Mary Hemenway, whose husband, Augustus, had made a fortune in shipping. When Cushing found himself again in the East several years later, on sick leave and at loose ends after his recall from Zuñi, Mrs. Hemenway came to the rescue with the offer of a cottage on her estate. This piece of good fortune was soon improved upon by her arranging for a second pilgrimage east by three Zuñi friends to pay homage to the Ocean of the East and to aid Cushing in his work. It was during this visit that the stories later collected in *Zuñi Folk Tales* were first recorded—by a stenographer who took down Cushing's impromptu translations in sessions with the Zuñi storyteller Waihusiwa.

Accompanied on the journey east by Cushing's elder brother Enos (who had joined Cushing in Zuñi and stayed on there after his departure), and hosted for a time by Cushing's parents at the family farm near Albion, New York, the Indians arrived at the Hemenway establishment on the Massachusetts coast in mid-August of 1886 for a stay which extended over several months. The following selections are taken from Cushing's extensive notes recording the conversation of his Zuñi friends during this visit—whose sequel was Mrs. Hemenway's sponsorship of the ambitious archeological explorations conducted by Cushing in Arizona in the late 1880s under the aegis of the Hemenway Southwestern Expedition. The notes, some eighty typewritten pages of them, are among the Cushing papers in the Southwest Museum. In them we see Cushing in the reverse role of host to the Zuñis—a role which entails at times an embarrassment rather like that of a country boy fallen into the decadent ways of the city and trying to look innocent before the parents who have found him there. More important, but still through the medium of Cushing's art as observer, translator, and storyteller, we see the Zuñis taking in—taking the measure of—the land of their colonizers. Their perceptions should have a place among the keenest of those recorded by foreign visitors to this strange North American republic.

Note

1. For an account of this tour, see Sylvester Baxter, "An Aboriginal Pilgrimage."

Notes Made during a Visit of Palowahtiwa, Waihusiwa, and Heluta at Manchester-by-the-sea, Massachusetts, 1886

August 13, 1886
... Mrs. Hemenway invited a party of friends to be present at my meeting with the Indians.... It may be imagined that I awaited with great interest this arrival. Mrs. Hemenway and her friends were gathered together in the drawingroom of Casa Romona, as we have named it, while I went forth to meet the carriage as we saw it turning the corner of the lawn. When the carriage stopped before the door, my old brother Palowahtiwa was the first to descend, closely followed by the others. Before he had fairly stepped to the porch, he extended his hands and grasped mine, and, withdrawing a little under the shade of the awning, he placed his arms around me, and began the usual prayer of greeting between two members of the priestly order of the Zuñi who have been long separated.

. . . .

[From Palowahtiwa's account of the journey east, translated by Cushing:]
"That night we came to [Albion, New York]. Here we rested very pleasantly all night. The next day sometime came your father, Thomasy Cushie, with your elder brother, younger than the other, and some friend or relative young man, in an ample wagon, and we understood that they had come to take us to the home of your mother. Said your father, Thomasy Cushie, to your elder brother (or so we supposed he said, 'Do these young men speak Mexican or Spanish?' 'No,' said your elder brother, 'but the oldest one' (myself) 'understands it well'—whereby we were

led to suppose, ah, ha!, in journeying to the home of his mother with his father, Thomasy Cushie, we will not go as people dumb for want of hearing, but entertained with conversation. Now, therefore, when we entered the wagon, and had driven on some way (I was sitting between your father, Thomasy Cushie, and your elder-brother-younger-than-the-other), we all turned our faces and eyes expectantly upon your father. And thus we drove on for a long way, and still with our eyes and faces turned expectantly in the direction of your father, Thomasy Cushie. Now, your elder-brother-younger-than-the-other is a man who does not speak much, but jokes much without speaking. When he saw how my ears were turned towards your father, Thomasy Cushie, who had his head bowed as though he were thinking of something he had forgotten, he, this brother of yours, who has a hard thumb, extended it out from his hand and punched my knees with it, and smiled under concealment with his eyes, whereat we all laughed exceedingly, and nodded our heads and intensified our expectancy. Still we drove along in silence, . . . on and on, would you believe it, until we reached the identical little valley that descends past the home of your mother, and when we had come to the home of the horses, which, as you know, is somewhat this side of the home of your mother, once in Spanish spake Thomasy Cushie, 'Aqui mi casa' ('Here my house'). 'Indeed, my poor father,' said I, 'do you live with your horses now?' 'Well,' we said to one another, 'when water or speech begins to flow, it is more likely to continue.' And we began to query as well as listen, but no other word did he say to us. . . .

"One day they took us away from the home of your mother in a wagon to Tchotchi's Village [Albion], where, towards evening, your brother Enosy placed us in a room all by ourselves, with large bowls of metal and wood, which they filled with hot water. Then they gave us foam cake and big brushes, and told us to wash ourselves, which we did with great pleasure. And that night, behold, we entered into a house of the iron road, with beds like the shelves in a wall, where we slept until morning. Now, here we are, thanks be to the beloved! After growing strong with anxiety many times and much, we behold one another, my younger brother, and grasp each other with warm hands. I know this country perfectly well. It is the border land of the world.

FIG. 71. The First Sight of the Atlantic, at Boston, 1882. (From Baxter, "An Aboriginal Pilgrimage")

Why, over yonder," said the old man, extending his hand exactly in the direction of Deer Island, "over yonder, out of sight from here, we made our first greetings and prayers to the beloved of the water."

. . . .

As soon as our pleasant party had broken up to prepare for dinner, I led the Indians to the suite of rooms in Casa Romona which Mrs. Hemenway had set aside for their use. They were delighted with them but thought them too many at first. They spoke of the rest and pleasure they would have in them; but lingering only a little to examine them, mentioned a wish to visit the rocky shore below and make their prayers to the Beloved of the Ocean. . . .

One characteristic of the Indians during the whole evening's conversation was conspicuous, namely, an apparent studied effort on their part to avoid all allusion to the natural features of the scenes by which they had been surrounded during the day. Later Professor Morse asked me why they did not speak of what they had seen. I told this to the Indians, on our way up from prayers at the waterside that morning. They were walking at my side. Both stopped, and turned, and looked at me intently for a moment. "What should one say," said Heluta, "if one should see so much water as this, having always believed that in all the world not so much could be seen, though having known all his life that there was this much and even much more? When an eater of food comes into the presences of the Beloved, though he see them not, is there anything to be said? What could we say, when to say anything would only show how little our thoughts, instead of how great?"

. . . .

August 19, 1886

For the first time since they arrived here, my Zuñi companions discussed at some length today the ocean. "You say," Heluta questioned me, "that one can cross these waters; that while they are not a river, yet they are not endless but in very truth the embracing waters of the world?" I said, "Yes, that is so." Said he, "In what particular direction is it shortest, this journey across these waters?" I pointed in the eastward direction. "How many days, were it possible, would a man journey on foot to cross them?" "I do not know," said I. Said he, "As many days as would be required for crossing from this country to Zuñi, and beyond to California—so many, I think." "No," said I, "more, certainly; as many days as would be required for going to and returning from the land of Zuñi." "And yet," said Palowahtiwa, "the great sailing chests which move by means of coal and steam, travel as fast, I am told, as the iron horses and their string of houses. This being so, the journey might be made much sooner, I conceive." "Yes," said I, "it may be made in eight days and nights of constant travel, providing the winds and water do not oppose their progress." "Ah, these Americans!" exclaimed Waihusiwa. "How far is it across these waters in a south-easterly direction, or a southern direction, through their middle?" asked Heluta. "Almost endlessly far," said I, "for a sailing chest of coal and steam might pass southward over the middle of these waters a full month without the appearance of land on any horizon." "Wonderful! Wonderful!" said he. "Yet probably," said I, "at the end of that time, perhaps sooner, it may be that something like land would be found, for at the extreme southern end of the world great mountains of ice sail amidst the waters and rear themselves from them; and beyond, over these mountains, are everlasting fields of snow. No one has passed into that region." "Not even the Americans?" asked Waihusiwa. "Not even the Americans," said I. "How is this?" said Palowahtiwa. "Towards the south, say our traditions, lies the land of everlasting summer and never cooling waters, and toward the north the land where the snows lie forever. How is this?" "What your ancients have said is true," said I. "But beyond the land of everlasting summer comes again, as in the north, the region where the snow lies forever, which is the end of the world." "I see," said Palowahtiwa, "neither by heat, nor by danger, nor by any difficulty whatever, can the wandering of the Americans be restrained, but by cold and snow and ice individually put to them." "Yes," said I, "that is true, and yet again and again have they tried to pass over the ends of the world. For instance, during the last year I spent in Zuñi, an expedition of many Americans was fitted out to penetrate into the great ice country of the north. They sailed away under a captain of the Army named Greeley. They sailed in the middle of summer, and at last entered the region of eternal ice and snow which lay upon those waters, and through a wide track broken in them proceeded further than ever before any American had done. But at last the ice closed in upon them, and broke some of their vessels, and cast others high in the air, as it were, so that some of the men died, and those who remained hastened to make houses of the wrecks of their sailing chests, and remained there month after month, consuming their substance until it was all gone. Some of them died of cold, others of starvation. They became like corpse demons in appearance, and like corpse demons at last began to consume one another." Here the attention of the three was absolutely rigid. "Yes, they consumed one another, and not long after I returned, vessel after vessel having sailed to rescue them, they were at last found, those remaining alive, five or seven of them, and were brought to their own country. I saw some of them, and they were fearful to look upon; their flesh was wasted away, and their eyes were sunken deep into their sockets. For this reason it is rare that Americans attempt to pass into the regions beyond; yet they sometimes so attempt it, and will until they either perish or find their way through."

"Strange people, strange people, these Americans!" said they. "And beyond these mountains of ice and snow is the home of the beloved gods," said Palowahtiwa. "True, no doubt," said the others; and Heluta added, "Yes, beyond those mountains of ice and snow are waters like these, and still beyond, no doubt, a great and beautiful world wherein the gods dwell in peace. Ah, the gods know full well the passions of the Americans, and they girdle their world about with barriers impassable by the eaters of food (mortals)." "Such indeed are the Americans," remarked one of them. "Though we Indians live in a poor and dried-up country, though we may love them not, and treat them despitefully, yet they gather around us and come into our country continually, and even strive to get our land from us. Is it possible for any one to say what they want? Where is there a country more beautiful than this we are sitting in now? Is there any water needed here? Without irrigation, on the very tops of the mountains and hills things grow green, and there is water to drink."

"Yes, and to spare," said Waihusiwa. "What a shame that so much water should be wasted as now lies before us, contributing neither to the good of men nor the sustenance of the earth!"

"In that water," said Palowahtiwa, "there are many other creatures, which may be quite as important as men. To their sustenance the water contributes; it is therefore not wasted."

"True! I had not thought of that," said Waihusiwa. "Yes, the Americans have all this; they have enough to eat and to spare; though their houses and villages lie scattered over the land as thickly as the pine woods and sage brush in Zuñi land, still they

FIG. 72. The Reception at Wellesley College, First Trip East, 1882. (From Baxter, "An Aboriginal Pilgrimage")

have enough to eat and enough to wear, and what they eat and what they wear are also of the best."

"Well, it is not only that," said Heluta, "but the sentiment of home affects them not; the little bits of land they may own, or the house they may have been bred in, are as nothing to them; and, more than all, their thoughts do not seem to dwell contentedly even on their own wives and children, for they wander incessantly, wander through all difficulties and dangers, to seek new places and better things. Why is it they are so unceasingly unsatisfied?"

"I think why," said Palowahtiwa; "above every people they are a people of emulation; above every kind of man or being a people of fierce jealousies. Is not this an explanation?"

"Why, even so," exclaimed the others.

"Most certainly so," said Palowahtiwa. "And if one American goes one day's journey in the direction of a difficult trail, it is not long ere another American will go two days' journey in the direction of a more difficult one. One American cannot bear that another shall surpass him. Ho! were it possible, no American would be taller than another one. Is it extraordinary, then, that the gods begirt their dwelling places with barriers of ice and snow, and fatal unceasing cold, or that they dwell in the lands above the skies or the regions under the world?"

. . . .

When Palowahtiwa had completed his evening meal, he rose from his chair and stood behind it as if waiting for something. He stood very quietly, eyeing me intently as I ate, but saying nothing. After a while I asked him what disturbed his thoughts. "You," said he. "Six days I have been here. So many days I have observed you. So far as I can see, you are an American, not a Zuñi. My younger brother, I am waiting for you."

"I will follow shortly," said I.

"It is well," said Palowahtiwa. "When you were in Zuñi you established an allegiance with the beloved of Zuñi" (referring to the gods); "you became their child, as we are their children. Are you not now as then, their relative? A father once, or a son, is forever a father or son. It occurs to me that you have not kept this in mind, and that you have neglected to sacrifice and pray to the gods."

"When my prayer meal gave out, I ceased to pray as a Zuñi," said I, "but according to the faith of my ancestors I have not failed to pray."

"Nor would I have you fail to pray according to the faith of your ancestors," said Palowahtiwa, "and even so I would not have you fail to pray according to the faith of our ancestors. You will and you must pray and sacrifice thrice daily hereafter. Why deceive yourself? You are still a Zuñi. In the morning you will cast forth to the gods prayer meal and sacred speeches, at midday while the sun rests, and at sunset. This you must do. I shall see to it."

. . . .

September 22, 1886

On the occasion of the third of the religious exercises at Mrs. Hemenway's home . . . I translated to the Zuñis a part of the selected readings of the day—preceding this translation by a short story of Christ, as follows:

"My brothers, younger and elder, this ancient record says that there was once a being, the God himself, as it were, who, that he might teach men the better ways of living, assumed the form of a man, the flesh of a man, and the ways of a man. He, one of the Beloved, for the sake of the children of the world, was content to submit to all manner of humiliation and the suffering consequent to poverty and the lowest estate of a man, and he went about on foot throughout the cities of the land, teaching, and was reviled, unloved, cast away, and even made captive and killed by men whom he had come to benefit."

"No other," said Palowahtiwa, "than the story of Poshai-ank'ya, the father of our sacred societies of worship."[1]

"This story is much the same," said I; "it may be some part of the same, for even as Poshaiank'ya was despised and cast away as he journeyed from one city of men to another, even as he was poor as the poorest, so indeed was this Beloved One, a man only in his disguise."

"Is it possible that this is so?" asked the two younger men, "that the Americans also have this ancient tradition?"

"It is of course possible; it is only to be expected," said Palowahtiwa, "for all ancient religion, unbroken by the interpolation of modern guesses, having one source, must be in effect at least the same."

. . . .

"In all councils of worshippers, amongst those who look on," said Palowahtiwa, "there are some young ones who are foolish. Are there not among you such unwise young ones, who might say, for example, that all this sacred writing of yours" (pointing to the great Bible which lay upon the table) "is but paper, common paper which any one might roll into cigarettes and smoke away? Even so, there are some among us who say of our ancient sacred plumes and medicines that they are nothing but old turkey feathers and eagle plumes, crumpled and broken, old cotton strings, musty and worn out, and broken bits of beads and shell stuck in a lump of clay and pitch mixed with cornmeal. But as the wise among you would say to these foolish ones of yours, 'This ancient writing is nothing but paper, it is true, yet wrapped up in its heart, as it were, is something else, with a wise and precious meaning.' So also our wise ones would say to these foolish ones, 'Ye see not into the hearts of these things. True it is that these are only musty old plumes, broken beads and cornmeal and pitch tied up with rotten cords; yet the gods gave these medicines and powers, which are still there, that we might through them supplicate for all the surrounding cities of men, from the sunrise even unto the sunset, the seeds of earth for food, the water of life for drink. So, verily, the meaning and potentiality that are wrapped up in these old plumes are such that they are too precious to be bought by the largest herd of horses in the world."

. . . .

Referring to a reverie which I had had as a vision during the year last past, I said to Palowahtiwa, "I heard the most wonderful and incomprehensible thing at the home of my friend on the island west of here. I would tell it to you if I thought you would understand it, but you will not, and it is better that I should not tell it to you."

After smoking a long time in silence, he said to me, "Why should it not be understood that a brother should be direct with his brother, and why should this brother not comprehend him in a straight and perfect way, even so that this foolish act, our hiding of important facts from one another, should not be done?"

"Very well," said I. "As many days ago as this (a year ago) I had been very ill, as you know, and I was sitting one day in front of my house, red all around me, for the trees were turning red and yellow with cold, and the sun was red in the smoky western sky; and it was said to me by some one, whom I seemed to see in the form of an ordinary man—as plainly and circumstantially as this it was said to me, 'You are not what you seem to be; you are not an American, you yourself, but you are an Indian, truly an Indian, disguised as it were in the flesh of an American. Do you not mind how you were born before your time, not being perfected in your mother's womb? You are the soul of an Indian of olden times, you yourself, in the flesh of an American. Therefore as a child you led the life of an Indian. Therefore you had eyes to see, as a dog on the trail has nostrils to smell, the places of your true people; and

FIG. 73. Burying the Sacred Plume-Sticks in the Ocean. (From Baxter, "An Aboriginal Pilgrimage")

you sought out where others could not find them their remains, and gathered them together, and placed them in your little room and slept surrounded by them. Therefore you went where others of your race had not gone, and lived the life of an Indian in Zuñi. Therefore you quickly learned to understand what others would not or could not understand, his thoughts and his language. Therefore you foresaw, years before, the finding of the shrine of Ahaiyuta and Matsailema in the caves of Arizona, where others had not found them, in a land which you knew of neither by sight nor by hearing. Was not this because you were to become one of the initiates, understanding the things pertaining to these shrines? I say to you, you are not an American, though you think yourself one, believe yourself one, and would laugh at this strange fancy, not understanding it; but sometime you will understand it well, when you shall have come to understand better the Zuñi language and Zuñi life, and all will be well, that it may be well.'

"This, my brother, did I hear, this strange and most incomprehensible speech. You laugh; I knew you would."

The old man had been leaning forward toward me as I recited this to him, and smiling, and he continued to smile and laugh in a low, perfectly satisfied sort of way. "Certainly," said he, "you don't understand it; and it was because you didn't understand it that you thought I could not. You don't understand and you don't believe what I perfectly understand and fully believe of what you yourself have told me. Was this a daylight being who spoke to you, did it seem such?"

"I don't know, my brother," said I. "It may have been a dream, it may have been a reverie. It was as if it were a man speaking to me according to the strange beliefs of other parts of the world than that which I live in."

"You don't understand it, I repeat," said he. "How long had it been since you had sacrificed any plumes, or properly and perfectly said the rituals relating to that part of our worship with which you were connected? You need not answer, for I know. You had not sacrificed one solitary plume after leaving Zuñi, and you had not prayed with any regularity whatsoever, nor had you ever prayed with any due sincerity, according to the forms of worship which you had deliberately adopted. Now, this is why you seemed to hear the things which were told to you; and it was fortunate on the whole that one of the Masters of Life and the World should deem it worth his while to instruct you with such a reverie, rather than let you be utterly cut off while a young man. You will get well. If this thing, and as I suspect other things like it, had not happened, we might conclude that you would not get well. It seems now that you did not understand your fathers, the priests of the Knife Order in Zuñi, when they performed over you the ceremonials which made you one of their children, a member of the Priesthood of the Bow. Do you remember the ritual and the incantation which they pronounced over you, saying that had you not been chosen, even before you were born, to become one of the number of the children of their gods and your gods, you would not have become so; saying that in the times most ancient you were of the membership of their family, like to them, because you were to become like them. This ceremonial of your fathers, the laying on of all the sacred black paint, the laying on of the yellow paint, the distributing over your person of the sacred apparel and the symbolic down of the eagle, this was only that you might be brought to the surface and see yourself in your relation with these the fathers, which you had not been aware of before, and which it seems, forsooth, you did not become aware of then. Don't you remember how they laid these things upon you, repeating the prayers and incantations, which should have informed you of as much as I have told you? And when you went not out from the dance, don't you remember how they took these things off from you, waving them up and down your person, that, knowing yourself to be, however humble, of the company of the gods, you might resume your relations with man as a man? With those prayers and incantations they placed in your hands the weapons of your order, symbolic of its functions and of your relations to those among the Beloved who have charge of those functions, placing across your breast the sacred badge of your membership, last of all crowning you and your being with the precious and sacred symbol, the head-plume, as it were, of avowal before men of this your relationship, which had existed, because it would become so in daylight, from the times when all things were new.

"Do you understand any better now the thing which you thought I could not understand?"

During this appeal to me, Palowahtiwa repeated long paragraphs of the rituals and incantations to which he referred, giving to them by the context, here so imperfectly written down, a newer and deeper meaning than I had ever attached to them before. Some excuse exists for this in the fact that they are couched in archaic forms of expression, which even now I understand only to a limited degree, notwithstanding the fact that I have been initiated.

Palowahtiwa continued: "I will now relate to you an incident which occurred long, long ago in my own life: My uncles and fathers and elder relatives, mostly all of them, had gone to Taya and Heshota-tsina (Los Ojos de los Pescados), to plant, it being spring time. I was very, very sick, therefore did not go with them. I was a comparatively young man then, and had not long since married the wife, who is your sister older, and we were living in a large room, part of the house of my father below, where she your sister was nursing and caring for me, as I lay there day after day, by the side of the fire-place; and my uncle, the father of Mana, whom you know, he brought wood for us from time to time. And I became worse and worse, day after day, and it was said that it was finally not well with me, and the message was sent to my elder relatives and others at Taya and Heshota-tsina. And before they had time to come, I was dying, it seems, for I was become but bones with skin over them, and weak of breath, and very slow of heart. And thus I was lying one day in the afternoon, and the light was coming in through the window at the end of the room, but I did not see it. In daylight it grew dark, and it was bad for me but a very short time, for I had forgotten all things. Then I saw again, and the light was coming through the window at the end of the room, brighter than before, so that all things were clear to me, very clear; and as I looked round the room, wondering that everything was so much better than it had been for so long, but still lying there by the side of the fire-place, yet feeling that I need no longer lie there, I saw a broad-shouldered, good-sized man coming towards me, he having opened and passed through the door. I did not know him. He was dressed in the ancient costume of my people, with red buckskin leggings, good and strong, red buckskin breeches, tight and smooth, with buttons of brass upon them—for you will remember that our people at one time had no silver and used brass for their buttons and bracelets and earrings—and he wore the olden coat of my people, woven by their own hands, and not of the thin cloth of the Americans; and round his head, stiff, like that which you have on your wrist," said Palowahtiwa, stretching out his finger and touching my cuff, "and white, was his head-band, which was the kind of head-band worn by our people when the cloth of foreigners was most expensive and rare. His hair was fine and heavy, and as black as the hair of a youth, though he was a somewhat old man. His head-knot was fine and large, and most properly arranged. He looked like a friend of mine and a relative, but I did not know him. He came toward me, holding in one hand, which was extended towards the door, a riata, as though he had led a horse behind him. Then he stood over me, and looked down at me and smiled, not greeting me in the least, except by this word, 'Keshi' " (which may be translated "Is everything arranged?" or "Is it all in readiness?"). "Then he said to me, 'Would you like to go with me?' And I looked at him and said, 'Why not? But I do not know you,' said I, looking at him, as though against a strong light, with my hand shading my eyes. 'I seem to know you, yet I do not.'

" 'My child,' said he, smiling, 'it is not surprising that you do not know me. I am your grand-grand uncle, and went away from Zuñi a long, long time ago, long enough surely before you were in the womb of your mother.'

" 'Ah, yes!' said I.

" 'Now, are you ready to go with me?'

" 'Yes,' said I.

" 'It is well,' said he. 'In order that this journey, which is long, might not seem strange to you, I have brought a couple of fine horses, such as my people used and I see your people use constantly now-a-days. Everything is in readiness for you. The horse is saddled and bridled, and is a good horse. Come, let us go.' And he turned to gather up the riata and lead me towards the door, and I was rising from my bed easily enough, when there appeared, not coming through the wall opposite, but already through the wall, the form of a little old man, dressed in the most ancient costume of my people. White was his apparel, with leggings of knotted cotton, soft and in figures, fringed down the front of the leg, with embroidered breech-clout, and embroidered wide-sleeved cotton coat; and his hair was as white as snow, and very long, falling down either side of his head in front, and done up in a strange old-fashioned knot behind. His face was surely pleasant, but very old, and he was short, not as high as the lower part of the window. Though so very old, he walked with an easy and majestic tread, noiselessly, more so than the wind. He came toward my uncle, reached out his hand and laid it on my uncle's sleeve, and said to him, 'What are you doing here, my son?'

" 'I have come for this, our child,' replied my uncle.

" 'Why!' said the old man, looking at him not sharply, but in a commanding way, 'he is not ready yet. You must not take him away. Go back! go back, my son!' said he. 'For many years he will not be ready.'

" 'But he is ready,' said my uncle, dropping his head on his breast and beginning to gather up the riata.

" 'We are not ready, if he be,' said the old man. 'Leave him and go.'

"My uncle turned, not sadly, but thoughtfully, and disappeared through the door.

"Then the old man turned towards me and came to where I was lying, looking at me. 'My son,' said he, 'it is not time for you to go yet. We do not wish it. One sometimes learns wisdom through great illness. Therefore you have been ill. You have been so ill that it has been said, "He will go." But you will not go, no. For many a long year you will not go; you will become old, even as I am, before you go. Your hair will be white, your face will be wrinkled, and you will grow shorter as you have heretofore grown taller, year after year. Were you to go now, one fewer would be those in the world where so many once dwelt who give us those attentions which we cherish, who sacrifice plumes of worship to us, as was directed in ancient times, who pray to us and greet us, and show that our children among men have not forgotten us. These things are most acceptable to us; we would not miss them from one individual, so few are they who are left among our priests, whose time is not measured out and who has not properly and in a finished manner reached the dividing line of the light of his life. Live, my child! live many a long year, until you, even as I am, are old. A few days, and your flesh will begin to gather upon your bones, and as you were, so will you become again. And although it may not be pleasant to you to think that you must endure illness and suffering, and many unhappinesses, yet know it is best that this should be so. Live! become well! and when the time has come for you to go, it will be said, "Yes," and we will come for you. Farewell. Be it even as I have said.' And the little old man turned, and I lost sight of him, and everything grew dark again, and in a moment I heard the people crying, crying, crying about me, and they began chafing my hands and feet, for they thought I had even died."

From "Notes Made during a Visit of Palowahtiwa, Waihusiwa, and Heluta at Manchester-by-the-Sea, Massachusetts, 1886." Box No. 1, Hodge-Cushing Collection, Southwest Museum, Los Angeles. Printed with the permission of the Southwest Museum.

Note

1. "*Pó-shai-an-k'ia*, the God (Father) of the Medicine societies or sacred esoteric orders, of which there are twelve in Zuñi, and others among the different pueblo tribes. He is supposed to have appeared in human form, poorly clad, and therefore reviled by men; to have taught the ancestors of the Zuñi, Taos, Oraibi, and Coconino Indians their agricultural and other arts, their systems of worship by means of plumed and painted prayer-sticks; to have organized their medicine societies; and then to have disappeared toward his home in *Shí-pä-pu-li-ma* (from *shí-pi-a* = mist, vapor; *u-lin* = surrounding; and *i-mo-na* = sitting place of—"The mist-enveloped city"), and to have vanished beneath the world, whence he is said to have departed for the home of the Sun. He is still the conscious auditor of the prayers of his children, the invisible ruler of the spiritual *Shí-pä-pu-li-ma*, and of the lesser gods of the medicine orders, the principal "Finisher of the Paths of our Lives." He is, so far as any identity can be established, the "Montezuma" of popular and usually erroneous Mexican tradition" ("Zuñi Fetiches," p. 15). [Ed. note]

Epilogue

On December 13, 1886, together with Cushing and others of
the Hemenway Expedition party, Palowahtiwa, Waihusiwa, and
Heluta set out on the return journey to Zuñi. Already it was not a
destination so distant from the East as it had been when Cushing
first made his way there in 1879, for the railroad had by now
advanced through Fort Wingate, a mere thirty miles from Zuñi.
Here, according to Hodge's diary of the expedition, the travelers
arrived December 18, and after a day's stopover proceeded on
their way, camping on the trail the night of the twentieth and
arriving in Zuñi on the twenty-first, to be greeted with much
embracing and hand shaking by the entire village.

For Cushing's group this was the beginning of a history-
making venture in southwestern archeology whose aim was to
unearth the keys to the Pueblo past linking Zuñi with the ancient
civilizations of Mexico and Central America. For the Zuñis, both
homecomers and welcomers, the occasion, from a different
perspective, could be seen as not quite the beginning any more
of a long process linking them with the civilization of the modern
Americans. Cushing, indeed, much as he identified with Zuñi
traditionalism and with the ways of the ancients whose remains
and ruins he studied, was himself, by his very presence in Zuñi,
not to mention his part in the Zuñi pilgrimages to the East, a force
in promoting this process. His own recognition of this aspect of
his role is explicitly conveyed in a speech he gave later before
the Board of Indian Commissioners, "The Need of Studying the
Indian in Order to Teach Him"—a piece reminding us that in

addition to the boy arrow chipper who went on, sanctioned by anthropological purpose, to become "truly an Indian," Bow Priest and War Chief, and to the anthropologist who lived with savages for the sake of knowledge and science, there was a third Cushing, at least, who saw himself as contributing to the eventual assimilation of the Indians as their own archaic culture inevitably gave way to the more advanced.

The speech to the Indian Commissioners, delivered two years before Cushing's death, testifies eloquently to the complexity of his position with respect both to the Indians and to his own role as scientist and government representative. Regarding as a foregone conclusion the outcome of the native Americans' "sadly unequal struggle," he took the government's proper task to be that of helping fit them "to survive among us and not be further degraded or utterly destroyed." However, nothing good could come, he argued, from trying to force them to give up their traditions in favor of Christianity and the ways of civilization.

> For with them, sociologic organization and government and the philosophy and daily usages of life are still so closely united with [their] religion that all their customs, which we consider so absurd and useless, grow from it as naturally and directly as plants grow from the soil. . . . We do not want to go to them, then, and weaken their sense of morality founded on the traditions they believe, and so venerate, by saying that these are wrong; for we never in a lifetime, with the utmost effort and labor, can blot out of their minds what their fathers and mothers have taught them, when young, of reverence for these traditions, and replace it with equally influential reverence for our own.[1]

What was needed, he urged, was true understanding, intimate acquaintance with the Indian's "very nature, his mood of mind, his usages, his attitudes." Approaching him in brotherhood, we must "learn how he came to be what he is, and thus learn how to make him other than what he is."[2]

Cushing's words, as Curtis M. Hinsley, Jr., perceptively comments, "expressed [a] deep sensitivity . . . based on intimate experience. It was mixed, to be sure, with visions and intellectual edifices that assumed the decline of the red man and celebrated the evolutionary supremacy of the white American. But within the seemingly undeniable general process, there remained much room for the individual human experience, like Cushing's."[3]

Cushing, in any case, was but the first of the anthropologists to be, more or less reluctantly, welcomed to Zuñi. So many have followed, down to the present day, that they themselves have become a phenomenon to study.[4] As for Zuñi itself, whatever else may be said, history continues. Longer under colonial rule than any other town in North America, Zuñi endures. It seems, as the old man told Palowahtiwa in his vision, that the ancients are not yet ready for it to go.

Notes

1. *The Need of Studying the Indian in Order to Teach Him*, pp. 10–12.

2. Ibid., p. 9.

3. Hinsley, "The Development of a Profession: Anthropology in Washington, D.C., 1846–1903," pp. 254–55.

4. Pandey, "Anthropologists at Zuñi." Pandey's list includes, besides Cushing, Matilda Coxe Stevenson, Jesse Walter Fewkes, Alfred Louis Kroeber, Elsie Clews Parsons, Frederick Webb Hodge, Leslie Spier, Ruth Benedict, Ruth Bunzel, Li An-che, Omer C. Stewart, John Adair, John M. Roberts, Tom F. S. McFeat, Bert Kaplan, Jean Cazeneuve, Stanley Newman, Willard B. Walker, and Dennis Tedlock.

Bibliography

Selected Bibliography

Frank Hamilton Cushing's Published Writings

"Antiquities of Orleans County, N.Y." In *Annual Report of the Board of Regents of the Smithsonian Institution, 1874*, pp. 375–77. Washington, D.C., 1875.

"Ancient Cities in Arizona." *American Antiquarian* 10 (1880): 325–26.

"The Zuñi Social, Mythic, and Religious Systems." *Popular Science Monthly*, June 1882, pp. 186–92.

"The Nation of the Willows." *Atlantic Monthly* 50 (1882): 362–74, 541–59. Reprinted in book form with introduction by Robert C. Euler, Flagstaff, Ariz.: Northland Press, 1965.

"My Adventures in Zuñi." *Century Illustrated Monthly Magazine* 25 (1882): 191–207, 500–511, and 26 (1883): 28–47. Edition in book form together with Sylvester Baxter's article "An Aboriginal Pilgrimage" and introduction by E. DeGolyer, Santa Fe: Peripatetic Press, 1941. Facsimile reprint in book form with introduction by Oakah L. Jones, Jr., Palmer Lake, Colo.: Filter Press, 1967.

"Zuñi Fetiches." In *Second Annual Report of the Bureau of American Ethnology, 1880–1881*, pp. 9–45. Washington, D.C., 1883. Facsimile reprint in book form with introduction by Tom Bahti, Flagstaff, Ariz.: KC Publications, 1966. Reprinted, Las Vegas, Nev.: KC Publications, 1974.

"Zuñi Weather Proverbs." *Weather Proverbs*, pp. 124–27. Washington, D.C., 1883.

"Zuñi Breadstuff." *Millstone* 9 (1884), nos. 1–12, and 10 (1885), nos. 1–4, 6–8. Edition in book form with introduction by John Wesley Powell, Indian Notes and Monographs, vol. 8, New York: Museum of the American Indian, Heye Foundation, 1920. Reprinted 1974.

"A Study of Pueblo Pottery as Illustrative of Zuñi Cultural Growth." In

432 SELECTED BIBLIOGRAPHY

Fourth Annual Report of the Bureau of American Ethnology, 1882–1883, pp. 467–521. Washington, D.C., 1886.

"Preliminary Notes on the Origin, Working Hypothesis, and Primary Researches of the Hemenway Southwestern Archaeological Expedition." In *Congres International des Americanistes, Berlin, 1888*, pp. 151–94. Berlin, 1890.

"Manual Concepts: A Study of the Influence of Hand-Usage on Culture Growth." *American Anthropologist* 5 (1892): 289–317.

"The Villard-Bandelier South American Expedition." *American Anthropologist* 5 (1892): 273–76.

"A Zuñi Folk Tale of the Underworld." *Journal of American Folklore* 5 (1892): 49–56.

"The Giant Cloud-Swallower." *Archaeologist* 1 (1893): 241–44.

"Commentary of a Zuñi Familiar." In Edna Dean Proctor, *The Song of the Ancient People*, pp. 25–49. New York: Houghton Mifflin Co., 1893.

"Primitive Copper Working: An Experimental Study." *American Anthropologist* 7 (1894): 93–117.

"The Germ of Shore-land Pottery: An Experimental Study." In *Memoirs of the International Congress of Anthropologists*, pp. 217–34. Chicago, 1894.

"Keresan Indians." In *Johnson's Universal Cyclopaedia*, vol. 4. New York, 1894.

"Pueblo Indians or Pueblos." In *Johnson's Universal Cyclopaedia*, vol. 6. New York, 1895.

"Tañoan or Tanoan Indians." In *Johnson's Universal Cyclopaedia*, vol. 8. New York, 1895.

"Zuñian Indians." In *Johnson's Universal Cyclopaedia*, vol. 8. New York, 1895.

Review of "As to Copper from the Mounds of the St. Johns River, Florida," from Part II of "Certain Sand Mounds of the St. Johns River, Florida." *American Anthropologist* 8 (1895): 185–88.

"A Preliminary Examination of Aboriginal Remains near Pine Island, Marco, West Florida." *American Naturalist* 29 (1895): 1132–35.

"The Arrow." *American Anthropologist* 8 (1895): 307–49.

"Outlines of Zuñi Creation Myths." In *Thirteenth Annual Report of the Bureau of American Ethnology, 1891–1892*, pp. 321–447. Washington, D.C., 1896.

"Discussion of J. Cheston Morris' Address ['The Relation of the Pentagonal Do-decahedron found near Marietta, Ohio, to Shamanism'] and Remarks on Shamanism." *Proceedings of the American Philosophical Society* 36 (1897): 184–92.

"Primitive Motherhood." In *Work and Words of the National Congress of Mothers: First Annual Session Held in the City of Washington, D.C., February 17–19, 1897*, pp. 21–47. New York: D. Appleton & Co., 1897.

"Scarred Skulls from Florida." *American Anthropologist* 10 (1897): 17–18.

"A Case of Primitive Surgery." *Science* n.s. 5 (1897): 977–81.

"The Need of Studying the Indian in Order to Teach Him." In *Twenty-eighth Annual Report of the Board of Indian Commissioners*, pp. 109–15. Washington, D.C., 1897. Reprinted, Albion, New York, 1897.

Tenatsali's Leaves. N.p., n.d. (ca. 1897). A pamphlet of poems, 10 pp.

"Exploration of Ancient Key Dwellers' Remains on the Gulf Coast of Florida," *Proceedings of the American Philosophical Society* 35 (1896): 329–448. Reprinted as *The Pepper-Hearst Expedition: A Preliminary Report on the Explorations of Ancient Key-Dwellers' Remains on the Gulf Coast of Florida*. Philadelphia: MacCalla & Co., 1897. Reprinted, New York: AMS Press, 1977.

"The Genesis of Implement Making." *Proceedings of the American Association for the Advancement of Science, 1897*, pp. 337–39. Salem, Mass., 1898.

Zuñi Folk Tales. Introduction by John Wesley Powell. New York: G. P. Putnam's Sons, 1901. Reissued with introduction by Mary Austin, New York: Alfred A. Knopf, 1931.

"Observations Relative to the Origin of the Flyfot, or Swastika." *American Anthropologist* n.s. 9 (1907): 334–37.

Contributions to Stuart Culin, "Games of the North American Indians." In *Twenty-fourth Annual Report of the Bureau of American Ethnology, 1902–1903*, pp. 212–17, 221–22, 374–81, and passim. Washington, D.C., 1907.

Contributions to Frederick Webb Hodge, ed. *Handbook of American Indians North of Mexico*. 2 vols. Washington, D.C.: Smithsonian Institution, 1907–10.

"Oraibe in 1883." In Jesse Walter Fewkes and Elsie Clews Parsons, "Contributions to Hopi History." *American Anthropologist* 24 (1923): 253–68.

"The Origin Myth from Oraibi." Edited by Elsie Clews Parsons. *Journal of American Folklore* 36 (1923): 163–70.

A Chant, a Myth, a Prayer; or, Pai-ya-ta-ma, God of Dew and the Dawn. San Francisco: Grabhorn Press, 1949(?).

434 SELECTED BIBLIOGRAPHY

Related Writings

Works marked with an asterisk (*) include a bibliography related to Cushing. See Brandes especially for a listing of unpublished Cushing material.

Bandelier, Adolph F. A. *The Romantic School in American Archaeology*, New York: Trow's Printing & Bookbinding Co., 1885.

———. *Contributions to the History of the Southwestern Portion of the United States*. Hemenway Southwestern Archaeological Expedition Monograph. Papers of the Archaeological Institute of America Series. Cambridge, Mass.: John Wilson & Son, 1890.

———. *The Gilded Man (El Dorado) and Other Pictures of the Spanish Occupancy of America*. New York: D. Appleton & Co., 1893.

———. *Pioneers in American Anthropology: The Bandelier-Morgan Letters, 1873–1883*. Edited by Leslie A. White. 2 vols. Albuquerque: University of New Mexico Press, 1940.

———. *Unpublished Letters of Adolph Bandelier*. Edited by Paul Radin. El Paso: C. Hertzog, 1942.

———. *The Southwestern Journals of Adolph F. Bandelier*. Vol. 1, 1880–82; vol. 2, 1883–84; vol. 3, 1885–88. Edited by Charles H. Lange, Carroll L. Riley, and Elizabeth M. Lange. Albuquerque: University of New Mexico Press, 1966–75.

Baxter, Sylvester. "The Father of the Pueblos." *Harpers* 65 (1882): 72–91.

———. "An Aboriginal Pilgrimage." *Century Illustrated Monthly Magazine* 24 (1882): 526–36.

———. *The Old New World: An Account of the Explorations of the Hemenway Southwestern Archaeological Expedition in 1887–1888, under the Direction of Frank Hamilton Cushing*. Salem, Mass., 1888.

Benedict, Ruth. *Zuñi Mythology*. 2 vols. Columbia University Contributions to Anthropology, no. 21. New York: Columbia University Press, 1935.

Bourke, John G. Diaries, 1872–96. U.S. Army War College Library, Carlisle, Pennsylvania.

Brandes, Raymond Stewart. "Frank Hamilton Cushing: Pioneer Americanist." Ph.D. dissertation, University of Arizona, 1965. (Available on microfilm, Ann Arbor, Mich.: University Microfilms, 1965)*

Brew, J. O., ed. *One Hundred Years of Anthropology*. Cambridge: Harvard University Press, 1968.

Bunzel, Ruth L. "Introduction to Zuñi Ceremonialism," "Zuñi Origin Myths," "Zuñi Ritual Poetry," "Zuñi Katchinas." In *Forty-seventh Annual Report of the Bureau of American Ethnology, 1929–1930,* pp. 467–1086. Washington, D.C., 1932.

———. *Zuni Texts.* Publications of the American Ethnological Society, 15. New York: G. E. Stechert & Co., 1933.

Curtis, William E. *Children of the Sun.* Chicago: Interocean Publishing Co., 1883.

Darnell, Regna Diebold. "The Development of American Anthropology, 1879–1920: From the Bureau of American Ethnology to Franz Boaz." Ph.D. dissertation, University of Pennsylvania, 1969.*

Dozier, Edward P. *The Pueblo Indians of North America.* Case Studies in Cultural Anthropology. New York: Holt, Rinehart & Winston, 1970.

Durkheim, Emile, and Mauss, Marcell. *Primitive Classification.* Translated by Rodney Needham. Chicago: University of Chicago Press, 1963.

Dutton, Bertha Pauline. *Sun Father's Way: The Kiva Murals of Kuaua.* Albuquerque: University of New Mexico Press, 1963.*

Eggan, Fred. *Social Organization of the Western Pueblos.* Chicago, University of Chicago Press, 1950.

Fewkes, Jesse Walter, ed. *Journal of American Archaeology and Ethnology.* 4 vols. Boston and New York: Houghton Mifflin, 1891–94.

Flack, James K. "The Formation of the Washington Intellectual Community, 1870–1898." Ph.D. dissertation, Wayne State University, 1968.

Fontana, Bernard L. "Pioneers in Ideas: Three Early Southwestern Ethnologists." *Journal of the Arizona Academy of Science* 2 (1963): 124–29.

Fuller, Clarissa P. "Frank Hamilton Cushing's Relations to Zuñi and the Hemenway Southwestern Expedition." Master's thesis, University of New Mexico, 1943.*

Gilliland, Marion Spjut. *The Material Culture of Key Marco, Florida.* Gainesville: University of Florida Presses, 1975.*

Green, Jesse D. "The Man Who Became an Indian." *New York Review of Books* 22, no. 9 (May 29, 1975): 31–33.

Haury, Emil W. *The Excavation at Los Muertos and Neighboring Ruins in the Salt River Valley, Southern Arizona.* Papers of the Peabody Museum of American Archaeology and Ethnology, vol. 24, no. 1. Cambridge, Mass.: Peabody Museum, 1945.*

Helm, June, ed. *Pioneers of American Anthropology: The Uses of Biography*. American Ethnological Society Monograph 43. Seattle: University of Washington Press, 1966.

Hinsley, Curtis M., Jr. "The Development of a Profession: Anthropology in Washington, D.C., 1846–1903." Ph.D. dissertation, University of Wisconsin, 1976.*

Hodge, Frederick Webb. *The History of Hawiku, New Mexico, One of the so-called Cities of Cibola*. Los Angeles: Southwest Museum, 1937.

———, ed. "In Memoriam: Frank Hamilton Cushing." *American Anthropologist* n.s. 2 (1900): 345–79.

Judd, Neil M. *The Bureau of American Ethnology: A Partial History*. Norman: University of Oklahoma Press, 1967.

Kennan, George. "Frank Cushing." "G.K.'s Column," *Medina* (N.Y.) *Tribune*, December 6, 13, and 27, 1923, and January 3, 1924. Copies in Cushing file, National Anthropological Archives, Smithsonian Institution, Washington, D.C.

Kroeber, Alfred L. *Zuñi Kin and Clan*. Anthropological Papers of the American Museum of Natural History, no. 18, p. 2. New York: Trustees of the American Museum of Natural History, 1917.

———. Review of *Zuñi Breadstuff*. *American Anthropologist* 23 (1921): 479.

———. "Frank Hamilton Cushing." In *Encyclopedia of the Social Sciences*. New York: Macmillan & Co., 1930.

Leighton, Dorothea C., and Adair, John. *People of the Middle Place: A Study of the Zuñi Indians*. Behavioral Science Monographs. New Haven, Conn.: Human Relations Area File Press, 1966.

Lévi-Strauss, Claude. "Social Structure." In *Anthropology Today: An Enclepedic Inventory*, edited by Alfred L. Kroeber. Chicago: University of Chicago Press, 1953.

———. *Structural Anthropology*. Translated by Claire Jacobson and Brooke Grundfest Schoepf. New York: Basic Books, 1963.

Lévy-Bruhl, Lucien. *How Natives Think*. Translated by Lilian A. Clare. London: George Allen & Unwin, 1926.

Mark, Joan. "Frank Hamilton Cushing and an American Science of Anthropology." *Perspectives in American History* 10 (1976): 449–86.*

Martin, Paul S. *Digging into History: A Brief Account of Fifteen Years of Archaeological Work in New Mexico*. Chicago Natural History Museum Popular Series, Anthropology, no. 38. Chicago: Chicago Natural History Museum Press, 1959.

Matthews, Washington. Review of *Zuñi Folk Tales. American Anthropologist* n.s. 4 (1902): 144.

Ortiz, Alfonso, ed. *New Perspectives on the Pueblos.* Albuquerque: University of New Mexico Press, 1972.

Pandey, Triloki Nath. "Anthropologists at Zuñi." *Proceedings of the American Philosophical Society* 116 (1972): 321–37.*

Parsons, Elsie Clews. *Pueblo Indian Religion.* 2 vols. Chicago: University of Chicago Press, 1939.

Powdermaker, Hortense. *Stranger and Friend: The Way of an Anthropologist.* New York: W. W. Norton, 1966.

Radin, Paul. *The Evolution of an American Indian Prose Epic: A Study in Comparative Literature.* Special Publications of the Bolingen Foundation, no. 3. Basel, Switzerland: Ethnographical Museum, 1943.

Spicer, Edward H. *Cycles of Conquest: The Impact of Spain, Mexico, and the United States on the Indians of the Southwest, 1533–1960.* Tucson: University of Arizona Press, 1962.

Stevenson, Matilda Coxe. "The Zuñi Indians." *Twenty-third Annual Report of the Bureau of American Ethnology, 1901–1902.* Washington, D.C., 1904.

Tedlock, Dennis. "On the Translation of Style in Oral Narrative." *Journal of American Folklore* 84 (1971): 114–33.

———. *Finding the Center: Narrative Poetry of the Zuñi Indians.* New York: Dial Press, 1972.

———. "Pueblo Literature: Style and Verisimilitude." In *New Perspectives on the Pueblos,* edited by Alfonso Ortiz, pp. 219–42. Albuquerque: University of New Mexico Press, 1972.

tenKate, H.F.C. "Frank Hamilton Cushing." *American Anthropologist* n.s. 2 (1900): 768–71.

———. "The Indian in Literature." In *Annual Report of the Board of Regents of the Smithsonian Institution, 1921,* pp. 517–18. Washington, D.C., 1922.

Tylor, Edward B. *Primitive Culture: Researches into the Development of Mythology, Philosophy, Religion, Language, Art, and Custom.* 2 vols. London: J. Murray, 1920.

———. *Researches into the Early History of Mankind and the Development of Civilization.* Edited by Paul Bohannan. Chicago: University of Chicago Press, 1964.

Vogt, Evon Z., and Albert, Ethel M., eds. *People of Rimrock: A Study of Values in Five Cultures.* Cambridge: Harvard University Press, 1966.

Wilson, Edmund. *Red, Black, Blond, and Olive: Studies in Four Civilizations: Zuñi, Haiti, Soviet Russia, Israel.* New York: Oxford University Press, 1956.

Wissler, Clark. *The Relation of Nature to Man in Aboriginal America.* New York: Oxford University Press, 1926.

————. *Indians of the United States.* New York: Doubleday Anchor, 1966.

The Zuñis: Self Portrayals by the Zuñi People. Translated by Alvina Quam. Albuquerque: University of New Mexico Press, 1972.

Acknowledgments

For permission to reprint in expanded form an earlier essay of mine on Cushing, I am grateful to the *New York Review of Books*. I am also grateful to the Southwest Museum in Los Angeles and to the Smithsonian Institution for permission to include selections hitherto unpublished. More particularly, I wish to express my thanks to Ruth M. Christensen, Librarian of the Southwest Museum, and James R. Glenn, Archivist of the National Anthropological Archives at the Smithsonian, for their generous helpfulness to me as a rummager in their respective collections and to Fred Eggan, Richard B. Woodbury, Nathalie F. S. Woodbury, Bernard L. Fontana, and William C. Sturtevant for their careful reading of the text, their many valuable suggestions, and their continued supportiveness in the face of my needs as a tourist in the land of the anthropologists. Obviously they cannot be held responsible for any gaffes they may have overlooked. For accepting the additional task of providing a foreword I am especially grateful to Professor Eggan. I wish also to thank Emlyn H. Hodge for contributing several rare photographs and for helpful recollections of her mother, Margaret Magill Hodge; her aunt, Emily Magill Cushing; and their stories of the Washington and southwestern worlds of the 1880s and 1890s. To Nancy Green I am grateful for the host of editorial helps, most notably for salutary advice in the difficult but necessary task of cutting down a Cushing mountain to the proportions of a readable book. I am also much indebted to Cartier J. Olson and John Smith of Chicago State University and to Morton Shapiro and Duncan Green for their help and advice in the photographic work required for reprinting the original illustrations included here, and to Richard C. Higginbotham, Ann Malone, and others of the Chicago State University Library staff for their many good services and sustained good nature. Finally, I am indebted to the National Endowment for the Humanities for a Summer Stipend and to Chicago State University for the leave time granted me to pursue this project.